THE WEST OF SCOTLAND IN HISTORY

Being Brief Notes Concerning Events, Family Traditions, Topography, and Institutions

by

Joseph Irving

Author of "The History of Dumbartonshire,"
"Annals of our Time," &c., &c.

HERITAGE BOOKS
2012

HERITAGE BOOKS
AN IMPRINT OF HERITAGE BOOKS, INC.

Books, CDs, and more—Worldwide

For our listing of thousands of titles see our website
at
www.HeritageBooks.com

A Facsimile Reprint
Published 2012 by
HERITAGE BOOKS, INC.
Publishing Division
100 Railroad Ave. #104
Westminster, Maryland 21157

Copyright © 2001 Heritage Books, Inc.

Originally published
Glasgow:
Robert Forrester, t Royal Exchange Square
1885

— Publisher's Notice —
In reprints such as this, it is often not possible to remove blemishes from the original. We feel the contents of this book warrant its reissue despite these blemishes and hope you will agree and read it with pleasure.

International Standard Book Numbers
Paperbound: 978-0-7884-1924-9
Clothbound: 978-0-7884-9241-9

TO

JAMES H. STODDART, Esq.,

Editor of the "Glasgow Herald,"

THESE BRIEF SKETCHES IN WEST COUNTRY HISTORY

ARE

RESPECTFULLY DEDICATED.

J. I.

PREFACE.

PREFATORY matter, or "Fore-words," as now sometimes used by scholars, better befits the language of explanation than apology. Over two centuries since a famous Episcopal Puritan, Archbishop Tillotson by designation, wrote of his once popular Sermons, "I shall neither trouble the reader, nor myself, with any apology for publishing of these Sermons, for if they be in any measure truly serviceable to the end for which they are designed, I do not see what apology is necessary; and if they be not so, I am sure none can be sufficient." Explanation in such a case may be made in terms equally brief. The slight desultory Sketches making up the following pages have for the most part already appeared in print, as prepared in the hurry of journalistic work for publication in the "Glasgow Herald," daily or weekly, and "Evening Times." The writer is not unconscious that in their imperfect form, and for which he is alone responsible, the Sketches only touch the edge of the subject—the mere hem of what is historical, and can in no sense be considered exhaustive. A certain picture, Goldsmith wrote, would have been better had the artist taken more pains. So of these Sketches; more and better may follow, should what is written meet with any moderate acceptance of public favour. Reference having occasion to be made from time to time in the articles as originally written to events of a passing or ephemeral nature, these in the following pages have been either omitted altogether, or explained, it is hoped with sufficient fulness, by the use of dates within brackets. Being rather Notes on History than History itself, the writer did not at first contemplate publication in a separate form, and even now only yields to the frequently expressed wish of a few friends that the Sketches might be placed in a handier and more permanent form than could be secured through their appearance in any newspaper of the day, however popular and widely circulated.

J. IRVING.

HILLHEAD HOUSE, NEAR PAISLEY,
ST. JAMES'S DAY,
1885.

CONTENTS.

	PAGE
QUEEN MARY AND DARNLEY IN GLASGOW,	1
COREHOUSE AND THE CRANSTOUNS,	10
BATTLE OF LANGSIDE,	16
AUCHINLECK AND THE BOSWELLS,	22
THE MURES OF CALDWELL,	29
JOHN GLASSFORD OF DOUGALSTONE,	36
CATHCART AND ITS EARLS,	43
THE STEUARTS OF COLTNESS AND ALLANTON,	50
A DAUGHTER OF THE HOUSE OF COLTNESS,	54
ANDREW STUART OF TORRANCE AND CASTLEMILK,	59
THE LOLLARDS OF KYLE,	65
THE EARL OF EGLINTON SHOT BY A POACHER,	72
CARNWATH AND THE LOCKHARTS OF LEE,	77
DALRYMPLE AND THE STAIRS,	81
THE MASTER OF STAIR AND GLENCOE,	85
KELBURNE, HAWKHEAD, AND EARLS OF GLASGOW,	91
DUNDONALD AND ITS EARLS,	98
COILSFIELD AND THE MONTGOMERIES,	103
THE EARLDOM OF CARRICK,	109
THE LOCKHARTS OF MILTON-LOCKHART,	113
ARDGOWAN: THE STEWARTS AND SHAW-STEWARTS,	119
POLLOK AND THE MAXWELLS,	125
SIR THOMAS MUNRO, K.C.B.,	133
JOHN KNOX AND THE ABBOT OF CROSSRAGUEL AT MAYBOLE,	140
THE STORY OF GLENFRUIN,	146
THE GREAT DOUGLAS CAUSE,	161
MONTROSE FAMILY DESCENT AND POSSESSIONS,	167
MONTROSE PEERAGE CONTEST,	176
CUMBERNAULD HOUSE AND THE FLEMINGS,	181

	PAGE
CUMBERNAULD HOUSE AND THE ELPHINSTONES,	186
GLASGOW BURGH RECORDS,	192
GLASGOW CHAMBER OF COMMERCE,	206
OLD GLASGOW HOUSES,	213
A GLASGOW CATHEDRAL RELIC,	217
THE SPREULLS OF GLASGOW,	221
ANDREW MELVILLE IN GLASGOW,	223
LORD PROVOST PATRICK COLQUHOUN, LL.D.,	229
SHERIFF ALISON,	232
GRAHAM OF THE MINT,	238
GENERAL ROY OF CARLUKE,	242
BURNS AND "HIGHLAND MARY,"	250
KILMARNOCK,	256
ST. MICHAEL'S, DUMFRIES,	260
DUMFRIES ROOD FAIR,	265
RENFREWSHIRE RECORDS,	268
THE RENFREWSHIRE WITCHES,	278
PAISLEY ABBEY,	284
PAISLEY GRAMMAR SCHOOL,	289
ALEXANDER WILSON, ORNITHOLOGIST,	293
MOTHERWELL AND CUNNINGHAM,	302
THE BARNS OF AYR,	306
RAMBLES IN GALLOWAY,	309
THE HERRIES PEERAGE,	315
A GALLOWAY CHARACTER,	320
DRUMLANRIG AND THE DOUGLASES,	324
THE SCOTTS OF BUCCLEUCH,	329
ST. COLUMBA,	335
CUNNINGHAM,	339
LEADHILLS AND WANLOCK,	343
THE FULLARTONS OF FULLARTON, &C.,	347
INVERKIP TO WEST KILBRIDE,	353

THE WEST COUNTRY IN HISTORY.

QUEEN MARY AND DARNLEY IN GLASGOW.

QUEEN MARY, beautiful, accomplished, and rich also in gracious, persuasive ways, was not more remarkable among Sovereigns of her own day than for the romance which has ever since surrounded the story of her life, from its chequered opening to that tragic close in the halls of her ancestors at Fotheringay. Partly through her connection with foreign Courts, and partly in spite of that connection, Mary's position as wife of the Dauphin, as Dowager of France, as Queen of Scotland, and as next in succession to her cousin Elizabeth on the English throne—all tended, whether consciously or unconsciously, to make her the centre round which were devised that series of cunning plots and counterplots which disturbed the peace of other nations than Scotland, and ultimately led to serve as excuses for her long, dreary imprisonment, for her unconstitutional trial, and for her cruel execution. "False witnesses did rise up; they laid to my charge things that I knew not," is the motto selected from the painful experience of the Psalmist by the most imaginative of modern painters for his portrait of the unhappy Sovereign, fitted more for adorning the gay Court of Bourbon than for controlling or even moderating the pretensions of her own rapacious nobles in the North. Queen Mary may have known innocence; peace but seldom. Cradled amid the storms of the Reformation, she was a prisoner even in infancy, and before she could speak must have been often alarmed by the contentions of violent, unprincipled men. The necessity of protecting her youthful person from seizure led to her first appearance in the West. The Protector Somerset, failing to follow up his success gained on the field of Pinkie in September, 1547, the Queen-Mother took advantage of the temporary quietness which succeeded that engagement to prepare for removing Mary to the French Court, where, it was thought, she would be safe from the machinations of England, and the no less dangerous factions which existed in her own country. With this object the young Queen was removed with her mimic Court from her retreat in the monastery of Inchmahome, where the remains of her child garden may yet be traced, and placed in Dumbarton Castle to await the arrival of a French fleet in the Clyde. An entry in the Exchequer Record (Register House) fixes the removal as on the last day of February, 1548, when the Queen was about three months over six years of age. Here she would appear to have sickened of small-pox, without, however, having her beauty impaired— an experience which enabled Mary twenty years afterwards to bestow sympathy with her sister of England on casting off a complaint which in these days was little short of a national scourge. It was not till the first week in August that the Queen could safely embark with her "Four Maries" and other attendants. The little Lady was observed to shed tears after she had received the maternal blessing and farewell kiss of the only parent she had ever known; but, trained even thus early in the regal science of self-control, she offered no resistance, but permitted herself to be carried on board the galley of the King of France, which had been fitted up and sent expressly for her accommodation by the father of her future husband. Suspicious of hostile ships at sea, the Admiral in charge (Villegaignon) selected a circuitous course to steer by, so that it was six days before Brest was made, when the Queen commenced her progress to the palace of St. Germain, where she was joyfully received by the French monarch, and a household appointed for her at the public expense. With Mary's residence in France, and her training at the Court of the Guises, little mention need be made here, beyond the brief facts that she married the Dauphin at sixteen (1558), was Queen of France for sixteen months, and a widow at eighteen. Never entirely trusted by the Guises, and anxious at the same time about affairs in Scotland, Queen Mary left France to land at Leith, 19th August, 1561. Hunting and other graver duties frequently led her afterwards to the West. Early in July, 1563, the Royal Household Book shows her to have been in Glasgow about a fortnight, during which time she visited her kinsman, Lord Claud Hamilton, at Paisley Abbey, and other members of the family at Hamilton. She next passed to Dumbarton and Rossdhu, and on the 19th set out for Inverary on a visit to her half-sister, the Countess of Argyll, daughter of James V., by Elizabeth, daughter of John Lord Carmichael. This Lady would not appear to have been blessed with the sweetest of tempers, inasmuch as her domestic troubles were reported to have given the Queen an opportunity for requesting the good offices of John Knox. The story is told in "Calderwood," vol. ii., p. 5. In this year of her visit, at the third conference between Queen Mary and Knox, Her Majesty requested him again to use his good offices on behalf of her sister, the Lady Argyll, who, she confessed, was not so circumspect in everything as she could wish; "yet," she added, "her husband faileth in many things." "I brought them to concord," said Knox, "that her friends were fully content; and she promised before them she should never complain to any creature, till I should first be made acquainted with the quarrel, either out of her own mouth, or by an assured messenger." "Well," said the Queen, "it is worse than you believe. Do this much for my sake, as once again to reconcile them, and if she behave not herself as becometh, she shall find no favour of me; but in no case let my Lord know that I employed you." Knox, in consequence, wrote to the Earl on the Countess' behalf, exhorting him to bear with the imperfections of his wife, seeing that he was not able to convince her of any crime since the last reconciliation, but his letter was not well received.

In this same year of grace, 1563, Queen Mary began to manifest increased feelings of respect for Matthew Earl of Lennox, then living under the protection of England with his Countess Margaret, daughter of Margaret Tudor, mother of James V., by her second marriage with the Earl of Angus. Their son, Henry Lord Darnley, had thus a common ancestry with the Queen, and might in certain contingencies be looked upon as a rival in the English succession. Marriage negotiations, which had been commenced almost upon the death of the Dauphin, were carried on with the most fruitless result till the summer of 1565, when the Queen put an end to all further suspense by announcing that she had resolved to unite herself in marriage with her cousin, Henry Lord Darnley. Darnley, a lusty, well-made young fellow, but totally devoid of judgment or dignity, met the Queen for the first time at Wemyss Castle, Fifeshire, 16th February, 1564. He was then 19 years of age, and the Queen in her 23rd year. The tradition of a courtship and residence at Cruikston Castle, Renfrewshire, rests on no foundation worth examining. The fabric would appear to have been even then in ruins, while all the letters known to exist from the Earl and Countess of that date are dated from Houston or Inchinnan. (See D. Semple's "Tree of Crocston," 1876.) The ill-starred marriage between Mary and Darnley was solemnised in the chapel of Holyrood House on the morning of 29th July, 1565. Up to this date Darnley had signed simply as "Lord HENRY DARNLEY," as King Henry of Scotland he afterwards signed "HENRY R." In conformity with other high honours bestowed upon him at marriage, a special seal was engraved for his use, bearing the familiar Scottish lion surmounted by a crown, and the less known initials, recalling the fact now not generally remembered that for a few months a Henry bore the title of King in Scotland. A coinage also was issued bearing the joint names of Mary and Darnley; but too much suspicion can hardly be entertained regarding what is known as the "Cruikston Dollar," or "Mary Ryall." The coin, well enough known to collectors, bears, not a yew-tree, either of Cruikston or elsewhere, but a palm-tree, as may be ascertained from the records of Privy Council authorising its issue, 22nd December, 1565. Immediately after her marriage, Mary took active steps to break up the faction headed by her natural brother the Earl of Murray, which had manifested great opposition to the match, and was generally believed to look to the English Court for direction and support. Darnley for a time aided her in this attempt, but with characteristic folly and ingratitude he afterwards allied himself with her opponents, and finally alienated all affection the Queen may ever have felt for him by consenting to, if not originating, that scheme of hostility to her government which led to the murder of her favourite, David Rizzio. From this period revenge dignified as far as such a passion can be dignified, and ill-concealed by either her levity or despondency, seemed to take possession of the mind of Mary; nor did the birth of a Prince, which took place on the 19th of June following, very seriously change the current of her thoughts. From playing false with Mary, Darnley, to secure the crown matrimonial, began to play false with his fellow-conspirators. The poor misguided youth was now encompassing his own destruction as swiftly as possible. The Queen was not likely to stop short in extreme measures of retaliation; nor were Morton, Maitland, Lindsay, or the grim Ruthven, the men to place themselves in the power of a fickle, soft-spoken and rather loose-living lad. At this crisis in his history he is smitten down with disease, brought on, it has often been said, through his own excesses, and he thereupon resolved upon a journey to Glasgow, that he might consult physicians and be at the same time beyond such personal danger from the Queen's friends or foes as he feared equally at Holyrood and Stirling. This brought the Queen to Glasgow, where the mysterious "Casket Letters" were alleged to have been sent by her Majesty to Bothwell—letters, whether genuine or not, which proved full of evil consequences in her after career.

Sick in mind and body, alienated from all friends at Court he ever had, and excluded, it is thought, at the Queen's express desire, from the ceremonies incident to the baptism of his son, Prince James, Darnley withdrew from his sullen seclusion at Stirling on or about Christmas-Day, 1566, and arrived at Glasgow certainly before the closing day of the year. His father, the Earl of Lennox, would not appear to have been in the City at the time; nor was even the Castle open to receive the King; so that it is inferred, but only inferred, that he took up his residence in the humble dwelling close at hand, long after known as Darnley's Cottage, and removed from Cathedral Square in quite recent years. Openly disclaiming any knowledge of the "Bond" entered into at Whittingham by Bothwell, Archibald Douglas, Secretary Lethington, and others, for the "removal" of Darnley, but in suspicious compliance with the spirit of its design, Queen Mary left Edinburgh on the 21st January, 1567, and, proceeding by way of Callendar, reached the bedside of her sick husband in Glasgow on the afternoon of the 23rd. That the design of the Queen was the removal of her husband to the east country is evident enough from the circumstance that she brought a "litter" with her for the purpose of facilitating the journey, or, as her defenders put it, for the purpose of making the journey less hurtful to the invalid than it would otherwise have been. Craigmillar was the place first suggested, but this came to be changed to Kirk-of-Field, Edinburgh, where the tragedy was to be consummated, and which Bothwell was at the moment preparing for the reception of the victim. Hearing that the Queen had been speaking of him with unusual severity, Darnley sent Captain Crawford, of Jordanhill, a trusted friend of his own, and of the Lennox family (and afterwards Lord Provost of Glasgow) to meet Her Majesty four miles from the city, with a message excusing himself for not waiting upon her in person. He was still infirm, he said, and did not presume to come to her until he knew her wishes and was assured of the removal of her displeasure. To this Mary briefly replied that there was no medicine against fear, and that he (Darnley) need have no fear if he did not feel himself faulty. The Queen then passed with her escort, being joined at this point by the Lairds of Luss, Houstoun, and Caldwell, with forty horse. The narrative at this point rests in a great measure on letters said to be her own, and afterwards referred to; but for conversations between the Queen and her sick husband in his Glasgow lodgings, much reliance came to be placed on a deposition made by Captain Crawford before the informal Commission at York in December, 1568, when Mary was a prisoner in Bolton Castle—a deposition, however, it may be proper to explain, not only sworn to as accurate, but based on conversations taken down at the time, and still existing as endorsed by Cecil. Crawford reports that Darnley asked what he thought of the Queen's taking him to Craigmillar? "They treat your Majesty," said Crawford, "too like a prisoner. Why should you not be taken to one of your own houses in Edinburgh?" "It struck me much the same way," answered Darnley, "and I have fears enough; but may God judge between us, I have her promise only to trust to, yet I have put myself in her hands, and I shall go with her though she should murder me." (Crawford's "Deposition," State Paper Office.) On another occasion Crawford heard Darnley say to the Queen, "If you promise me on your honour to live with me as my wife, and not to leave me any more, I will go with you to the end of the world, and care for nothing; if not I shall stay where I am." "It shall be as you have spoken," she replied, and thereupon gave him her hand and faith. The Queen remained in Glasgow from the 23rd to 27th January, and between these dates, mostly in the evening, four of the eight celebrated "Casket Letters" purport to have been written by the Queen to Bothwell. That these letters may have been obtained surreptitiously, or even stolen from the page Dalgleish when conveying them from Edinburgh Castle to his master Bothwell; that they were irregularly, and therefore improperly, used in evidence against the Queen at York (and about this there cannot be much doubt), and that they were improperly destroyed as implicating the memory of his mother by King James after ascending the English throne—all this may be true, but not necessary to discuss here. It is not even necessary in a light sketch of this kind to discuss their authenticity—whether they were written by the Queen in French, or forged originally in Latin or Scots by Buchanan at the instance of Murray and other Lords, whether they were ever intended for, or sent to Bothwell at all, or whether some of them at least were not letters from Mary intended for her husband Darnley, and therefore removed from the region of censure. It is sufficient that the letters, genuine or not, existed at one time, and exercised a powerful influence in the Queen's condemnation. Buchanan describes the casket in his "Detection" as "ane small gilt cofer not fully ane foot long, beying garnishit in sondry places, with the Romaine letter F under ane Kyngly crowne (presumed to be the arms of Mary's first husband, the Dauphin, Francis II.) quhairin were certain letters and writynges well knawin, and by othes to be affirmit, to have been written with the quene of Scottes awne hand to the Erle Bothwell." This casket, intercepted as mentioned above, contained letters written from Glasgow, Stirling, Linlithgow, and the Kirk-of-Field, a series of twelve sonnets, and two contracts of marriage. These important documents were presumed to have been preserved by Bothwell both as pledges of her affection and as proofs of her assent to the murder of Darnley, and also of her own abduction at Cramond Bridge. The casket, it is further presumed, was lodged with other papers by Bothwell in Edinburgh Castle when he brought the Queen from Dunbar. These letters, first produced when Mary was a prisoner, were never submitted to the Queen herself or to her Commissioners, and were uniformly disclaimed as authentic by all concerned in her defence. Constitutional lawyers, naturally jealous of the rights of individuals as against the power of the Crown, have generally condemned this feature in the proceedings against Queen Mary. Some of them, indeed, have gone the length of saying that they only desired to be as assuredly convinced of her innocence as that she had an unfair trial. The first and longest letter, from Glasgow, bore the initials of Elizabeth, as well as Mary's arch-foe, Cecil, indicating that it was inspected by the Queen, for whom, perhaps, it was translated or transcribed. The most damaging evidence against their authenticity is the coarseness of thought and suggestion pervading them. "Cursed be this pocky fellow (she is represented as writing from Darnley's bedside), who troubleth me thus much, for I had a pleasanter matter to discourse unto you but for him. He is not much the worse, but he is ill arrayed. I thought I should have been killed with his breath, for it is worse than your uncle's, and yet I was set no nearer to him than in a chair by his bolster, and he lieth by the further side of the bed." Again—" I have taken the worms out of his nose. You have heard the rest. We are tied to two false races. The good year untie us from them. God forgive me, and God knit us together for ever for the most faithful couple. I am ill at ease, and glad to write you when other folks be asleep, seeing that I cannot do as they do, according to my desire, that is between your arms, my dear life, who I beseech God to preserve from all ill and send you good rest, as I go to seek mine, till to-morrow in the morning." Such

"Night Thoughts" in Glasgow came to an end on the 27th January, when Darnley was conveyed by way of Callendar and Linlithgow to the "prepared" lodging in the ruined premises at Kirk-of-Field, Edinburgh. On Sunday, 9th February, according to what is known as the Regent's Diary, the Queen and Bothwell supped with the Bishop of the Isles, and passed afterwards with Argyll and Huntly to the King's chamber, where Bothwell and his accomplices "putt all things to order." About two hours after midnight (Hepburn confessed), when the Queen had retired from Bastian's wedding festivities in Holyrood, "a loud noise like the bursting of a thunder-cloud awoke the sleeping city. The King's House was torn in pieces and cast into the air, and the King himself slain." Whether suffocated beforehand or killed by the explosion, it is impossible now to determine from the conflicting testimony of the ruffians concerned in the outrage. With indecent haste Bothwell was acknowledged by Mary as her friend, and before she had been three months a widow was accepted by her as a fitting successor to that husband whom he was believed to have murdered. But so unfortunate was the issue of Mary's affairs from the date of her union with Bothwell that, in little more than four weeks afterwards she was compelled to surrender to the nobles confederated in arms against her at Carberry Hill; and on the day following that surrender she was, in violation, as some think, of a solemn promise to the contrary, conveyed a captive to the castle of Lochleven. Bothwell himself contrived to escape at Carberry, scouring the northern seas afterwards as a pirate, and dying a maniac in the lonely Danish prison of Draxholm. The remains of certain minor conspirators executed were conveyed to Glasgow and hung up, in token of at least a small measure of justice meted out to the murderers of one so intimately associated by descent and title with the West of Scotland as Henry, Lord Darnley. The lands of the lordship of Darnley, which includes the mill of the barony, make up the south-west corner of Eastwood Parish, Renfrewshire, and passed from the Darnley Stewarts first to the Montrose family, by purchase, from the Duke of Lennox and Richmond, and then about fifty years later, or in 1757, to Sir John Maxwell of Nether Pollok, whose descendants are still in possession.

COREHOUSE AND THE CRANSTOUNS.

SPRUNG from the old house of Crailing, near Jedburgh, George Cranstoun may be thought to belong more to the East than the West, but the fine residence close on Corra Fall, Lanark, is so closely identified with the life and leisure of one of the foremost men of his day at the bar, that little apology is required for recalling the memory of a scholar profound as well as witty, an advocate full of enthusiasm for his client, and a judge whose judgment could always be relied on. Without the slightest pretension to the literary culture or many-sided readiness of Jeffrey, or even to the crisp conversational power of the great critic, it is not too much to say that, with the exception of Jeffrey alone, George Cranstoun stood in the very front of that group of young Whig lawyers which made the early years of the present century so memorable in the history of the Parliament House. He may not have had the homely familiarity of Cockburn with a jury, but Cranstoun had persuasive powers of another kind in grace and culture which rivalled in effect the delicious humour of "Henry," and kept him abreast in the race with the gay, light-hearted Fullerton, as well as of the silver-tongued Maitland. In matters of feudal law he was acknowledged to have no rival, either on the bench or at the bar—no rival at least which he needed to fear; and there were in his day either on the bench or at the bar names so historical as Robert Blair of Avonton, Robert Macqueen of Braxfield, and Ilay Campbell of Succoth. Cranstoun's career is at once an illustration and explanation of what has often appeared a puzzle to readers trying to make themselves familiar with the inner life of these harsh exclusive Tory days. How, it is asked, if public life was then made so very irksome—how did the young Whigs find their way to such high distinction and such great practice? No doubt, they got on; but they had to force their advance, and in hands less competent success would have been impossible, even although aided by the spell which seemed to have fallen on the Tories since they excluded Erskine from the office of Dean of Faculty, and elected Robert Dundas of Arniston. Step by step the resolute youths beat their foe, but it died hard and made a mighty commotion in its death-throes. Sydney Smith was neither joking nor exaggerating when he wrote that his chief desire to know Horner proceeded from a caution given him by some excellent but feeble people who represented him as a person of violent political opinions. "I interpreted this to mean a person who thought for himself, who had firmness to take his own line in life, and who loved truth better than he loved Dundas." Tyrant as he was in all things political, Henry Dundas was personally and socially one of the most delightful men of his time, and we cease to wonder that his power became all but irresistible when he had practically unlimited power of patronage in almost every department of His Majesty's service—patronage in the army and navy, in the Customs, and in the Post Office, at home and in India—places suited for everybody, from a tide-waiter to a colonial governor. Representative freedom Scotland had none. Dundas named the sixteen peers, and forty-three out of forty-five commoners sent by counties and burghs to Parliament. The county voters or freeholders, few in number, were generally managed by some intriguing local magnate, while the burgh members were chosen by a self-elected council, generally steeped in servility and jobbing corruption. In this way the party of progress came to be not only avoided in society, but were rudely treated by the bench, and, indeed, for the most part, by those holding other official stations. Second son of George of Longwarton, who was in turn seventh son of the fifth Lord Cranstoun, George passed as advocate in 1793, the year after Scott, and one year before Jeffrey; so that he may be said to have entered on professional life when Pitt and the Dundas dynasty lay heaviest on Scotland. Pitt had been ten years First Lord of the Treasury; his friend, Henry Dundas (afterwards Viscount Melville) was leaving the Home Office to take up the duties of War Secretary, which he held for seven eventful years; a nephew, Robert of Arniston, before referred to, was Lord-Advocate, anxious, it may be, concerning the trial of Muir of Huntershill for alleged seditious practices, which took place in August. George Cranstoun was originally intended for the army, and during his first year or two at the bar was so annoyed with the bitterness of party feeling that he had serious thoughts of carrying out the earlier determination. The story goes, whether true or only meant to torment the decorous young advocate it is neither easy to say nor necessary to inquire, but it runs that he intended to enter the Austrian army, and consulted his friend Lord Swinton as to the propriety of joining a service in which it was said officers were liable to be flogged. His Lordship, who had a sound horror of a Jacobin, replied—" 'Deed, Mr. George, ye wad be muckle the better of being whuppit." But, truth or jest, the step indicated was never taken. Solicitors and clients began to feel confidence in the abilities of the young advocate who had spurned the written "test" proposed by David, afterwards Baron Hume, nephew of the historian; and the whip, instead of being applied to his own back, was laid with inimitable cleverness on the shoulders of most of the grave "Fifteen," who then looked down on the bar from the bench. Mr. Cranstoun was generally credited with the authorship of the famous "Diamond Beetle Case," being an imaginary report of a preposterous action given out as raised by a well-known Edinburgh jeweller for having had his Diamond Beetle described as only an Egyptian Louse. The involved style of Bannatyne, the predilection for Latin quotation of Meadowbank, the brisk manner of Lord Hermand, the anti-Gallic feeling of Lord Craig, the broad dialect of Polkemmet and Balmuto, and the hesitating manner of Lord Methven, are all playfully but admirably caricatured. There is room for only a few sentences here. Craig—" By an Egyptian louse I understand one that has been formed in the head of a native Egyptian, a race of men who, after degenerating for many centuries, have sunk at last into an abyss of depravity in consequence of having been subjected for a time by the French. I do not find that Turgot or Condorcet or the rest of the economists ever reckoned the combing of the head a species of productive labour, and I conclude therefore that wherever French principles have been propagated, lice grew to an immoderate size, especially in a warm climate like that of Egypt. I shall only add that we ought to be sensible of the blessings we enjoy under a free and happy constitution where lice and men live under the restraint of equal laws, the only equality that can exist in a well regulated State." Hermand—" I should have thought the defender would have gratified his spite to the full by comparing the beetle to a common louse, an animal certainly vile enough for purpose of defamation

—[shut that door there]—but he adds the epithet of Egyptian; and I well know what he means by that epithet. He means, my lords, a louse that has fastened on the head of a gipsy or tinker, undisturbed by the comb and unmolested in the enjoyment of its native filth. He means a louse ten times larger and ten times more abominable than those with which your Lordship and I are familiar. The petitioner seeks redress for an injury so atrocious and so aggravated, and, so far as my voice goes, he shall not ask in vain." Balmuto—"Awm for refusin' the petition. There is more lice than beetles in Fife. What they ca' a beetle is a thing as lang's ma airm, thick at the ae end and sma' at the ither. I thocht when I read the petition that the beetle, or bitill, had been a thing that women ha'e when they are washing towels or naipery, a thing for dadding them wi'; and as the petitioner is a jeweler to his trade, I thocht he had ane o' the beetles, and set a' roun' wi' diamonds; and I thocht that a fuilish and extravagant idea; and I saw nae resemblance it could ha'e to a louse. But I find I was mistaken, my Lord; that now the beetle clock the petitioner has, but in my opinion it's the same as it was before, and I am, my Lord, for refusing the petition; and I say, "——. Polkemmet—" It should be proved, my Lord, that what is called a beetle is a reptile well known in this country. I ha'e seen mony o' them on Drumshorling Muir. It is a little black beastie about the size o' my thoomb nail. The country folk ca' them cloks, and I believe they ca' them also 'Maggie wi' the mony feet,' but it is not a bit like ony loose I ever saw; so that in my opinion though the defender may have made a blunder through ignorance in comparin' them, there does not seem to have been any *animus injuriandi*. Therefore I am for referrin' the petition." Among the greatest speeches of Cranstoun at the Bar, prominence has generally been given to that on behalf of Edgar, a Glasgow teacher tried with another (1817) before the High Court of Justiciary for administering unlawful oaths to members joining a Parliamentary Reform Society, in so far as it implied a design to upset the Constitution by either physical or moral force, as the case might require. In addition to certain technical objections as to the form of the libel, Mr. Cranstoun contended specifically that even on the supposition that the oath purported what the public prosecutor said it did, still it would not imply an obligation on the part of the prisoner to commit treason. It must be proved, he held, in such treason cases that there was an expressed intention to accomplish the King's death or to levy war against him, and in the latter case the possession of arms must be proved, as well as meetings for drill. Twenty or thirty individuals doing particular things by force was not a levying of war; and though they were doing what would constitute treason if they were armed, still it would not be treason if they were not. The Lord-Advocate (Colquhoun) withdrew the indictment. The opinion of Lord Corehouse, delivered from the bench, on academical subscriptions was worthy of his judicious forethought and enlightened liberality of spirit. "I dissent," he said, "from that resolution, that all professors shall be required to subscribe the Confession of Faith of the Church of Scotland. It is proper and necessary that the Theological Faculty should belong to the Church established in this part of the kingdom; but to extend the same rule to the other Faculties by which not only dissenters of every denomination, but members of the Church of England, are excluded from teaching science and literature, appears an inexpedient restriction in the choice of professors. It is true that subscription is enjoined by the Act of Parliament cited in the Report, but the circumstances and opinions of the country have materially changed since that period; and, in particular, the number of Episcopalians has increased among the best educated classes in the community. Accordingly, the practice of subscription has, for a long time, been generally discontinued in the Universities; and I am of opinion that those statutes, now fallen into disuse, instead of being enforced should be repealed." Cranstoun's practice at the bar became in a few years steady and lucrative, while his official promotion was reasonably rapid. He was appointed a Depute-Advocate during the short Grenville Administration of 1806; chosen Dean of Faculty in room of Matthew Ross, of Candie, 1823, and in 1826 elevated to the bench on the death of George Fergusson, Lord Hermand, when he took the title of Lord Corehouse from his estate situate amid the Falls of Clyde, a few miles south of Lanark, but in the east of Lesmahagow parish. The beautiful mansion of the name, in the manorial style of Queen Elizabeth's reign, was begun in 1824 from designs by Blore, and the grounds afterwards laid out in a style so exquisite as to make it difficult to say whether the tasteful fittings of the house corresponds more with the fabric than the winding walks and flowery parterres do with the exquisite scenery bordering them on every hand. Here Lord Corehouse was visited by Sir Walter Scott in 1827, the friendship between the two dating as far back as the College class days of 1788. They had also been associated together on a committee appointed to make inquiry concerning the method and expense of transplanting trees practised by Sir Henry Stewart of Allanton. Bowed down as he was by the death of Lady Scott in the summer of the preceding year, pleasing reference is made in "The Diary" regarding this visit to his old friend at Corehouse. The ruined tower, originally the fortified residence of the proprietors, stands a few hundred feet from the present mansion, and, though often looking as if it would topple over with some heavy spate in Clyde, it is thought the foundations are not greatly weakened since its erection, many centuries since.

Relatives of Lord Corehouse have been often referred to in records far removed from mere family or local history. His cousin James, eighth Lord Cranstoun, was a distinguished naval officer under Rodney and Cornwallis, came home with despatches announcing the great victory over De Grasse, 12th April, 1782, and three years later received the thanks of Parliament for his skilful handling of the "Bellerophon" in another action with the French fleet. One sister, Helen D'Arcy, author of "The tears I shed must ever fall," became the second wife of Professor Dugald Stewart; another, Margaret, married William Cunningham of Lainshaw, Ayrshire; and a third, Jane Ann, one of the earliest friends and literary advisers of Scott, became Countess of Purgstall, Styria. After the death of her husband, and of a son, the hope of her life and the last of his illustrious line, the Countess shut herself up in a solitary mountain Schloss, and all but forsook intercourse with the world. Captain Basil Hall fared better than others who had sought refuge in these Styrian Valleys. He was warmly invited, hospitably entertained by the somewhat eccentric lady, and not permitted to go back to the world beyond the valleys with either his wife or family, till he had fulfilled a promise, given under extreme pressure, of seeing her laid in the grave. Many interesting particulars of this visit, and of the Countess herself, will be found in that author's "Schloss Hainfield; or a Winter in Lower Styria." The uncle of Lord Corehouse, then Captain W. H. Cranstoun, was mysteriously, but, as it turned out, innocently mixed up with the affairs of the notorious Mary Blandy, executed at York for poisoning her father—one of her allegations being that the captain sent her poison from Scotland, after an acquaintanceship made when recruiting with his regiment at Henley.

Stricken with paralysis, and otherwise in poor health, Lord Corehouse retired from the Bench in 1839, but survived in retirement, at his beautiful seat, till 26th June, 1850, when death removed the old Judge, whom it is difficult to over-estimate in his zeal as an advocate, for his impartiality as a judge, or even for his scholarship, so full, ready, and informing. Corehouse fell to be possessed by E. Cranstoun Charles Harris, fourth son of J. Cunningham of Lainshaw, who, in 1869, succeeded his aunt, under the entail. The present possessor of this historic seat is C. E. H. Edmonstoune-Cranstoun, Esq., born 1841, succeeded 1869.

BATTLE OF LANGSIDE.

EARLY in May, 1568, the news of Queen Mary's escape from Lochleven flashed through Scotland, and across the Borders to England and the Continent. On the evening of the 2nd, through the connivance of a page known as "Little Douglas," the keys of her prison were abstracted from the castellan, and a boat being in readiness she was rowed across the Loch, with one of her young lady attendants, to the lands of Caldon, where she was received by Lord Seaton, John Beaton, (brother of James, Archbishop of Glasgow), and other friends. Tytler writes of her as then taking horse to ride at full speed south to the Ferry, which she crossed, and held on her gallop, accompanied part of the way by Lord Claud Hamilton with fifty horse, till Niddry Castle was reached, where the royal fugitive passed her first night of freedom. Here a hurried despatch was sent to France, and Hepburn, of Riccarton, instructed to proceed in the first instance to Dunbar for the purpose of demanding delivery of the castle, and then to pass seaward to Denmark, that his master Bothwell might be made aware of her deliverance. Next day a south-western course was taken by way of Mid-Calder and Shotts, till Hamilton was reached, a distance somewhat over thirty miles. Here Mary felt herself in safety, and had hardly halted till plans were being devised for summoning friends to her assistance. The Earls of Argyll, Cassillis, Eglinton, and Rothes, the Lords Somerville, Yester, Livingstone, Herries, Fleming, Ross, Borthwick, and many others, all crowded into the camp at Hamilton with their followers.

Nor were the lesser barons overlooked, the Laird of Nether-Pollok (Sir John Maxwell), among the rest, being written to on the 5th :—"We dowt not bot ye know that God of his gudness has put us at libertie, quhome we thank maist heartlie. Quhairfore desires you wt all possible diligence fail not to be heir at us in Hamylton with all yor folks, friends and seruands bodin in feir of weir, as ye will do us acceptable service and pleasure. Because yor constance. We need not at this put to mak langer Lyr, but will byd you fairweill.—(Signed) Mary, R. Dated off Hamylton, ye v. of May, 1568." Tradition, generally of a very loose kind, has connected many places with the presence of Mary during her few busy days in and around Hamilton— pre-eminently Castlemilk (Stuart) and Craignethan, then occupied by the infirm Earl of Arran, third of the name, whose reason had become affected by the Queen's refusal to accept him for a husband. Unlike most of the other members of his family, he was in early life actively inclined to favour the Reformers. It is on the whole difficult to see why Mary should for any purpose remove beyond the bounds of the protection afforded by her kinsmen and supporters at Cadzow or in and around Hamilton proper, where in a very few days about six thousand men mustered in her cause. Mary's letters during her stay are all dated like the above, as from or "off" Hamilton, and it was certainly at Hamilton she held her great Council to declare that consent to the coronation of her son had been extorted by the fear of death. An Act of Council was thereafter passed to make treasonable all the proceedings by which Moray had become Regent, and a Bond drawn up in defence of their Sovereign which, in the enthusiasm of the moment, was signed by nine earls, nine bishops, eighteen lords, twelve abbots and priors, and nearly one hundred barons. Two versions have come down to us of Mary's proceedings at this time. In one she is opposed to civil war, and is said even to have made overtures to the Regent for reconciliation and forgiveness. Another will have it that she was no way averse to the Hamilton policy of striking a decisive blow at the Regent's party, and would certainly make no effort to avoid a conflict.

Since a day or two before Mary's escape on the 2nd May, the Regent had been in Glasgow with a small following administering justice and holding courts of various kinds. Anxious to attack at once before either Huntly or Ogilvy, with their northern followers, could join the royal forces, but wishful at the same time for a breathing space to gather men, Moray issued a proclamation declaring his determination to support the King's Government. Mar thereupon despatched reinforcements and cannon from Stirling. Grange took command of the horse; Hume, after foiling Hepburn in his attempt to seize Dunbar, joined the Regent with six hundred; Edinburgh sent a small force of hagbutters; and important as any, Andrew, chief of Arrochar, marched in from Lochlomondside, followed by six hundred of "the wild Macfarlane's plaided clan." It thus came about that between Sunday, 2nd May, the day of Mary's escape from Lochleven, and Thursday, 13th May, an army, irregular it is true, but full of enthusiasm, and numbering at least four thousand, had gathered round the Regent. Thursday was the day fixed by the Queen to advance towards Dumbarton Castle, kept all along in her interest by John, fifth Lord Fleming. Their design, if one can gather it from dubious authorities, was to avoid the City of Glasgow, where they well knew the Regent lay encamped with his men, and cross the Clyde lower down, probably at Renfrew or Dunglass, the river then being easily crossed at these points during low water. With roads hardly existing in the sense now understood, it is not known what route the Queen and her army took on leaving Hamilton, but from what followed it may be presumed to have been by way of Blantyre and Cambuslang, where a westward movement was effected in the direction of Langside. At anyrate the Regent was fully informed that through the village of Langside the Queen's forces must pass. Had it been sincerely intended to avoid a contest, a safer road to the Clyde, south of Cathcart, might have been found.

Early in the morning, Grange had examined Langside and neighbourhood, while the Regent was mustering his men on the Burgh Muir, off the Gallowgate. Informed of the intention of the Queen's party to march along the left or south bank of the Clyde, he returned in haste to the muster-ground, mounted a hagbutter behind each horseman, and having rapidly forded the Clyde, a little above the frail old bridge, he placed them advantageously among the cottages, hedges, and gardens skirting each side of the narrow rising lane up which the Queen's troops must defile ("Melvill's Memoirs," pp. 200-201.) Moray with the main body, and Morton with the advance, crossed Clyde by the bridge, and, ascending Camphill and Langside Hill from their western slopes, out of view of their opponents, arrived on the ground just in time to meet the Queen's forces. The vanguard, two thousand strong, was commanded by Lord Claud Hamilton, but the disposal of the troops generally was in the hands of Mary's brother-in-law, Archibald, fifth Earl of Argyll, whose commission as Lieutenant of Scotland had been signed at Hamilton early in the morning. The writer of the "Diurnal of Occurrents" mentions that the advance of Hamilton got involved within narrow passages, or "fauld dykes," when rushing to attain the crest of the hill, and being fired on in this disorganised state, they "gaif bakis and fled." Others in the rear sought to push on, and so far succeeded, but were nearly exhausted when they found themselves face to face with the

Regent's advance, well rested and in firm order. Tytler, relying on Melvill, describes this portion of the force as composed of the choicest Border pikeman, led by Hume, Kerr of Cessford, and other barons of the Merse, who all fought on foot. Obeying Grange's command to keep pikes shouldered till the enemy had levelled theirs and then push on, the most severe struggle of the day now took place for possession of the hill-side. Melvill (the Queen's secretary), who was present, describes the long pikes as so closely crossed and interlaced that, when the soldiers behind discharged their pistols and threw them on the staves of their shattered weapons in the face of their enemies, they never reached the ground, but remained lying on the spears. Reinforcing the Barons of Renfrewshire, with the followers of Lindsay and Balfour, a sharp united attack on the Queen's party was made by Moray and Grange, with disastrous results to their opponents. They wavered, broke up, cast aside their weapons, and fled. The route was completed by a charge on the part of the Macfarlane men, with the leaps and yells peculiar to their mode of fighting. Even the Hamilton cavalry, greatly superior as it was to anything on the side of the Regent, became mixed up in the confusion, and when relieved, could do little but turn and disperse, although every incitement to renewed effort was given by the presence of the Queen, who witnessed the scene with sorrow from an eminence adjoining Cathcart Castle. About 300 were set down as being slain on the Queen's side, and many distinguished leaders captured—among them Lords Seaton and Ross, the eldest sons of the Earls of Eglinton and Cassillis—and the Sheriff of Linlithgow, a Hamilton, who bore the royal standard in the vanguard. The Regent's loss was trifling—not more, it is thought, than half-a-dozen, but three of his trusty supporters—Hume, Ochiltree, and Andrew Car of Faudonside, were severely wounded.

With much humanity, the Regent checked his followers in pursuit, and even liberated certain of the captives condemned to death. One so released was that John Hamilton of Bothwellhaugh, destined within two years to cause the death of his deliverer by shooting him when passing in triumph through the streets of

Linlithgow. The authorities on which reliance can be placed for information regarding the battle or "Field," as it was called, of Langside, are neither weighty nor very informing. No letter or despatch from the Regent regarding the encounter is known to exist. The "Memoirs of Melvill" and the "Diurnal," published by the Maitland Club, as well as the "Herries' Memoirs," issued by the Abbotsford Club, although each in their way pretending to the authority of observers or actors concerned in the events narrated, have all had their accuracy questioned. Among the Scottish documents in the State Paper Office, London, is a printed "Advertisement of the Conflict in Scotland," bearing date three days after the engagement; but it is brief, and otherwise imperfect through decay. On only one point are all agreed—that the encounter lasted only a short time, not many minutes over half-an-hour. It was long enough, however, to check, if not dispel, any notion Queen Mary might have indulged in of again ascending the throne of her ancestors. Wrung in spirit by disappointment, yet resolute as any Guise of them all, she turned hastily from her exposed resting-place to urge her horse southward, accompanied by a few valued friends like Herries, Melvill, Fleming, and Livingstone, not forgetting even in her grief the page "prettie" George Douglas. Her route and destination on the evening of that day are still matters of conjecture. Historians have said Dundrennan Abbey, near Kirkcudbright. Herries writes of a halt as being made at Sanquhar before proceeding to his own house at Terregles, not far from Dumfries, but on the Galloway side of the Nith. Mary herself, in the pathetic letter to Elizabeth, written from Workington, Cumberland, three days after the battle, says she rode sixty miles across country the first day :—"It is," she writes with touching simplicity, "my earnest request that your Majesty will send for me as soon as possible, for my condition is pitiable, not to say for a Queen, but even for a simple gentlewoman. I have no other dress than that in which I escaped from the field. My first day's ride was sixty miles across the country; and I have not since dared to travel except by night." Sixty miles agrees better with the Herries narrative than any other theory, and it may be that Sanquhar was the first place halted at, and reached by routes not known now, but roughly marked out by the present road leading through East Kilbride, Strathaven, and Douglas, from which Sanquhar is distant only about twelve miles. Dundrennan could be easily reached the second day from Lord Herries's residence at Terregles, and beyond Dundrennan the Queen's movements can be traced almost daily during the long years of imprisonment which followed on carrying out the ill-advised scheme of submitting her troubles to the gracious consideration of her "Sister" Elizabeth, of England. The Regent, on returning to Glasgow with his forces, received a warm welcome from the inhabitants, attended a special thanksgiving service in the Cathedral, and was afterwards entertained by the Magistrates. Besides renewing or extending former privileges enjoyed by certain crafts, the Regent, before leaving the City, and in consideration of the uncommon exertions made by the bakers, to supply bread to the troops, working as they did not only in the mills but in their own houses, gave them a grant of what was known as the Archbishop's mill at Partick, which had then become the property of the Crown, and also a piece of land adjoining, annexed to the Royalty of Glasgow in the first session of the first Parliament of Charles II.

AUCHINLECK AND THE BOSWELLS.

LYING almost longitudinally across mid Ayrshire, but slightly to the east or Lanark side of the country, the little strip of Auchinleck parish appears as if likely to be crushed down on Cumnock by Sorn, were it not for the soft mossy barrier which "serves it in the office of a wall, or moat defensive." This dreary upland waste, bleak and barren in itself, is yet classic as Marathon to the descendants of those who there contended to the death for religious liberty. Beginning about a mile and a half east by north-east of Auchinleck village, this battle-ground of the Covenant extends nearly six miles north-eastward towards the course of Ayr Water, a small portion projecting into Muirkirk parish as a boundary on the east, and corresponding so far with the sinuous division made by "winding Lugar," which divides the west point of Auchinleck from Ochiltree, and most of the south from Cumnock. Poor, cold, and thin, even as pasture land, the Lugar in modern days may be looked upon as another Pison compassing treasures beneath the surface more precious than the gold of Havilah. Nor is the parish quite without antiquarian remains of interest, as within its bounds stand the ruined Castle of Kyle, a few miles south-east of the village; and within Auchinleck policies there is what remains of the Boswell's ancient family "keep," along the mouldering walls of which Dr. Johnson himself clambered. Auchinleck (the "Affleck" of natives and neighbours) may claim even a slight additional literary distinction, in so far as it is the birth-place of that keen controversial Protestant, William M'Gavin, and of the smooth-flowing, if somewhat colourless, essayist and divine, "A. K. H. B." Cameron fell on its dark heath, and Peden, after innumerable escapes, was laid in the churchyard, but not before visiting his young friend's lonely grave in the moss, where he knelt and prayed fervently, while "Oh! to be wi' Ritchie" was "still his bitter cry." To the shame of any Government, except the shameless Government of Charles, the remains of the brave old Covenanter, whom Providence had permitted to breathe his last, concealed in the house of "one of his own people," were disinterred, removed to Old Cumnock, and flung with ignominy into a pit beneath the public gallows.

In the first years of the sixteenth century the lands of Auchinleck, corresponding, it may be presumed, with something like the present parish boundaries, as two-thirds of its rental still remain in the Boswell family, was granted by James IV. to Thomas Boswell, of the Balmuto line, who had married a daughter and co-heiress of Sir John Auchinleck of that ilk. The early history of the land or family is not necessary to be set forth here. Exactly 200 years after Auchinleck had passed to the Boswells, or in 1704, the James Boswell of the day, a lawyer of some eminence, married Lady Elizabeth Bruce, daughter of Alexander, second Earl of Kincardine, by whom, besides other children, he had an heir and successor, Alexander, who was trained for the bar, and admitted advocate 29th December, 1729. He acted for two years as Sheriff-Depute of the county of Wigtown, but resigned in 1750; and on the resignation of David Erskine, of Duns, in 1754, was elevated to the bench as Lord Auchinleck. On the death of Hew Dalrymple of Drummore, a few months later, he was nominated a Lord of Justiciary. He resigned the latter appointment in 1780, but retained the former till his death, which took place on 25th August, 1782, in the seventy-sixth year of his age. This old gentleman seems to have experienced no greater grief in the world than that his son should have become the companion of Dr. Johnson. "There's nae hope for Jamie, mon," the Judge said to a friend, "Jamie is gaen clean gyte. What do you think, mon? He's done wi' Paoli—he's aff wi' the land-louping scoundrel of a Corsican; and whose tail do you think he has pinned himsel' to now, mon?" Here old Auchinleck summoned up a sneer of most sovereign contempt. "A *dominie*, mon—an auld dominie; he keeped a schule, and cau'd it an academy." When Johnson was at Auchinleck the conversation one evening became more than usually animated between the Covenanting Judge and his Tory guest. "And pray," the latter asked, "what good did Cromwell ever do to his country?" "God, doctor! he gart Kings ken they had a *lith* (joint) in their neck." The Judge and his son appear to have been two very different men, the one being solid, composed, and slow; the other vain, frivolous, and volatile. Riding together one day James appeared impatient to get on a little faster, "for," said he, "it is not the exercise that fatigues me, but the hinging upon a beast." "What's the matter, mon," his father replied, "What's the matter, mon, how a chield hings, if he dinna hing upon a gallows?" Lord Auchinleck died 25th August, 1782, aged 76. Towards the later years of his life (or about 1771), he pulled down the old family mansion, and built a new, elegant, and comfortable residence.

James Boswell, son and heir of Lord Auchinleck, and author of one of the most esteemed biographies in the English language, was born in 1740, studied at Glasgow and Utrecht for the bar, and passed advocate 1766. Visiting London in

1763, he made the acquaintance of Johnson at the hospitable table of Mr. Dilly, and though they were never together so long nor so frequently as might be inferred from the "Life," Boswell, in spite of his many frailties, and probably in a great measure because of these frailties, was able to make such good use of his opportunities as to cause all readers to be thankful that one so prone to talk as Johnson, and who talked so well, should have been brought into close contact with one so zealous and able to record. But Boswell did more than record. He suggested and planned for Johnson schemes which Johnson himself would never have thought of, or, if thought of, would have been cast aside through his habitual or rather constitutional indolence. But for Boswell, who suggested the whole project, and accompanied his friend from first to last, there would have been no "Journey to the Western Islands of Scotland," where as a denizen of Fleet Street the sage saw so much that was "surprising in modes of life and appearances of nature." In Boswell he admits to have found "a companion whose acuteness would help his inquiry, and whose gaiety of conversation and civility of manners were sufficient to counteract the inconveniences of travel in countries less hospitable than those through which they passed." To have earned such praise, Boswell must have been something more than a mere fussy, obsequious gossip, the meanest and the feeblest of mankind—"a fellow," the Doctor said, in one of his cross moods, "who missed his only chance of immortality by not being alive when the 'Dunciad' was written." That he was indolent there is other evidence besides his own excessively frank and frequent confessions. Through various causes not necessary to explain here, the casual introduction at Dilly's table began to ripen so soon into close friendship that Johnson that very season insisted on accompanying Boswell as far as Harwich, from which he was to proceed to Utrecht for the purpose of continuing his law studies. A lady passenger with them spoke of never permitting her children to be idle. Johnson replied—"I wish, madam, you would educate me, too, for I have been an idle fellow all my life." On her rejoining that she was sure he had not been idle, he resumed, "Nay, madam, it is very true; and that gentleman there (pointing to Boswell) has been idle. He was idle at Edinburgh; his father sent him to Glasgow, where he continued to be idle. He then went to London, where he has been very idle; and now he is going to Utrecht, where he will be as idle as ever." Besides passing as advocate in Edinburgh, James Boswell was called at the English Bar, and went the Northern Circuit, where many droll stories were circulated regarding him, particularly one invented at Lancaster Assizes, where, at the instigation of a waggish brother, he is said to have moved the Court for a writ "Quare adhærit pavimento." "I never heard (said the Judge) of such a writ; what can it be that adheres *pavimento?* Are any of you gentlemen at the Bar able to explain this?" The Bar laughed. At last one of them said, "My Lord, Mr. Boswell last night *adhærit pavimento*. There was no moving him for some time. At last he was carried to bed, and he has been dreaming about himself and the pavement." With the exception of the "Douglas Cause," in which he was mixed up as a kind of volunteer on the winning side, Boswell had little call to appear often in Court, although he had all his life the esteem and friendship of the Scottish Bench and Bar. Of a festive, convivial turn of mind, he was simple and unconstrained to an almost reprehensible degree, and occasionally, it would appear, he found those as high in social station as himself willing to minister to his vanity. His great work (for his books of travel have been forgotten), the "Life of Dr. Samuel Johnson," appeared in two volumes 4to, 1790—nearly six years after the death of his hero. Boswell himself died June 19, 1795, aged 55, leaving Alexander, his heir, with James, a barrister, and friend of Malone, Shakespearian commentator.

Alexander Boswell (shortly before his melancholy death, Sir Alexander, Bart.), was one of the most popular Scottish gentlemen of his day, and in the course of his too brief life there came to gather round him an interest as varying in kind as it was unique in character. Efficient as a magistrate, he was also foremost in all that related to the public business of his native county of Ayr, while his accessibility to the humblest neighbour, joined to an unaffected appreciation for good-humoured social enjoyment, made him one of the most delightful of companions in the hunting-field or the race-course. His favourite riding colours, blue and white stripes, were often landed first at the post, and none ever received warmer or more sincere congratulations on victory. He was not only the writer of two or three Scottish songs of far above average merit, but he sang them socially with a polished humour and fiery earnestness all his own. A sound scholar, not either public or private business—not even the exacting demands of the Muses, lessened his appreciation of these family treasures of old Scottish lore which he had inherited in the family library at Auchinleck, and which the luxury of a private printing-press he indulged in made familiar to more readers than would otherwise have been the case. There Scott picked up the romance of "Sir Tristram," and there Sir Alexander himself re-issued his interesting reprint of the discussion at Crossraguel between John Knox and Quentin Kennedy, 1562. Sir Alexander, born October 9th, 1775, was educated at Westminster and Oxford, and created a baronet for his patriotic zeal during the threatening Radical disturbances of 1821. He was not spared to enjoy the honour for any long season. The political atmosphere was charged with influences unusually exciting. Men given far less than Boswell to either light-heartedness or humour were led to think, and say, and write things not to be defended. One or two "squibs" from his pen, printed in the "Glasgow Sentinel," bore somewhat ungraciously on a leading Whig of the day, James Stuart, W.S., younger, of Dunearn. The most offensive was in the form of a Whig song, "supposed to be written by one of the Jameses, certainly not by King James I. or King James V., but probably by one of the house of Stuart." A few of the lines appear to have been studiously calculated to give offence:—

"There's stot-feeder Stuart,
Kent for that fat cow-art,
How glegly he kicks ony ba', man,
And Gibson, lang chiel, man,
Whose height might serve weel, man,
To read his ain name on a wa', man.
Your knights o' the pen, man,
Are a' gentlemen, man,

> Ilk body's a limb o' the law, man;
> Tacks, bonds, precognitions,
> Bills, wills, and petitions,
> And ought but a trigger some draw, man."

The manuscripts given up by the printer Borthwick, and the editor Alexander, were afterwards sworn to as in the handwriting of Auchinleck. A hostile meeting thereafter took place on 26th March, 1822, on the farm of Auchtertool, Fifeshire, when John Douglas, brother to the Marquis of Queensberry, acted as second to the Baronet, and the Earl of Rosslyn for Mr. Stuart. The principals stood at twelve paces distant. The Earl of Rosslyn gave the word, and the parties fired, when Sir Alexander received Mr. Stuart's ball in the right shoulder, which broke the clavicle of the bone and injured the spine. Sir Alexander immediately fell, and was carried to Balmuto House, the seat of his relative Lord Balmuto, where every professional assistance possible was rendered, but without avail, and the unfortunate Baronet, then only forty-seven years of age, gradually sank, and expired on the afternoon of the following day. Sir Alexander, in his last moments, expressed regret for not making his intention to fire in the air more distinct; but admitted that Mr. Stuart took the only course open to him in insisting on a "meeting." It had been intended to arrange matters in the neighbourhood of Edinburgh, but the Sheriff of that county bound the parties over to keep the peace, and Fife was only thought of at the last moment, as preferable to the Continent, which had been partly arranged for. Mr. Stuart left the ground, after an ineffectual attempt to express his sympathy with the wounded Baronet. He surrendered for trial before the High Court of Justiciary on 10th June, same year (1822), where he was defended with unrivalled ability by his friends Jeffrey and Cockburn. The jury, after the address of counsel and a summing up by Lord-Justice Clerk Boyle, returned a verdict unanimously finding Mr Stuart not guilty. In relief of mental distress, he afterwards travelled in America, and returning to London edited the Liberal "Courier" for some years, when he was appointed Inspector of Factories, which position he held at his death in 1849, aged 74 years. Certain circumstances connected with the above hostile meeting were reproduced by Scott in the duel scene of "St. Ronan's Well." Sir Alexander Boswell left one daughter, married to Sir W. F. Elliot of Stobs and Wells, and a son, James, who succeeded him; born 1806, and married, 1830, Jessie Jane, daughter of Sir J. Montgomery Cunningham, Bart., with issue, two daughters. Young Sir James died in 1857, a few years after he had succeeded in reducing what was intended to be a very strict entail of the family estate, as designed by Lord Auchinleck and his son, James, on the ground that certain letters written on or over an erasure were not referred to in the testing clause of the deed. Lady Boswell died March, 1884. The valued rental of lands composing Auchinleck parish is entered at £24,797, about two-thirds being held by the Boswell family, and the rest divided among the Marquis of Bute with ten other proprietors.

THE MURES OF CALDWELL.

MURE, Moore, More, for the same name has in process of time assumed all these and at least as many other forms, carry the mind back to public transactions in Scotland earlier than to what well-authenticated history can testify, and earlier also than the time when any uniformity in spelling was observed. A settled nomenclature has justly been described as one of the niceties of modern orthography. Of the Mures it may be said with literal exactness, "Kings have come of us, not us of kings." Smitten by the charms of his cousin, the "Beauty of Rowallan," while living in retirement at Dundonald, the young Stewart, Earl of Strathaven, afterwards Robert II., by marrying Elizabeth Mure, under a dispensation from Holy Mother Church, made her the maternal head of the whole Royal race of Stewart. Without making any pretensions to be the parent stem of this ancient family the house of Caldwell has ever ranked high for the public spirit and energy

of its representatives—in later days for judicial wisdom and intellectual culture.
Early in the fourteenth century, Easter Caldwell passed from the family of that
name to the Mures through the marriage of Gilchrist Mure with the last heiress of
her race, whose ancient ruined tower may still be seen within the grounds of
Caldwell.

One of the earliest existing family documents (1496) is an instrument of
sasine of Sir Adam Mure's—*Noblis viri Adæ Mur de Cauldvel*—peaceably and
legally conveying a small hamlet called Kempisland, otherwise "Breadsorrow," so
named because of the "grate sorrow it bred in debating and contesting for the
hereditable right thereof." The term "kemping" has been explained as an old
Scottish word for striving and fighting—a commentary, it is further explained, of a
disputatious age, when Border chiefs, great coveters of Naboth's vineyard, converted
many an adjoining field into a *campus belli*, of which the strongest man reaped the
harvest with his claymore. This Adam is described by contemporary annalists as
"a gallant, stout man, having many feuds with his neighbours, which were managed
with great fierceness and much blood-shed." Hector, a son, is mentioned as killed
in 1499 by the Maxwells of Pollok, whose laird narrowly escaped the wild justice of
Hector's brother John in retaliation. The feud remained long an heirloom in the
families, but that it ultimately came to be "staunched" may be noticed from a
pleasant adventure mentioned below. John Mure was not only indicted for
laying an ambuscade to capture Maxwell and "his man" with "wikid malice,
wrongwislie and violentlie;" but in 1515 we find him paying so little respect to
the Church as to engage with Lennox for sacking the palace of Archbishop
Beaton at Glasgow, and breaking down the same with artillery. An inventory,
curious enough in its way, but too long for quotation here, will be found in the
"Caldwell Papers" (vol. 1, p. 54) of the "guids and geir," the scarlet gowns
lined with fur, the gold rings and precious stones, the plate, ordnance, and
"vivers" seized on the occasion. The dying voice of another of the family
recorded in 1640 expresses with a quaint solemnity not to be misunderstood the
fast-approaching troubles of the Cromwellian period :—" For so mickle as at this

tyme thair is great appeirance of trubles and warres in this land, whilk God of His infinit mercie prevent, and grant ane happie and guide reformationie to the glorie of His name. Howbeit, I, Robert Mure of Cauldwell, am now baith weill and haill in bodie, spirit, and mynd; yet, considering there is nothing more certaine nor death, and nothing more uncertaine nor the tyme and manor yrof. . . . thairfore I heirby mak my latter will and testament."

Good and thoughtful Robert of Caldwell might well think of "trubles and warres" when the Commons in London were not only refusing subsidies to the King, but impeaching Strafford and Laud. Robert, the testator, would seem to have been soon "called away," for when the storm burst the owners were minors, and it may be said to have passed with comparative gentleness over the house of Caldwell. Putting aside at this time any account of the part taken by the Caldwell Mures in the great national commotions which followed the Reformation, the oppression to which they were subjected for supporting the Covenant party, and their Hanoverian loyalty during the Jacobite "risings," the date of 1753 is easily reached, when Wester Caldwell was again joined to the old estate by William Mure, Baron of Exchequer. It is mainly with this William Mure, and partly with his grandson, the accomplished historian of Greek literature, the present article is concerned.

According to Professor Jardine—who, however, it should be remembered, had been the youth's tutor in Paris—William Mure came nearer up to his idea of a wise man than any he had ever known. Born in 1718, his father, also William, died suddenly a few days after his election for Renfrewshire; so that the infant heir was left under the sole guardianship of his mother, a woman of sense and piety, who, in course of time, wisely introduced into the house as teacher, William Leechman, promoted in after life, partly by the interest of his pupil, to be Principal in the University of Glasgow. A Continental tour was undertaken in due course, but schemes being already devising to send him to the House of Commons as member for his native county, his time there was more limited than might otherwise have been the case. One incident in it affords a happy illustration, that long before that time the feud of ancient standing between the Mures and Maxwells had been buried in oblivion as a cause of strife. Thirty years afterwards the Baron's son, Colonel William, recorded in his journal that he remembered going to see the Chateau de Sceaux, belonging to the Count d'Eu, a descendant of Louis XIV., almost a rival to Versailles at the time, but plundered and destroyed at the Revolution. In the fine park was a large piece of water which led the guide of the party to mention that many years ago two impudent Englishmen, who had been permitted to see the place on a very hot day, took advantage of not being observed, as they supposed, to bathe in the lake. The Countess, however, got word of what was going on, much to the consternation of the bathers, who had just time before she came up to regain their clothes and effect a retreat into the wood. The guide added that the strangers were both above six feet high, and that as they hurriedly dressed themselves and slunk away, the Countess remarked, "What fine fellows they are." On repeating this story to my father at home, he asked if our cicerone had told us the names of the two tall Englishmen, and on my answering that he had not, he said: "Then I will tell you; the one was the late Sir John Maxwell of Pollok; the other, myself."

From a very early period in life, at least long before his elevation to the Exchequer Bench, William Mure displayed, in addition to other excellent qualities, an agreeable faculty for forming and maintaining the friendship of distinguished men—"*Principibus placuisse viris non ultima laus est.*" Among these, foremost in the front rank, were John, Marquis of Bute, Prime Minister, and David Hume, historian and philosopher. From the year of his election for Renfrewshire, on the death of Alexander Cunningham, of Craigends (1742), till his promotion to the Bench in 1761, William Mure spoke but rarely in the House; but his solid sense and cautious ways made him so much of an informal chamber-counsel on Scotch politics, commerce, and manufactures that Lord Bute not only handed him over the management of much of his own dilapidated property, but placed at his disposal a very considerable amount of Government patronage in Scotland—an influence great at the time, "and preserved by his own personal character long after political power had passed away from his patron." Short as Lord Bute's tenure of office was, he writes to Mure :—" I was long tired of the anxiety, envy, and disgust of a situation ill-suited to my temper or habitudes of life." His physical powers unfitted him for battling with the active, and sometimes unscrupulous, opponents by whom he was beset :—" Many reasons," his Lordship again wrote, " justify this resignation in a prudential light, but none of these should have had weight with me at present if my health had permitted my continuance; the state of that made it impossible, and I yield to necessity." ("Caldwell Papers," vol. i., p. 175-6.) Again, he writes on the death of one of his brothers :—" Attachment, gratitude, love, and real respect are too tender plants for Ministerial gardens: attempt to raise them, and they are either chilled on their first springing, or, if they once appear, they fade with the very nourishment that is given them." This fairly corresponds with, and even justifies, Macaulay's description of the mixed motives which he surmises may have led to Bute's sudden resignation. His habits, the historian explains, had not been such as were likely to fortify his mind against obloquy and public hatred. He had reached his forty-eighth year in dignified ease without knowing by personal experience what it was to be ridiculed and slandered, when all at once, without any previous initiation, he found himself exposed to such a storm of invective and satire as had never burst on the head of any statesman. But to linger with Mure and Bute detains us from a historical character of still greater and more permanent interest. Born seven years before William Mure, David Hume survived the Baron only a few months, but sufficiently long to deplore "as a loss irreparable the death of the oldest and best friend I had in the world;" adding, "I should be inconsolable, did I not see an event approaching which reduces all things to a level." The friendship appears to have been of a most cordial description in the philosopher's Paris days, when he acted as Secretary to the Embassy of Lord Hertford, and where, as Walpole puts it, Hume, Whist, and Richardson (of "Pamela" fame) was the only Trinity in fashion. The intimacy was renewed and kept up by personal intercourse in

Edinburgh, Mrs. Mure, who professed, no doubt sincerely, to "admeer" David, being always at home in her own house on the Abbey Hill when he called for a rubber at whist, or a friendly informal chat. His proficiency in the history of card kings, as set down in the "Caldwell Papers," would not appear to have been rated high by the professors of Hoyle in these days, although on this point Hume did not willingly bear criticism; Mrs. Mure, keen in the game as Sarah Battle herself, was often "down" on the philosopher without mercy. One night it is recorded they got into such a warm discussion on his play that even the good-natured Hume lost his temper, and would stand it no longer. Taking up his hat, and calling a pretty Pomeranian dog accompanying him, "Come away, Foxey," David walked out of the house in the middle of the rubber. The family were to start next morning for Caldwell; and Hume, who then lived in St. Andrew's Square, a good mile distant, was at the door before breakfast, hat in hand, with an apology.

Another card story connected with an intimate friend of the Mures, and showing David in another light, although hardly new at this time of day, should not be omitted. Before building his house in the New Town, Hume occupied a lodging in the lofty block, known as St. James's Court, on the Mound. On the floor below lived Mrs. Campbell, of Succoth (a Wallace of Elderslie), mother of the Lord President, Sir Ilay Campbell. One Sunday evening, Hume, who was on friendly habits with Mrs. Campbell's family, stepping down to take tea with her, found assembled a party of pious elderly ladies, met to converse on topics suitable for the Sabbath. David's unexpected entrance on such an occasion caused some dismay on the part of the landlady and her guests; but he sat down and chatted in so easy and appropriate a style that all embarrassment soon disappeared. On the removal of the tea-things, however, he gravely said to his hostess—"Well, Mrs. Campbell, where are the cards?" "The cards, Mr. Hume! Surely you have forgot what day it is." "Not at all, madam," he replied; "you know we have often a quiet rubber on a Sunday evening." After vainly endeavouring to make him retract this calumny, she said to him, "Now, David, you'll just be pleased to walk out of my house, for you're not fit company in it to-night." When young, Hume is said to have courted a well-born beauty of Edinburgh, and was rejected; but, records the historian of the house of Caldwell, several years afterwards, when he had obtained celebrity, it was hinted to him by a common friend that the lady had changed her mind. "So have I," dryly replied the philosopher. As became the best-natured man of his day, Hume quitted the world and his lady friends at peace. On taking leave of Mrs. Mure, with whom he had had many a critical rubber, he gave her as a parting gift a complete copy of his history. This tradition is circumstantially confirmed by the existence in the Caldwell library of his own last edition of the great work (8 vols. 8vo, 1773), inscribed on the title-page of the first volume, "From the Author." She thanked him, and added in her native dialect, which Mrs. Mure and the historian spoke in great purity, "O, David, that's a book you may weel be prood o'; but before ye dee, ye should burn a' your wee bookies!" To which, raising himself on his couch, he replied with some vehemence, half-offended, half in joke, "What for should I burn a' my wee bookies?" But feeling too weak for further discussion of the point, he shook her hand and bade her farewell. David Hume died August 25, 1776, fully five months after his friend, Baron Mure, who died the preceding 5th March.

When Baron Mure retired from Parliament to ascend the Exchequer Bench in 1761, he was succeeded in the representation of Renfrewshire, at the general election of that year, by Patrick Crawford of Auchinames. Three years afterwards Baron Mure was elected Lord Rector of Glasgow, an honour likewise conferred upon his son and successor, Colonel William of Caldwell (1793-4), friend of Sir John Mure, and by Anne, daughter of Sir J. Hunter Blair, Bart., of Dunskey, father of William Mure of Caldwell, D.C.L., another Lord Rector (1847-8), but wider known among students at home, on the Continent, and over Europe as one of the most profound scholars of the century, especially in all that concerned the language and literature of ancient Greece. It was intended to have noticed at some length the writings of this distinguished ornament of the house of Caldwell, the minuteness of his researches, and the extent to which they have been appreciated, of his place and influence among Homeric scholars, and to give a glimpse, in addition, of the entirely new "setting" into which he fixed early legends, and of the clear light his researches have thrown on ancient customs and ancient habits of thought. But the space already occupied warns us at present from entering on such enchanted ground. One sentence more must suffice. Dr. Wm. Mure, who sat, as his grandfather had done, for Renfrewshire in Parliament, was succeeded on his death in April, 1860, by his eldest son, Lieut.-Colonel Wm. Mure, who twice successfully contested the county (1874, 1880), and died 9th November, 1880, leaving by his wife, Constance Elizabeth, third daughter of the first Lord Leconfield, one son, Wm. Mure (born 1870), the present youthful representative of his ancient and distinguished house.

Situate in parts of three parishes, Beith, Dunlop, and Neilston, the lands of Caldwell mark the boundary line of North Ayrshire and South Renfrewshire. The mansion house was commenced by Baron Mure in 1773 from designs by Robert Adam.

JOHN GLASSFORD OF DOUGALSTONE.

ALONG with William Cunningham of Lainshaw, James Ritchie of Busby, and Alexander Speirs of Elderslie, each to be noticed on another occasion, John Glassford of Dougalstone has always been reckoned as one of the merchant princes who planted the tree of commercial prosperity in Glasgow, and was happily spared not only to see it spread and flourish, but to enjoy an abundant store of its rich fruit. And yet neither his origin nor upbringing was in any way superior to that of hundreds of others who were then trying to cultivate such small trade as was carried on in the City. His father, James Glassford, was a worthy but not wealthy Magistrate and trader in Paisley, and, like many more in his walk of life, the best aid John ever received towards future greatness, was a fair education at the ancient Grammar School of his native town. A peaceable man himself, and engaged in commercial pursuits which should always tend to peace, Glassford's life touches curiously enough upon some of the more threatening turbulent occurrences of his day. Born in 1715, a year when the peace of the country was seriously menaced by a Jacobite "rising" in favour of the exiled Stuarts, his earliest days corresponded with the period when Glasgow undertook to send into the field 500 men armed and provisioned, and also protected the City so skilfully by entrenchments, as to lead to a Royal recognition for the first time of the chief magistrate (Provost Bowman) as "My Lord." So much for the old Pretender. While one of Glassford's early Glasgow residences was the then superb mansion of Whitehill, north from Duke Street, he latterly, when still more prosperous, purchased the great fabric in Argyll Street, known as the Shawfield Mansion, which had been so seriously injured by the malt-tax rioters in 1725 as to warrant compensation money being paid almost equal in amount to what the owner, Daniel Campbell, paid for a large portion of the Island of Islay. Here, curiously enough, the old Pretender's son, Charles Edward, took up his quarters on entering Glasgow with his ragged, starved, retreating followers, that dismal day after Christmas, 1745.

Again, the revolt of the colonists in Virginia, and ultimate independence of the States, affected few merchants more seriously than John Glassford, whose tobacco trade, which this new "rising" ultimately ruined, was amongst the most extensive in the world. Writing to a friend regarding his appearance before a committee of the House of Commons, selected to consider the involvements likely to arise through the resistance by colonists to pay claims made on them by British merchants, William Rouet of Belritero (now Auchindennan, Lochlomondside), records in February, 1766—"I heard Glassford say that his mere private debts in the colonies amounted to £50,000." In connection with an introduction to the great merchant, Smollett mentions in "Humphrey Clinker," the latest of his novels, that during the last war Glassford, whom he took to be one of the mightiest merchants in Europe, "was said to have had at one time five-and-twenty ships, with their cargoes—his own property—and to have traded for above half-a-million sterling a-year." Great Britain had so much strife on hand in these days, that "the last war" may be judged as of uncertain meaning; but as the novel was partly written and published in 1771, it may have been the expulsion of the French from Lower Canada, when Wolfe fell fighting so bravely on the heights of Abraham above Quebec, or the war with Spain of 1762, when Havana, Trinidad, and Manilla were seized.

Like most other merchants of his time, John Glassford took a deep interest in the construction of a Canal between the Forth and Clyde, although he was satisfied it could not be altogether so successful as its more sanguine promoters represented. For mineral, stone, timber, and general miscellaneous traffic, its utility, he thought, could hardly be overrated; but he doubted if the manufacturers of either Glasgow or Paisley would much avail themselves of that mode of transit. The cost of cartage to them from point to point appeared to him as trifling compared to what they were likely to reckon on as possible damage from water and delay in transhipment. Glassford's correspondence shows him to have been in frequent communication on this subject, and also on the Scotch paper currency, with his friends William Mure of Caldwell, Baron of Exchequer, ex-Provost Cochrane, Ritchie, and Colin Dunlop. Writing in 1762 to Baron Mure, Glassford expressed a hope that when the Baron came to Glasgow the Canal scheme might be a little riper for judging as to the expediency of taking any concern with others in carrying out the project. "I hope then to have the pleasure of seeing you, and that you will do me the favour of lodging in my house, as you lately gave me some reason to expect. You will be entirely at your own freedom. (Signed), JOHN GLASSFORD." In the course of the year above-mentioned (1762), Francis, Fifth Lord Napier, employed two surveyors to examine the ground from Carron at Abbotshaugh, about two miles from the place where that river discharges itself into the Forth, to the Clyde at Yoker Burn, about five miles below Glasgow, and his Lordship likewise caused accounts to be taken of the quantities of goods carried between the two friths, and of the expense of carriage. In 1764 Smeaton declared himself strongly in favour of the route now so familiar to travellers by road and rail, and Lord Dundas, one of the leading promoters of the scheme, pushed an Act through Parliament for its construction. The works, the most difficult of the kind undertaken in the kingdom up to that time, were commenced in 1768, but lack of capital led to a delay of nearly twenty years, the canal not being finished till 1790 (by Whitworth, one of Brindley's pupils), when the opening of the new communication between east and west was celebrated with great rejoicing, the chairman of the Canal Committee, Archibald Speirs of Elderslie, symbolically performing the feat by launching a hogshead of Forth water into the Clyde at Bowling Bay terminus. It is but right to say that the name of John Glassford does not appear in the original list of the company formed under the Act of 1768 to carry out the canal works. There, however, will be found John, Earl of Glasgow, George Murdoch, Lord Provost of Glasgow, James and Richard Oswald, Archibald Stirling, and Patrick Miller of Dalswinton.

Powerful in the City as a "Tobacco Lord" alone—for he might daily be seen marching in front of the Tontine in his scarlet cloak, with curled wig, cocked hat, and gold-headed cane—John Glassford had also a large share in such lucrative concerns as the Cudbear Purple-dye Manufactory, the Pollokshaws Dyeworks, and the Glasgow Tanwork Company, the largest business of the kind then known. All these were in addition to his interest as a shareholder in the Glasgow Arms Bank, established 1753, and the Thistle Bank, set on foot some five years later. When Glassford commenced business on his own account in Glasgow about 1740, the population was put down at a little over 17,000, while the Clyde shipping made up an aggregate carrying power of 5,600 tons, represented by sixty-seven vessels, fifteen of which traded to Virginia, four to Jamaica, and six to London. For some years after the tobacco trade was opened up by the Union, Glasgow had only one ship of its own, a vessel of sixty tons, built at Greenock, and the precious weed had to be conveyed from the Plantations for the most part in vessels built at Whitehaven. Notwithstanding the pawky rule laid down by Bailie Nicol Jarvie about "pickling in their ain pockneuk," so far as concerned home-made goods for exportation, or at the worst, being able to buy English north-country wares cheaper even than English merchants, the principle, if desirable, could not always be carried out. Dr. Carlyle of Inveresk, a student for two years at the University (1743-44), and a shrewd observer, found that while the chief branches of trade in Glasgow then was with Virginia in tobacco, and with the West Indies in sugar and rum, there were often not enough manufactured goods either in the City or Paisley to make up a sortable cargo to such foreign markets, and for that purpose shippers were obliged to have recourse to Manchester. The merchants, he admits, were men of honour, industry, and enterprise, ready to seize with eagerness and prosecute vigorously every new scheme in commerce which promised success; but manufactures among themselves were in their infancy, the single Inkle factory commenced in 1732, and extended in 1743 by the purchase of land in Ramshorn Yard, being shown cautiously to strangers as a great curiosity.

The tobacco trade may be said to have reached the height of its prosperity in 1773 and 1774. In the first-mentioned year, when the Clyde shipping was over 60,000 tons, thirty-eight Glasgow firms imported the unprecedented quantity of 43,970 hogsheads (over 35,000 from Virginia), and, with stock-on-hand, were able to export to France, Holland, and other countries 47,778 hogsheads. Next year forty-six firms imported 40,543 hogsheads, and exported 34,146, leaving a stock on hand at the close of the year of 6,347 hogsheads. Matters in the States took a threatening turn in September, when the first Congress assembled at Philadelphia; but reconciliation with the mother-country can hardly be described as hopeless till April, 1775, when the first blow for independence was struck at Lexington. In June following Washington was appointed Commander-in-Chief of the American Continental Army. In October of this eventful year Franklin requested one of his correspondents to inform a common friend that Britain, at an expense of three millions, "has killed 150 Yankees this campaign, which is £20,000 a-head; and, at Bunker's Hill, she gained a mile of ground, half of which she again lost by our taking part in Ploughed Hill. During the same time 60,000 children have been born in America. From these data his mathematical head will easily calculate the time and expense necessary to kill us all and conquer our whole territory." No foreign force, however brave, numerous, or well equipped, could strive successfully against the grim determination here shadowed forth. The tobacco trade in Glasgow was not only doomed, but, so far as monopoly was concerned, had already become a thing of the past. The leaf or "weed," it is true, on hand rose first from 3d. to 6d. per lb., and, greatly to the profit of Lainshaw, ultimately to 3s. 6d. per lb.; but the time was fast hastening when the proud "Tobacco Lords" could hardly find their favourite stock in the market at any quotation. Fortunately for Glasgow, the West Indies at this juncture could be kept open for sugar, as well as material for the favourite punch beverage, and a powerful impulse was at the same time given to the mineral and manufacturing industries of the district.

John Glassford, as has been mentioned, removed from his pleasant residence at Whitehill to the more spacious Shawlands mansion in Argyll Street. It had been built in 1712 by Daniel Campbell of Shawfield, M.P. for the Clyde Burghs 1716–1734, and sacked by the mob in 1725 from resentment at his vote in Parliament for extending the malt-tax to Scotland. Campbell, who had acquired a large fortune through farming the Customs in the Firth of Clyde, was awarded £6000 as compensation, to be paid by the City from a tax on ale and beer, and, investing his money in the Islay property, sold the dilapidated Argyll Street house to M'Dowall of Castle-Semple. Although occupied by the Young Pretender during his brief, unwelcome visit to Glasgow in 1745, the rooms would never appear to have been restored to their early splendour, as in 1760 M'Dowall sold it to Glassford, with all the ground stretching to the Back Cow Loan, now Ingram Street, for 1700 guineas. Here the enterprising merchant, still in the prime of life, lived and dispensed a wide hospitality for six or seven years, or till 1767, when he purchased Dougalstone estate (originally probably Dougal's town, seat of Dougald of the Lennox family), in New Kilpatrick parish, from

John Graham, advocate, the representative of a branch of the Montrose family whose chief residence, before Buchanan House came to be built, was at the old Castle of Mugdock, near to Dougalstone, although in a different parish. The east side of New Kilpatrick parish and the west side of Strathblane touch each other in this neighbourhood, the first being mostly within the county of Dumbarton, the other in Stirlingshire. The mansion-house, which stood upon the site of the fine new one erected by the present owner, Robert Ker, Esq., merchant, had been built in 1707 by John Graham, then of Dougalstone. Besides possessing property in the east end of Glasgow, this branch of the Montrose Family owned the western suburb of Grahamston, extending from what is now the south-west corner of Union Street west to a little past Hope Street, and backward to a line slightly north of Gordon Street. (See paper on Grahamston by C. D. Donald, Jun., "Glas. Archæological Pro.," pt. 2, vol. II.) On entering Dougalstone as his country residence, John Glassford laid out the grounds anew in the most ornamental style, and at the same time greatly enlarged the mansion. As appears from a memorial tablet in the western wall of the Ramshorn burying-ground, Mr. Glassford was three times married, his last wife being Lady Margaret Mackenzie, daughter of George, last Earl of Cromartie, whose son, James Glassford, raised an unsuccessful claim to the ancient Cromartie peerage, dormant for a time, but now held in her own right by Anne, present Duchess of Sutherland. John Glassford died in Glasgow, August 27th, 1783, aged 68. His son, Henry, sat in the Commons for Dumbartonshire, 1802–6, when he resigned, and again 1807–10, when he was succeeded by Archibald Colquhoun of Killermont, Lord Advocate of Scotland. Henry Glassford died unmarried, 19th May, 1819, aged 54. In 1792 he sold the family town mansion of Shawfield to a builder for £9,850. The fabric, not very old as we have seen, but which had experienced strange vicissitudes, was then removed for the purpose of opening up the well-known street stretching northward from the junction of Argyle Street with Trongate, and which now bears the name of the greatest merchant of his time.

CATHCART AND ITS EARLS.

"I WAS told the other night (wrote Horace Walpole to the Countess of Ossory) that Lady Cathcart, who is still living, danced lately at Hertford, to show her vigour at past four score." The Lady Cathcart of that day (1770) was originally Sarah Malyn, daughter of a Southwark landowner, who married first James Fleet, lord of the manor of Tewing, Hertfordshire; secondly, Captain Sabine, also of Tewing; and, thirdly, in 1739, Charles, eighth Lord Cathcart, whose first wife, and mother of the ninth Earl, also Charles, had been Marion, only child of Sir John Shaw of Greenock, an honorary title still enjoyed by the eldest son of the Cathcart family. In May, 1745, fully four years after the death of her husband, Lord Charles, at sea, Lady Cathcart, then fifty-four years of age, married Hugh Macguire, an Irish officer in the Hungarian service, who, alarmed, as her fourth husband at the suggestive motto round one of her wedding rings—" If I survive, I shall have five "—took her ladyship over to Ireland, and kept her in confinement till his death, which, to her great satisfaction, happened in 1764, when she returned to England, and eight years later, when over four score, showed much of her old native sprightliness by dancing, as mentioned above, at the Welwyn Assembly. In the novel of "Castle Rackrent," the Edgeworths published many interesting particulars regarding the harsh treatment of Lady Cathcart by Colonel Macguire. She appears to have survived her imprisonment of nearly 20 years by living on in high spirits for another quarter of a century. Lady Cathcart died 3rd August, 1784, in her 98th year, having lived under the reign of five English Sovereigns—viz., William and Mary, Queen Anne, and Georges I., II., III. It may also be added that she enjoyed the life-rent of the manor of Tewing for six years over half a century. She was born in the year after the Battle of the Boyne, and lived to hear the first peal of the French Revolution in the taking of the Bastile a fortnight before her death. Lady Cathcart had no issue by any of her husbands. Her first alliance, she is said to have remarked, was for the purpose of pleasing her parents; the second for money; the third (with Lord Cathcart) for title; and the fourth, with the fortune-hunting Hibernian, "because the devil owed me a grudge, and must punish me for my sins."

This Charles, the eighth Lord Cathcart, born in 1686, or five years before his second wife, who survived him nearly 50 years, came of an old distinguished stock, who, taking their title from the pleasant lands south of Glasgow, marking the junction of North Lanark with East Renfrewshire, won high distinction in countries far removed from their own as servants of the Crown. So early as 1178 Rainaldus de Kethcart (Cart Castle), founder of the house, was witness to a charter by Alan, son of Walter the Steward, "dapifer regis" of the patronage of the church of Kathcart to the monastery of Paisley. A succeeding Sir Alan of Cathcart gave Bruce unwavering support throughout all the fierce struggle for independence. At Loudonhill, where Pembroke was defeated in 1307, he was next year with Edward Bruce in Galloway, and joined in the engagement against St. John. Barbour writes of

> "A knight that then was on his rout,
> Worthy and wight, stalwart and stout,
> Courteous and fair, and of good fame,
> Sir Alan Cathcart was his name."

The wife of a modern descendant, as we have seen, took to herself four husbands in succession, so Sir Alan's wife, of the house of Wallace of Sundrum, was fourth husband of Eleanor Bruce, Countess of Carrick. A grandson, another Alan, the first Lord Cathcart, added largely to the family estate by the purchase or gift of property in Ayrshire—Auchincruive being obtained in 1465, while Dundonald, with the keepership of the Royal Castle there, was granted by James III. in 1482. The ancient fortress of the family overlooking the Cart, and of which a ruined ivy-covered tower above the village is now all that remains, is thought to date as far back at least as the early part of the fourteenth century. With walls about ten feet in thickness throughout, loop-holed windows, and lofty battlements, Cathcart Castle not only gave a secure shelter to the inmates with such "gear, plenishing, and supplies" as was deemed essential to a household in these unsettled times, but its position as a watch-tower, overlooking the pleasant valley below, now studded with evidences of industry and comfort, made it serve a purpose favouring the peace of the country for miles around. On a neighbouring eminence, now known as Camphill, within two miles northward, and also, like Cathcart, overlooking Langside, traces still exist of another stronghold, older far than the age of Bruce or Wallace; older even, there is some reason for thinking, than the period of Roman occupation in Scotland, and dating, in all probability, back to a time in Caledonian history impossible to illustrate by any other memorial than is furnished in its own design and manner of construction.

Successors to Alan, first Lord Cathcart, were his grandson, John, second Lord, and father of three sons (slain with their Sovereign at the fatal field of Flodden); Alan, killed at Pinkie, 1547—a year after he had conveyed the lordship to a kinsman connected with the Sempill family; and another Alan, fourth Lord, one of the Reforming nobles, who sallied out with his vassals to fight for the Regent Murray on his own ancestral domain of Langside, where, from a site still pointed out by tradition as "Court Knowe," within the shadow of the old castle walls, Queen Mary saw her last array of armed men beaten back in confusion by barons like Cathcart, who waged war against her in name of the infant King. Three other Alans of the family, less prominent than predecessors in public affairs, brings the family pedigree down to Charles, eighth Lord Cathcart, already mentioned as son of the seventh Earl, by Elizabeth Dalrymple, second daughter of James, first Viscount Stair, and Margaret Ross of Balneil, Wigtownshire, the reputed original of Scott's Lady Ashton, mother of the "Bride of Lammermoor." Born in 1686, Earl Charles was trained early for military service, and obtaining a captain's commission when only seventeen years of age, passed across to Flanders, where he obtained a company in Macartney's regiment, and rapid promotion afterwards under his relative John, second Earl of Stair, then engaged with the allies against France in the war of the Spanish Succession. Colonel Cathcart joined Argyll's forces during Mar's "rising" of 1715, and, as might have been expected, rendered efficient service on the doubtful field of Sheriffmuir. Later in life (1740), and eight years after he had succeeded his father as eighth in succession to the honours of the house, Lord Charles was appointed Commander-in-Chief of the British forces sent out to attack the Spanish dominions in South America. About two months after leaving Spithead he was seized with sudden illness, and died at sea, as already mentioned, being buried on the beach of Prince Rupert's Bay, Dominica, where a monument was erected to the memory of the gallant soldier. By his first marriage with Marion, only daughter and heiress of Sir John Shaw of Greenock, Lord Cathcart had, besides other sons and daughters, Charles, who succeeded as ninth Lord, famous as any of his family for services in the field and as a diplomatist at foreign Courts. Earl Cathcart's second wife, by whom he had no issue, was the Mrs. Sabine, or Malyn, referred to in the opening sentence of this article. The young Earl Charles, for he was only 19 years of age when he succeeded his father, served under Stair at Dettingen, and under Cumberland at Fontenoy, where he was severely wounded, and his only brother, Shaw Cathcart, slain. Present and active on the field of Culloden, his Lordship was next year at Laffeldt, where he was wounded once more; and within a few months passed to the Court of France, where he resided as one of the hostages for the delivery of Cape Breton to Louis XV., under that Treaty of Aix-la-Chapelle which concluded the war of the Austrian Succession, waged originally between Marie Theresa and Frederick II. of Prussia, afterwards known as Frederick the Great. On returning home, Lord Cathcart, who was then promoted to the rank of colonel, represented the King for many years in succession as Lord High Commissioner to the General Assembly, and in 1763 was invested with the Order of the Thistle, having two years earlier been appointed Governor of Dumbarton Castle. In 1768 at a critical point of the struggle between Russia and Turkey, Lord Cathcart was appointed Ambassador Extraordinary to the Court of St. Petersburg, where he resided for three years. Lord Charles died, August, 1776, aged not more than 56 years; but over thirty of which had been spent in active service at home or abroad. Lady

Cathcart was Jane, daughter of Lord Archibald Hamilton of Riccarton and Pardovan, sister of Sir William Hamilton, K.B., eminent as an antiquarian and art collector, who married the beautiful but humble-born Emma Harte, famous afterwards for her connection with Lord Nelson. Lady Cathcart bore a family of nine children—five sons and four daughters—William Shaw becoming tenth lord, and a younger brother, the Hon. Charles Alan, serving with distinction in America and in India, being especially prominent on duty against the French in the trenches at Cuddalore. Charles Alan, like his grandfather, died at sea, being overtaken with a fatal illness in the Straits of Banca, on his way to open up commercial intercourse with China, under instructions from the East India Company. He was then (1783) only 29 years of age. Of the daughters, the eldest, Jane, became Duchess of Athol. The next daughter was that Mary destined to become famous, not only for her beauty and accomplishments, but whose early death, in 1792, led her husband, Thomas Graham of Balgowan, to temper his sharp sorrow, by throwing himself at middle age into that military career in which he became for ever famous as Lord Lynedoch, victor of Barossa, and otherwise one of the ablest of Wellington's lieutenants, as he proved at Victoria, San Sebastian, and the Bidassoa. William Shaw, tenth Lord Cathcart, also won high honour for services in the field, his most prominent achievement being the bombardment of Copenhagen in the summer of 1807, when the Danish fleet, with its wealth of ammunition and stores, was seized and brought to England. Before the year had closed he was elevated to the British peerage as Baron Greenock of Greenock, and Viscount Cathcart of Cathcart, the higher title of Earl following in 1814, after his return from a special mission to St. Petersburg. Full of years and honours—he was 88—yet vigorous, the Earl passed away in June, 1843, being at the time senior General in Her Majesty's service. His eldest son, William, who commenced a naval career under Nelson in the Medusa frigate, died young, from yellow fever, at Jamaica, nearly forty years before his father. The succession thereby passed to the second son, Charles Murray Cathcart, who became eleventh Baron and second Earl. As Lord Greenock, he served with the army in Ireland, the Mediterranean, at Flushing, and through most of the Peninsular war, till Waterloo, where he was present and took part in the action. Soon after succeeding to the Earldom, he was appointed Commander-in-Chief of the forces in Canada, and Colonel of the 3rd Dragoon Guards. Dying in July, 1859, Earl Charles was succeeded by his son, Alan Frederick, Lord Greenock, the present Earl of Cathcart, born 1828, and married, 1850, Elizabeth Mary, eldest daughter and co-heiress of the late Sir Samuel Crompton, Bart., with issue five sons and five daughters. Frederick, third son of the first Earl, served in the Scots Greys, was present with his father at the surrender of Copenhagen, and brought home the despatches relating thereto. He married Jane, daughter of Quentin Macadam of Craigengillan, Ayrshire, taking thereafter the additional surname of Macadam. The fourth and youngest son of Earl Charles was the well-known Sir George Cathcart, who served with his father in Germany and France, being also present at Quatre-Bras as aide-de-camp to the Duke of Wellington. Sir George commanded at the Cape in 1851, but on the breaking out of the Crimean War became Lieut.-General of Fourth Division of the British army, and, to the regret of all who knew him, fell fighting at Inkermann on a hill which has since borne the name of the brave soldier.

About the lands of Cathcart, it may be thought proper to say a word or two. The parish itself, as arranged in modern times, makes up portions of two counties, Renfrewshire east, Lanarkshire west, and includes the pleasant districts, suburban to Glasgow, of Langside, already referred to, Mount Florida, Crossmyloof, New Cathcart, and Prospect Hill. The territory originally formed part of the extensive estates conferred by David I. on Walter, founder of the house of Stewart, before the middle of the twelfth century. The church with all its pertinents passed to the Monastery of Paisley, and remained under the control of that richly-endowed religious house till the Reformation, when the monastic possessions were broken up, with the exception of that portion sold about 1546 by Alan, third Lord Cathcart, to his wife's kinsman, Gabriel Sempill of Ladymuir. In this branch of the Sempills, the lands then known as Cathcart, although shorn of their original extent, continued till about 1720, when they were sold to John Maxwell of

Williamwood. Towards the close of the century the old family possessions were still further broken up, the castle and principal messuage being acquired by James Hill, from whom in 1801 they appropriately passed by purchase to the first Earl Charles, who afterwards added the property of Symshill, another portion of the original Cathcart estate. Regarding the date when the old castle was reared on the steep height above the Cart nothing is known, and conjecture therefore useless. For probably 500 years at least, we may repeat, the original square tower frowned over the valley below, and afforded protection not only to its inmates, but to the fruitful gardens round about, of which mention is made by various writers. So strong and thick were the walls, that the systematic attempt made to demolish it about the middle of last century had to be abandoned in despair. Not far from the castle stands Cathcart Cottage, the modern residence of the family, and where some sixty years since there was built into the front wall a sculptured stone, removed from Sundrum, showing the arms of Cathcart quartered with those of Stair, indicating the marriage connection already referred to between Alan, seventh Lord, and Elizabeth Dalrymple, daughter of Viscount Stair. Dull and polluted as the White Cart now is in many of its reaches, it flows through Cathcart parish amid scenes of natural beauty, well fitted to suggest pleasant memories to poets like Grahame, of "The Sabbath," and Thomas Campbell, who had each played on its banks. The poet of "Hope" almost becomes the poet of "Memory" when he recalled those

> "Scenes of my childhood, so dear to my heart,
> Ye green waving woods by the margin of Cart;
> How blest in the morning of life have I strayed,
> By the stream of the vale, and the grass-covered glade.
> * * * * * *
> But hush'd be the sigh that untimely complains,
> While Friendship and all its enchantment remains,
> While it blooms like the flower of a winterless clime,
> Untainted by chance, unabated by time."

THE STEUARTS OF COLTNESS AND ALLANTON.

FEW properties in the upper Ward of Lanarkshire, or, indeed, few properties in any part of the county, have continued to present in our own time so much of their early sylvan amenity as Coltness, and this, although surrounded in every direction with coal and iron works, sending out continuously suggestive if not attractive evidence of the mineral wealth being wrought beneath the surface. Within Cam'nethan parish, but on its extreme northern limit, where the winding South Calder divides it from Shotts, Coltness passed through the Somervilles to the Logans of Restalrig, and from them to the Steuarts, at a time when coal and iron were in but little use, and not dreamt of in the way of a national industry, as the term is now understood. The Jacobite Laird of the family, too gracious with the Prince at Holyrood, returned from an eighteen years' exile in 1763 to cultivate his favourite science of political economy in the pleasant shades of Coltness—a harmless pursuit varied frequently by a personal superintendence of improvements made in his time on the paternal acres and the pleasant mansion they still surround. His son, General Sir James, educated for the most part abroad during the period of exile, was guilty of two serious errors during his long life—an expensive intimacy with George IV. and the Duke of York, and a zeal surpassing even the zeal of his father for agricultural improvements. Between the constant hospitality of a great country-house and the usual results of gentleman-farming on a wide scale, Sir James contrived to dissipate the whole of the goodly inheritance that had devolved on him. He died a landless man at Cheltenham; but it is recorded he appeared unconscious of what had occurred as to his worldly fortunes, and might be seen now and then marking trees in the Long Walk of the Old Spa, as if he were still at Coltness.—("Qr. Rev.," vol. 70, p. 372.) This Sir James, the last in the direct line of Coltness, was born so far back as 1744, the year preceding that which wrought his father so much trouble, and when he died in 1839, at the great age of 95, was, as colonel of the Scots Greys, the senior general officer in Her Majesty's service. He is not yet quite forgotten as the inventor of certain improved tactics in cavalry warfare. His cousin, Sir Henry B. Steuart, of Collairnie, Fifeshire, succeeded as fifth Baronet of Coltness, the property itself passing, by purchase, in 1842 to Thomas Houldsworth then M.P. for Nottingham. Mr. Houldsworth died in 1852, when Coltness went first to his eldest brother, William, then to Henry, father of another Henry, at whose death, in 1868, the property passed to its present owner, James Houldsworth, Esq., born 1825. (See W. Promphrey's "Old Lairds of Coltness." Wishaw, 1879.)

The adjoining property of Allanton (or Allerton), another possession of a still more ancient branch of the house of Steuart, was long the seat of Sir Henry, of the name, celebrated for his skill as an arboriculturist, and as the first who practised on any considerable scale the art of transplanting trees, with a success which even to an experienced planter like Sir Walter Scott appeared almost marvellous. Sir Henry was enabled to cover a whole park at once with groups and single trees, combined with copse and underwood of various sizes, all disposed in exquisite taste. Independent in circumstances, as has been mentioned, and attached by taste and habits to rural pursuits, Sir Henry resided for the most part at Allanton, to which, little distinguished by nature, his wonderful exertions gave within a comparatively short period of time all the beauty that could, according to the usual modes of improvement, have been conferred in the course of forty tedious years. The soil naturally is described as moorish, and the view from the front of the house must, before it was clothed with wood, have consisted of irregular swells and slopes, presenting certainly no striking features either of grandeur or beauty—probably "just not ugly."

Allanton was visited by many intelligent judges disposed to inquire with sufficient minuteness into the reality of the changes effected there, and so far as an opportunity was afforded for knowing, the uniform testimony of those visitors corresponded with the account given by Sir Henry Steuart himself. Rather over sixty years since, or in September, 1823, a committee of gentlemen, supposed to be well acquainted with country matters, was appointed by the Highland Society to inquire into the management of Allanton plantations, particularly with reference to (1) single trees and open groups on lawn which might appear to have suffered from the operation of transplanting; (2) inclosed groups or masses of wood planted together; and (3) the cost of transplanting. From the facts which they witnessed the committee reported it as their unanimous opinion that the art of transplantation, as practised by Sir Henry Steuart, was calculated to accelerate in an extraordinary degree the power of raising wood, whether for beauty or shelter. The committee consisted of Robert, eighth Lord Belhaven; Sir Archibald Campbell of Succoth, Sir Walter Scott, George Cranstoun (afterwards Lord Corehouse), and Alexander Young of Harburn. Five years later, or in 1828, Sir Henry published his "Planters' Guide," describing in detail the measures employed by the author to anticipate in such a wonderful manner the march of time, and "to force, as it were, his woodlands in somewhat the same manner as the domestic gardener forces his fruits, upsetting thereby the old saying, 'Heu! male transfertur senio cum indurnit arbor?'" Sir Henry, son of James, tenth baron of Allanton, was created a baronet of the United Kingdom, 1814, with remainder to his son-in-law, Reginald Macdonald of Staffa, who succeeded as second baronet on the death of Sir Henry in March, 1836, and whose son, the present Sir Henry James Seton Steuart, is now the third in descent of the new Allanton creation, and represents, besides the Setons of Touch, hereditary armour-bearers to the Sovereign and squire of the Royal body. The learned author of "The Planters' Guide" was an F.R.S., an LL.D., and well known among scholars for his edition of "Sallust." He died, as has been just mentioned, in 1836, aged 77. The area of Allanton is put down at 2,673 acres, and the rental at £4,076, fully one-half being for minerals.

But it is now necessary to say something of an earlier member or two of the house of Coltness than any yet noticed. The first of the line was Sir James

Steuart, merchant, and Provost of Edinburgh, 1649-50, and who, although a strait and rather intolerant Presbyterian, protested against the execution of Charles I. but presided officially at that of Montrose. He is said by the family genealogist to have treated the illustrious victim with personal courtesy and decorum, rebuking even "the grim Geneva ministers" for their savage rudeness on the scaffold. All this, however, did not save him at the Restoration from being fined and imprisoned as "stiff and pragmatic." The family genealogist, indeed, admits with a kind of stern satisfaction that it was lucky for the Provost he was confined in Edinburgh Castle when the rash insurrection of Pentland Hill took place. His domestic chaplain, the youthful Hugh M'Kail, was prominent among the leaders of the outbreak, and being seized armed on his way to Libberton, was subjected to the form of trial then gone through, put to the torture of the "boot," condemned and executed, two grandsons of Provost Steuart attending him to the place of execution at the Cross of Edinburgh, and receiving his Bible from the youthful martyr (he was only 26), a memorial long treasured at Coltness.

When Sir James turned his attention to the Coltness property, within two miles of his elder brother's hereditary lairdship of Allanton, the lands were described as having "a convenient little tower-house, freehold of the Crown and giving a vote at elections." Obtaining his liberty by paying a fine so heavy as almost to ruin his estate, the old knight paid a brief visit to Coltness during his last illness, when well advanced in years. At Muiryet, a rising ground about two miles east from Allanton, where he had often halted, he is recorded to have turned his horse, looked around, and remarked, "Westsheild, Carnewath Church, and Lanrick, my early home and haunts, farewell! Alertoun, Coltness, and Cambusnethan Church, my later abodes, farewell! ye witnesses of my best spent time, and of my devotions! 'Tis long since I bid to the vanities of the world adieu." Sir James died soon after, and was interred with honour as one of the Fathers of the City in Greyfriars' Churchyard.

The eldest son, Sir Thomas, or "Gospel Coltness," as he came to be called, made great additions to the old tower, and otherwise added to the beauty of the grounds; but his zeal as a Covenanter so far imperilled the family estate as to make him flee to Holland, from which country he was permitted to return in poverty (1696) through the good offices of William Penn, who had made his acquaintance at the Hague. A younger brother, James Steuart, more compliant, rose to eminence at the bar, filling, as he did, the post of an Under Secretary of State and of Lord-Advocate from 1693 till his death in 1713. The "Gospel" laird's line failing in the person of Sir Archibald, family genealogist, the honours fell on the lawyer's descendant, James Denham Steuart, of Goodtrees, already referred to as involved in the Jacobite rising of 1745, influenced a good deal, it is believed, by his wife, Lady Frances, a daughter of the Earl of Wemyss, and sister of the attainted Lord Elcho. Sir James was well known in his day as a lawyer and political economist—thought, indeed, by many to have anticipated principles laid down by Adam Smith in the latter department of knowledge. His reputation as one of the founders of the modern science of political economy, symptons of regret for rashness in 1745, as also for his subsequent scheming at the French Court, and the general appreciation of the amiable qualities of Lady Frances and himself in private life, procured for him a free pardon from George III., in 1763, when he returned to Coltness, to live in retirement, after an exile of 18 years. Sir James's works, complete in six vols., were published in 1805 by his son, General Steuart, who also published in 1818, at Greenock, the correspondence between his father and Lady Mary Wortley Montague, whom he had met at Venice in 1758.

A DAUGHTER OF THE HOUSE OF COLTNESS.

LEARNED as Sir James Stewart was in his day, his books, on the whole, now interest readers less than that "Diary" of home and foreign travel left by his sister, wife of Mr. Calderwood of Polton, a gentleman of moderate estate in Mid-Lothian. Her mother was a daughter of Lord-President Dalrymple, created Viscount Stair, so that she was niece of that other daughter of the Lord-

President, famous in history and romance as the "Bride of Lammermoor." Mrs. Calderwood's own sister, Agnes Stewart, was married in 1739 to Henry David, tenth Earl of Buchan, and mother, therefore, of the eccentric Earl David, and his two celebrated brothers, Henry and Lord Erskine. Earl David, the story goes, enlarging on one occassion to the Duchess of Gordon regarding the abilities of his family—"Yes (sharply remarked her Grace), yes, my Lord, I have always heard that the wit came by the mother's side, and was settled on the younger branches." Mrs. Calderwood was also grandmother of Admiral Sir Philip Calderwood Durham, G.C.B., a naval officer who saw much service in his day, and at his death full of years, in April, 1845, was thought to be the last surviving officer, if not the last of all the crew, of the "Royal George," sunk at Spithead in 1782, the year he joined the great but unfortunate ship as one of the four lieutenants saved. But to the "Diary" of Mrs Calderwood, the record of a carriage journey to London, undertaken with her husband in 1756, for the purpose of visiting her brother, the political economist, then taking the waters of Aix-la-Chapelle. Mrs. Calderwood, who appeared to have managed all the business of the road, although never on the Continent, most likely never out of Scotland before, had, as her father's daughter, been brought up in the best of Edinburgh Society, and was in addition naturally of a quick, lively, observing disposition. It is her quaint audacity, her narrow prejudices, national as well as personal, her lofty preference for everything Scottish as against England or the Continent, and her shrewd, sarcastic, self-complacent readiness, which makes her "Diary" one of the most delightful records known of travel or criticism by a lady who had strong "views" about all her experiences and all persons she saw or conversed with.

The route was the familiar east road from Edinburgh to London, by way of Dunbar, Berwick, Durham, York, and Stamford. The couple travelled in their own post-chaise, attended by John Rattray, a steady serving-man, on horseback, with pistols in his holsters and a good broad-sword at his belt. There was also a case of pistols in the carriage, which it has been shrewdly fancied the lady, notwithstanding the mild and elegant countenance hanging on Polton walls, would have been more likely to make fit use, had there been any occasion for it, than the worthy laird with his pocket Horace. The party does not appear to have been encumbered by any Abigail or lady-attendant. From 12 to 14 hours were occupied with each day's travel. At Durham, Mrs. Calderwood gives indisputable evidence that she had never passed the threshold of any place of worship where Christian people kneel when they pray, or think it more decent to stand than to sit when they sing psalms.

June 6, it is recorded—" We dined at Durham, and I went to see the Cathedral ; it is a prodigious bulky building. It was on Sunday, betwixt sermons, and in the piazzas (cloisters) there were several boys playing at ball. I asked the girl that attended me if it was the custom for the boys to play at ball on Sunday? She said, 'They play on other days as well as on Sundays.' She called her mother to show me the church, and I suppose, by my questions, the woman took me for a heathen, as I found she did not know of any other mode of worship but her own ; so, that she might not think the bishop's chair defiled by my sitting down in it, I told her I was a Christian, though the way of worship in my country differed from hers. In particular, she stared when I asked what the things were that they kneeled upon, as they appeared to me to be so many Cheshire cheeses. I asked the rents of the lands about Durham, and was told by the landlord they were so dear he had no farm, for they let at 30s. or 40s. per aiker near that toun; that a cow was from £4 to £6 sterling, and they gave (at the best) about eight Scots pints per day. That night we lay at Northallertoun. . . . . . I could have little conversation with the people I saw, for though they could have understood me, I did not them, and never heard a more barbarous language, and unlike English as any other lingo. I suppose it is the custom in a publick-house for strangers to roar and bully, for I found when I spoke softly they had all the appearance of being deaf. I think the Cathedral of Durham is the most ridiculous piece of expense I ever saw—to keep up such a pageantry of idle fellows in a country place, where there is nobody either to see or join with them, for there was not place for above 50 folks besides the performers."

Again—"Any of the English folks I got acquainted with I liked very well. They seem to be good-natured and humane ; but still there is a sort of ignorance about them with regard to the rest of the world, and their conversation runs in a very narrow channell. They speak with a great relish of their publick places, and say, with a sort of flutter, that they shall to Vauxhall and Ranelagh, but do not seem to enjoy it when there. As for Vauxhall and Ranelagh, I wrote you my oppinion of them before. The first, I think, but a vulgar sort of entertainment, and could not judge myself in genteel company, whiles I heard a man calling, 'Take care of your watches and pockets.' I saw the Countess of Coventry at Ranelagh. I think she is a pert, stinking-like hussy, going about with her face up to the sky, that she might see from under her hat, which she had pulled quite over her nose that nobody might see her face. She was in dishabile, and very shabby drest, but was painted over her very jaw-bones." [The editor of Mrs. Calderwood's "Journal," the late James Dennistoun of Dennistoun, makes no particular mention of this "pert hussy," but it may be well for the reader to keep in mind that the Countess of Coventry, whom the good lady encountered, was none other than Maria, one of the three "beautiful Miss Gunnings," married four years previously to George William, sixth Earl. These ladies will come across us again in connection with the Hamilton and Argyll Families.] "I saw only three English Peers, and I think you could not make a tolerable *one* out of them. . . I saw very few, either men or women, tolerably handsome. . . The ladies pass and repass each other with very little appearance of being acquainted, and no company separates or goes from those they come in with, or joins another, and, indeed, they all seem to think there is no great entertainment ; but, however, they are there, and that is enough. . . . I went one morning to the park in hopes to see the Duke—'Culloden' Cumberland, son of George II.—review a troop of the Horse Guards, but he was not there. The Guards were very pretty. Sall Blackwood and Miss Buller were with me; they were afraid to push near for the crowd, but I was resolved to get forward, so pushed in. They were very surly; and one of them asked me where I would be; would I have my toes trode off?

'Is your toes trode off?' said I. 'No,' said he. 'Then give me your place, and I'll take care of my toes.' 'But they are going to fire,' said he. 'Then it's time for you to march off,' said I; 'for I can stand fire. I wish your troops may do as well.' On which he sneaked off, and gave me his place. I paid some visits, and went to see Greenwich Hospital, which is a ridiculous fine thing. The view is very pretty, which you see just as well in a rary-show glass. No wonder the English are transported with a place they can see about them.

"Kensintoun Palace looks better within than without, and there is some very fine marbles, pictures, and mirrors in it. But I could not see the private apartment of the old goodman [George II.] which they say is a great curiosity. There are a small bed with silk curtains, two sattin quilts and no blanket, a hair mattress; a plain wicker basket stands on a table, with a silk night-gown and night-cap on it; a candle with an extinguisher; some billets of wood on each side of the fire. He goes to bed alone, rises, lights his fire and mends it himself, and nobody knows when he rises, which is very early, and is up several hours before he calls anybody. He dines in a small room adjoining, in which there is nothing but very common things. He sometimes, they say, sups with his daughters and their company, and is verry mery, and sings French songs, but at present he is in very low spirits. Now, this appearance of the King's manner of living would not diminish my idea of a king. It rather looks as if he applied to business, and knew these hours were the only ones he could give up to it without having the appearance of a recluse, and that he submitted to the pagantry rather than make it his only business."

Mrs. Calderwood on English dinners is especially notable as well as quotable:—"As for their victualls they make such a work about, I cannot enter into the taste of them, or rather, I think they have no taste to enter into. The meat is juicy enough, but has so little taste, that, if you shut your eyes, you will not know by either taste or smell what you are eating. The lamb and veall look as if it had been blanched in water. The smell of dinner will never intimate that it is on the table. No such effluvia as beef and cabbage was ever found at London." [Alas! alas!] "The fish, I think, have the same fault. As for the salmond, I did not meddle with it, for it cut like cheese. Their turbet is very small by ours, but I do not think it preferable. Their soll is much smaller, and not so much meat on them; they are like the least ever you saw; were it not that they are long and narrow, I should think them common flounders. Their lobsters come from Norway or Scotland."

The views of Mrs. Calderwood on the future of Scottish trade may excite a smile among Glasgow merchants and shipbuilders, particularly as coming from the pen of one whose brother was a master in the principles and exposition of political economy :—"Most of the reproaches our country meets with can only be the want of inquiry or reflection. I once thought that Scotland might carry on a greater trade than it does, from its advantageous situation for the sea; but if they should import, who is to take it off their hands? There is no country behind them to supply who has not the advantage of seaports, which is the case of Holland, who has all Germany to supply; neither have they a great demand at home, like England, which is a great country, and most part of it inland, that must be supplied from the trading towns on the coast. Or to what country can they transport their merchandise, when they have imported more than serves themselves, that cannot be as cheap served by nearer neighbours? They have no East India goods, which are almost the only goods that are demanded by all the world; so that no country which has not one or more of these advantages can ever become a country of great trade."

ANDREW STUART OF TORRANCE AND CASTLEMILK.

PROMINENT as he was in his day, influential too, and useful withal, Andrew Stuart of Torrance almost requires a process of restoration to be made familiar to present-day readers. To all Scotland, and England too, for the matter of that, he was known in his own time as an accomplished lawyer of indefatigable industry and of undaunted courage, as a politician unswerving to the principles he professed, and, as a member of society, distinguished by birth and education. Andrew Stuart was indeed no common man. He carried two elections for his native county of Lanark; he was Keeper of the Signet, and Commissioner of Trade and Plantations; he fought a duel with a lawyer so eminent as Thurlow, afterwards Lord Chancellor; and he was an exact historian and antiquary, when neither branch of learning was cultivated with exactness or even with thoughtfulness. But it was in the great "Douglas Cause" he won his spurs, and with this stupendous law-plea his name must remain for ever associated as the supreme working agent in the interest of the infant Duke of Hamilton and his guardians. That he was unsuccessful in the final Court of resort militates nothing against the prudent zeal and weighty knowledge of the agent on whose shoulders the Case against the house of Douglas largely rested. Lord Mansfield himself, "long enough his country's pride," did not quail more under the envenomed attacks of Junius than under the brisk fire of Stuart directed by common sense, and arising from a knowledge of the Case far more profound than his own, Chief-Justice though he was. Although considerable obliquy was incurred in high quarters during the progress of the suit, men like Dunning, Wedderburn, and Adam Ferguson did not fail to do justice to the high honour and the gallant zeal, almost romantic in its self-denial, with which the Hamilton agent carried on the case through its intricate windings and varied fortunes. Second son of Archibald of Torrance (who was the seventh son of Alexander), by Elizabeth, daughter of Sir Andrew Myreton of Gogar, Andrew Stuart was educated for the law, and passed as a W.S., or Writer to the Signet, 1759. He early secured official notice, fully as much, however, from his own ability as from the accident of his connection with a branch not far removed from the main stem of the ancient Royal house of Scotland. Having for some years carried through much of the Edinburgh business connected with the Hamilton estates, it was found, on the early and unexpected death of James, sixth Duke, in March, 1758, that Mr. Stuart was named in his settlement as one of the guardians of his son, James George, seventh Duke, then only three years old, and he naturally fell thereby to be the chief agent in carrying on the business portion of the trust. The other guardians were the wife of the deceased Duke, or Dowager-Duchess as she came to be called (the second of the three "beautiful" Miss Gunnings, mother of the boy, and afterwards Duchess of Argyll, and mother of the sixth and seventh Dukes of that house); Alexander, sixth Earl of Galloway; and William Mure of Caldwell, afterwards a Baron of Exchequer. "Ah! that Baron Mure," threatened the Duchess of Douglas on one occasion, and, shaking her dainty little fist in the air, as if in the face of the guardian of her antagonist— "Ah! that Baron Mure, if I catch him, I'll mak' him as barren a muir as ony in Scotland." On the death of Archibald, first and only Duke of Douglas, in July, 1761, a somewhat eccentric old nobleman, who had married Miss Margaret Douglas, of Mains, late in life, but left no issue, the guardians of Archibald Stewart, a reputed surviving son of his sister, Lady Jane Douglas, proceeded without delay to vest him in the feudal right of his uncle's estate by getting him served heir of entail before a jury of competent witnesses. The case was one of unusual delicacy, clear proof being required that Archibald Stewart, then 13 years of age, was a surviving twin born in Paris when his mother, the deceased Lady Jane, was 50 years of age. The jury found in favour of Lady Jane's reputed son, who soon after completed his title by a charter from the Crown, and thereupon entered formally into possession of the wide Douglas estates in Lanarkshire, Renfrewshire, and other counties. Dissatisfied with the verdict of the jury, the guardians of the Duke of Hamilton resolved to investigate the matter thoroughly in his interest, and also of his brother, Lord Douglas Hamilton, as heirs-male of the Duke of Douglas through his great-great-grandfather, Lord Selkirk. Andrew Stuart now commenced his researches in earnest; nor was he long in submitting important results to his brother guardians. His discoveries appeared to himself and his colleagues to amount to nothing short of a proof that the whole story of the pretended birth, as set forth in the service of Mr. Douglas, was an absolute fraud; and in December, 1762, an action was raised in the Criminal Department of the

Parliament of Paris, accusing Sir John Stewart of Grandtully, husband of Lady Jane, and Mrs. Hewitt, her travelling companion, of the crime of *partus suppositio*, or procuring false children when in France. This action was taken secretly against Sir John, and the witnesses bound over to give evidence in Scotland, while the charge, being of a criminal nature, precluded him from interfering in favour of his son. As instructed by Stuart, the Hamilton lawyers now took up the position that Lady Jane was never confined at all; in particular, that she was not confined in the house or in the presence of Madame La Brunne, inasmuch as no such person existed; and that there was imposture, mystery, and concealment regarding the movements of all the principal parties in and around Paris during the July of 1748. Stuart was also able to establish on indubitable evidence the all-important fact that two children, answering to the description of the twins, were stolen from their parents in Paris on or about the date in question. In due course, in the summer of 1767, the great "Cause" came before the Court of Session, or "The Fifteen," as it was commonly called, the "advising" taking up seven days in July. On the 15th the Court gave judgment, when seven voted on each side. Lord-President Dundas thereupon gave his casting vote in favour of the pursuer, the Duke of Hamilton. Among the lawyers engaged at one time or another in the case, besides many elevated to the Bench during its progress, were, for the pursuer, Andrew Crosbie, the reputed original of Scott's "Counsellor Pleydell," Sir Adam Ferguson, Sir David Dalrymple, afterwards Lord Hailes, and Thomas Miller, then Lord-Advocate, afterwards Lord Justice-Clerk; for the defender (Douglas), Islay Campbell, Robert Macqueen, afterwards Lord Braxfield, Francis Garden, afterwards Lord Gardenston, and James Boswell, friend of Johnson, a contributor to the prolific literature of the contest in the form of what he called "The Essence of the Douglas Cause." Following this failure in the Court of Session, an appeal was immediately entered upon for Mr. Douglas before the House of Lords. A year and six months afterwards (27th February, 1769), a decision was given in that last Court of Appeal in favour of Mr. Douglas as pursuer, which secured him the estates as lineal heir of Duke Archibald.

Such a finish did not take Mr. Stuart by surprise. "Last night (he wrote to a friend the following day) our fate was decided agreeable to the prediction I sent you." The decision was received in Edinburgh with much rejoicing and some tumult. The counsel who spoke before the Lords were—For the appellant (Douglas), the Lord-Advocate (Montgomery) and Sir Fletcher Norton; for the respondents, Wedderburn and Dunning. The Lord-Chancellor (Camden) and the Chief-Justice (Mansfield) spoke with marked ability in favour of Mr. Douglas. A man of quiet, retired habits, and an excellent landlord, he was raised to the Peerage as Lord Douglas of Douglas, 1790, and died universally respected, December, 1827. Stuart's "Letters to Lord Mansfield" on the case, a weighty, dignified, and closely-reasoned remonstrance regarding the opinions expressed by his Lordship, appeared in January, 1773, with many apologies for unavoidable lateness. In the later stages of the "Cause," when papers were being prepared for the House of Lords, Mr. Stuart took objection to the quaint Gallicism used by Thurlow, "*a mean cominer.*" As a lawyer, equal in education and character, and greatly his superior both in birth and social connection, Stuart resented the phrase, and a hostile meeting in Hyde Park with swords and pistols was the result. According to the cautious prints of the day, he was attended as second "by his brother, Colonel ——," Thurlow having for his "Mr. L——, member for a city in Kent." The first may readily be identified as Colonel J. Stuart of Torrance, younger brother to Andrew, the other, probably, was Mr. W. Lynch, member for Canterbury. Both gentlemen discharged their pistols, which, however, did no harm. They then drew their swords, but their seconds interposed and put an end to the affair.

In the summer of 1767, when the decision of the Court of Session stood in favour of the Hamilton family, Mr. Stuart contested Lanarkshire in anticipation of the dissolution of Parliament the following year, the sitting member, Daniel Campbell of Shawfield (and Islay) being expected to retire. His opponent was John Ross (Lockhart) of Balnagowan, Ross-shire. That the contest was conducted keenly enough is apparent from a short note by Mr. Stuart (then

generally described as of Craigthorn) to a friend, dated September 13th, 1767:—
"My brother and I have been consorting here with our father (who, I have the pleasure to tell you, is much better) the plan of operations for the contest. We sally forth early to-morrow morning by different routes in order that the applications may be made as rapidly as possible in all the different corners of the county,— Yours most sincerely, ANDW. STUART." Mr. Stuart was unsuccessful at the poll, as he mustered only 26 freeholders against 41 who voted for Ross. Mr. Stuart was successful at next general election, 1774, and again in 1780, holding the seat till 1784, when he was succeeded by Sir J. Stewart Denholm of Coltness.

Mr. Stuart's great achievement in the way of literature was his "Genealogical History of the House of Stewart," published in 1798, and still an authority in its own special department. While a subsidiary object of the book was to refute the pretensions of Lord Galloway as representing the Royal House, and establish the claim of Castlemilk, which the author came to represent, there is much collateral information concerning successive generations of Stewarts of Darnley, Lennox, and Aubigny, supported by abundance of valuable "proofs" and "references." In particular, and more important than all the rest, there are the documents long lost sight of, but discovered by Mr. Stuart in the Vatican, in the form of two Dispensations relating to Robert the Stewart of Scotland (Robert II.) for his marriages with Elizabeth Mure and Euphemia Ross, settling once and for ever the question of the legitimacy of the Stewarts, so fiercely debated among the genealogists of last century. Mr. Stuart's position in the claim for family honours was that on the death of Cardinal York, then living, the representation of the male line of the Stuarts of Darnley and Lennox must devolve upon the person who was able to prove himself descended from Sir William Stuart, the next brother of Sir John Stuart of Darnley and first Lord of Aubigny. The necessary conditions, Mr. Stuart contended, were found, not in the Galloway family, but in his own ancestor, Sir William Stuart of Castlemilk. Over 40 years since the most learned genealogists of the day contended that the early Stewarts were clearly represented by Christian-Anne, Elizabeth, and Charlotte, daughters of Andrew of Torrance. His succession to the older and larger portion of the family estates came late in life and were enjoyed for only a brief season. The eldest brother of the family, Alexander, died 23rd March, 1796, when Andrew succeeded to the romantic estate of Torrance; and in January of next year (1797) his cousin, Sir John of Castlemilk, died, when Andrew again succeeded as nearest heir-male to the deceased. The latter days of his life were spent largely in keeping up a wide correspondence, and in those congenial antiquarian researches which had occupied so much of his active career. It only remains to be mentioned that Andrew Stuart married Margaret Stirling, daughter of Sir William Stirling of Ardoch, and latterly sat in the House of Commons as one of the members for Weymouth. He died at his London residence, Berkeley Square, 18th May, 1801, aged 73. Major-General James Stuart, brother of Andrew, saw much active service in India, as well as in North America, and the west India Islands, and after having bravely won the highest honours in his profession, returned to Castlemilk, where he died, 2nd February, 1793, without issue. The present proprietor of Torrance is Lieut.-Col. Robert Edward Harrington-Stuart, eldest son of Robert Harrington of Crutherland, by Charlotte, daughter and co-heiress of the above Andrew Stuart of Torrance and Castlemilk. Lieut.-Colonel Harrington-Stuart married, 1863, Louisa-Alice, daughter of the Hon. Robert Arthur Arundell, and succeeded to Torrance on the death of his aunt, 1879.

THE LOLLARDS OF KYLE.

SEPARATING Cunningham on the north from Carrick on the south, the third ancient middle division of Ayrshire, known as Kyle, is itself divided by Ayr Water into two rather unequal portions, Stewart-Kyle and King's-Kyle, the former stretching in one direction to the fertile holms along the Irvine, the latter from the Ayr southward towards Maybole and Dailly in Carrick. Kyle district comprehends in all twenty-one parishes, Tarbolton, Symington, and Dundonald lying north of the Ayr, while southward is Dalrymple, Coylton, Ochiltree, and Stair. Richly cultivated, beautiful in itself, and full of associations in romantic and legendary lore this old district of Kyle has an interest of a still higher order for the historical student wishful to enlarge his knowledge by adding to stores already collected one of the most interesting chapters in ecclesiastical annals concerning the great movement carried on against the Papacy by Reformers before the Reformation. The blood of martyrs has been affirmed on high authority to be the seed of the Church; and so, no doubt it has proved on many occasions; but Persecution, when relentless enough, and well directed, has also had its evil victories. A war distinguished, Macaulay writes, even among wars of religion by its merciless atrocity, destroyed the Albigensian heresy in the early part of the thirteenth century, and with so-called heresy perished the prosperity, the civilisation, the literature, and even the national existence of what was once the most opulent and enlightened part of the great European family. Then also arose as part of a system designed to strengthen the Church, that dreaded Inquisition, whose tribunals completed on system the destruction of such remnant as might by accident have escaped the sword. For about a century and a half, or till 1380, the Church did not judge itself to be seriously annoyed by heresy, and largely through the aid of her new order of Mendicant Friars, Rome became once more the mistress of the world, with kings for her vassals.

Next came the great Schism of the West, with two Popes, each having a doubtful title, and fulminating anathemas against each other from Avignon and Rome. By this time Wickliff, who was reared in the Church, and only kept from expulsion, if not a worse fate, through the help of powerful friends, had protested against Transubstantiation. He also declared that pilgrimages and monastic vows had no authority from Scripture. More important than all, the judicious, if not very courageous Rector of Lutterworth completed a translation of the Bible into the language of his countrymen in the year above-mentioned. Although known to a few only by manuscript fragments, there can be no doubt that it powerfully influenced the reforming movement among the common people in this country, as well as on the Continent. The most recent researches among such of his manuscripts as have escaped the destructive zeal of enemies show Wickliff to be justly entitled to dignity as Day Star of the Reformation; and such praise is now doubly deserved, as for more than two centuries after his death all that was recorded of him was set down by adversaries. The earliest, Netter of Walden, reputed author of the "Zizaniorum," published some years since in the "Rolls" series, was Wickliff's bitterest opponent, as might almost have been expected from his official position as Provincial of the Carmelite Order in England. Wodeford in his answer to the "Trialogus" was unwearied in setting down calumnies; and Nicholas Harpsfield used an Ecclesiastical History largely for the purpose of defaming his memory. Dr. James, the first librarian appointed by Sir Thomas Bodley to his newly-founded library at Oxford, 1602, was amongst the earliest scholars who undertook to vindicate the memory of the great divine.

The fears of the Church as to the effect of the new doctrines were not ill-founded. The instinctive dread of Rome that Scripture knowledge in any other than her own form should be imparted to the people once more roused her "from idle torpor to unholy zeal. Laymen and even priests secretly discussed the new doctrines in England, while missionaries, in the guise of students or merchants, carried them to France, Saxony, Bohemia, and the distant towns of the Lower Danube." A Council, as usual, was called—this time, however, for the threefold purpose of healing up schism, reforming ecclesiastical abuses, and condemning heresy as well as heretics. This important gathering, ranked among the great Councils of the Church, sat down to business in November, 1414, the place of meeting selected being the fortified but still beautiful City of Constance, on the Swiss side of the Lake bearing the same name. This Council, known in Church history as that of Constance, is said to have been reluctantly opened by the anti-Pope himself (John XXIII.), in presence of the Emperor Sigismund, 26 princes, 140 counts, more than 20 cardinals, 7 patriarchs, 20 archbishops, 91 bishops, 600 other prelates and doctors, and about 4000 priests. The Council lasted three years and a-half, or till April, 1418, the anti-Pope having by that time abdicated, and been succeeded by Cardinal Colonna as Martin V. In the course of various sessions held during 1415, John Huss and Jerome of Prague were condemned to the stake, and suffered death for teaching the new doctrines, sometimes called after Wickliff, but more commonly known as "Lollard." Forty-five articles said to have been extracted from the writings of Wickliff were condemned as heretical and erroneous, while the Reformer's dust, which for over 30 years had been lying within the quiet churchyard of Lutterworth, was with senseless malignity, ordered to be separated from the "faithful," if possible, and cast upon a dunghill. Thirteen years later this sentence was executed by the Bishop of Lincoln, as demanded by Pope Martin. Instead, however, of being thrown on a dunghill, the disinterred bones were burned, and the ashes thrown into a neighbouring brook called the Swift, which, wrote Fuller in his quaint way, "conveyed them into the Avon, the Avon into the Severn, the Severn into the narrow seas, and they to the main ocean; and thus the ashes of Wickliff are the emblem of his doctrine, which is now dispersed all over the world." The rage of the Council also fell heavily on such disciples as its far-reaching power could grasp. Some, it would appear, submitted; some fled; some sealed their faith with their blood; some received the wages of apostasy. Sawtrey was burnt; Repingdon died a cardinal ("Qr. Rev.," vol. 104, p. 148). The flame which Wickliff lighted is admitted by his enemies never to have been quite trampled out even by the iron heel of persecution. But to those who have examined the position most carefully, it seems that the flame kindled by Wickliff, which burnt so brightly, was nearly all but extinguished, because neither England nor Scotland, for a century and a-half following his death, were so well prepared as in his own time for shaking off the most corrupt form of the most corrupt church ever known to exist. So utterly had the new doctrines been trampled down, that in 1451, when Cade put himself at the head of a revolutionary population, not one of the demands made touched upon religious reform.

Among the disciples who fled northward, and sought to propagate the new doctrines, the two best known are John Reseby, and Paul Crawar, a Bohemian, both executed for holding Lollard principles—the first at Perth, 1407, the other at St. Andrew's, where he had taken up his residence, 1433. The opening sentence of Knox's "History of the Reformation" is to the effect that in one Record, vaguely described, in some now unknown Register, as the "Scrollis of Glasgu," mention is made of one "whais name is not expressed, that in the year of God, 1422, was burnt for heresye; bot what war his opinions, or by what ordour he was condempned, it appearis not evidentile." Historians have frequently fixed upon Reseby as the name intended to be "expressed," but the dates vary so widely that it is safer to conclude reference is made to some other poor Lollard, nameless, no doubt, but doubtless also, like so many of his brethren, zealous and venturesome.

Where or when the term "Lollard" came to be first applied to those who held the new doctrines, or even how the word itself came to be so applied, are points far from clear. Antwerp would seem to have been the early home of the sect, and the word may be taken from Low-German "lollen," as expressive of a lullaby or chanting of prayers. It has, however, affinities with the English "loll" and "lollers," equivalent to loungers or idle vagrants. In this sense "Lollard" might be used by orthodox Churchmen as a term of reproach towards the followers of Wickliff. From such terms in the language of scorn it is known we have "Puritan," "Quaker," and even "Christian" itself, the disciples being first so called in derision by the nimble-witted citizens of Antioch. But how originated or when first applied need not occupy more space. By the early part of the fifteenth century the name had come to express in Scotland a well-defined set of religious principles hostile to the Church as it existed, and also to the priests who ministered at her altars. Wyntoun, in his "Metrical Chronicle," composed about 1420, writes of Robert, Duke of Albany, appointed fifteen years earlier Governor of Scotland, as "a constant Catholike, all Lorrard he hatyt, and Hereticke." The execution of Reseby at Perth during his exercise of power, shows that the compliment such as the worthy Prior of Lochleven intended was not ill merited. The prevalence of Lollard opinions is still more evident from the terms of an oath framed for the newly-founded University of St. Andrews in June, 1416, requiring that all who commenced Masters of Arts should swear, among other things, that they would resist all adherents of the sect of Lollards. Again, in 1424, and suggestively enough in Perth, the city of Reseby's martyrdom, a Parliament of James I. passed an Act "Anentis Heretikis and Lollardis," providing that " Ilk Bischop sall ger inquyr be the Inquiscione of Heresy, quhar ony sik beis fundyne, and that thai be punnyst as lawe of Haly Kirk requiris ;" and, finally, that secular power be called in for helping of the Kirk.

It is under the conditions provided for in this Act of Parliament that we are brought face to face with the Lollards of Kyle. In 1494, the sixth year of the reign of James IV., when Luther was a lad at Mansfeldt School, and 23 years before he had nailed his famous challenge thesis to the church door of Wittenberg, information was conveyed to Robert Blackadder, Archbishop of Glasgow, that about 30 people within his jurisdiction, most of them in Kyle, but a few in Cunningham, were infected with the Lollard leprosy, introduced into that quiet pastoral district, it was unknown by whom, but spreading with alarming haste. Blackadder, of the house of Tulliallan, who had been Prebendary of Cardross and Bishop of Aberdeen before his elevation to the see of Glasgow, was much engaged in his day in missions to the Papal Court, and must have known well all about the rise and progress of Lollardism in his native country as well as on the Continent. The daring heretics were instantly summoned to answer for their offence at a Council, held in presence of the King. Among those who answered to the charge were George Campbell of Cessnock, Adam Reid of Barskimming—(of "Blaspheming," Vautroullier transcribes in his very defective edition of Knox's "History")—John Campbell of Newmilns, Andrew Shaw of Polkemmit, the Lady Polkellie, related to Cessnock, and Marion (or Isabella) Chalmers, Lady Stair, from whom descended Lord-President Stair.

The charges made before the Council against these early Worthies of Kyle amounted to 34 in number. Briefly stated, they were accused of believing that neither images nor the relics of saints were to be worshipped; that the "power of the keys" ended with the Apostle Peter himself; that tithes ought not to be paid;

that every faithful believer was a priest; that the Pope was not the successor of St. Peter, and deceived the people by bulls and indulgences; that the blessing of a Bishop was of no value; that excommunication was not to be feared; that priests might marry; that prayer ought not to be offered up to the Virgin; and, worse still, for it lay at the core of all heretical teaching, that the pretended sacrifice of the mass was idolatry. "Adam Reid (said the Bishop) believe ye that God is in heaven?" Reid answered—"Not as I do the Sacraments seven;" "whairat the Bischop (we now follow Knox), thinking to have triumphed, said—'Sir, so he denys that God is in heaven;' whairat the King, wondering, said, 'Adam Reid, what say ye?' The other answered—'Please your Grace to heir the end betwixt the churle and me.' And thairwith he turned to the Bishope and said, 'I nether think nor beleve, as thou thinkis, that God is in heavin; but I am most assured that he is not only in heavin, bot also in the earth. Bott thou and thy factioun declayre by your workis, that eyther ye think thair is no God at all, or ellis that he is so shut up in the heavin, that he regardis not what is done into the earth; for yf thou formerlie believed that God war in the heavin, thou should not mack thy self check-mate to the King, and altogether forgett the charge that Jesus Christ the Sone of God gave to his Apostles, which was to preach his Evangell, and not to play the proud prelatts, as all the rabill of yow do this day. And now, sir (said he to the King), judge ye whither the Bischop or I believe best that God is in heavin.' Whill the Bischope and his band could not weill revenge thame selfis, and whill many tantis war gevin thame in thair teith, the King, willing to putt ane end to farther reasonying, spoke to the said Adam Reid, 'Will thou burne thy bill?' (a sign of recantation). He answered—'Sir, the Bischope and ye will.' With these and the lyik scoffis the Bischop and his band war so dashed out of countenance that the greatest part of the accusatioun was turned to lawchter." Bishop Blackadder, it may be mentioned, who is described by Lesly as "ane noble, wyse, and godlie man," died in the summer of 1508, soon after he had set out on a pilgrimage to the Holy Land.

No more prosecutions for belief are heard of till the youthful Patrick Hamilton acquired the undying distinction of being the first Scottish martyr for Reformation principles by suffering at the stake in front of the College of St. Salvador, St. Andrews. Ayr, however, was not much later in furnishing a confessor "faithful unto the death" in the person of young Kennedy—he was only eighteen—who in 1539 was burnt in Glasgow at the instance of Bishop Gavin Dunbar, and certain assistants, whom Knox described as "beasties," sent west by Cardinal Beaton. Young Kennedy, whose Christian name is conjectured to have been Thomas, suffered along with Jerome Russell, a learned and pious Cordelliere Friar. They both met death with great heroism, each inciting the other to endurance at the stake here for the life of blessedness to come—"Playing the man," as honest Hugh Latimer expressed it to his fellow-sufferer, "Master" Ridley, and, too, like these later martyrs for the same principles, "lighting a candle in Scotland which should never be put out." "I am ready to die (said Kennedy), and free from the fear wherewith I was once oppressed."

THE EARL OF EGLINTON SHOT BY A POACHER.

IN the prime of life, high in official station, popular wherever he was known, and esteemed by his tenantry, as most of the house of Montgomery have ever been, few deaths could have been more unlooked for, and none less likely to be the result of violence, than Alexander, tenth Earl of Eglinton. In the fatal altercation with his assassin on the shore at Ardrossan, it almost seemed as if humane confidence led him for a moment to forget the cautious motto of his house—"Gardez Bien"— "Take good care." His father was that Alexander, ninth Earl, less known probably for his exertions in favour of the Hanoverian succession during Mar's Rebellion in 1715, or even for having cleared the estate of encumbrances and added to its extent, than for having as third Countess the amiable Susannah Kennedy of

Culzean, whose perfect beauty and charming manner may still be recalled in a distant way through the pages of Allan Ramsay and Hamilton of Bangour. Her family became distinguished for what was known as "the Eglinton air;" nor was her eldest son, the tenth Earl, less distinguished than the others for manly grace and a frank, accessible manner. These, however, could not be discerned when he succeeded to the wide inheritance of the family in 1729. The new Earl was only three years old. Minorities are usually favourable for "nursing" an estate when in the hands of judicious guardians, nor is there any reason for thinking that his youthful Lordship was in any other hands than the most competent. But, as the unexpected always happens, so does the unforeseen sometimes occur. In the summer of 1730, the year after his succession, a desolating storm of hail spread over three baronies of the earldom to the almost utter destruction of the crop. The calamity gave rise to a litigation extending over several years, but at its weary close the Court of Session decided that the tenants were not entitled to pay rent for that year. Even the miller obtained compensation for deficiency in multures.

Being only sixteen years of age at the Jacobite "rising" in the perilous '45, the Earl was able to avoid personal involvement on either side; but, as his father's son, he must often have heard of the narrow escape made by his Wintoun relative after Mar's attempt in 1715. Following the troubles of '45 came the Act for abolishing heritable jurisdictions, under which the Earl got £7,800 in full payment of a larger claim made for the redeemable Sheriffship of Renfrew, the bailairy of the regality of Kilwinning and the regality of Cunningham. Governor of Dumbarton Castle, a Lord of the Bed-Chamber at the Court of George III., he was also a Scottish representative Peer, and took an active part in passing through Parliament a useful measure abolishing the optional clause permitting the Scotch banks to refuse payment of their notes in cash for six months. But it was as an improving agriculturist that he made his most memorable mark, inasmuch as he thereby not only benefited his own estate but set an example which was soon copied all round. Regarding the preservation of his game, he was neither more strict nor less considerate than his neighbours. That he intended having a shot on his own grounds the day he met with his death is evident enough from a gun being placed in his carriage on setting out in the forenoon. He not only planned but personally superintended much work in the way of planting, reclaiming, enclosing, and building. Earl Alexander, indeed, was seldom off the estate, and it was in the course of inspecting such operations that he came to his untimely end. The murderer and his victim had encountered each other at least once before.

Mungo Campbell, described as an excise officer at Ardrossan, was born at Ayr in 1712, and reputed to be one of twenty-four children. His father was at one time Provost of that burgh, but meeting with heavy losses in business, the family were left only indifferently provided for at his death. Mungo was taken charge of in infancy by his godfather, Cornet Campbell, and on growing up enlisted into the Scots Greys, went with them to Dettingen, was discharged in 1744, and on returning to Scotland received a commission in the excise through the patronage of the Earl of Loudoun, whom he had accompanied in a humble capacity to the Highlands. Esteemed on the whole for his military experiences as well as his gentle descent, and fond of the gun, he had a loose kind of permission to ramble over various properties in that portion of Ayrshire where he lived. On Eglinton's ground Campbell was not permitted to encroach. The Earl had come across him on one occasion at Parkhead after shooting, and only let him off with a stern warning, incited thereto, it was said, by one of the Castle servants named Bartlemore, who had been detected by Campbell in assisting to smuggle inland a quantity of rum. On the 24th October, about ten o'clock forenoon, Campbell, carrying a gun, and accompanied by a tide-waiter named Brown, set out from Saltcoats to walk to Montfode Bank by a common road leading through the Eglinton grounds, the primary object of the journey, it was alleged for Campbell, being the detection of smugglers either at Montfode or Castlecraigs.

They were returning by the sands, and within flood mark, when Earl Alexander passed them in his carriage on the Largs and Saltcoats road. Informed, or knowing otherwise, that they had been poaching over his grounds his Lordship left the carriage, mounted a horse, and accompanied by some of his servants, rode up to Campbell, charging him with faithlessness after the promise he had made to abstain, and demanding at the same time possession of the gun. Campbell refused, declaring, with an oath, that he would rather part with his life than his gun. The Earl now dismounted, and although unarmed sought to circle round and gradually close in on Campbell. Campbell, on his part, followed every movement of his Lordship, and slightly stooping kept the gun closely and firmly by his thigh, always pointing full in the direction of the Earl. Exasperated and like to be beaten, for one of the servants had hurried to the carriage for the gun, Campbell shouted, "Keep off, my lord, or (with another oath) I will shoot you!" Nothing daunted, his Lordship replied, "I, too, can use a gun" (although the servant had not yet brought up the weapon), and kept pressing in on Campbell. The latter, retreating a few steps, yet still looking full at Eglinton, stumbled and fell. Gathering himself together, in a moment he aimed direct at his Lordship, pulled the trigger, and lodged the charge in his left side. Campbell then rushed on the servant, who had reached the ground with his Lordship's gun unloaded, seized it from him, and took aim in a general way, but as if intent on more mischief. After some little rough usage, which the wounded nobleman sought to moderate, Campbell was secured and conveyed to Irvine prison, then to Ayr, and finally, under a strong guard, to Edinburgh, to be tried before the High Court of Justiciary. Finding himself mortally wounded, Lord Eglinton rested for a few minutes on a stone by the shore, and then desired to be conveyed to his carriage, that the Castle might be reached as soon as possible. The party arrived there a little after two o'clock, but, although skilful physicians were there before him, it was found that any effort to save his Lordship must be fruitless. He employed the few remaining hours of his life in giving orders and written directions about his affairs, in making provision for his servants, and comforting with much self-possession the mourning friends around his bed. He died about ten o'clock next morning, or as near as possible twelve hours after the encounter.

Campbell's trial came on in Edinburgh before the High Court, February 26, 1770—the Lord Justice-Clerk presiding. Certain technical objections had previously been taken to the libel, but its relevancy was supported by all the Judges, who, however, allowed the panel full liberty to prove any facts in exculpation or which might alleviate his guilt. The evidence presented to the Court by the Crown Prosecutor was in substance according to the facts mentioned above. The only statements of any importance made in defence were that the Earl was hasty, threatening, and angry, none of which were proved. The jury, by a majority, returned a verdict of guilty, and Campbell was sentenced to be executed, 11th April—a doom which he avoided by hanging himself in prison on the evening of conviction.

Alexander, tenth Earl of Eglinton, was succeeded by his brother Archibald, a military officer of considerable repute, and M.P. for Ayr county, 1761–68. As tending to modify the grief caused by the great calamity which overshadowed the house of Eglinton, it is pleasant to remember that the mother of the two young Earls, the Countess Susannah mentioned above, was spared, with what was thought almost increasing attraction, till 1780, when she died in the house of Auchans at the great age of 91. Late in life she was visited by Dr. Johnson on his return from the Hebrides, when it came out in conversation that she was married the year before he was born, upon which she pleasantly said to him that she might have been his mother, and that she now adopted him. When we were going away (Boswell records), the Countess embraced him, saying, " My dear son, farewell." "My friend (continues Boswell) was much pleased with this day's entertainment (November 1, 1773), and owned that I had done well to force him out."

An interesting Memorial of the tragedy on Ardrossan Sands still exists in the form of a gold finger ring, presented by the dying Earl to Andrew Wilson, Fiscal of his Barony Court of Beith, and land-steward for that portion of the Eglinton property. Mr. Wilson accompanied his lordship on the fatal day, was present at the encounter, and so became naturally one of the chief witnesses relied on by the Crown, to secure a conviction against Campbell. After the Earl was shot, Mr. Wilson assisted him home to Eglinton Castle, and remained there till he died. Shortly before the end came, the Earl asked Mr. Wilson if he would like to have anything from him as a keepsake. Mr. Wilson replied, that he would prize very highly any little reminder of his lordship, on which the Earl took off a ring from his finger, and put it on Mr. Wilson's finger, asking him to wear it for his sake. This ring is now in the possession of a great-grand-son of Mr. Wilson's, and owing to its interesting history has been handed down as an heirloom in the family. Mr. Wilson gave it to his daughter, Janet, who married Robert Faulds, Banker, Beith, from whom it came to their only son, James Faulds, Writer and Banker, Beith, who gave it to his son, Andrew Wilson Faulds, and in whose possession it now is.

CARNWATH AND THE LOCKHARTS OF LEE.

HAD no "Talisman" ever cast the glow of romance over the House of Lockhart, the family, in any other country than Scotland would have been held noble, dating back, as it does at the least, to that Sir Simon of the name knighted by William the Lion, and who held under Walter the Stewart of Scotland the lands in two counties, now known as Symington of Kyle and Symington of Lanarkshire. The cradle of the race, so far as known to history, would appear to have been the east side of the Upper Ward, the Lanarkshire Symington, abutting close on the county of Peebles. Carnwath acquired from the Somervilles, Lords of Carnwath, in comparatively recent times, is so far north on the same side of the county as to be divided from Dunsyre by the southern range of the Pentland Hills. Lee, again, the present delightful seat of the family, is almost in the centre of Lanarkshire, being only three miles from the county town, and two from those Cartland Crags bridged over by the genius of Telford.

In 1329, the young Sir Simon of his day accompanied Sir James Douglas in his expedition to the Holy Land with the heart of Bruce, and, undeterred by the loss of the precious relic in a conflict with the Moors near Tebas, Andalusia, continued his journey eastward, but added then, it is recorded, a heart to the original armorial padlock on his banner, with the motto still used, "Corda serata pando"—"I lay open locked hearts." It is this Sir Simon whom tradition identifies as the Lockhart who brought home from Palestine the famous charm known afterwards as the "Lee-penny," and used with such dramatic effect by Scott in his novel of "The Talisman," generally acknowledged as the best of his Crusader tales. What is historical in the tradition may not be of surpassing accuracy, but it is at least interesting, and is briefly set forth by the great novelist in the introduction to his story. Fighting as a soldier of the Cross, Sir Simon Lockhart had on one occasion taken prisoner an Emir of considerable wealth and consequence. The aged mother of the captive came to the Christian camp to redeem her son from his state of captivity. Lockhart is said to have fixed the price at which his prisoner should ransom himself; and the lady, pulling out a large embroidered purse, proceeded to tell down the ransom like a mother who pays little respect for gold in comparison of her son's liberty. In this operation, a pebble inserted in a coin, some say of the Lower Empire, fell out of the purse, and the Saracen matron testified so much haste to recover it as gave the Scottish knight a high idea of its value, when compared with gold or silver. "I will not consent," he said, "to grant your son's liberty unless that amulet be added to his ransom." The lady not only consented to this, but explained to Sir Simon the mode in which the talisman was to be used, and the uses to which it might be put. The water in which it was dipped operated as a styptic, as a febrifuge, and possessed several other properties as a medical talisman.

Sir Simon Lockhart, after much experience of the wonders which the charm wrought, brought it to his own country, and left it to heirs, by whom, and by Clydesdale in general, it was, and is still, distinguished as the Lee-penny, from the name of his native seat of Lee. The most remarkable part of its history, perhaps, was that it so especially escaped condemnation when the Church of Scotland chose to impeach many other cures which savoured of the miraculous, as occasioned by sorcery and censured the appeal to them, "excepting only that to the amulet, called the Lee-penny, to which it had pleased God to annex certain healing virtues which the Church did not presume to condemn." The efficacy of the charm is said to have been tested with fair success even during the present century, but the risk of injury or loss, when out of proper custody, was so great that the "Talisman" was dipped in water at home, the water being sent out in bottles to patients or others who desired to test its power.

Sir James Lockhart of Lee, the sixth in descent from the above Sir Simon, and son of Allan, slain at Pinkie, became in 1630 one of the Commissioners of Estates for the county of Lanark, and in 1645 a Commissioner of Exchequer. The following year he was made a Lord of Session, succeeding on the Bench that Sir

Alexander Gibson, Lord Durie, deceased, who was scarcely better known in his day from a ponderous volume of "Decisions," than for having been kidnapped by a daring moss-trooper known as Willie Armstrong, or "Christie's Will," and carried off to a lonely "peel" or fortress in Annandale, where he was kept in confinement till my Lord Traquair, Lord High Treasurer, had got some law case in which he was concerned settled after his own mind. After taking part in the exploit known as the "Engagement" to relieve King Charles from captivity in England, Lord Lee was himself taken prisoner at Alyth, August 1651, shipped off to England, and confined for years in the Tower, till relief came through the intercession of his eldest son, Sir William Lockhart, Governor of Dunkirk, and otherwise prominent as a diplomatist during the Commonwealth. Mazarine is said to have offered him the baton of a marshal of France if he would favour the plans of Louis XIV. regarding the cession of Dunkirk and Mardyke. Lord Lee's second son was that distinguished lawyer, Sir George Lockhart, President of the Court of Session, shot on Sunday, March 31, 1689, in a close off High Street leading to his own residence, by John Chiesley, of Dalry, in consequence of having given a decision in favour of Chiesley's wife as one of the arbiters in a suit for aliment. Chiesley, known in his day as a regardless ruffian, was first put to the torture by warrant of the Estates, and, confessing the crime, had his right hand struck off the Wednesday following. He was hanged immediately thereafter, and his body hung in chains between Leith and Edinburgh. The Lord President, known as Sir George of Carnwath, purchased that estate from the Earl of Carnwath, to whom it had come from the Somervilles through the Mar and Buchan families. The eldest son of the Lord President, also a George, known from his intrigues with the Jacobites as "Union Lockhart," acted as a sort of confidential agent between the Pretender and his Scottish adherents. Exiled to Holland for a brief period, he was permitted, in 1728, to return to Carnwath, where he lived unmolested till 1732, when he was unfortunately killed in a duel. George Lockhart wrote "Memoirs of Scotland, from the Accession of Queen Anne till the Union," published, but without his consent, in 1714; and left behind him "Papers on the

Affairs of Scotland, 1720-25," printed 1817. A younger brother, Philip, shot as a rebel at Preston, was father of Alexander of Craighouse, raised to the Bench under the title of Lord Covington. Carnwath, since 1639, has given the title of Earl to the family of Dalzell of Dalzell, presently represented by Henry Burrard Dalzell, eleventh in descent from Sir Robert, first Earl.

From Lord Lee the family succession was carried on by Sir William Lockhart, whose second wife, Robina Shouster, was niece by her mother of Oliver Cromwell, Lord Protector. Cromwell Lockhart, their eldest son, succeeded to Lee, but, failing issue, the estate reverted for the third time to a brother, James, on the death of whose son, John, the succession opened up to Count Lockhart Wishart. After him came another George of Carnwath, a strong partisan of the House of Stuart—James, who added the name of Wishart to his own, and became a Count of the Holy Roman Empire. A younger brother, Charles, married Elizabeth, only child of John Macdonald of Largie, and from them descends the present representative of the Lee and Carnwath Lockharts. On the death of John Lockhart, last of Lee, in 1777, James succeeded to that estate; but his son, Charles, dying in 1802 without issue, the foreign honours of the family became extinct, and the estates of Lee and Carnwath devolved upon his cousin, Alexander Macdonald, eldest surviving son of Charles Lockhart and Elizabeth Macdonald of Largie.

On inheriting the estate and representation of the family, Alex. Macdonald resumed the name of Lockhart, and was created a baronet of Great Britain, 24th May, 1806. With two daughters, he had three sons—namely, Sir Charles, second baronet; Sir Norman, third baronet; and Alexander, M.P. for Lanarkshire from 1837 to 1841. The eldest son, Sir Charles Macdonald Lockhart, married Emilia Olivia, daughter of Sir Charles Ross, sixth baronet of Balnagown, and had two daughters. On his death, 8th December, 1832, he was succeeded by his brother, Sir Norman Macdonald Lockhart, who died in 1849, when his son, Sir Norman Macdonald Lockhart, born 1845, became the fourth baronet. Sir Norman died 1870, and was succeeded by his brother, the present Sir Simon Macdonald Lockhart, fifth baronet, born 1849. Lee House, greatly enlarged and improved in 1822 from designs by James Gillespie, Edinburgh, stands in an extensive and well wooded valley, near the bottom of the sloping hills which form its northern boundary. Technically speaking, it may now be described as an extensive building of a square castellated form, having circular embattled turrets at each corner, and an embattled parapet top. The principal entrance is in the lower part of a central tower in the east front, and immediately above is a square window, which lights the entrance hall. The building is surrounded with a high, broad terrace walk. The best view of this stately mansion and the fine woods around is thought to be from the road carried over Cartland, which passes along the brow of the hills on the north, and gives the spectator some idea of "a giant fortress in fairyland."

DALRYMPLE AND THE STAIRS.

SEPARATED from the western corners of Dumfries and Galloway by the wide parish of Dalmellington, and from the sea by Maybole, Dalrymple, lying along the north or right bank of the Doon, is like Stair, on the south or left bank of the Ayr, included within that subdivision of central Ayrshire known as King's Kyle. The one point marks the northern, the other the southern, limits of this portion of the country, and are only separated from each other by portions of Ochiltree and Coylton. With the exception of Craigie, north of the Ayr, Stair is the least thickly-peopled parish in Kyle, and, with the exception of Barr, in the centre of Carrick, smaller in point of numbers than any within the entire county. The figures in the last census show 734 for Stair and 1412 for Dalrymple, the latter coming thus to be classed also among the minor parishes so far as population is concerned. Yet, insignificant as these two Ayrshire parishes may appear under the application of a mere statistical test, it is within their bounds we must search for the cradle of a race devoted beyond most families to the public service of their country. No way overlooking or extenuating the dark crime of Glencoe, it is still to the Dalrymples the historian must turn for some of the brighter examples of eminence in literature and law, in arms and diplomacy. It is indeed hardly open to doubt that we have in the career of James, first Viscount Stair, the highest example of a race of statesmen in which Scotland, up to his time, had by no means been so prolific as might be supposed, if judged only by what she won through her sturdy spirit of independence. From evidence not to be put lightly aside, it would appear that about the middle of the fifteenth century (1450), the year when King James, second of the ill-starred line, brought home Mary of Gueldres as his bride, a certain William, son of John of the barony of Dalrymple, acquired the lands of Stair, or Stair-Montgomery, through his marriage with the heiress, Margaret Kennedy, daughter of Malcolm of Carrick. Their son, William Dalrymple of Stair, is set down as having married Marion, daughter of Chalmers of Gadgirth, a lady who, as we have already described, was summoned before the King's Council as belonging to that religious reforming band known as the Lollards of Kyle. A grandson, James of Stair, was among the first who openly professed the reformed doctrines. In later years his enemies—and he had many of them—did not fail to taunt James, first Viscount Stair, with his lowly descent; but, if an offence was intended, it did not appear to disturb either his equanimity or his dignified bearing as President of the Court of Session. The place of his birth is thought to have been Drummurchie, Barr parish, Ayrshire, and the date 1619.

The future Lord-President's father was James of Stair, and his mother Jannet Kennedy of Knockdaw. Stirring as his career was, it may be stated in a very few lines from the period when he passed from Mauchline school to Glasgow University, till his elevation to the peerage a few years before his death. Commanding for three years a company of foot in Glencairn's regiment, he afterwards turned his attention to philosophical studies, and in 1641, after a competitive examination, he became a professor or regent of the logic class in his old University. This appointment, however, would appear to have been only a preliminary step towards the perfecting of his legal studies, which enabled him to pass as advocate in 1648. Although one of the Commissioners to Breda for the purpose of inviting Charles II. to Scotland, Dalrymple was made a Judge by Cromwell on the recommendation of Monk. The appointment was confirmed at the Restoration, and the dignity of a baronetcy added, to be followed at no distant interval by promotion to the chair of the Lord-President. The work known as "Stair's Institutes," long familiar to lawyers, judges, and statesmen, and hardly yet superseded, appeared in 1681, a year otherwise of evil import to the great jurist, since his resistance to the ensnaring Test Act, pressed on by the Duke of York, led to his removal from the bench and flight to Leyden for safety. This step was taken on a hint from Sir George Mackenzie, Lord-Advocate, to the effect that if the bigoted Royal Duke pressed matters as he threatened, even the author of the "Institutes" could not be saved from imprisonment at least. His tenantry and dependants were also at this time much harassed by soldiers, and sharply fined for non-conformity or church irregularities.

At Leyden, Dalrymple made the acquaintance of Claudius Salmasius, a now all but forgotten controversialist, whose defence of King Charles would, in the author's own day, have fallen into oblivion had it not called forth Milton's stinging but scarcely less abusive "Defence of the English People.'" The Revolution of 1688 brought such measure of relief and honour to Dalrymple, as is best indicated by his restoration to the Presidentship of the Court of Session, and his elevation to the peerage as first Viscount Stair, Lord Glenluce and Stranraer. Death took place at Edinburgh, November, 1695, when Lord Stair had reached the age of 76. As opposed to the bitter judgment of Burnet, Sir George Mackenzie left on record that what he most admired Stair for was that in ten years' intimacy he never heard him speak unkindly of those who had injured him. Scott writes of Stair as one of the most eminent lawyers who ever lived, though the labours of his powerful mind were unhappily exercised on a subject so limited as Scottish Jurisprudence.

With the original of Scott's "Lady Ashton" for a wife, the domestic life of Lord Stair is interwoven with that painful tragedy of Fate known as "The Bride of Lammermoor," elaborated with unwearied care and skill by novelists, musicians, and dramatists. Lady Stair was originally Margaret Ross, co-heiress of Balneil,

Wigtonshire. She has been described as an able, politic, and high-minded woman, so successful in what she undertook that the vulgar, no way partial to her husband or her family, imputed her success to necromancy. According to the popular belief, as mentioned by Scott, this Dame Margaret purchased the temporary prosperity of her family from the master she served under a singular condition, narrated in these words by the historian of her grandson, whose descent leads Macaulay to add an additional touch of blackness to his portrait of the son, Master of Stair, first Earl, and the execrated of Glencoe. Lady Stair lived, writes an "impartial hand," to a great age, "and at her death desired that she might not be put under ground, but that her coffin should be placed upright on one end of it, promising, that while she remained in that situation, the Dalrymples should continue in prosperity. What was the old lady's motive for such a request, or whether she really made such a promise, I cannot take upon me to determine; but it is certain her coffin stands upright in the aisle of the church at Kirkliston, the burial place of the family." The daughter of the family, and original of "Lucy Ashton," the "Bride" was Janet Dalrymple, betrothed to Lord Rutherford, but compelled by her mother to marry a new suitor in the person of David Dunbar, son and heir of David of Baldoon. The bridal feast was followed by dancing, during which, as was usual, the bride and bridegroom retired to the nuptial chamber. Suddenly wild and piercing shrieks were heard proceeding from the apartment. It was then the custom, writes Scott, to prevent any coarse pleasantry which earlier times tolerated, to entrust the key of this room to the bridesman or "best man." He was called upon, but at first refused, to give up the keys till the shrieks became so hideous that he was compelled to hasten with others to learn the cause. On opening the door, they found the bridegroom lying across the threshold, dreadfully wounded, and streaming with blood. The bride was then sought for. She was found in the corner of a large chimney, having no covering save her shift, and that dabbled in gore. There she sat grinning at them, mopping and moaning, as I heard the expression used; in short, absolutely insane. The only words she spoke were "Tak up your bonny bridegroom." She survived this horrible scene little more than a fortnight, having been married on the 24th of August, and died on the 12th of September, 1669. The unfortunate Baldoon recovered from his wounds, but sternly prohibited all inquiries respecting the manner in which he had received them. The satirists of the day did not fail to turn the tragedy to the discredit of the house of Stair, one lampoon of exceptional bitterness writing of "Stair's neck, mind, wife, sons, grandson, and the rest," as "wry, false, witch, pests, parricide, possessed."

Besides the unhappy Miss Janet Dalrymple, Lord Stair left issue, John "Master" of Stair, second Viscount and first Earl, who will be written of at length next chapter in connection with Glencoe; also Sir James, designated first of Borthwick and afterwards of Cousland, progenitor of the present Earls; Sir Hew, the first baronet of North Berwick; and Sir David, founder of the Hailes family, and grandfather of the distinguished historian, Lord Hailes. The Hailes offshoot from the Stair prolific stem is now represented by Charles Dalrymple, Esq. of New Hailes, M.P., younger brother of Sir James Fergusson of Kilkerran, through the second marriage of Lord Hailes with Helen, youngest daughter of Lord Kilkerran, senator of the College of Justice, a learned jurist, elevated to the Bench on the death of Adam Cockburn of Ormiston.

THE MASTER OF STAIR AND GLENCOE.

ELDEST son of the first Viscount Stair, Sir John Dalrymple, or the "Master," as he was commonly called, had about twenty years' experience at the Bar or on the Bench, when, in 1691, he was promoted by King William from the position of Lord-Advocate to be one of His Majesty's Principal Secretaries of State. An unnatural alliance happened to exist at the moment between Jacobites and Presbyterians, the one writhing as much through loss of power as for the fall of the hierarchy; the other sullen and discontented at the promotion of time-serving politicians like the Stairs, who had suffered little or nothing in the "good cause," and even held office when that "cause" was being subjected to its most trying ordeal. But Dalrymple was not to be daunted, either by such a combination, or by the personal hatred of intriguers like Hamilton and Athole. The tolerant King, it is well known had no particular objection to Episcopacy even for Scotland; indeed, his earliest schemes for settling the peace of the North would seem to have proceeded on the assumption that the system might be continued as the established form of belief. But Carstairs knew the temper of his countrymen better, and exercised the great influence he justly possessed with the King in private to promote the design openly advocated by Dalrymple for setting up Presbyterianism on a just, rational, and moderate footing. The settlement of 1690 was never put to a more severe trial than during the discussions which took place three years later on the Oath of Assurance, providing for the admission of Episcopalians within the fold of the new Establishment, provided they acknowledged William as King *de jure* and *de facto*. Those whom it was intended to relieve clamoured for a far greater measure of relief, while the Church it was intended to strengthen looked askance at the proposal as full of Erastianism—nothing short of bending the knee to Cæsar. The part taken by Dalrymple at this precise stage has never been made very clear, but it is fairly open to infer that he promoted the resolution ultimately arrived at, of leaving the settlement of 1690 undisturbed.

The tragedy of Glencoe, standing alone as it does in Scottish history for cool treachery and merciless atrocity, may yet be said to have a kind of remote connection with events of over two years preceding its consummation. It was even connected in no indistinct way with that great confederation of princes concerned in protecting the liberties of Europe under the direction of William of Orange. Wishful to transport to the Netherlands such troops as could be spared, the King declined following up the advantage gained at Killiecrankie in the summer of 1689, with the result that the clans became more disorderly and threatening than ever, and perplexed statesmen with far higher scruples than any to which Dalrymple ever pretended. To get some measure of peace restored in what was to him a remote and worthless part of the kingdom, William gladly listened to a proposal for securing the allegiance of the chiefs by the offer of an indemnity and the division among them of £12,000 as a gratuity. To Lord Breadalbane was committed the invidious task of distributing the fund, and, though no doubt was ever cast on his honesty in this matter, it is certain there was never any real justification for his sharp retort to Nottingham on being asked to account for the money—"The Highlands, my Lord, are quiet, and the money spent; that is the best accounting among friends." The Highlands were not quiet even when the oaths came to be taken at the close of 1691. Tarbat's gratuity plan was from the first opposed by the Master of Stair, who plainly said that the only way to restore and maintain order in the Highlands, was to enforce with a firm hand obedience to law, and to draft off a large portion of the population kept up by rival chiefs for purposes of pride or robbery. His natural hatred of the Highland race as turbulent and troublesome was roused to fury as he saw chance after chance pass away of suppressing what he described as "a thing deplorable in any Christian country." The taking of the oath gave the Master another opportunity for which he was watching. He seems to have originally contemplated nothing less than breaking up and extirpating the entire clan system. In a letter to Sir Thomas Livingston, dated January 7, 1692, he says, "You know in general that the troops posted at Inverness and Inverlochie will be ordered to take in the house of Invergarrie, and to destroy entirely the country of Lochaber, Lochiel's lands, Keppoch's, Glengarie's, and Glencoe." He adds, "I assure you your power shall be full enough, and I hope the soldiers will not trouble the Government with prisoners." In sending Livingston the instructions, signed and countersigned by the King on the 11th January, "to march the troops against the rebels who had not taken the benefit of the indemnity, and to destroy them by fire and sword," he said in his letter as a hint to Livingston how to act—"Just now my lord Argyle tells me that Glencoe hath not taken the oath, at which I rejoice. It is a great work of charity to be exact in rooting out that damnable sect, the worst of the Highlands." Additional instructions, bearing date 16th January, were sent to Livingston, and in the letter containing them, Secretary Dalrymple said, "For a just example of vengeance, I entreat the thieving tribe of Glencoe may be rooted out to purpose." A duplicate of these instructions was at the same time sent by him to Colonel Hill, governor of Fort-William, with a similar letter.

The oath fell to be taken on or before the 1st January, 1692. Old MacIan Macdonald of Glencoe offered to comply at Fort-William on that day, but found the Sheriff had gone to Inverary, and the inclement season made the second journey unusually tedious. The roll was ultimately returned with a certificate explaining the cause of delay. The certificate was first suppressed and Macdonald's name afterwards deleted from the roll—a fraud for which the Master of Stair has had to bear even a greater share of the odium than his Royal Master who signed an order to the Commander of the Forces in Scotland:—"As for MacIan of Glencoe and that tribe, if they can be well distinguished from the other Highlanders, it will be proper for the vindication of public justice to extirpate that set of thieves." In his defence of William, generally admitted to be more ingenious than convincing, Macaulay discusses "extirpation" as in itself an innocent legal term, expressive of the primary duty of a Government to extirpate all clans whose chief business was to steal cattle and to burn houses. This, however, does not meet the case, evading as it does, and not very adroitly, the graver portion of the charge made against King William and his government in Scotland. It may, and no doubt is, as the historian insists in many passages of his writings, one of the primary duties of a Government to protect life and property, and therefore, naturally, to take all proper means for "extirpating" thieves. But this surely cannot be set down as meaning that every thief is first to consider himself as pardoned, then to be entrapped into a display of friendly hospitality to his rulers, and finally to be murdered in his sleep without the pretence of even a form of trial. It is the mingled treachery and ruthless cruelty which burned the recollection of Glencoe into the hearts of all Scotsmen at home and abroad, and even threatened complications with Continental allies.

The soldiers appointed to carry out the deed of darkness were 120 in number, and mostly Campbells, hereditary foes of the Macdonalds. They entered the glen early in February, were received with unsuspecting hospitality, and basely repaid the kindness by rising at a concerted signal about four o'clock on the morning of the 12th to carry through their bloody mission of "mauling them in the long nights of winter." Men, women, and children, to the number of 38 in all, were treacherously put to death, many of them in their bed unconscious, and about 150 escaped to the hills, to endure hardships worse to face than death. The body of the old chief himself was found among the slain, his gray hair dabbled in blood. During the month of March, as mentioned before, it was known in a general way in Edinburgh that the Macdonalds had come to an untimely end, but it was not till April that the "Paris Gazette" published the news to the world. Even then theerwas so little popular excitement on the subject that Dalrymple continued to hold unmolested the offices of Scottish Secretary and Lord-Advocate. But details of the treacherous outrage could not be long concealed. Public indignation rose in proportion as each terrible fact got whispered about; and to anticipate as far as possible any action which might be taken in the Scottish Parliament, Dalrymple resigned his offices before the end of that year so fatal to the reputation of King William and himself. With a dilatoriness not creditable to the King the Report of a Royal Commission regarding the massacre was delayed for over three years, when a resolution was come to "that William's instructions afforded no warrant for the measure;" but, "considering that the Master of Stair's excess in his letters against the Glencoe men has been the original cause of this unhappy business, and hath given occasion in a great measure to so extraordinary an execution, by the warm directions he gives about doing it by way of surprise, and considering the station and trust he is in, and that he is absent, we do therefore beg that your Majesty will give such orders about him for vindication of your Government as you in your royal wisdom shall think fit. And likewise, considering that the actors have barbarously killed men under trust, we humbly desire your Majesty would be pleased to send the actors home, and to give orders to your Advocate to prosecute them according to law." It is but right to say that letters to and from Breadalbane, in the charter-chest at Taymouth, give colour to the opinion that King William was cognisant of all that passed in Scotland, discussing in particular this Highland matter so frequently with Stair, Queensberry, and Tarbat, as to make it all but certain that Glencoe fell into the trap prepared really for Keppoch and Glengarry. "Tarbat (writes Stair) thinks that Keppoch will be a more proper example of severity, but he hath not a house so proper for a garrison, and he hath not been so forward to ruin himself, and all the rest. But, I confess,'both's best to be ruined."

The Lord-President succeeded his father as second Viscount in November of the same year (1695), but public feeling regarding the Glencoe outrage had increased to such a pitch that he declined taking his seat in Parliament for five years. Soon after the accession of Queen Anne he was sworn a Privy Councillor and created Earl of Stair. As one of the Commissioners for framing the Treaty of Union the Earl of Stair gave it powerful support in its passage through Parliament. The Earl died suddenly January 8, 1707, his last speech being delivered that day in the course of an animated debate on one of the closing articles of the treaty providing for the election of representative Peers and the number of members to be sent to the Commons. Active and prominent as Stair had always been in the public service of his country (except during the Glencoe retirement), he had yet not reached the age of more than fifty-nine years at death.

An evil destiny still seemed to follow the family, notwithstanding all their gifts and worldly prosperity, John, second son of preceding, and successor in the Earldom, having the misfortune when a mere boy to shoot his elder brother by accident. Earl John had seen service under Marlborough at Ramilies and Malplaquet. As British Ambassador at Paris he manifested considerable hostility to the schemes of Law, the Finance Minister, which led to his being recalled, when he took up his residence at Newliston, to pass his leisure time in planting trees and cultivating cabbages in the open air for the first time in Scotland. On the dissolution of Walpole's Ministry in 1742, Lord Stair was recalled to public life, appointed Commander-in-Chief of the allied army in Flanders, and fought with King George at Dettingen. Earl John died at Edinburgh, 1747, aged 74. Among his successors were Captain John Dalrymple, fifth Earl (cousin of William, fourth Earl of Dumfries, and also fourth Earl of Stair, under the patent), author of various political treatises, and John, eighth Earl, son of Sir John Dalrymple of Cranston, author of "Memoirs of Great Britain and Ireland." The present holder of the honours is John, tenth Earl of Stair, who, when Lord Dalrymple, sat as M.P. for Wigtownshire, 1841–56; and was Lord High Commissioner to the General Assembly of the Church of Scotland, 1869–72. His eldest son, Viscount Dalrymple, unsuccessfully contested Wigtownshire in the Liberal interest, when he was defeated by Sir Herbert Maxwell (Conservative), the voters polled being 768 to 782.

KELBURNE, HAWKHEAD, AND EARLS OF GLASGOW.

DESCENDED from a house famous over five hundred years since for its long descent—famous even among houses of such high repute as the Comyns and Mures, the Boyles of Kelburne have for generation after generation taken a prominent part in the public business of Ayrshire and Renfrewshire, and, indeed, of the West of Scotland generally. Seated almost as early as authentic records reach at Kelburne, Largs parish, the most northerly in Cunningham or North Ayrshire, a marriage with an heiress of George, Lord Ross, brought, about the middle of last century, the lands of Hawkhead, Renfrewshire, to the Boyle of his day (1754), then John, third Earl of Glasgow. A Richard Boyle, of Kelburne, is known to have married, about 1260, Anicia, daughter of Sir Gilchrist Mure, of Rowallan, by his wife, daughter and heiress of that Walter Comyn who had early in the reign of Alexander III. (1249-86) succeeded in expelling the Mures from their Ayrshire possessions. Sir John Boyle, a descendant in the sixth generation, adhered to the cause of James III. as against his son, put forward by the discontented nobles, and fell on the field of Sauchieburn, near Stirling, where the King himself was treacherously murdered, 1488. As the houses of Cochrane and Boyle came to have an early as well as a late connection through marriage, so had the Boyles a double connection with the Rosses, Lords of Hawkhead, for in addition to the heiress, Elizabeth, mentioned above, John Boyle, son of the John who fell at Sauchie, married Agnes, daughter of the first Lord Ross of Hawkhead. He afterwards fell at Flodden (1513), where his brother-in-law, John, Lord Ross, was also slain. A son, John Boyle, got a charter of the lands of Ballehewin, Meikle Cumbrae, and was also made hereditary coroner of the island. An only surviving son was John Boyle of Halkshill, whose great-grandson, David, married his cousin, the heiress of Kelburne, and carried on the family succession. This heiress was Grizel Boyle, daughter of John of Kelburne by Agnes, only daughter of Sir John Maxwell of Pollok, and Margaret, daughter of William Cunningham of Caprington; issue three sons and one daughter. The eldest, John of Kelburne, sat as member for Buteshire in the Parliament of 1681. By his marriage with Marion, daughter of Sir William Steuart of Allanton, John Boyle, left with a daughter, two sons, David, raised to the peerage as first Earl of Glasgow, and William, a Commissioner of Customs for Scotland, who died in 1685.

David Boyle of Kelburne, after sitting as member for Bute in the Convention Parliament of 1689, was sworn of the Privy Council, and on 31st January, 1699, created a Peer by the title of Lord Boyle of Kelburne, Stewarton, Cumbrae, Largs, and Dalry, with remainder to his issue, male and heirs-male whatsoever. By patent, dated 12th April, 1703, Lord Boyle was advanced to the dignity of

Earl of Glasgow, the Crown acknowledging thereby his zeal for the Protestant succession and patriotic endeavour to check the plots of disaffected Jacobites. Earl David some years earlier had succeeded the Duke of Lennox as Bailie of the Regality of Glasgow, an office which empowered the holder to appoint the Provost as well as the lesser Magistrates of the City. In 1706 Earl David was appointed Lord High Commissioner to the General Assembly of the Church of Scotland, and filled that office for four successive years afterwards. Chosen for a second time a representative Peer at the general election of 1708, he was the same year constituted Lord-Clerk Register for Scotland, and discharged for six years the duties of that high office of State, which has since again fallen to his descendant, the present George Frederick Boyle, sixth Earl of Glasgow. At a threatening period of Mar's rebellion in 1715, Earl David made offer to George I. of 1000 men at his own expense for the service of the Government, and personally took an active part besides, in training the fencible men of Ayrshire. His Lordship died 1st November, 1733. Earl David was twice married, first to Margaret Crawford, eldest daughter of Patrick of Kilbirnie, sister of John, first Viscount Garnock, and in whose right, under an entail, the estates of Crawford Priory, Kilbirnie, &c., came into the possession of George Boyle, fourth Earl of Glasgow, on the death of Lady Mary Lindsay Crawford, unmarried, 1833. By this, his first marriage, Earl David had four sons, the eldest being John, his successor and second Earl, born 1697; a younger, Patrick, studied for the law, passing advocate 1712, and was elevated to the bench as Lord Shewalton on the death of James Elphinstone, Lord Balmerinoch, December, 1746. Lord Shewalton died at Drumlanrig, 31st March, 1761, unmarried. Earl David married secondly, Jane, daughter and heiress of William Mure of Rowallan, and by her had two daughters—(1) Anne, who died unmarried, and (2) Jane of Rowallan, married to Sir James Campbell of Lawers, a distinguished military officer who fought at Dettingen, and fell at Fontenoy, commanding the British horse, 29th April, 1745. Their son, James Mure-Campbell of Lawers, succeeded as Earl of Loudoun, and assumed the additional surname of Muir on inheriting the Ayrshire estates of his grandmother, the second Countess of Glasgow, mentioned above, who died September, 1724. Earl David died 1st November, 1733, and was succeeded by his eldest son, John, as second Earl.

John, second Earl of Glasgow, born 1687, died at Kelburne, May, 1740, aged 53 years, leaving by his wife Helen, daughter of William Morrison of Prestongrange, with other issue, two sons—(1) John, his successor, and (2) Patrick, father of David Boyle, Lord Justice-General, and President of the Court of Session (1811–1852), from whom descended that family of the Boyles of Shewalton, presently represented by David, Captain R.N., son of Patrick, of Shewalton, born May, 1833, and married July, 1873, Dorothea, eldest daughter of Sir Edward Hunter Blair, Bart., with issue three sons and three daughters.

John, third Earl of Glasgow, born 4th November, 1714, entered the army, in which he rose to the rank of captain, and was severely wounded in two historical engagements—Fontenoy, April, 1745, and Laffeldt, July, 1747. In 1764 he was called upon to fill the office, previously in his family, of Lord High Commissioner to the General Assembly of the Church of Scotland, and continued the same for eight successive years. Earl John died on 7th March, 1775, the memory of the brave soldier being affectionately commemorated at the desire of his widowed Countess by the erection of a marble memorial in a romantic situation within the grounds of Kelburne, on the banks of Kelburne Water. Earl John married Elizabeth, second daughter of George, thirteenth Lord Ross of Hawkhead, and sole heiress of her brother William, fourteenth Lord Ross, who died August, 1754, after enjoying the honours of that very ancient lordship for only a few weeks. In a settlement made by the above George Lord Ross, in 1751, the destination was confined first to heirs-male of his body, and, failing them, to his daughters and their heirs. The Ross Barony of Hawkhead thereupon passed to John, third Earl Glasgow, and has ever since remained in the family, the succeeding Earl George, father of the present Earl, being in 1815 made a Peer of the United Kingdom as Baron Ross of Hawkhead. The other Ross property of Balnagowan, Ross-shire, passed, after a brief litigation, to his Lordship's cousin, Sir James Lockhart, second baronet of Carstairs, whose mother, Grizel, was the third daughter of William, twelfth Lord Ross. In the Parliamentary Return of Owners of Lands and Heritages (1874), Hawkhead is entered as comprising 4453 acres, with a gross annual rental of £6811, exclusive of minerals, £480. The mansion-house—originally a plain, square tower—built near a bend of the White Cart, but well screened from that now scarcely pure stream, and with ground on every side otherwise well wooded, was greatly added to in 1634 by James, fourth Lord Ross, and his lady, Dame Margaret Scott, eldest daughter of that Walter, first Lord Scott of Buccleuch, by Mary, daughter of Sir William Kerr of Cessford, and sister of Robert, first Earl of Roxburghe, her husband being celebrated also in Border minstrelsy as directing the rescue of "Kinmont Will" from Carlisle Castle. At Hawkhead an entertainment is said to have been given in October, 1681, by the loyalist William tenth, Lord Ross, to James, Duke of York (afterwards King James II. of England), kinsman to that Countess Anne of Buccleuch who, "in pride of youth and beauty's bloom, had wept o'er Monmouth's bloody tomb." This Countess Anne was grand-niece of Dame Margaret Scott, mentioned above as having married James, fourth Lord Ross, progenitor of the noble host who entertained Monmouth's uncle at Hawkhead. For much of its modern attractions—its trim gardens, its pleasant walks, and its shaded bowers—Hawkhead, house, and grounds, is indebted to the care and munificence of Elizabeth Ross, Countess of John, third Earl, who in 1782 gave her old family mansion such thorough repairs and seemly additions as has made it one of the most desirable residences in the county. It was lately (1884) occupied by the Hon. T. Cochrane and his wife, the Lady Gertrude Boyle, eldest daughter of the Earl of Glasgow.

Succeeding John came George, fourth Earl of Glasgow, G.C.H., F.R.S., born 26th March, 1766, and elevated to the British Peerage as Baron of Hawkhead, Renfrew, 11th August, 1815; a Captain in the West Lowland Fencibles; Colonel of the Renfrewshire Militia; Lord-Lieutenant of that county, and afterwards of Ayrshire; a representative Peer prior to his elevation as Baron Ross of Hawkhead; and Lord Rector of Glasgow University, 1817. On the death of his relative, Lady

Mary Lindsay Crawford, unmarried, 1833, Earl George succeeded to her inheritance in the lands of Crawford Priory, Fifeshire, as well as to others in Kilbirnie parish, Ayrshire. The first mentioned is entered in the Parliamentary Return already referred to as consisting of 5625 acres, with a gross annual value (exclusive of £60 10s. for minerals) of £9024. An addition to the family property was also made about this time by the acquisition of the Garrison lands, Isle of Cumbrae, in addition to others already in possession of the family. The "Garrison" is so named from the original residence slightly fortified, built there in the middle of last century by Andrew Crawford, commander of the first revenue cutter placed on that station. George, fourth Earl, who died 6th July, 1843, married twice—(1) 4th March, 1788, Augusta, daughter of James, fourteenth Earl of Errol, and had issue, John, Viscount Kelburne, a naval officer, born 1789, died 1818; James, fifth Earl; William, born 1802, died 1819; Isabella, Elizabeth, and Augusta, the latter married to Lord Frederick Fitzclarence. Earl George married (2) November 1824, Julia, daughter by a second marriage of the learned and patriotic statesman, Sir John Sinclair, Bart. of Ulbster; Earl George died 6th July, 1843, and the Countess Julia 19th February, 1868, leaving George Frederick, present Earl, and Diana, who in July, 1849, married the Hon. John Slaney Pakington, second Lord Hampton, eldest son of Sir John Pakington, first Lord Hampton, an esteemed servant of the Crown, 1852-68. The Hon. Lady Diana Pakington died 1st January, 1877.

James, fifth Earl of Glasgow, born 10th April, 1792; entered the navy, 1807; became lieutenant, 1814; and subsequently captain. As Lord Kelburne he in 1837 contested Ayr county unsuccessfully against Sir John Dunlop of Dunlop, but on the death of the latter in 1839, Lord Kelburne again came forward against Mr. Campbell of Craigie, whom he defeated by a large majority, and held the seat till called to the House of Lords on the death of his father in 1843. His Lordship was master of the Renfrewshire hounds, and an ardent, honourable, although never a very lucky, patron of the turf. Earl James died 10th March, 1869, when, there being no issue by his marriage with Miss Mackenzie, daughter of Edward Hay of

New Hall, Cromarty, the succession devolved upon his half-brother, the sixth or present Earl of Glasgow.

George Frederick Boyle, born 9th October, 1825; educated at Christ Church, Oxford, taking his B.A. degree 1847, and M.A. 1850—represented Buteshire in Parliament for a few months during 1865, having defeated his opponent, J. Lamont of Knockdhu, on the elevation of David Mure to the bench, but was in turn defeated in the second contest which took place on occasion of the general election in autumn of the same year. Before this date, or in 1843, Mr. Boyle had not only erected the beautiful little church of St. Andrew's within the Garrison policies, Cumbrae, but built at his own charge from designs by Butterfield, and on a commanding site within the bounds of the same family property, the extensive, costly, and ornate Cathedral Collegiate Church of the Isles, intended for the threefold purpose of giving assistance to the clergy of the diocese, to afford a retreat for a limited number of aged or infirm clergymen, and to prepare a few students for the service of the Church, more especially in Gaelic districts. The College, governed by a Provost, with the Bishop of Argyll as visitor, was taken possession of by students and choristers in November, 1850, the church being opened for service the following year, and consecrated 1876. Succeeding to the family honours on the death of Earl James in 1869, Lord Glasgow had restored to him on the death of Sir W. Gibson-Craig (1878) the high honour held by an ancestor of Lord-Clerk Register of Scotland, and keeper of the Signet. His Lordship is also convener of the county of Bute (succeeding the late A. B. Stewart, Esq. of Ascog, 1880), and Chief Magistrate of the Burgh of Millport—duties which he discharges with unwearied attention and courtesy, the latter none the less from the circumstance that the Garrison residence on the Island was long occupied and much improved by his mother, the Dowager-Countess, and himself. The Earl George Frederick, married 29th April, 1856, the Hon. Miss Montagu Abercromby, only daughter of George Ralph, third Lord Abercromby, and has issue Gertrude Julia Georgiana, born 15th November, 1861, who married Hon. Thomas H. A. E. Cochrane, with issue a son and daughter; and Muriel Louisa Diana, born 18th November, 1873.

DUNDONALD AND ITS EARLS.

UNLIKE the square divisions or plots into which land is parcelled out in new and thinly-peopled countries, parishes in Scotland—nor is England much different —have been made to assume every variety of odd fantastic shape. In some cases, indeed, they are made up of portions of land quite detached from each other, and not unfrequently in different counties. An explanation of this apparent irregularity both as to shape and size, must be sought for, at least partly, in the conditions under which the land came to be laid out in distinct portions, parishes, or townships. There is first, if any reliance is to be placed on the most recent researches into early land tenures, the village commune, where the inhabitants not only held the soil in common, but frequently stocked and cultivated it in common. Then, when we come down with clearer vision to a point almost touching authentic history, there is possession of the soil by the Crown alone, often gifted with wonderful munificence to relations and followers; but the origin of the possession, not even yet understood with certainty. After this the inquirer gets a more stable footing within the period of documents, or at the very least of assured tradition. Next comes the feudal period, when the baron held land, doing suit and service for the same to the sovereign, and dividing it again among his own retainers on nearly the same condition of mustering under his banner in the field. Running parallel with this feudal tenure, but having interests of its own of a more beneficent character, there was the parish as a diocese or district assigned to a particular Church, and where, in process of time, the teinds in its support could only be collected within strictly defined limits. After this, and as presently existing, the parish boundaries came to be affected by the necessities for local self-government, and the administration of the law relating to parochial relief. All these conditions have helped to make parishes what they are in shape and size. Dundonald, with which we are more immediately concerned, presents an outline so irregular as to make the "beating of its bounds," were such a ceremony necessary, an undertaking requiring the nicest observation and thorough parochial experience. Its broadest, or northern part, extending from Riccarton to Fullarton, a distance of some seven miles, marked wholly by the course of the Irvine, is touched by no fewer than four parishes—Irvine, Dreghorn, Kilmaurs, and Riccarton, Kilmarnock almost edging in within the last two. Along its eastern side there is Symington and Monkton, but on the west, bending for the most part smoothly inland, there is nothing but the sea or Firth of Clyde for another seven miles from Fullarton to Monkton, which Dundonald overlaps for a short distance on the south. The only break on the westward line may be said to be Troon Point, which with the port lies within Dundonald parish.

Crowning the summit of a pleasant hill west of Dundonald village, the now ruined Castle, so closely identified with the history of the parish, and dating as it does from the thirteenth, or probably the twelfth century, may be said to correspond in time with the arrival of the first Norman Stewarts in Scotland, and was certainly occupied by them long before any succession to the throne had opened up to that high official in the Royal household which gave name to the family. Here, till he was long past middle age, lived Robert II., first of the Royal race, raised to the throne under an Act of Settlement as son of Walter the Stewart and Marjory Bruce, daughter of the great King Robert and half-sister of Bruce's son, David II., who died in February 1371. At Dundonald Robert II. married, under a Papal dispensation, that Elizabeth Mure of Rowallen who had become attached to the Stewart while he was living at the old castle in retirement during the brief usurpation of Edward Baliol. Here, too, full of years, the first sovereign of the Stuart race died in peace, 1390, having withdrawn from Dunfermline when the power of the Crown was practically wielded by a son, Earl of Fife, in name of the heir, an elder brother, John, known better in history under the more popular title of Robert III. A loose tradition has been handed down that a still earlier castle, on the site, was built of wood by a certain Donald Din or Dun Donald, who acquired great fame in this part of Kyle through discovering a pot of gold as revealed in a dream, like so many similar stories of sudden riches current in lands far beyond Ayrshire. The present castle, greatly dismantled by the Cochranes to build their new house of Auchans adjoining, still presents, even in ruin, many traces of its ancient grandeur. It is two stories in height, and measures 130 feet by 40 feet. On its western wall traces may still be found of the Stewart armorial bearings, as also of a "keep" or prison, and a wide protecting moat. The fabric, with a few roods of land adjoining, is the last remnant of Ayrshire property possessed by the Cochrane Earls of Dundonald, famous in Renfrewshire before being ennobled as lairds of the Barony of Cochrane, an estate on the west side of Paisley Abbey Parish, now mostly included within the lands owned by G. L. Houstoun, Esq. of Johnstone.

In addition to Cochrane, the Sir William of the day (1640) possessed the Ayrshire lands of Dundonald and Auchans, and, in consideration of his loyalty and munificence to the Crown during the civil war, was in 1647 created a Peer as Lord Cochrane of Dundonald. The higher title of Earl of Dundonald, with that of Baron of Paisley and Ochiltree, was conferred in 1669 by Charles II. A few years before this date Earl William had, for 160,000 pounds Scots, acquired the rich lordship of Paisley from the Earl of Angus, trustee for James, second Earl of Abercorn, who in 1621, fell heir as grandson of the Commendator, Claud Hamilton, "grey Paisley's haughty Lord." Earl William resided at the Place of Paisley, and from memorial stones still to be seen there, would appear, in or about 1675, to have made important additions to the original fabric. In 1658 he disposed of the superiorities of the burgh to the Bailies and community, and gave them power at the same time to elect their own magistrates, up to that date nominated by himself, in terms of clauses contained in the charter of 1488 granted to Abbot Shaw, by which Paisley was erected into a free burgh of barony. A charter was obtained for the burgh from Charles II. in 1665. The Earl died in Paisley, 1686, and was buried at Dundonald, leaving, by his wife Euphame, daughter of Scott of Ardross, Fifeshire, one son, known early in life as Sir John Cochrane of Ochiltree, much mixed up with the Presbyterian plots of his day, and uncle of John, second Earl, whose father William had predeceased the first Earl. The daughter, Lady Grizel Cochrane, became first wife of George, tenth Lord Ross of Hawkhead, Renfrewshire, a family connection to be renewed in after years by the marriage of the Hon. Thomas Cochrane, second son of the present Earl, with Lady Gertrude, eldest daughter of George Frederick Boyle, present and sixth Earl of Glasgow.

Among later members of the family who greatly distinguished themselves were William, seventh Earl, sprung from the Cochranes of Kilmaronock, Dumbartonshire, killed in 1758 when engaged in the siege of Louisbourg; Thomas, of the house of Ochiltree, eighth Earl, engaged in the fight at Prestonpans, and who left at death eleven sons, by his wife Jane, eldest daughter of Archibald Stuart of Torrance. Charles, third son, was killed while serving in America under Sir Henry Clinton; James, fifth son, was vicar of Mansfield, and author of various treatises in theology and chemistry; Basil, also an author, purchased the barony of Auchterarder, Perthshire; while Sir Alexander was a prominent naval officer in his day, and wrote several esteemed books of travel. Archibald, ninth Earl, is now less known for his numerous scientific treatises than as the father of the great Thomas, Lord Cochrane, tenth Earl of Dundonald.

Born in 1775, Lord Cochrane entered the navy when only ten years of age, and while but a youth was promoted by admiral Keith, for exceptionally courageous services, to the command of a sloop of fourteen guns, in which many daring and successful feats were undertaken against Spanish ships of war. Early in 1806, when commanding the Pallas frigate, of 32 guns, he ascended the Gironde, 20 miles above the Cordovan shoals, and boldly cut out a frigate lying under the protection of two heavy batteries. But the crowning achievement of this period (1809) of Lord Cochrane's life, was his attack on the French fleet then being blockaded by Admiral Gambier in the Basque Roads. Here he personally conducted the explosion ship with such terrific results to the enemy that popular enthusiasm was no more than satisfied when he was created a Knight of the Bath. Lord Cochrane had been previously twice returned to Parliament—first for Honiton, and in 1807 for Westminster. Opposing as a Radical Percival's Tory Ministry; and disliked otherwise in Parliament through a misunderstanding of certain charges he had brought against

Admiral Gambier, advantage was taken to try, fine, and imprison the gallant officer on a charge, erroneously made, as was afterwards proved, of being mixed up with certain Stock Exchange transactions connected with a false report of Napoleon's defeat by the allies. Lord Cochrane was also deprived of his honours and dismissed the service. Returned again for Westminster, he found it hopeless at the time either to serve his constituents or vindicate himself as he wished, and an offer therefore was gladly accepted to command the Chilian fleet on the coast of South America. The new flag under which he served once more triumphed over Spain, and towards the close of the war of Independence Lord Cochrane passed, with increased honour, into the service of Brazil. In 1830, when the Whigs got into power, and a year before succeeding his father in the Earldom, Lord Cochrane, then looked upon as the victim of party spite, was restored to his rank in the British navy. Years brought additional honours to the harshly used officer, being made a Vice-Admiral in 1847, Commander on the North American and West Indian stations 1848-54, and Rear-Admiral of the United Kingdom 1854. Thomas, tenth Earl of Dundonald, died October 31, 1860, leaving by his wife—daughter of Thomas Barnes, Essex—four sons and a daughter. A nephew, Captain J. D. Cochrane, was well known in his day as an eccentric pedestrian traveller over most of the continent of Europe and Siberian Tartary.

The eldest son of Admiral Dundonald, Thomas Barnes, Lord Cochrane, present Earl, born 1814, succeeded on the death of his father, and by marriage (1847) with Louisa Harriet, daughter of W. A. Mackinnon of Mackinnon, his issue two sons and four daughters, the eldest being Douglas Mackinnon, Lord Cochrane, born October, 1852, and married (1858) Winifred, only surviving daughter of Robert Bamford Hesketh, Gwyrch Castle, Denbigh, with issue one daughter, Grizel Winifred Louise, born May, 1880. A second son, the Hon. Thomas Horatio Arthur, late Lieutenant of Scots Guards, born 2nd April, 1857, married 2nd December, 1880, Lady Gertrude Boyle, daughter of George Frederick, 6th and present Earl of Glasgow, with issue Louisa Gertrude, born 8th January, 1882, and Thomas George Frederick, born 19th March, 1883. The Hon. Mr. Cochrane, with Lady Gertrude and family, lately (1884) occupied Hawkhead, the barony brought to the Boyles, Earls of Glasgow, through the marriage of John, third Earl, with Elizabeth, daughter of George, Lord Ross.

COILSFIELD AND THE MONTGOMERIES.

WHETHER the old Eglinton mansion of Coilsfield was renamed altogether out of deference to Burns's fine lines, descriptive of those "banks and braes and streams around the Castle o' Montgomery;" or whether it was to keep fresh those tender memories of "Highland Mary," so closely associated with the house; or whether it was judged to be a seemly compliment to the name of its early owners—whether for any of these reasons, or for all of them, with others added, the substitution of "Montgomery Castle" for Coilsfield has at least avoided the possible degradation of the name to "Culsfield," as has happened with a parish only a few miles south, but on the other side of Ayr water. Coylton years ago had degenerated in the common speech of its natives to "Culton," an unmeaning corruption, having no sort of apparent affinity, as it should have, with either Kyle or Coila. Coilsfield itself, as has been mentioned, although nearly in the centre of Kyle district, is not in Coylton, but in Tarbolton parish—on the right bank of the Feale, below the Abbey ruins, greatly altered since Burns's day by modern classic additions, but still embowered in those woods where "Simmer first unfaulds her robes." The traveller in this region of song may catch a glimpse of Montgomery Castle by approaching coastward from Tarbolton village, from which the mansion is distant only a good mile, or, if more convenient, he may travel westward from Mauchline, by way of Failford, a good deal longer but equally romantic route. The estate, within which tradition affirms the remains of "Old King Coil" were laid, is now in the possession of Mr. William Paterson.

Putting aside mere minute genealogical details, with which these sketches are not much concerned, it may be stated generally that Hugh, third Baron of the family, and first Earl of Eglinton, was fourth in the line from that Sir John Montgomery, seventh laird of Eaglesham, who distinguished himself at Otterburn by capturing the fiery Hotspur, as detailed in the familiar old ballad of the fight :—

> "The Percy and Montgomery met,
> That either of other were fain,
> They swapped swords, and they twa swat,
> And aye the blood ran down between."

The patent of creation in favour of Earl Hugh was dated 20th January, 1508. After him came a succession of four Hughes, all Earls of Eglinton, the last of this early line of Montgomeries, Hugh, fifth Earl, being succeeded in 1612 by his cousin, Alexander Seton, father, among others, of James of Coilsfield, who, by his wife, daughter of John Macdonald, Kintyre, had a son, Hugh, from whom descended the present Earls of Eglinton. Hugh married twice—(1) Jean, daughter of Sir William Primrose, with issue three daughters; (2) the famous beauty, Katherine Arbuckle, widow of John Hamilton of Letham. By her first marriage Mrs. Hamilton had, among other sons, Basil, who married Margaret, daughter of Clerk of Brackleken, whose family held large estates in Argyllshire as far back as the reign of James II. Their daughter, Bazill, married Captain Henry Beatson, of Glasmont, Fifeshire, grandfather of the Beatsons and Lacys of Campbeltown. By her marriage with Hugh Montgomery of Coilsfield, Katherine Arbuckle bore, with two daughters and three sons, Hugh, who took up the honours of the family on the death (1796) without male issue, of Archibald, eleventh Earl, brother of Alexander, tenth Earl, shot on Ardrossan sands by a poaching exciseman, named Mungo Campbell, as described in a former paper. The elder Hugh of Coilsfield was also father of that James Montgomery, a Lieutenant-General in the army, Grand Master in the masonic lodge of Tarbolton, of which Burns was made Depute-Master, 1784–5. In one of his early Edinburgh letters (March 8, 1787), addressed to Gavin Hamilton, the poet makes reference to his right worshipful brother, the General, in connection with an aliment case before the Supreme Court, of some interest in its day to Ayrshire people.

Coilsfield House, purchased by the Montgomeries from Cunningham of Caprington, is connected with the life of at least two of Burns's heroines. "Montgomery's Peggy," whom he had met first at Kirkoswald, when attending Rodger's school, passed afterwards into the Coilsfield family as a housekeeper or upper servant, and permitted herself to be wooed and sung of by the youth of twenty for some six or eight months, when she informed him that her heart had already been given to another. Peggy Thomson, with whom the good lass has been identified, became the wife of a person named Neilson, and lived long in Ayr. But it is with "Highland Mary" that the most tender memories of Coilsfield are entwined. Burns himself threw such an air of mystery and perplexing fancy over his connection with Mary Campbell that little more than surmise regarding either her movements or position is now possible; but it is not going far beyond what is known to presume that some time in the summer of 1785 she passed from service in Gavin Hamilton's house to Coilsfield, there to act as dairymaid, or, it may be, as nurse to some of the younger children of Hugh Montgomery. Within the grounds, and not far from the junction of the Faile with the Ayr, it is almost certain that romantic meeting and parting took place on the second Sunday in May (14th May, 1786), when they swore everlasting fidelity to each other, as recorded in the famous Bibles now appropriately placed in the monument at Brig o' Doon after a curious enough history. This brief episode—for it was little more—in the poet's career—was closed by the death of "Highland Mary" in her father's house at Greenock sometime, it is thought, during the month of October following.

When Hugh Montgomery succeeded as twelfth Earl of Eglinton, only a portion of the then wide estates passed to him with the title, a valuable share falling to Lady Montgomerie, elder and only surviving daughter of the preceding Earl, Archibald. Born in 1739, Hugh Montgomerie entered the army in 1755, and, after serving with distinction in America, was appointed major in the Argyll or Western Fencibles when hostilities broke out with France in 1778. Six years later, when known as Hugh of Skelmorlie, his father living at Coilsfield till 1783, he succeeded Sir Adam Fergusson of Kilkerran, in the representation of Ayrshire, and sat till 1789, when, on being appointed inspector of military roads, he was succeeded in turn by Sir Adam. Hugh Montgomerie again entered the Commons for a few months in 1796, but on succeeding to the Earldom that year as heir-male, the seat was won by Colonel Fullerton of Fullerton. Earl Hugh had some years before this been appointed Lieut.-Governor of Edinburgh Castle, in room of Lord Elphinstone, and Colonel of the Western Fencibles, a Lowland regiment noticeable for having worn the Highland dress. A representative Peer from 1798 to 1806, Earl Hugh was in the last-mentioned year raised to the British Peerage as Baron Ardrossan. He was now becoming known as one of the most munificent, patriotic, and enterprising noblemen of his time, carrying out as he did valuable improvements on the estate, especially in the neighbourhood of Kilwinning, commenced, so far as planting was concerned, by a predecessor, Alexander, tenth Earl. Between 1797 and 1800 Earl Hugh also rebuilt Eglinton Castle, from designs by Paterson, on a scale of princely magnificence, worthy at once of his own long-descended house, and of the beautiful site it occupies on the banks of the Lugton. But even this was to be surpassed by his noble ambition to construct a grand harbour at Ardrossan for the purpose of making that place a principal port of Glasgow, with which it was to be connected by a canal passing through Johnstone and Paisley. Only a portion of this latter scheme was carried out, the application of steam to purposes of navigation, as well as to the conveyance of goods by land, coming to supersede the original scheme contemplated by the Earl. Commenced in 1806, the works at Ardrossan were brought to a standstill in 1815, when, although £100,000 had been expended, the Engineers, Telford and Rennie, indicated the likelihood of £300,000 more being required. The works were resumed in 1833, when Archibald William, thirteenth Earl, came of age, and then completed on a reduced scale, but not before the entire expenditure was found to have reached £200,000. This lavish expenditure on public projects, without any return in his day, began to exhaust even Earl Hugh's rent-roll, and various properties were sold to meet pressing obligations. Now, it is thought, also commenced the burdening of that wide Eaglesham estate, sold outright to Mr. Gilmour about 1840 by Earl Archibald, after having been in possession of the Montgomery family for over five hundred years. A brave soldier, but a strict disciplinarian, his easiness of access to tenantry, and an unbounded hospitality, suggesting more of the ancient baron than the modern nobleman, made Earl Hugh extremely popular among all classes in the West Country. An enthusiast in music, even to the extent of keeping a family piper, the Earl had no great taste or desire for public speaking. In his "Earnest Cry and Prayer," Burns describes his patron as

> "Sodger Hugh, my watchman stented,
> If bardies ere are represented,
> I ken that if your *sword* were wanted
>   Ye'd lend your hand;
> But when there's ought to *say* anent it
>   Ye're at a stand."

Earl Hugh died 15th December, 1819, having had by his wife Elenora, daughter of Robert Hamilton of Bourtreehill, two sons and two daughters. The elder son, Archibald, Lord Montgomery, a Major-General in the army, predeceased his father, leaving two sons, Hugh, who died young, and is commemorated by a marble column erected by his grandfather in a retired part of Eglinton woods, and Archibald William, who became thirteenth Earl.

Born at Palermo in 1812, Earl Archibald had a long minority, not unfavourable to the nursing of his estate, and which enabled him, as has been mentioned, to complete some of Earl Hugh's schemes in a moderate way. A leading patron in all manly sports, Lord Eglinton was much liked in the hunting-field as well as on the race-course, where a fair measure of luck fell to horses he had trained or purchased, the fame of Flying Dutchman, and the match with Lord Zetland's Voltigeur at York Spring Meeting in 1851 being still a landmark in turf annals. An attempt, sadly marred by the weather, was made by his Lordship in August, 1839, to recall even the by-gone splendour of the Tournament by a display within Eglinton grounds which kept society in talk for months, and drew countless visitors from all parts of the kingdom, and many from the Continent. The hospitality at the castle far surpassed anything ever seen in the best days of Earl Hugh, but at a cost which touched heavily on the well-gathered savings made in by-gone years for the young Earl. Served heir to the attainted title of Winton in 1840, the Earl of Eglinton twice filled, with an acceptance amounting to enthusiasm, the office of Irish Viceroy in the Ministry of Lord Derby—1852–58. As early as 1842 he was appointed Lord-Lieutenant of Ayrshire, and in 1852 Earl Archibald William was elected Lord Rector of Glasgow University, the Order of the Thistle being conferred upon his Lordship the following year. High-born, Lord Eglinton was also high-minded, and, with a handsome figure, allied to fascinating manners, all Scotland may be said to have felt proud of her son, whether he was discharging public duties at home, improving the holdings of his tenantry and promoting education among them, or smoothing down the asperities of Irish life by his winning courtesy at Dublin Castle—a courtesy, it is but right to say, manifested equally to all, of whatever creed or political profession. His death occurred with startling suddenness in the house of his friend, Mr. Whyte Melville, St. Andrews, 4th October, 1861. By his first marriage with Theresa Newcomen, widow of Commander R. H. Cockerell, R.N., Earl Archibald left two sons, the eldest being Archibald William, present Earl, born 3rd December, 1841, and married Lady Sophia, only daughter of second Earl of Yarborough, with issue four daughters. At present, therefore, the heir-presumptive to this ancient house is his Lordship's brother, Hugh Seton-Montolieu, late lieutenant in Scots Fusilier Guards, born 1846, and married 1870, with issue one daughter, deceased.

THE EARLDOM OF CARRICK.

LESS in size than many of the northern earldoms, none of them—not even Angus, Fife, or Huntly, not Strathearn itself, the patrimony of the mighty Malise—can be made to render up a more romantic or interesting story than is connected with that Carrick division of south Ayrshire, lying between the Doon and the northern boundary of those princely feudatories in Galloway who more than once held the Crown in check. The Carrick district makes up only about a third part in the area of one county, and that only seventh in size among the counties in Scotland. From Bridge of Ness, Loch Doon, following the river course north-west to the sea or Ayr Bay, the distance is about sixteen miles; from the mouth of Doon, mostly southward, but tending a little west, to Galloway Burn, Glenapp, the distance is not much, if anything, over forty-five miles. Carrick district first comes under the notice of historians about the middle of the twelfth century, when it was held by a succession of Uchtreds and Gilberts as part of the lordship of Galloway. Towards the close of the same century Carrick was erected into an independent Earldom, and granted by William the Lion to Duncan, held to have founded the Abbey of Crossraguel about 1240. Following Duncan came a son, Nigel, or Neil, second Earl of Carrick, one of the Regents and Guardians of Alexander III., who died in 1256, leaving by his wife Margaret, daughter of Walter, High Stewart of Scotland, an only child, a daughter, named also Margaret, or Marjory, who became Countess of Carrick in her own right. Legend and tradition now get mixed up with anything that ever was historical in the early history of the Earldom. The Norman, or rather the Yorkshire, Bruces had acquired the Lordship of Annandale from David I. as early, it is thought, as 1140, the honours of the family being held when Marjory succeeded to Carrick by Robert de Bruce, fifth Lord, who came to be known in after years as the Competitor, in virtue of being heir nearest the Crown in degree through his grandmother, Isabella, second daughter of the Earl of Huntingdon, younger brother of

William the Lion. John Baliol claimed as great grandson of the eldest daughter Margaret. The Competitor's eldest son, also Robert, accompanied Edward I. of England (then Prince Edward) in his crusade to Palestine (1270-72), where he is presumed to have fought along side of an Adam de Kilkonath, husband of Marjory of Carrick, but slain on the field when charging the infidel hosts of the Sultan. Returning to Scotland with the shattered remnant of Prince Edward's expedition, young Bruce is reported to have been riding on one occasion near the Carrick fortress of Turnberry, when the widowed Countess was out hunting with a retinue of squires and fair dames. Struck, so the story goes by the nobility of his appearance, Countess Marjory invited the young knight to join her in the chase and be her guest for a time in that family stronghold, the ruins of which still overlook the sea from Turnberry Point. Aware of the peril incurred by paying undue attention to a King's ward, as the Countess then was, Bruce courteously evaded the invitation, but the gallant lady's wish was not to be so easily put aside, and on a signal, given, it has been recorded, by herself, the retinue closed in around him, while the Countess seized his bridal reins, and led him off with gentle violence to her castle. Within a fortnight they were married, and King Alexander soon afterwards was induced to overlook the youthful indiscretion on payment of a heavy fine. The second Robert Bruce thus became Earl of Carrick in right of his wife, and she became mother of that still more famous third Robert Bruce, the hero of Bannockburn and restorer of Scottish independence, born 11th July, 1274.

It was within the walls of Turnberry that the most powerful Scottish and English barons met on the death of King Alexander III., 1286, to subscribe that bond declaring that they would henceforth adhere to and take part with one another, on all occasions, and against all persons, "saving their allegiance to the King of England, and also their allegiance to him who should gain the kingdom of Scotland by right of descent." The Countess Marjory died some time before 1292, as in November of that year Bruce, then in full possession, to avoid homage to Baliol, resigned the Earldom of Carrick into the hands of his son Robert, then seventeen, and afterwards retired to his English estates. Besides Robert, King of Scots, the Countess bore her husband five sons and seven daughters—among them being Edward, sixth Earl and King of Ulster; Thomas and Alexander, captured in Galloway when bringing supplies to their eldest brother, and executed at Carlisle by order of Edward I.; and Neil, a young man of exceptional comeliness, taken at Kildrummie in 1306 and also executed. Of the daughters, Lady Christian married Bruce's attached friend, Sir Christopher Seton, also put to death at Dumfries by the English in 1306.

As the career of the great King Robert belongs more to the history of Scotland generally than to Carrick in particular, two circumstances only fall to be specially mentioned. It was to Turnberry Bruce fled with his wife and children after wasting the lands of William, Lord Douglas, Knight of Liddesdale; and it was from the towers of his own paternal inheritance that a fire, accidentally kindled, became a signal for him to cross the firth from Arran for the purpose of attempting the delivery of his country. One of the earliest feats to carry out the resolve was a successful attack on Percy's English troops in Turnberry before Bruce withdrew for safety to the mountain fastnesses of Carrick, but not before he had put almost the entire garrison to the sword.

After King Robert the Earldom of Carrick was held by Edward Bruce, and in succession by three of his illegitimate sons—Robert, slain at Dupplin, 1332; Alexander, who fell at Halidon Hill, 1333; and Thomas, on whose death in 1334, without issue, the honours reverted to the Crown in the person of David II. Held for a very short time by Sir William Cunninghame, the King made a new grant to John Stewart, Lord of Kyle, great grandson of King Robert I., and son of Robert Stewart of Scotland, Earl of Strathearn. Succeeding to the throne as Robert III., the title fell to his eldest son, the unfortunate Duke of Rothesay, who became twelfth Earl of Carrick. In 1404 the King last mentioned granted in free regality to his second son, James Stewart of Scotland, afterwards James I., the whole lands of the Stewartry of Scotland, including the Earldom of Carrick. The title thus came to be hereditary in the Royal Family as Princes and Stewarts of Scotland; and since the union of the Crowns has been borne, as at present, by the Sovereign's eldest son. The Welsh dignity is conferred from life to life by patent, but it is in virtue of the Scottish Act of Settlement of 1469 that Albert-Edward, present Prince of Wales, is by hereditary descent also Duke of Rothesay, Earl of Carrick, Baron of Renfrew, and Lord of the Isles. An attempt was made in the early part of the seventeenth century to get the Carrick honours revived in the person of John Stewart, second son of Robert, Earl of Orkney, a natural son of James V.; and, although King Charles did not seem disinclined to favour the suit, especially as Stewart had got possession of certain lands in the Earldom, yet, when the patent came up for discussion, Sir Thomas Hope, Lord-Advocate, had courage to remind the Council that the title of Earl of Carrick belonged to the King's eldest son, the Prince of Scotland, and was not communicable to any subject. He therefore recommended the Council to advise with His Majesty on the subject before anything "forder wer proceedit herein." The difficulty was partly got over by the elevation of Stewart to a similar title, but alleged to be taken from lands in Orkney. His Lordship died in 1652, without male issue.

In mentioning the boundaries of the Earldom it has been judged best to treat it as making up the district known as Carrick in modern times, for purposes civil, ecclesiastical, and legal. But there is some reason for thinking that long after its separation from Galloway the Earls had jurisdiction far north of the Doon into Kyle, and probably into Cunningham. The Kyle men especially were ever valiant and faithful to the Bruce cause, and are often noticed by historians as mustering with alacrity to defend the patriot king, either when he was concealing himself among them or raised his standard elsewhere. Speaking topographically, the Carrick locality of Ayrshire, as understood in modern times, is made up of nine parishes—Ballantrae, Barr, and Colmonell; Daily, Girvan, and Kirkmichael; Kirkoswald, Maybole, and Straiton. Each of these parishes has a history interesting in itself, apart from any connection with the old Earldom, and, if not already noticed, will come up for future illustration. Maybole and Kirkoswald are especially rich in associations with the past—the first mainly ecclesiastical as relating to its once richly endowed and beautiful Abbey, now in ruins; the other as having Turnberry and Culzean within its bounds, and Cassillis mansion on its borders, famous in the history of the Kennedies, from the wicked Gilbert, "King of Carrick," downwards. Kirkoswald, besides its memories of the exciting smuggling days and the building of smuggling craft, is also pre-eminently a Burns portion of Ayrshire. Here, under the very shadow of Turnberry ruins, was the farm of Shanter, thrown into another in recent years, but occupied in the poet's day by that Douglas Graham, the original of the stalwart, thoughtless, and undying "Tam." In the village adjoining, too, Burns himself for some months attended Rodger's mathematical school, and is likely to have written there one of his very earliest pieces, "My Father was a Farmer upon the Carrick Border." In population the district of Carrick has rather fallen off during late years, the census for 1831 showing 25,536, and 1881 only 23,566.

Certain other minute particulars concerning the Earldom of Carrick—especially touching the legitimacy in succession of the three sons of Edward Bruce—will be found in a small volume issued at Edinburgh, 1857 (T. G. Stevenson), entitled "Some Account of the Ancient Earldom of Carric," by Andrew Carrick, M.D. Edited by James Maidment.

THE LOCKHARTS OF MILTON-LOCKHART.

WITH a pedigree reaching as far back as Stephen of Cleghorn, armour-bearer to James III. (1460–88), the family of Milton-Lockhart may be looked upon as among the oldest, if not the very oldest, offshoot of the house of Lee. Another Stephen, great-grandson of the founder, married Grizel, daughter of Walter Carmichael of Hyndford, and had a family of three sons—(1) William, who fell at Rullion Green, supporting the cause of the Covenant, and whose line became extinct in 1776 on the death without issue of his grandson, Sir Wm. Lockhart

Denham, Bart.; (2) Robert, of Birkhill, who also supported the Covenant, and having first had a horse shot under him at Bothwell Bridge, afterwards died from exposure, a fugitive, in the wastes of his own parish of Lesmahagow; and (3) Walter of Kirkton and Wicketshaw, who, after espousing, like his brothers, the cause of the Covenant, entered the Royal army, in which he rose to the rank of captain, became paymaster of Forces in Scotland, and died in Edinburgh Castle, 1743, aged eighty-seven. William, a successor in Birkhill, married Violet Inglis, niece and heiress of James Somerville of Corehouse, and left among other sons and daughters, Major-General William Lockhart, who died 1817; and John, who studied for the Church and became a D.D. of Edinburgh University.

Licensed by the Presbytery of Stirling, 1785, the Rev. John Lockhart was ordained minister of Cam'nethan parish the following year, in succession to Alexander Ranken, translated to Ramshorn (now St. David's), Glasgow. In 1796, about ten years after his ordination, Dr. Lockhart was presented by the Town Council of Glasgow to the church of Blackfriars or "College Kirk," vacant by the death of John Gillies, who had ministered there for the long period of fifty-four years. Dr. Lockhart himself may be also classed among the aged ministers of his day, surviving, as he did, till December, 1842, when he had reached the eighty-second year of his age and the fifty-seventh of his ministry. He published "The Covenant of God, the Hope of Man," and one of many sermons preached on the death of the Princess Charlotte. Twice married, Dr. Lockhart had by his first wife, Elizabeth Dinwoodie of Germiston, William, his heir, born 1787, who acquired part of the old family estates adjoining the barony of Milton-Lockhart, and represented the county of Lanark in Parliament from 1841 till his death in 1856, when he was succeeded for a brief period by A. D. Baillie-Cochrane of Lamington. William Lockhart, esteemed in his day as one of the most useful public men in the county, was Lieutenant-Colonel Commandant of the Lanarkshire Regiment of Yeomanry Cavalry, and Dean of Faculties of the University of Glasgow. Dr. Lockhart married secondly Elizabeth, daughter of the Rev. John Gibson, of St. Cuthbert's, Edinburgh. By this marriage there was issue, with other sons and daughters, John Gibson Lockhart, born in 1793, to be afterwards referred to; Lawrence, born 1796, who succeeded to Milton-Lockhart, and Robert, who entered upon a mercantile career.

Lawrence Lockhart, second son, as above-mentioned, studied, like his father, for the Church, and like him also came to be honoured with the degree of D.D. He was licensed by the Presbytery of Glasgow, 1822, and ordained to the charge of Inchinnan, in succession to William Richardson, D.D., in August of same year. Dr. Lawrence Lockhart filled the charge of Inchinnan from 1822 till 1860, when he resigned the living and took up his residence at Milton-Lockhart, to which he had succeeded on the death of his half-brother, William. Dr. Gillan, of St. John's, Glasgow, succeeded to the charge of Inchinnan. Like his father in many other respects, Dr. Lawrence Lockhart was also twice married, his first wife being Louisa, daughter of David Blair. Dr. Lawrence married secondly, 1849, Marion, eldest daughter of William Maxwell of Dargavel, and on his death in 1876 left issue David Blair, now of Wicketshaw and Milton-Lockhart, referred to below. Dr. Lockhart's second son was the well-known Colonel Lawrence William Maxwell, of the 92nd Highlanders, who served with distinction in the Crimea, and, like his uncle, John Gibson, occupied an honourable position in the literature of his day. He acted as correspondent for the "Times" in the Franco-Prussian war, wrote various popular novels, "Fair to See" among the rest, and was a contributor to "Blackwood," highly appreciated by readers, and most sincerely respected by the publisher. Colonel Lockhart died at Mentone in March, 1882, leaving issue by his marriage with Katherine, younger daughter of Sir James Russell of Ashestiel, Selkirkshire, one son, Lawrence Archibald Somerville.

The eldest son of Dr. John Lockhart, Blackfriar's Church, by his second marriage with Miss Gibson, was the eminent critic and novelist, John Gibson Lockhart, biographer of his illustrious father-in-law, Sir Walter Scott. Born in the manse of Cam'nethan, 1795, he was educated at the University of Glasgow, and passed on a Snell Exhibition to Baliol College, Oxford. Selecting law as a profession, he passed advocate in 1816, but made an appearance in Court only on rare occasions. Even during the legal studies necessary to qualify for the Bar, Lockhart showed such a strong leaning towards literature, that after forming the acquaintance of Scott in 1818, little persuasion was needed to make authorship his chief reliance, his first work being issued the following year in the form of "Peter's Letters to his Kinsfolk." Known as the "Scorpion" of the Chaldee MS. inserted in an early number of "Blackwood," Lockhart may be said to have been from the commencement of that magazine the leader of that mischievous band of young Tories who furnished its most biting and brilliant papers. His connection with the periodical, of which he was erroneously reputed to be editor, led, in 1821, to a hostile correspondence with John Scott, of the "London Magazine," the quarrel ending in a duel, in which Scott fell mortally wounded by Lockhart's "friend," Mr. Christie, who had got himself involved in the unhappy quarrel when negotiating for an apology. After "Valerius," Lockhart's first novel, sent out 1821, "Adam Blair," "Reginald Dalton," and "Matthew Wald" followed in quick succession; till in 1826 he succeeded Gifford as editor of the "Quarterly Review," which he was spared to conduct, with rare ability, for the long period of twenty-eight years. Proud in spirit, and rather cynical and disdainful in his manner, Lockhart's domestic life was severely tried by affliction, first through the death of his favourite son, the "Hugh Littlejohn" of Scott's "Tales of a Grandfather;" then of his wife Sophia, Scott's eldest daughter, in 1837; and finally of his only surviving son, a cornet in the 16th Lancers, who, after ruining a fine constitution, died unmarried, January 10, 1853, at the early age of twenty-seven. Mr. Lockhart's only surviving child, Charlotte, named after her grandmother, Lady Scott, became the wife of J. R. Hope, Q.C., who assumed the name of Scott, and had an only child, Mary-Monica, who became wife of the Hon. J. Constable-Maxwell (now Scott) of the Herries family, present proprietor of Abbotsford through his wife, great-grand-daughter of Sir Walter. Of this marriage there is issue several sons and daughters.

In addition to the writings above referred to, Lockhart translated a collection of "Ancient Spanish Ballads," about the accuracy of which critics differ, although none dispute the flowing rhyme or animated descriptive power. He also wrote a few pieces of a patriotic and humorous character—the best known being "The Broadswords of Old Scotland," the inimitable "Captain Paton," and, probably, "The Great Glasgow Gander" in the "Noctes." One or two other occasional pieces in the form of "Epitaphs" on friends may also be mentioned. That on the accomplished but unfortunate Dr. Maginn has been much admired for its neatness. It is dated simply—

WALTON-ON-THAMES, AUG., 1842.

Here, early to bed, lies kind William Maginn,
Who, with genius, wit, learning, Life's trophies to win,
Had neither great Lord nor rich cit of his kin,
Nor discretion to set himself up as to tin;
So, his portion soon spent (like the poor heir of Lynn),
He turn'd author, ere yet there was beard on his chin—
And, whoever was out, or whoever was in,
For your Tories his fine Irish brains he would spin,
Who received prose and rhyme with a promising grin—
"Go ahead, you queer fish, and more power to your fin!"
But to save from starvation stirred never a pin.
Light for long was his heart, though his breeches were thin,
Else his acting, for certain, was equal to Quin;
But at last he was beat, and sought help of the bin—
(All the same to the Doctor from claret to gin),
Which led swiftly to gaol, with consumption therein.
It was much, when the bones rattled loose in the skin,
He got leave to die here—out of Babylon's din.
Barring drink and the girls, I ne'er heard of a sin—
Many worse, better few, than bright broken Maginn.

A companion epitaph on Theodore Hook is less known, but those familiar with it think it not quite so genial, while one or two lines make the piece less suitable for publication. Broken, as has been said, in spirit, and shattered in health, Lockhart laid aside the cares of the "Quarterly" in 1853, and, like Maginn, turned his back on "Babylon's din," proceeding northward in the summer of next year, with the view of recovering some measure of physical vigour, and, it may be, of recalling the early delightful days spent with his wife, her father, and her father's friends at Chiefswood. Halting for a short rest with his relative at Milton-Lockhart, the invalid passed on to Abbotsford, but, so far from recruiting amid scenes full of agreeable associations, he gradually became weaker, and died there, 25th November, 1854. The remains of J. G. Lockhart were laid within the ruins of Dryburgh Abbey, beside those of his father-in-law, Sir Walter, and with much appropriateness, for it is not too much to say that the Memoir of the one from the pen of the other will live as long as "Waverley" novels are read. The memoir appeared in 1837-38.

The present proprietor of Milton-Lockhart is David Blair Lockhart, also of Wicketshaw, a Lieutenant-Colonel in the 107th Foot, eldest son of Rev. Lawrence Lockhart, D.D. He represents two other old families—the Cleghorn branch in the male line, and in the female line the Somervilles of Cam'nethan. Allan Eliot Lockhart of Cleghorn, Lanarkshire, and Borthwickbrae, Selkirkshire, son of William Eliot, was descended from another Allan Lockhart, said to have witnessed charters in the reign of James II. (1437-60). The later Allan studied for the bar, passed advocate 1824, and sat as member of Parliament for Selkirk county from 1846 till 1861, when he accepted the Chiltern Hundreds, and was succeeded in the representation by Lord Henry John Scott, after a contest with the Hon. W. Napier.

ARDGOWAN: THE STEWARTS AND SHAW-STEWARTS.

IF what was once a chief fortalice of those early Stewarts descended from Robert III. is now the ruined, grim, and roofless tower at Blackhall, close on Paisley, the splendour of the new residence at Ardgowan gives not only manifest tokens of more peaceable times, but suggests much otherwise concerning the Royal race from which the lairds, knights, and baronets of the old castle sprung. It should also be kept in mind that while Ardgowan has long been the principal mansion of the family, the property, with its own old fortress, now forsaken like Blackhall, was amongst the earliest of their possessions in Renfrewshire. Certain antiquaries make mention of it as the first property granted by King Robert to his son John Stewart; but more exact inquiry would fix the charters as passing the Great Seal in the following order :—Auchingown, 1390; Blackhall, 1395; Ardgowan, 1403, or three years before the King died in Rothesay Castle, partly, it is thought, through grief at the capture on the high seas by the English of his only surviving legitimate son, Prince James, while being conveyed to France for safety. The Greenock and other acquisitions of the Blackhall Stewarts will be noticed below in connection with the Shaw family. Situated on a fine natural terrace on the left or south bank, about two miles below the Cloch Lighthouse, and therefore beyond the point where Clyde bends from its westward course southward to the Firth, Ardgowan commands magnificent views along both shores of the estuary, and as far down as the rugged peaks of Arran. The present mansion, designed by Cairncross, was built early in last century by the then Sir John Shaw-Stewart, fourth baronet, and fifteenth in direct male descent from John, son of Robert III., and founder of the house. Blackhall then (1710) became the farm-house of that property. Sir John also enclosed the beautiful grounds amid which the mansion-house stands, and planned the gardens, walks, and plantations. Unlike Blackhall Tower, now little more than an unseemly encumbrance within an ordinary farm-yard, the old and only remnant of the first family residence at Ardgowan has been so far cared for as to impart interest to the landscape. Mouldering and ivy-clad, the ruin yet carries the mind back even beyond the days of that James Stewart who, in 1576, obtained from James VI. a charter creating the three properties mentioned above into a barony. John Stewart had by Margaret, daughter of Stewart of Castlemilk, one son, Archibald, of Blackhall, who sat in Parliament as Commissioner for the shire of Renfrew. He was also chosen as a Privy Councillor by Charles I., and advanced to the dignity of knighthood. By his first wife, a daughter of Bryce Blair of Blair, Sir Archibald had issue three sons and two daughters—(1) John, who predeceased his father, but left by his wife Mary, daughter of the house of Keir, among other sons, Archibald, who succeeded to the family honours in 1658; (2) Archibald, who obtained the lands of Scotston through his wife Margaret, daughter and heiress of John Hutcheson; (3) Walter, who married Elizabeth, daughter and heiress of Robert Stewart, and succeeded thereby to the lands of Pardovan, leaving issue one son, Walter, prominent in the Church Courts of his day as a debater, and frequently in correspondence with Woodrow. Of the two daughters of Sir Archibald Stewart, Annabel married Sir George Maxwell of Pollock, while Margaret married Sir David Boswell of Auchinleck. Sir Archibald, first knight, was succeeded, as mentioned above, by his grandson, also Archibald, who was created a baronet of Nova Scotia. Married to Anne, eldest daughter of Sir John Crawford of Kilbirnie, the second Sir Archibald had, with other issue, a son, John, father of Archibald, second baronet, and of Michael, third baronet, who succeeded to the title and estates on the death of his elder brother, without issue, in 1724. It is now necessary to turn to the Ardgowan connection with the family of Shaw, of Greenock, through the marriage of the Sir Michael just mentioned as third baronet, with Helenor, eldest daughter of Sir John Houstoun, third Baronet of Houstoun, and Margaret Shaw, his wife, daughter of Sir John Shaw, second baronet of Greenock, and Eleanor, eldest daughter and co-heir of Sir Thomas Nicolson, Bart., of Carnock.

Tracing their descent, in common with the Wemyss family, to Duncan, fifth Earl of Fife, the Shaws of Sauchie, Stirlingshire, are early found making alliances with the best families in Scotland. One member, during the fourteenth century, married a daughter and co-heiress of Malcolm Galbraith, described as "of Greenock," but Lennox in descent, and thereby acquired a moiety of the barony known as Wester Greenock, the other co-heiress carrying Easter Greenock into the family of Crawford of Kilbirnie, from whose descendant it was purchased in 1669 by Sir John Shaw. Wester Greenock passed first to a younger son of Shaw of Sauchie, but, on failure of that line, Greenock eventually succeeded to Sauchie, and became chief of the name. John Shaw of Greenock and Sauchie (son of James Shaw of Wester Greenock, by Margaret Montgomery, and grandson of John and Elizabeth Cunningham), was knighted on the field of Worcester, 1651, and created a baronet, 1687. By his wife, Jean Mure, daughter of the house of Rowallan, Sir John left one son, Sir John, second baronet, and five daughters, one of them marrying into the family of Smollett of Bonhill. By Eleanor, eldest daughter and co-heir of Sir Thomas Nicolson of Carnock, as mentioned above, the second baronet of Greenock had issue besides John, his successor, other four sons, all killed in the wars of the Low Countries, and one daughter, Margaret, who in 1714 married Sir John Houstoun, third Baronet of Houstoun. Lady Margaret Houstoun died in 1750, leaving issue one son, Sir John, the fourth and last baronet of Houstoun, who married Eleanora, eldest daughter of Charles, eighth Lord Cathcart, without issue; and two daughters, (1) Helena, who married, as already mentioned, Sir Michael Stewart, third baronet of Blackhall; and (2) Anne, who married Colonel William Cunninghame of Enterkine. Joanna, sister of Margaret, died unmarried. Sir John Shaw, second baronet of Greenock, was succeeded by his son, also Sir John, who in 1700 married Marion (or Margaret), eldest daughter of Lord-President Dalrymple, by whom he had one daughter, Marion, who in 1718 became wife of Charles, eight Lord Cathcart, ancestor of the present Alan-Frederick, Earl Cathcart, heir-general of the house of Shaw of Sauchie. Sir John died at Sauchie Lodge, Clackmannan, April 5, 1752, without male issue. The unentailed estate of Sauchie passed to his daughter, Lady Cathcart, while the Greenock, or entailed property, fell to the heir of his sister, Lady Houstoun, John Stewart, eldest son of Sir Michael, third baronet of Blackhall.

John Stewart thus came to represent the families of Nicolson of Carnock, and Houstoun of Houstoun, as well as that of Shaw of Greenock. Sir John Shaw-Stewart, fourth baronet of Greenock and Blackhall, represented Renfrewshire in Parliament from 1785, when William M'Dowall of Garthland resigned, till his death in 1796, when he was succeeded by Boyd Alexander of Southbar, who held the seat for six years. Dying in 1812, and leaving no issue by his wife, Frances Colquhoun, widow of Sir James Maxwell of Pollock, Sir John was succeeded by his nephew, Michael Shaw-Stewart, only son of Houstoun, younger brother of Sir John, by Margaret, daughter of Boyd of Porterfield.

Sir Michael Shaw-Stewart, fifth baronet, Lord-Lieutenant of Renfrewshire, and to whom Ardgowan owes many of its charms, married in 1787 his cousin, Catherine, youngest daughter of Sir William Maxwell of Springkell, by whom he had six sons and three daughters, the eldest being Michael-Shaw, sixth baronet referred to below. Houstoun-Stewart, K.C.B., third son, was born at Springkell, 1791, and educated chiefly at Chiswick, near London. Entering the navy when little more than fourteen years of age, he served under the daring Thomas, Lord Cochrane, afterwards tenth Earl of Dundonald. He was at the siege of Flushing (1809), and commanded the "Benbow" at the bombardment of St. Jean d'Acre. In November, 1846, Captain Houstoun-Stewart was appointed Comptroller-General of the Coastguard, an office which he held till February, 1850, when he became a Lord of the Admiralty. In 1851 he attained the rank of Rear-Admiral, and in February, 1852, was elected M.P. for Greenwich, but only retained his place in Parliament till July of that year, and in the following December, on the fall of the first Derby Ministry, Admiral-Houstoun Stewart ceased to be a Lord of the Admiralty. In 1855 he was created a Knight-Commander of the Bath, for his services as second in command of the naval forces off Sebastopol in that year. In 1858 he was appointed a Vice-Admiral. Dying December 10, 1875, Admiral

Sir Houstoun-Stewart left issue by his wife Martha, daughter of Sir William Miller, Lord Glenlee, among other sons and daughters, the present Sir William Houstoun-Stewart, K.C.B. Entering the navy, like his father, when about fourteen years of age, he served with distinction in operations on the north coast of Spain, 1836–37; in Syrian war, and bombardment of St. Jean d'Acre, 1840; at bombardment of Sebastopol, 1854, and operations in the Baltic, and bombardment of Sweaborg, 1855; was successively Superintendent of Chatham, Devonport, and Portsmouth dockyards, and Comptroller of the Navy. Admiral Stewart was among the few permitted to accompany the Czar's yacht "Lividia" on her first cruise from the Clyde to the Black Sea. Admiral William Houstoun Stewart has been twice married, with issue, besides other sons and daughters, Lieutenant Houstoun, R.N., born 1854.

The fifth son of Sir Michael Shaw-Stewart, fifth baronet, Patrick Maxwell, born 1795, sat as M.P. for Lancaster from 1831 till 1837, and for the county of Renfrew from 1841, when he carried the election against Colonel William Mure by a narrow majority, till his decease in October, 1846, when Colonel Mure was elected without opposition.

Sir Michael, sixth baronet of Greenock and Blackhall, eldest son of Sir Michael, fifth Baronet, succeeded Lord Archibald Hamilton in the representation of Lanarkshire, 1827, and held the seat for three years, when he was elected for his native county of Renfrew, in succession to Sir John Maxwell, younger of Pollok. In the first Reformed Parliament, Sir Michael, who had been a consistent supporter of "the Bill," was re-elected for Renfrewshire by 700 votes against 412 tendered in favour of R. C. Bontine of Ardoch, and held the seat till his decease in 1836, when it fell to George Houstoun (Conservative), who held it over a second contest till 1841, when Patrick Maxwell Stewart, mentioned above (described as a Liberal) was returned by 959 votes against 945 recorded in favour of Colonel William Mure, Liberal-Conservative. Sir Michael, sixth Baronet, married, 1819, Elizabeth Mary, only child of Robert Farquhar of Newark, and had issue, with other sons and daughters, Robert, the present

Sir Michael Shaw-Stewart, born 1826, and, rare in the history of Scottish families, the seventeenth in direct male descent from the John Stewart first mentioned as son of Robert III., whose reign extended over 1390–1406.

Presently Lord-Lieutenant of Renfrewshire, Sir Michael succeeded to the representation of the county in Parliament, 1855, when Colonel William Mure accepted the Chiltern Hundreds, and held the seat as a Liberal-Conservative without a contest till 1865, when it was won by Mr. A. A. Spiers of Elderslie (Liberal), with 938 votes against 836 tendered in favour of Sir Michael. Born in 1826, the present Baronet married in December, 1852, Lady Octavia Grosvenor, sixth daughter of Richard, second Marquis of Westminister, K.G., and has had issue five sons and four daughters, the eldest and heir-apparent being Michael Hugh Stewart-Nicolson of Carnock, born 11th July, 1854, a Captain in the Argyll and Sutherland Highlanders, married, 14th November, 1883, Lady Alice Thynne, daughter of John Alexander, fourth Marquis of Bath.

Among the more recent additions to the Ardgowan property there falls to be mentioned Finnock, Leven, Duchal, Flattertoun, and Dunrod, the latter famous in Renfrewshire history as a resort of witches who kept company with that "auld Dunrod" who sold the barony in 1619 to Archibald Stewart of Blackhall. Making up, as it does, over two-thirds of the parish of Inverkip, Sir Michael's Renfrewshire property is entered in the Parliamentary Return of Owners and Heritages (1874), as consisting of 4,773 acres, with a rental of £13,012, exclusive of £458 for quarries and £700 for minerals.

NOTE.—It cannot, in the nature of things, happen frequently for the local or family annalist to record events of permanent historic interest as mere news. Yet it would be ungracious, less far than dutiful, not to make special mention of the fact that young Lieutenant Houstoun-Stewart, R.N. (born 1854), mentioned above as son of Admiral Sir William, K.C.B., cousin of the present Sir Michael of Ardgowan, fell in the Soudan so recently as the forenoon of Thursday

(March 13, 1884), while commanding the guns of the Naval Brigade, opened with such stern purpose against the desert troops of Osman Digma, fighting in name of the Mahdi, otherwise known as the False Prophet. Houstoun-Stewart was senior lieutenant at the time of H.M.S. "Dryad." Son of Sir William, presently Commander-in-Chief at Devonport, Houstoûn-Stewart, who has fallen so nobly, entered the Navy as cadet 1866, became midshipman two years afterwards, and Lieutenant in September, 1876.

POLLOK AND THE MAXWELLS.

OF the five baronetcies held by families named Maxwell—Pollok, Calderwood, Cardoness, Monreith, and Springkell—the first named has been long esteemed the most ancient, starting as it does with that Aymer de Maxwell (son of Sir John, Sheriff of Teviotdale), who in the reign of Alexander II. appears as witness to a charter proceeding from Walter the Great Stewart, gifting the churches of Dundonald and Sanquhar to the Monks of Paisley Abbey. Aymer, Chamberlain of Scotland (or his son John, for genealogians are not agreed on the point), would appear from such slender evidence as exists to have married Mary, the heiress of Roland of Mearns, and thereby brought into the family that portion of the Renfrewshire property, as well as Nether Pollok, or Polloc, which now makes up a large portion of the parish of Eastwood. Herbert, the eldest son of Aymer, is claimed as ancestor of the Maxwells of Caerlaverock, afterwards Lords Maxwell and Earls of Nithsdale, now represented in pursuance of a decision in the House of Lords (1858) by Marmaduke Constable-Maxwell, baron Herries of Terregles. From John, second son of Aymer, the family of Nether Pollok would appear to be more immediately descended. His name appears as witness to two donations of land in the Mearns which Herbert gave to the monks of Paisley in the end of the thirteenth century. In one deed the Abbey Cartulary makes mention of him as "Johannes de Maxwell, dominus de Polloc inferiori," while in the other John Maxwell is simply described as the brother of Herbert. (Cart., pp. 104-380.) The name has generally been accepted as coming from that Macus who, about the year 1116, witnessed the inquisition made by David, Prince of Cumberland, afterwards King David I., into the possessions of the Church of Glasgow. Thus there would be first "Macus" only; then "Macus' vil," or town of Macus; until mere superfluity appears in the now familiar "Maxwelltown" of the Herries barony. Other derivations, however, have not been wanting, and are yet maintained by scholars of high reputation, as the Gaelic "Pollag," a little pool, and "weil," or circling eddy in a stream, as also "well" itself. In any case, such names as Undwyn, father of Macus, and of Liolf, his son, may be accepted as indicating a Saxon origin for the family.

Pollok proper, or Upper Pollok, as it was frequently called, was held possession of by a family of that name for over six hundred years, or from 1163 till 1794, when, on the death of Sir Hew Crawford of Jordanhill, the baronetcy was taken up by his eldest son, Robert, in whose person the families of Pollok, Kilbirnie, and Jordanhill became united. Dying without issue in August, 1845, Sir Robert was succeeded by his nephew, Hew, in the properties of Pollok and Kilbirnie, and also in the baronetcy of Kilbirnie, which last dates from 1638. By his wife, Elizabeth Oswald, daughter of Matthew Dunlop, Sir Hew Crawford had, besides one daughter, Jane, a son, Hew Crawford-Pollok, born 1843, the fifth and present baronet of Kilbirnie, who succeeded to the family honours on the death of his father, 5th March, 1867. Tracing a common ancestor in the very earliest of the Maxwells of Nether Pollok, the house of Calderwood springs more immediately from Sir John Maxwell, who, under a deed, dated at Dumbarton, 18th December, 1400, settled the family lands on his eldest son John, by Isobel, daughter of Sir James Lindsay, and the barony of Calderwood, with other lands, on his younger son Robert, who in 1402 married Elizabeth, daughter and co-heir of Sir Robert Dennistoun of Dennistoun, by whom he had two sons—one, John, his heir; and George, ancestor of the Maxwells of Newark. The present Sir

William Maxwell of Calderwood, born 11th August, 1828, is the tenth in descent of the Nova Scotia baronets, an honour first conferred on Sir James of Calderwood, March, 1627—Sir James being at the time heir presumptive of Sir John of Pollok, but afterwards passed over in favour of George Maxwell of Auldhouse. The present Sir William of Calderwood succeeded on the death of his father, Sir Hugh Bates, ninth baronet, February, 1870.

Third in descent from that Aymer de Maxwell of Caerlaverock, mentioned above, was Sir John, son of Sir Robert of Pollok, who, by his marriage with Isobel Lindsay of Crawford, daughter of Walter the High Steward, had, with other sons and daughters (1) John, his successor, who greatly distinguished himself at Otterburn (1388) by capturing Sir Ralph Percy, brother of the noted Hotspur; and (2) Robert, ancestor of the Maxwells of Calderwood. Another John Maxwell is found afterwards succeeding to Pollok, and leaving by his wife, Elizabeth, a daughter of Sir Patrick Houstoun of Houstoun, an only child, Elizabeth, sole heiress of Pollok, who brought the estate to her husband, Sir John, son of George Maxwell of Cowglen. This Sir John was knighted by Queen Mary, summoned to repair in her support to the muster-ground at Hamilton after the escape from Lochleven, with all his servants "bodin in feir of war," and fought in her army at Langside, on the borders of his own estate, May, 1568.

The Sir John Maxwell, last mentioned, fell at Dryfe Sands while aiding his chief, Lord Nithsdale, Warden of the West Marches, in an attack on the Johnstons, Scotts, Elliots, and other Border clans, 7th December, 1593. Sir John had some eight years previously finished building the now ruined castle of Haggs, as appears from an inscription all but illegible on a triangular stone over the main doorway :—

"1535,
NI DOMIN,
ÆDES STRVXE,
RIT FRVSTRA STRVIS,
SIR JOHN MAXWELL OF POLLOK, KNIGHT,
AND D. MARGARET CONYNGHAM,
HIS WIFE, BIGGIT THIS HOUSE."

The Dame Margaret Cunningham here mentioned was Sir John's first wife, a daughter of the Laird of Caprington, and mother of one daughter, Agnes, who married John Boyle, of Kelburne, ancestor of the Earls of Glasgow, and one son, Sir John of Pollok, at whose death, in 1647, without male issue, the estate, heritable and moveable, went to his cousin George of Auldhouse, although not without several attempts on the part of the Calderwood branch to disturb the succession. The Springkell Maxwells, who acquired the barony of Kirkconnel and Springkell, Annandale, 1609, and were created Baronets of Nova Scotia, 1683, claim to represent the male line of the Pollok family through an earlier George of Auldhouse. The second wife of Sir John, founder of Haggs Castle, so long a jointure-house in the family, was Marjory, daughter of Sir William Edmonstone of Duntreath, descended from Robert III. through the Princess Mary. This Royal connection was again renewed in the family by the above George of Auldhouse marrying (1646) Annabella, daughter of Sir Archibald Stewart of Blackhall and Ardgowan.

The name of Sir George Maxwell is associated with a case famous in the superstitious annals of Renfrewshire in connection with the reputed crime of witchcraft. Nearly twenty years before the local Presbytery had its attention directed with such fatal results to the deplorable case of Christian Shaw, of Bargarran. Sir George was taken suddenly ill while in Glasgow on the night of October 14, 1677, and afterwards confined to his mansion at Pollok, suffering severe bodily pain. A vagrant girl named Janet Douglas, who pretended to be dumb, was considered a clever witch-finder, and owing some of his tenants a grudge, accused several of them of bewitching Sir George. To confirm her assertions, she contrived, in one or two instances, to secrete small wax figures of the suffering knight, stuck with pins, in the dwellings of the accused persons. A special commission was issued for the trial of the case on the spot, and after a long investigation, at which were present, besides some of the Lords of Justiciary, most of the leading men of Renfrewshire, the following unfortunate creatures, namely, Janet Mathie, widow of John Stewart, under-miller in Shaw Mill; John

Stewart, her son; and three old women, the parties accused, were condemned to be strangled and burned; and Annabil Stewart, a girl fourteen years old, the daughter of Mathie, ordered to be imprisoned. A local ballad on the tragedy makes mention of the story as

> "Told by legends old,
> And by withered dame and sire,
> When they sit secure from the winter's cold,
> All around the evening fire.
>
> "How the faggots blazed on the Gallow-green,
> Where they hung the witches high,
> And their mouldering forms were grimly seen,
> Till darkened the lowering sky."

Besides three daughters who married into the families of Dreghorn, Upper Pollok, and Calderwood, Sir George left at his death in 1677 one son, Sir John Maxwell of Pollok, created a Baronet of Nova Scotia by Charles II., April 12, 1682, with extension of the title, in virtue of another patent, March 27, 1707, to his heirs-male whatsoever. In July, 1683, Sir John Maxwell was imprisoned for refusing to take the test, and December 2, 1684, he was fined £8000 by the Privy Council for allowing recusants to live on his lands, and refusing the Bond and Test. The Council, however, declared that if paid before the end of the month the fine would be reduced to £2000. In 1689 Sir John was sworn a Privy Councillor to King William. The same year he represented the county of Renfrew in the Convention of Estates. He was afterwards Commissioner for the same county in the Scots Parliament. In 1696 he was appointed one of the Lords of the Treasury and Exchequer. On the 6th February, 1699, he was admitted an Ordinary Lord of Session, and on the 14th of the same month nominated Lord Justice-Clerk. In the latter office he was superseded in 1702. He died July 4, 1732, in his ninetieth year, without issue.

His cousin, Sir John Maxwell, previously styled of Blawerthill, succeeded as second Baronet of Pollok. He was the son of Zecharias Maxwell of Blawerthill, younger brother of Sir George Maxwell of Auldhouse and Pollok. He married, first, Lady Ann Carmichael, daughter of John, Earl of Hyndford, and had a son, John, and two daughters; secondly, Barbara, daughter of Walter Stewart of Blairhall; issue, three sons—(1) George, of Blawerthill, who died unmarried; (2) Walter; (3) James; and two daughters; thirdly, Margaret, of the family of Caldwell of Caldwell, without issue. He died in 1753.

His eldest son, Sir John Maxwell, became third Baronet. On his death, his half brother, Sir Walter, succeeded as fourth Baronet, and died in 1761.

Sir Walter's only son, Sir John, became fifth Baronet, but died nine weeks after his father.

The title and estates reverted to his father's youngest brother, Sir James, sixth Baronet. This gentleman married Frances, second daughter of Robert Colquhoun of St. Christopher's, of the family of Kenmure; issue, two sons— (1) John, his successor; (2) Robert, a Captain in the army, died without issue; and two daughters—(1) Frances, wife of John Cunningham of Craigends; (2) Barbara, married Rev. Greville Ewing. Sir James died in 1785.

Sir John, seventh Baronet, was the first M.P. for Paisley under the Reform Act of 1832, as many as 777 votes being tendered for him in opposition to 180 given in favour of Mr. M'Kerrell of Hillhouse. He held the seat, however, for only two years, when he accepted the Chiltern Hundreds, and was succeeded by Professor Sir D. K. Sandford, after a contest with John Crawford, another Liberal, and Lieutenant J. E. Gordon, Conservative. He married (1788) Hannah-Anne, daughter of Mr. Richard Gardiner of Aldborough, Suffolk, by whom (who died 21st July, 1841) he had issue—John, eighth Baronet; Harriet-Anne, died unmarried 1841; Elizabeth, marrried 1st June, 1815, Mr. Archibald Stirling of Keir, and died 5th September, 1822; leaving (with two daughters, who both died unmarried) a son, Mr. William Stirling of Keir, M.P., the late Sir William Stirling-Maxwell, ninth Baronet of Pollok.

Sir John died 30th July, 1844, and was succeeded by his only son, Sir John, who was born on the 12th May, 1791, and married 14th October, 1839, Lady Matilda-Harriet Bruce, daughter of Thomas, Earl of Elgin and Kincardine, which lady died 31st August, 1857. Sir John sat in Parliament successively for the counties of Lanark and Renfrew. He died without issue, 6th June, 1865, when the Baronetcy devolved, in pursuance of the limitation of the patent of 1707, upon his nephew, Sir William Stirling-Maxwell, K.T., who assumed the surname of Maxwell, after his patronymic, Stirling.

William Stirling, only son of Archibald of Keir, was born at Kenmure, near Glasgow, 1818, educated at Trinity College, Cambridge, where he took his degree in 1839. Succeeding to the estate of Keir and Cadder on the death of his father, 1847, he took an early opportunity of disentailing these properties, and, besides greatly enlarging Keir House, built the beautiful memorial church of Lecropt, near his family inheritance. Stirling Maxwell married at Paris, 26th April, 1865, Anne-Maria, third daughter of David, eighth Earl of Leven, and by her (who died 8th December, 1874) had issue—(1) John Maxwell, present Baronet; (2) Archibald, born 1867. He married secondly, 1st March, 1877, the Hon. Caroline Norton, daughter of the late Thomas Sheridan, and widow of Hon. George Chapple Norton, brother of Fletcher, third Lord Grantley. She died 15th June following. Sir William was highly esteemed as one of the most accomplished scholars of his day, especially in the department of Spanish art and literature. With strong natural artistic tastes, refined by study and travel, Sir William made many important contributions to critical and historical literature, and published also a volume of "Songs of the Holy Land," 1846. Among his best known works are:—"Annals of the Artists of Spain," 1848; "Cloister Life of Emperor Charles V.," 1852; "Velazquez and his Works," 1855; two sumptuous privately printed books, relating to the victories and processions of Charles V.; "Don John of Austria;" "Essays concerning Proverbs, &c., and the Arts of Design." It was remarked concerning Sir William's "Processions" of Charles V. that, while the greatest and most illustrious historians had vied with each other in preserving the likeness of the Emperor's person, another in preserving the record of his famous achievements, it was no small addition to even his fame that in this our age, the taste, the learning, and the munificence of a Scottish gentleman, aided by the arts of the nineteenth century, should have raised such a literary monument to his greatness. Sir William was a trustee of the British Museum, 1872, and of the National Portrait Gallery; Lord Rector of Edinburgh University, 1871; Chancellor of Glasgow University, 1875; a Member of the Scottish Education Board; a D.C.L. and LL.D. As a Commoner, he also received the exceptional honour of being created a Knight of the Thistle. He sat in the House of Commons as a Conservative for Perthshire (1852-68), and from 1874 till his lamented death, which took place somewhat suddenly at Venice, 16th January, 1878, when the succession to Pollok opened up to his eldest son, Sir John Maxwell Stirling-Maxwell, the tenth and present Baronet, born 6th June, 1866.

The house of Nether Pollok—a large and handsome structure of four storeys—is situated on the right bank of the White Cart amidst highly-embellished pleasure grounds and beautiful plantations. The building was completed in 1753 by the then Sir John Maxwell, second Baronet, a few weeks before his death. The castle which had been previously occupied by the family was demolished about the same time. It stood on the site of the offices attached to the present mansion. Upon an eminence about 300 yards to the eastward of the house there stood a still older castle, the remains of the drawbridge and fosse belonging to which were in existence in Crawfurd's time.

In the Parliamentary Return of Owners and Heritages (Scotland, 1874), Pollok estate is entered as consisting of 4,773 acres, with a rental of £13,012, exclusive of £458 for quarries, and £700 for minerals. Sir William's other properties were entered—Stirlingshire (Keir), 1,487 acres; rental, £2,370. Lanarkshire (Cadder, &c.), 5,691 acres; rental, £8,741; minerals, £3,231. Perthshire, 8,863 acres; rental, £5,731.

SIR THOMAS MUNRO, K.C.B.

UNCOMMEMORATED as yet by any statue in the city of his birth, of his upbringing, and of his education, the fame of Sir Thomas Munro has been otherwise well cared for by a still fresh affectionate regard which connects him with all that was brave and of good report as a soldier, no less than with what was wise and humane as an Indian Governor. An equestrian memorial, carved out by the skilful hand of Chantrey for the inhabitants of Madras—a memorial which even native chiefs have been seen to salute with affection—recalls one phase of Governor Munro's career; a choultry and tank at Gooty for the accommodation of travellers, another; while a third is conspicuous as a tomb at Putteecondah, where the hero of the Maharatta war fell a victim to his zeal in that service of the Crown which had been the pride of his life for the long period of eight-and-forty years. His moderation in war was not more remarkable than his homely, disinterested career during such brief periods of peace as service in the East during his time permitted any of the Company's officials to enjoy. Forty years a soldier, for the most part high in command, and eight years a Governor in the wealthy Presidency of Madras, Sir Thomas Munro, with the uncontrolled management of provinces larger than many European kingdoms, died as he had lived, faithful to his public trust, and possessed of only a modest competence. But still more should be remembered to his credit. Founded as English rule in India was by the matchless bravery of Clive, and built up by the policy of Hastings, the India of Munro's day was a country still looked upon by most Europeans as a place to get rich in as soon as possible; so that every greedy factor, however petty his station, thought it no shame to extort from the poorest peasantry in the world whatever could add to his dreams of boundless wealth. Burke was scarcely exaggerating when he declared in the Commons that Indian civil servants were almost universally sent out to begin their progress and career in active occupation and in the exercise of high authority at that period of life which, in all other places, was employed in the course of a rigid education. "To put the matter in a few words," said the orator, "these civil servants are transferred from slippery youth to perilous independence, from perilous independence to inordinate expectations, from inordinate expectations to boundless power. Schoolboys without tutors, minors without guardians, the world is let loose on them with all its temptations, and they are let loose upon the world with all the powers that despotism involves." Munro has been fitly classed with Elphinstone and Metcalfe as having done their best to supersede such gangs of public robbers by a body of functionaries not more distinguished for ability and diligence than by integrity and public spirit.

The absence of any memorial here to a citizen so distinguished as Major-General Munro is apt to excite increased surprise when it is remembered that he was a son of Glasgow, not alone by the mere accident of birth or education, but it was a locality seldom absent from either his waking thoughts or dreams. Even when exercising supreme power over the dusky myriads of his Presidency, and amid scenes altogether different, he never forgot or ceased to be influenced by recollections of his early home at North Woodside, on the banks of the then silvery Kelvin. "The Father of his People," never appeared in happier mood than when writing or speaking regarding the land of his fathers and the old house at home, removed in 1869, when the ground was being laid out for the thriving new suburb of Kelvinside. To Munro the comfort of his parents, their country house and their garden, remained with him as fresh as if he had never left the paternal roof. But his sister (afterwards Mrs. Henry Erskine) would appear on the whole to have been his favourite correspondent. His tone has been noticed as changing whenever he addressed her, and the recollections and expectations of his heart to well out in their greatest fulness. One written from the camp before Cuddalore, on the eve when General Stuart (of the house of Torrance and Castlemilk) was making his successful attack on the fort kept by the French, supported with native troops under Tippoo Saib, may still be read with interest and profit:—"I have never yet been able to divest myself of my partiality for home; nor can I now reflect without regret on the careless, indolent life I led in my father's house, when time fled away undisturbed by these anxious thoughts which possess every one who seeks earnestly for advancement in the world. I often see my father busied with his tulip beds, and my mother with her myrtle pots; I see you drawing, and James lost in meditation: and all these seem as much present to me as they did when I was amongst you. Sometimes, when I walk on the sea-shore, I look across the waves and please myself with fancying that I see a distant continent amongst the clouds, where I imagine you all to be." Replying on another occasion to his sister, who had proposed a visit to Ammondell during his first return home in 1808, after an absence in the East of nearly thirty years, Colonel Munro wrote playfully:—"I have been twice at North Woodside, and though it rained without ceasing on both days, it did not prevent me from rambling up and down the river from Clayslap to the aqueduct bridge. I stood above an hour at Jackson's Dam, looking at the water rushing over. The rain and withered leaves were descending thick about me, while I recalled the days that are past. The wind whistling through the trees, and the water tumbling over the dam, had still the same sound as before; but the darkness of the day, and the little smart box perched upon the opposite bank, destroyed much of the illusion, and made me feel that former times were gone. I don't know how it is, but when I look back to early years I always associate sunshine with them; when I think of North Woodside, I always think of a fine day, with the sunbeams streaming down upon Kelvin and its woody banks. I do not enter completely into early scenes of life in gloomy, drizzling weather. I mean to devote the first sunny day to another visit to Kelvin, which, whatever you may say, is worth ten such paltry streams as your Ammon." Sentiments like these show that Munro was something more than a Scotchman; he was a Glasgow Scotchman, fully as much as either Lord Clyde, Sir John Moore, or Thomas Campbell, or, indeed, any other whose image has been judged worthy of being set up in George Square.

Munro came of a good old Glasgow family, his grandfather being Daniel and his father Alexander, both merchants of note in the City when the lucrative tobacco trade was reaching its greatest height. It is, indeed, more than probable that but for commercial fluctuations arising out of the unnatural warfare carried on by British troops and German mercenaries in America, the future Lieutenant-General and Governor of Madras might himself have paced along the Tontine pavement as a scarlet-cloaked and periwigged tobacco lord or Virginia Don. The desire of his father and mother was that Thomas, their third son, should be trained for mercantile pursuits; nor did their wish appear likely to be interfered with till the Act of Confiscation, passed by the American Congress in 1776, involved the ruin of his tobacco house, and reduced Alexander Munro to a state of distress which in after life it remained for his sons, Thomas, and an elder brother, John, a writer in Madras, to completely alleviate.

Born in May, 1761, Thomas Munro was at the period of his father's calamities fifteen years of age, and had been fully two years attending Glasgow University. His progress there cannot be set down as very marked. Like Outram, the Lawrences, and other Indian heroes, his boyhood was distinguished less for book learning than as a leader in athletic and other healthy sports, particularly swimming in Jackson's mill-stream, near his father's house, an exercise for which he retained a great partiality in after life. It appeared distressing to the lad that young ideas should be stifled by logic. "A few pages of history (he wrote in after life) give more insight into the human mind, and in a more agreeable manner, than all the metaphysical volumes that ever were published. The men who have made the greatest figure in public life, and have been most celebrated for their knowledge of mankind, probably never consulted any of these sages, from Aristotle downwards." Munro was now a devourer of books; and at sixteen, being justly told that no English translation can convey an adequate notion of "Don Quixote," he made himself a sufficient master of Spanish to relish his favourite romance in the original—a trait of zeal and enthusiasm which ought to have been more valuable in the eyes of his parents than a whole hamper of prize books. The first step in the career of Munro was to get himself rated as a midshipman on board the East India Company's ship "Walpole;" but this was, soon after, fortunately commuted for a Madras cadetship, and in the year 1779 he proceeded to the scene of his future useful and distinguished life. Hyder Ali, the most formidable single enemy that ever threatened the Company's possessions, then hung over the Carnatic; and Munro, after passing six months at the Presidency, most part beneath the hospitable roof of David Halliburton, Persian interpreter, was attached, in 1780, as ensign to the 16th Madras Native Infantry, under the immediate orders of the Commander-in-Chief, General Stuart, before referred to. The unfortunate defeat of Colonel Baillie's detachment, on its march to join the main army, is related in a letter from Sir Thomas to his father.

Munro's dauntless bearing all through the Mysore war waged by Lord Cornwallis against Hyder Ali attracted the notice of his superiors, and, after he had been promoted to the rank of Lieutenant, his talents and discretion obtained for him, in August, 1788, the appointment of assistant in the Intelligence Department. In this capacity he served under the orders of Captain Alexander Read, in the occupation of the ceded district of Guntoor, until the breaking out of the war with Tippoo Saib in 1790, when he again took the field with the army, and remained with it till the hollow peace of 1792. On the cession by Tippoo of the Baramahl, he was again employed under Captain Read in the civil administration of that district till 1799. In the ensuing campaign Captain Munro served in the army of Lord Harris as secretary to his friend, then Colonel Read, who commanded a detached force; and, after the fall of Seringapatam, he was appointed, with Captain, afterwards Sir John, Malcolm, joint-secretary to the Commissioners for the settlement of Mysore. Next he was nominated by Lord Mornington (afterwards Marquis Wellesley), then Governor-General of India, to the charge of the civil administration of Canara, a wild and rugged province on the western or Malabar coast of the peninsula.

Lieutenant Munro wisely described Tippoo as incomparably the most powerful and dangerous enemy of the English at that time, and condemned as preposterous the notion, then prevalent, of attempting to preserve a balance between Powers so unequal as Mysore and its neighbours. "But everything now is done by moderation and conciliation; at this rate, we shall be all Quakers in twenty years more. I am still of the old doctrine, that the best method of making all princes keep the peace, not excepting even Tippoo, is to make it dangerous for them to disturb your quiet." During all this dangerous and harassing period, the young officer's letters home continued to be of the most minute, playful, and affectionate character. His sister had advised him to get married, but he judged on the whole that such a step would add but little to his happiness. "Would it not be a very comfortable matter, about the end of the century, to read in the 'Glasgow Courier'— 'Yesterday was married Lieutenant Munro, the eldest subaltern in the East India Company's service, to Miss——, one of the eldest maiden ladies of this place. The ceremony was performed by the Rev. Mr——, in the Ramshorn, and immediately after the happy couple,' &c. I have no relish, I suspect, for what is called domestic felicity. I could not endure to go about gossiping, and paying formal visits with my wife, and then coming home and consulting about a change in our furniture, or physicking some of the squalling children that Providence might bless us with. You will say—'You will be a more respectable character at home, settled with your family, than wandering about India like a vagabond.' But I cannot perceive that the one situation is more creditable than the other. . . In a place like Glasgow I should be tired in all companies with disputes about the petty politics of the town, of which I know nothing; and anecdotes of families, in whose concerns I am in no way interested. Among the merchants I should be entertained with debates on sugar and tobacco, except when some one touched upon cotton, which would give me an opportunity of opening my mouth, and letting the company know that I had been in India, and seen one species growing on bushes, and another on trees taller than any that adorn the Green. After thus expending all my knowledge, I should not again venture to interrupt the conversation." After the fall of Seringapatam and the final overthrow of Tippoo's power (1799), Captain Munro was raised to the rank of Major and made Governor, as mentioned above, of the disturbed district of Canara, ceded by the Nizam in commutation of subsidy. He was in frequent communication with Colonel Wellesley (afterwards Duke of Wellington), who forwarded to Munro a long account of one of his earliest successes in India—the defeat and death of the daring usurper known as Dhoondee, "King of the Two Worlds," near Yepulpurry, in the Kistra country. In 1808, after an absence of 28 years, Major Munro obtained leave of absence on a visit to his native country, and renewed acquaintance with his early haunts at and around North Woodside. A notice of his reference to them in a letter to his sister has already been given. He was at this time also examined by a Commitee of the House of Commons regarding a renewal of the Company's Charter, and the judicial as well as the commercial features of recent Indian legislation. After a sojourn here of about six years, Munro, then enjoying the full rank of Colonel, re-embarked for India, having shortly before, in oblivion of his early diatribes against matrimony, been united to Jane, daughter of Richard Campbell of Craigie, Ayrshire, a lady whose society formed the comfort and delight of his after life. Colonel Munro distinguished himself in the Pindaree and Maharatta wars (1817-19), and led Mr. Manning to express in the House of Commons his warm appreciation of the plans carried out by him for the subjugation of these troublesome neighbours. Europe, it was said, never had produced a more accomplished statesman, nor India, so fertile in heroes, a more skilful soldier—words, Munro wrote in a private letter, making it "worth while to be a Governor to be spoken of in such a manner by such a man." At the conclusion of the Maharatta War, Colonel Munro resigned his military command, and, accompanied by his family, again visited England, where he arrived in 1819. In November of that year he was invested with the insignia as a Knight Companion of the Bath. In 1820, with the rank of Major-General, he returned to Madras as Governor of that Presidency in succession to the Hon. Hugh Elliot; and, as a farther reward for his distinguished services, he was created a Baronet of the United Kingdom, June 30, 1825. The Burmese war prevented him from retiring from India so early as he wished; and, sacrificing his personal wishes and convenience to the public service, he retained office till its conclusion. At length, in 1827, Sir Thomas made every arrangement for returning to enjoy well-earned honours in his native land, but before his departure proceeded to pay a farewell visit to the people of the ceded districts, for whom he had continued to feel a strong interest, but was attacked with cholera on 5th July, then prevalent in the country, and expired next day at Putteecondah, near Gooty, where he lies buried. Sir Thomas was then in his sixty-sixth year. He left a family of two sons—(1) Thomas of Lindertis, Forfar county, second and present Baronet, some time a Captain in the 10th Hussars, born 1819; and (2) Campbell Munro of Fairfield, Lyme Regis, late a Captain of the Grenadier Guards, married, with issue sons and daughters. Lady Thomas Munro survived her illustrious husband twenty-three years, dying in September, 1850. Concerning the property of North Woodside, so intimately, and—as has been shown—so affectionately, associated with the memory of Sir Thomas Munro, a few sentences will be given in another chapter.

JOHN KNOX AND THE ABBOT OF CROSSRAGUEL AT MAYBOLE.

CONNECTED, it is thought not very remotely, with the Renfrewshire Knoxes of Ranfurly and Craigends, it is only in a secondary degree the aim of this paper to give local significance to that remarkable passage in the life of the Reformer generally described as the "Crossraguel Disputation"—the only debate of the kind known to have taken place in Scotland during the great strife between the Churches. The aim of the writer is twofold, and on the whole wider in purpose than anything merely local. He desires, in the first place, to show how such a discussion became possible through the condition of the Church in Scotland immediately prior to the Reformation; second, to give some account of the discussion itself, known only in a general way to other than special students in Church history. That the Roman Church in Scotland was in the early part of the sixteenth century corrupt and inefficient beyond all precedent at home, indolent and ignorant beyond anything heard of in either Italy or Spain, requires little argument beyond the plain statement of fact that, when her fall came, she fell almost without a struggle, and with hardly the honour of a dissolution. Had the old Church not reformed herself in a degree second only to what was pressed for by the Reformers, she would have died and made no sign—crumbled away to forgetfulness under the pressure of her own incompetence. But she did reform herself, and won through poverty and persecution a spirit of toleration and a wealth of learning to which for generations earlier she had either been a stranger or a remorseless foe. This made the Romanism of later years something altogether different from the Romanism by which it was preceded—different in character as well as different in influence—and the good change has been carried on with ever-increasing force till our own day. A like "revival," but on a more gigantic scale, took place in the south of Europe after the preaching of Luther. Almost at the moment when "Friar" Martin was challenging Romish doctrine at Worms (1521) under protection afforded by the Elector, there passed out from the Theatine Convent of Venice that Ignatius Loyola, in early life a Spanish hidalgo, but now poor, lame, and obscure, yet destined to found an Order famous in the histories of Churches as well as of States, for infusing new zeal into every department of knowledge—the pulpit, the press, the confessional, and the academies. As scholars, physicians, merchants, and missionaries, the Jesuits came to be found everywhere and under every disguise, uniting philosophy, literature, and science to the early orthodox teaching in religious belief and personal subjection to the will of the Church. Loyola was born 1491, eight years after Luther, and died 1556, when Knox was preaching the reformed doctrines in Geneva.

Long before the year last mentioned the fair ecclesiastical system built up by King David was tottering to ruin. Nor can it be said that the foundation of even such seats of learning as St. Andrews, Glasgow, and Aberdeen could either save it or vindicate its existence. The later Provincial Councils of the Church appeared heartless in procedure or divided in council—sometimes both—and thus sounds of only an uncertain kind came to be given out for the guidance of the faithful. With one half of the land in possession of the Church, prelates had naturally become arrogant and indolent, and lay nobles discontented, while the rapidly rising middle class, strongly favouring for the most part the " new learning " from Germany, were severely hostile. This unhappy state of matters was but ill compensated for by swarms of wandering friars, who usurped the place of parochial priests without discharging any duty to the common people. In the higher ranks of the clergy immorality had become so common that it ceased to be spoken of as a vice, and the illegitimate children of archbishops, as well as of the lesser dignitaries, ranked so high among the nobility as to make even Royal alliances, of which descendants boasted. It is not quite correct to say that this corrupt system was overthrown by the influence of a rapacious nobility. In the unjust division made of Church property at the Reformation most of them no doubt exhibited all the greed of sacrilegious zealots, eager to share the spoil; but the reforming lords were few in number—not more than half-a-dozen—the most notable being Argyll, Glencairn, Cassillis, and Rothes. The Hamiltons, Gordons, Douglases, and Athols—the Regent himself till the eve of the Reformation—all remained on the side of the old Church, or were identified in only a remote degree with the establishment of Presbytery. In Scotland the Reformation was in the main effected through a few resolute scholars, backed by the lesser barons, gentry, burghers, and the great body of the common people a degree or two above mere serfdom, whose rising power the Church so blindly failed to recognise. It was to such classes the keen satires of Lindsay and Dunbar specially appealed. Failing to assimilate itself to the new complicated conditions of life, and remorselessly as she put forth her power early in the struggle, Romanism fell in Scotland when the weapons of carnal warfare were withdrawn from its grasp. Blind enough herself, but full of suspicion towards the people, she sought in a hesitating way at first to check the fury of the storm bursting over her by cautioning the clergy to avoid controversy with any one assailing either her purity or her proud pretensions. This advice, cunningly enough devised, as she well knew, is thought to have been all but universally observed. The only known exception now falls to be noticed as occurring in the experience of Quentin Kennedy, last Abbot of the rich foundation at Crossraguel, near Maybole, Ayrshire.

In the summer of 1562, when Knox was labouring in the West Country, denouncing Popery as Antichrist, Quentin Kennedy, with more bravery than discretion, stepped forward to dispute the point with the dauntless Reformer. The Abbot belonged to one of the first families in Scotland, his father being the famous Gilbert, second Earl of Cassillis, and his nephew, also Gilbert, third Earl, the pupil and patron of George Buchanan, who wrote one of his early satires against the Franciscans while residing with the young Earl at Cassillis. The Abbot's grandnephew was the rapacious and unscrupulous fourth Earl Gilbert, best known as "King of Carrick," but still more notorious in the annals of violence for having roasted Quentin's successor in the Abbey lands, Allan Stewart, Commendator, before a fierce fire in the dark vault of Dunure Castle, for the purpose of extorting a grant of that property, as lying contiguous to his own estate. Abbot Quentin Kennedy also possessed what many of his brethren lacked: he was of blameless life, and something of a scholar. With but narrow notions of statecraft, and even little of that dialectic or theological skill which distinguished Knox, Abbot Kennedy was yet probably the foremost champion at the time Rome could have expected to appear in Scotland in her defence. His first appearance as a polemical writer was in 1558, four years before his encounter with Knox, when he published a short synopsis of Catholic belief, known still to collectors of curiosities as the "Compendious Tractive," showing "the nerrest and onlie way to establish the conscience of a Christian man" in all matters which were in debate concerning faith and religion. This, as explained, was nothing else than implicit faith in the decision of the Church. When any point of religion was controverted, Scripture might be cited as a witness, but holy mother Church was to be the judge. It was held to be sufficient for those who did not occupy the place of teachers that they had a general knowledge of the Creed, the Ten Commandments, and the Lord's Prayer, according to the sense in which they were explained by the Church; while as to the Sacraments and all other secrets of Scripture every Christian man was to "stand in the judgment of his pastor." On the 30th August, according to M'Crie, Abbot Kennedy read in his chapel at Kirkoswald a number of articles respecting the mass, purgatory, praying to saints, and the use of images, which he said he would defend against any who challenged them; but in the meantime promised to declare his mind more fully respecting them on the following Sunday. Knox, who is presumed to have been living at the time with Lord Ochiltree (whose daughter became the Reformer's second wife), no way reluctant to accept the challenge, set out for the scene of controversy on the day indicated. In the morning he sent forward certain gentlemen who accompanied him to inform the Abbot of the purpose in view, and desiring him either to preach according to promise, or to attend a sermon to be delivered by the Reformer himself. The Abbot did not appear, but on coming down the pulpit stairs a letter from him was put into Knox's hand. This led to an epistolary correspondence almost as curious as the "Disputation" itself, but too lengthy for quotation or even further reference. Knox wished the debate to be conducted publicly in St. John's Church, Ayr. The Provost's house in Maybole was afterwards mutually agreed upon. "Ye sall," writes Knox, "be assured I sall keip day and place in Mayboill, according to my writing, and I haif my life, and my feit louse." The date was fixed to be September 28, at eight o'clock in the morning; forty persons to be admitted by each champion as witnesses, with "as many more as the house might goodly hold, at the sight of my Lord of Cassillis." Notaries or scribes were also chosen on each side to record the papers which might be given in by the parties, and the arguments put forward. The particulars of the controversy were printed at the time in a now unique black-letter tract, entitled "Coppie of the Resoning which was betwixt the Abbote of Crossraguell (Quentin Kennedy) and John Knox, in Mayboill, concerning the Masse, in the year of God a thousand five hundred three score and two yeires. Edinburgh [printed by]: Robert Lepraik, 1563." A copy of this original, very rare black-letter pamphlet was discovered by Sir Alexander Boswell in the Auchinleck Library, and reprinted at Edinburgh in *facsimile*, 1812. Even this reprint is now a choice curiosity difficult to obtain.

The opening scene of the controversy was highly characteristic. When parties on each side were duly gathered together, Knox desired the Abbot to offer up public prayer; "whereat the Abbot was soir offended at the first; but when the said John wold in nowise be stayed, he and his gave audience, which being ended, the Abbote said, 'Be my faith, it is weill said.'" The debate itself was entirely confined to the interpretation of that text in the Old Testament, where it is said that Melchisedec brought out bread and wine in presence of Abraham and his company; the Abbot asserting that those elements were brought out as an oblation to God; and Knox, that they were produced merely for the refreshment and consumption of the visitors, contending that the mysterious King of Salem was the figure of Christ in that he offered bread and wine unto God; so, continued the Abbot, it behoved Christ to offer in His Last Supper His own body and blood under the forms of bread and wine. The second day was again mostly taken up with Abbot Kennedy, who urged against Knox that Abraham and his company had a sufficiency of provision in the spoil taken during their late victorious engagement at Dan, and did not therefore need Melchisedec's bread and wine. When parties met on the third day the Abbot presented a paper, in which he stated certain other objections to the view taken of the text by Knox, who in turn pressed his opponent to produce proof for the final argument on which he intended to rest his case. The Abbot appeared indisposed to do this verbally, but put into Knox's hand a small book on the subject, presumed to have been, although Knox does not mention it distinctly, Kennedy's "Familiar Commune on the Mass," printed the preceding year. By this time the audience expressed feelings of weariness. The gentlemen present had not been able to find suitable entertainment either for themselves or retinue in Maybole, so that, remarks M'Crie, had any person brought in wine there and then among them it is thought they would not have debated long concerning the purpose for which it was intended. Knox proposed that they should adjourn to Ayr, and there finish the dispute; but to this the Abbot objected. He expressed himself, however, as willing on some future occasion to proceed to Edinburgh for the purpose of renewing the debate, provided he could obtain the Queen's permission. Upon this the company dismissed, never again to have the privilege of listening to a debate in which Rome staked the issue on appeal to reason as distinguished from tradition and authority. The dispute was never resumed, although Knox writes of having applied to the Privy Council for the necessary permission. Abbot Kennedy died in August, 1564, and is mentioned by Dempster as having been canonised—"Aug. 22.—Monasterio Crucis regalis obitus Beati Quintini Kennedii Abbotis," &c. The name, it is but right to say, does not appear in the Roman Calendar. Among the objects of interest in and around Maybole, and there are many—some to be afterwards referred to in these pages—not the least suggestive is the still existing fabric known as "The Provost's House," in which the singular encounter above described took place.

THE STORY OF GLENFRUIN.

IT has been the fashion lately among historians who think lightly of James VI. as a statesman, to contrast to his disadvantage the famous Settlement, or Plantation, as it was called, of Ulster, with the disorder he permitted to exist at the same time along his own Highland line, better known, it has been argued, and even easier of access. This story of the

THE STORY OF GLENFRUIN. 147

Raid or "Conflict" of Glenfruin, may be taken as at least one pregnant illustration of the difference in disposition prevailing among the quiet thrifty emigrants of the North of Ireland and the turbulent chieftains of Western Scotland, who despised alike the peace of their neighbour and the power of their Sovereign. The year 1603, memorable in British history from the Union of the Crowns, is especially conspicuous in this western part of the island by an encounter of unusual fierceness, even for these days, which took place between the Clangregor and the ancient family of Colquhoun of Luss.

That the Macgregors for many years prior to 1603 were considered a disorderly clan is not seriously disputed, except, it may be, among a few family enthusiasts whom the grace of Parliament in the reign of George III. permitted to resume their own name. In 1563, their excesses had reached such a height that Queen Mary, by an Act of Privy Council, granted permission to several noblemen to pursue them with fire and sword, and prohibited the lieges from receiving or assisting them in any way whatever. In 1589 the murder of John Drummond in the forest of Glenartney—a murder attended with circumstances of appalling atrocity—again let loose the terrors of the law against the clan; but to so little purpose that in 1594 the Macgregors, along with the Macfarlanes of Arrochar, occupy the unenviable distinction of being the first-mentioned clans against whom the statute for the punishment of "theft, reiff, oppression, and sorning" was directed. It has been alleged that the extensive possessions held by the Macgregors in Perthshire and Argyllshire had been iniquitously wrested from them by the Earls of Argyll and Breadalbane, and that, therefore, the clan was justified in treating with contempt those laws from which they so often experienced severity, and never protection. But this allegation, even if correct, could have only a secondary bearing in their dispute with Colquhoun of Luss, as it is not even hinted that this family either shared in the plunder or abetted others in their attacks upon the Clangregor.

In order to strengthen their position, the Macgregors, about the close of the sixteenth century, entered into alliances, offensive and defensive, with certain families reputed to be connected with them by "auld descent" or otherwise. One was concluded at Kilmorie, on the 6th June, 1571, between James Macgregor and Lauchlan Mackinnon of Strathardill; and another, twenty years later, between Alexander Macgregor of Glenstray and Aulay M'Aulay of Ardincaple. The latter, "understanding our name to be M'Calppins of auld," bound himself to assist Macgregor, and to pay the "calpe" in token of submission. Before the close of the year in which this last "bond" was signed, the King's Secret Council were called to listen to a complaint by Buchanan of Culcreuch, that, under pretence of revenging the slaughter of certain of his men by the Buchanans, M'Aulay had conceived deadly hatred against the complainer, and under colour of His Majesty's charge, had brought within the Buchanan territory a great number of Macgregor's men, all of them "broken men and sorners, to sorn, harry, and wrack the complainer's lands and possessions."

Regarding the origin of the feud between the Macgregors and Colquhouns, no very precise information has ever been forthcoming. Sir Walter Scott tells a story on which, however, much reliance cannot be placed. Two of the Macgregors (he says) being benighted, asked shelter in a house belonging to a dependent of the Colquhouns, and were refused. They then retired to an out-house, took a wedder from the fold, killed it, and supped off the carcase, for which they offered payment to the owner. The Laird of Luss, so goes the story, unwilling to be propitiated by the offer made to his tenant, seized the offenders, and, by the summary process which feudal barons had at their command, caused them to be condemned and executed. The Macgregors confess to verify this account of the feud by appealing to the proverb current among them, execrating the hour (mult dhu an carbail ghil) that the black wedder with the white tail was ever lambed.

If the dying declaration of Macgregor of Glenstray can be believed—and there seems no strong reason to question his veracity—the feud was kept up, if not originated, by the artful machinations of Archibald, Earl of Argyll, who in January,

THE STORY OF GLENFRUIN.

1593, obtained a commission for repressing the violence of "the wicked Clangregour, and divers other broken men of the Hielands;" with power to charge "all and sindrie personis of the surname of Macgregour, thair assisstars and pairt takaris, to find souirtie, or to enter plegeis as he sall think maist expedient, for observatioun of his hieness peace, quietness, and guide reule in the countrey;" and, if necessary, to "persew and assege their housis, and strengthis, raise fyre, and use all kynd of force and weirlyke ingyne" against that clan. In these circumstances (says Pitcairn, whose valuable "Criminal Trials" throw so much light upon the "Raid of Glenfruin") it might be supposed that it was Argyll's interest, as it certainly was his duty, to have done all in his power to retain the Clangregor in obedience to the laws; but, on the contrary, it appears that from that time he first, as King's lieutenant, acquired complete control over the Macgregors, the principal use he made of his power was artfully to stir up the clan to various acts of aggression and hostility against his own personal enemies, of whom, it is well known, Colquhoun of Luss was one. It is therefore to be remarked that at the period of the conflict at Glenfruin both parties were in a manner equally armed with the royal authority—the Laird of Luss having raised his forces under a commission emanating from the King himself, while the Macgregors marched to invade the Lennox under the authority of the King's lieutenant.

With "Commissions of Pursuit" in the hands of leaders like Argyll, and subordinates, like the Laird of Culcreuch, it is little wonder that the restless, though brave, Clangregor had recourse to desperate measures, both of defence and retaliation. In 1602, their forays upon the lands of Luss became so frequent and aggravated, that the King, upon complaint being made to him, issued the following warrant, dispensing, in favour of Sir Alexander Colquhoun, with the provisions of the Act anent the wearing of guns and other weapons:—

"We vnderstanding that sindrie of the disorderlie thievis and lymmaris of the Clangregour wyth utheris thair complices dailie makis incursions vpoun and within the boundis and landis pertaining to Alexander Colquhoun of Lus, stealls, reiffs, and awataks divers gret herschipps fra him and his tenants; likeas thay tak greater bauldness to continew in thair said stouth and reiff becaus thay ar inarmit wyth all kynd of prohibit, and forbidding weapponis. Thairfor, for the bettir defense of the Laird of Lus and his saidis tennants, guidis, and gear, fra the persewit of the saidis thievis and broken men, we have given and grantit, and be the tenor heirof give and grant licence and libertie to the said Alexander Colquhoun ot Lus, his househald men and servantis, and sic as sall accompany him, not onlie to beir, weir, and shuitt wyth hagbuttis and pistolettis in the following and persewitt of the said thievis and lymmaris, quhilk is lauchful be the act of parliament, but alas to beir and weir the same hagbuttis and pistolettis in ony pairt abune the water of Levin, and at the said Laird's place at Dunglas and landis of Colquhoun, for the watching and keeping of thair awn guidis without ony crime, scaith, pains, or dainger to be incurred be thaim thairfra, in thair personnis, landis, or guidis in ony manner of way in tyme coming, notwithstanding our acts, statutes, or proclamations in the contrar thafranent or pains therein conteinit, we dispens be thir presents. Given under our signet and subscrivit wyth our hand at Hamiltoun, the fyrst dai of September, and of our reign the xxvj year, 1602. JAMES."

In the early part of 1603, the Macgregors and Colquhouns are described in several works as desirous of terminating their feud by a friendly conference; but, with characteristic imprudence, they each seem to have made secret preparations to follow up that conference with instant measures of hostility if its results were not satisfactory. Judging from the records of the burgh of Dumbarton, the alleged peaceable intention of the Macgregors does not appear to have made a strong impression on the burgesses. On the 8th January of that year (1603)—

"It is ordained that all burgesses within the burgh be sufficientlie furnissit with armor, and that sik persones as the baillies and counsall think fitt sall be furnissit with hagbuttis, that they haif the samyn with the furnitear thairto, uthirs quha sall be appointit to haif jak speir and steil-bonnat, that thay be furnissit with the samyn, and that the Baillies and counsall on the xxi of this instant make ane catholok of the saidis personis names with their armor, and they be chargeit to haif the said armor redey, and to present thame with the samyn at muster, and this to remaine in all tymes under the pane of x punds, the ane half to the Baillie, the uthir to the use of the burgh. Item, that ilk merchand or craftisman keipand buith haif ane halbart within the samyn under the pane of v punds. Item, that na burgess be maid heirefter without productioun of his armor at his creatioun, and that he sweir the samyn is his own."

As no record relating to any conference between the families at feud has been preserved, it is more than doubtful if it ever took place; and the allegation made against the Laird of Luss, that he treacherously attacked the Macgregors at its termination, is not substantiated by documents of the slightest value. Neither, on the other hand, can more credence be attached to the statement that the Macgregors on this particular occasion were the assailants. All that can safely be affirmed of the occurrence is, that on the 7th of February, 1603, both parties, fully prepared for hostilities, met in the Valley of the Fruin, or Glen of Sorrow—a name singularly suggestive of the events of the day, as the victory proved not more fatal to the vanquished than the victors. This now quiet retreat, so familiar to the angler and botanist, runs west from Loch Lomond in the direction of Dumfin and Drumfad, and then slightly north towards the source of the Fruin, near Strone Hill, in Row parish.

Regarding the force by which each chief was supported, various contradictory statements have been made. Alexander Ross, the historian of the Sutherland family, puts down Macgregor's force at 300 footmen; and, notwithstanding the manner in which the clan was broken up, there is no room to doubt that he would be able to raise at least that number to attack such an enemy as the Laird of Luss. But when the same authority states Luss' force to have been 300 horse and 500 foot, the assertion must be received with great caution, as it is not likely, even with the aid he received from the burgh of Dumbarton, that this chief could, in a single district of the Lennox, raise an army equal to what on some occasions obeyed the behest of the King. His footmen are not likely to have much outnumbered Macgregor's, and if any horsemen were foolhardy enough to accompany Luss to the scene of the conflict, the nature of the ground must have made their services perfectly useless. The locality was of the worst possible description for a fair trial of strength, but admirably suited for such desultory attacks as the Clangregor had been long in the habit of waging. The only wonder is how the Laird of Luss, who must have known the place thoroughly, ever ventured to encounter an enemy in such a place. With great forethought Allister Macgregor divided his force into two divisions—one led by himself, which advanced against the vanguard of Luss' party; and the other led by his brother, John Macgregor, who attacked them in the rear. The possession of the glen was stoutly contested for a short time, but Colquhoun's force, finding itself unable to contend with success against the enemy, commenced a retreat which was almost as disastrous to them as a conflict; for, besides having to fight their way through the force led by John Macgregor, they were closely followed by Allister, who, finding his brother slain, reunited the two divisions, and hung upon the fugitives to the very gates of Rossdhu. Numerous stragglers who had become detached from the main body in the flight, were seized and slain without mercy, while the weak and the defenceless, who had taken no share in the conflict, were also sacrificed by the infuriated Macgregors. When the flight had terminated a scene of murder, robbery, and destruction commenced which finds no parallel in even the bloody raids of the period. In the language of the indictment against their chief, the Macgregors seized six hundred kye and oxen, eight hundred sheep and goats, fourteen score of horse, set fire to the houses and barn-yards of the tenantry, and, in a word, carried off or destroyed the "haill plenishing, guids, and gear of the fourscore pund land of Luss." In the conflict and retreat, the Colquhoun party lost about one hundred and forty, while the Macgregors, it is said, did not lose more than two men—a slender excuse for the atrocities with which they disgraced their victory. Among those slain while aiding the Colquhouns were—Peter (or Patrick) Napier of Kilmahew; Tobias

Smollett, bailie of Dumbarton (an ancestor of the novelist); David Fallisdaill, burgess there; his two sons, Thomas and James; Walter Colquhoun and John Colquhoun, Barnhill; and Adam and John, sons of Colquhoun of Camstradden.

In addition to the slaughter in the open field, the Macgregors are accused of massacring in cold blood a party of students whose curiosity had led them from Dumbarton to the scene of the conflict in Glenfruin. Some doubt is certainly thrown upon this statement from the circumstance that it is not mentioned in the indictments against the Macgregors; but it seems not indistinctly alluded to in the record of the Privy Council proceedings against Allan Oig M'Intnach of Glencoe, who, in 1609, was accused of assisting the Clangregor of Glenfruin, and of having, with his own hand, there "murdered without pity the number of forty poor persons, who were naked and without armour." The Macgregors themselves did not deny there was a massacre of unprotected people who were present as spectators, but they impute the cruel deed to the ferocity of a single man of their tribe—Dugald Ciar Mhor, or the dun coloured, who is said to have been an ancestor of Rob Roy's. The deed is said to have been committed during the time of the pursuit; and on the chief of the Macgregors asking after the safety of the youths on his return, the Ciar Mhor drew out his bloody dirk, exclaiming in Gaelic, "Ask that, and God save me."

Hardly had the pursuit ceased and the plunder been secured, when justice in its most relentless form was let loose upon the track of the Macgregors. The measures taken against them, from their very severity, often defeated the object they were designed to serve; and hence, in seeking to extinguish the clan and abolish the name, more was done to keep alive a knowledge of both than anything the Macgregors themselves could have accomplished. Almost as soon after the conflict as the bodies could be stripped, Sir Alexander Colquhoun appeared before the King at Stirling, accompanied by the female relatives of the slain, each clad in deep mourning, and bearing aloft the bloody garments of their kinsmen. The idea of this impressive spectacle seems to have originated—not with Sir Alexander Colquhoun, but with some of his advisers, Sempill of Fullwood, and William

Stewart, Captain of Dumbarton Castle, being referred to in an epistle, addressed to Sir Alexander, immediately after the conflict, by Bailie Fallisdaill, Dumbarton :—

"Ryt honorable Sir,—My deutie wyt service remembrit. Plass you the Lard of Fulwood and the Capatine thinking that you ma adres yourself wyt als monie bludie sarks, as ather ar deid, or hurt of your men, togetter wyt als mony women, to present them to his Majesetie in Stirling upon Tysday, for thai ar boyth to ryd thair upoune Tysday, quha will assist you at thair power. The meitest time is now becaus of the French Imbassador that is wyt his Majestie."

King James, peculiarly susceptible of such emotions as this spectacle was calculated to produce, vowed vengeance against the lawless clan. By an Act of the Privy Council, dated 3rd April, 1603, it was made an offence punishable with death to bear the name of Macgregor, or to give any of the clan food or shelter. After this they were hunted like wild beasts, their dwellings were destroyed, they were loaded with every epithet of abhorrence, and every corner of the country was ransacked where there was the least possibility of them taking refuge.

As it was the Earl of Argyll who was responsible to the Privy Council for the conduct of the Macgregors, to him was chiefly intrusted the execution of the severe measures adopted towards them. Amongst the first against whom he directed the full force of his new powers was Aulay M'Aulay of Ardincaple, who, as has been seen, so far back as May, 1591, had entered into a bond of clanship with Allister Macgregor, admitting that he was a cadet of his house, and promising to pay him "The Calp." Proceedings were therefore instituted against him for having aided and abetted the Macgregors at Glenfruin; but as he was among the train of the Earl of Lennox in the King's journey to England to take possession of the Throne, a seasonable warrant was issued by His Majesty to the Justice-General and his deputies, commanding them to "desert the dyett" against M'Aulay, as he was "altogeddir free and innocent of the crymes allegit agains him." To other offenders no such leniency was shown. On the 28th of April, Allister M'Kie, Gilchrist Kittoche, and Findlay Dow M'Lean were "dilattet of certaine poyntis of thefts," and for "cuming to the Laird of Lussis boundis in companie with the

Laird of Macgregour, and being airt and pairt of the murthour and reiff committat thairin" in February. Being found guilty, "the justice be the mouth of James Hendersone, dempster of Court, ordaint thame, and ilk ane of thame, to be tane to the Borrowmure of Edenborough, and to be hangit vpone the galloise thairof quhill they be deid; and all thair moveable guedes to be escheit." On the 20th May, Gillespie M'Donald, M'Innis Dow, Donald M'Clerich or Stewart, and John M'Coneill M'Condochie, were severally accused of being "airt and pairt in the lait grit slauchter and crewall murthour of sevin scoir persones in the Lennox, all friendis and servandis to the Laird of Luss; and of the thiftous steilling and reiffing of aucht hundreth oxin, ky, and ither bestiall, and herrieing the haill cuntrie;" and being found guilty, were sentenced "to be tane to the Castell-hill of Edinburghe, and to be hangit thair on ane gibbit, quhill they be deid." On the 5th of July, Gilliemichell M'Hissock with Nicoll M'Pharie Roy M'Gregor; on the 14th, John Dow M'Oncoalich M'Gregor; and on the 12th August, Dugall M'Gregor with Neil M'Gregor Prudache, were dealt with in a similar manner; but the most of these being merely servants, the Privy Council found it necessary to take still more stringent measures than they had yet done, to bring some of the leaders within reach of the law. This appears more distinctly from a document among the law papers, in the form of a deliverance of the Council regarding a supplication presented by "the gentlemen of the Lennox," who seem to have been afraid that proceedings would be adopted against them for having "intromittit with the guids and gear of the Macgregors."

Notwithstanding the close manner in which he was hemmed in, Allister, the Chief of the Macgregors, contrived to elude the vigilance of his pursuers for nearly a twelvemonth. The Sheriff of Argyllshire (Campbell, of Ardkinlass) attempted his capture, by inviting him to a banquet, but, detecting the trick before it was accomplished, Macgregor sprang out of the boat in which he was placed, and swam to the shore in safety. With the Earl of Argyll he was not so fortunate. Under pretence that he would either obtain a pardon from the King or convey him safely out of Scotland, Argyll managed to bring the wily old Macgregor from his hiding-place; but, as Birrel says, the Earl kept only a Highlandman's promise, for he first marched out of Scotland with his guest as far as Berwick, and then, having satisfied himself that he had fulfilled the letter of his engagement, carried him back as prisoner to Edinburgh. They arrived there on the evening of the 18th January, and next day Macgregor made a confession, in which—making due allowance for the irritation he must have felt at being entrapped by Argyll—a fair account appears to be given of the affray at Glenfruin. The document itself is much too long for insertion here, but he specifically declared that since he was first His Majesty's man he had never been at ease on account of Argyll's falsehood and inventions—" He moveit my brother and some of my friendis to commit baith hership and slauchter upon the Laird of Luss; also, he persuadit myselfe with messages to weir agains the Laird of Boquhonene, quilk I did refuse, for the quilk I was contenowalie bostit that he sould be my unfriend; and quhen I did refuse his desyre upon that point, then he intysit me with uther messingeris, as be the Laird of M'Knachtane and utheris of my friendis, to weir and truble the Laird of Luss, quhilk I behuffit to do for his fals boutgattis." On the 20th January—two days after his arrival in Edinburgh—Allister Macgregor, along with four of his party, was brought to trial; and, as appears from the Books of Adjournal, they were all found guilty and executed the same day—the gibbet of Allister, it is said, being his own height above that of his friends. As the bodies were at once dismembered, the inhabitants of Dumbarton now enjoyed a savage kind of revenge in ornamenting their Tolbooth with the heads of the Macgregors:—

1604.—13 Feb.—The Baillies and Counsall of Dumbarton " concludit and ordanit that the Laird of Macgregor's heid wt Patrick Auldochy his heid be put up in the tolbuith on the most convenient place the baillies and counsall thinkis guid." [From another entry it appears that a sum of 24 merks was paid as part of the expense incurred in carrying this order into effect.]

1604.—17 April.—" Feiring the creueltie of the tyrannous persons of the name of the Clangregor and fyring of the toune be thame Thairfore it is statut and ordanit that the toun be devydit in aucht pairts and ilk aucht pairt to watche ane nycht. The watches to be armit and placit nytly by the quarter-master chosen by the baillies. And quha keipis nocht watche according to the Baillies ordinance gif he bes at hame himself and in his absence ane sufficient man, to paye ffourtie sh for his disobedyances and the samyn to be payit to the watchers and that the baillies cheis aucht quarter-masters. Item that na dwellers wtn this toun ressaif ony straingers puir or rich wtout making the baillies foreseen undir the paine of ffourtie sh toties quoties, the tua pts to the toun and the third to the baillies."

In April, 1605, the Privy Council urged on the pursuit of the Macgregors by ordaining that whoever should present any of that clan quick (alive), or failing that, the head of any of them, should have possession for nineteen years of all the lands and goods belonging to such Macgregor, or a money recompense, to be paid by the landlords of the district.

As it is not intended to detail at length the trials of the other Macgregors (seeing that nearly the same form was observed in each), it may be stated generally that from the number executed under form of law, and the still greater number slain as outlaws, the survivors in 1612 were described as "bot unworthie miserable bodyis." Indeed, the "Raid of Glenfruin" seems to have been a last desperate effort on the part of the clan, for very soon afterwards Lord Fyvie wrote to King James that if all the great Highland clans were reduced to a like point, he "wold think it ane grait ease to the commonn weill, and to his Majestie's guid subjects in Scotland;" while, about the same time, the Lords of Privy Council state that the Clangregor is so impoverished that it is impossible to extract from them what will pay for their removal to other countries. Still Luss seems to have had cause for anxiety, as he writes to the King in November, 1609, that his enemies had entered upon their former courses, and praying that "tymous remeid" might be provided. Next year, accordingly, in September, we find the Privy Council at the old work of extirpation, an enactment being then issued prohibiting owners of boats from transporting any of the "rebellious and barbarous thieves and lymmaris," or their "wives, bairns, or servands," across Lochlong, Lochgoil, or Lochlomond.

In January, 1611, the Council eclipsed all its former encouragements to revenge by enacting that

"Whatsomevir person or persones of the name of McGregour who sall slay ony persone of the same name being of als good ranke and qualitie as him self and sall prove the same slaughter befoir the saidis Lordis That everie suche persone slayar of ane McGregour of the rank and qualitie forsaid sall hai ane free pardoun and remissioun for all his bygane faultis, he finding suirtie to be ansuerable and obedient to the Lawis in tyme comeing; And siclike that whatsomever uther persone or personis will slay ony of the particular personis underwritten Thay are to say Duncan McEwne McGregour now callit the Laird, Robert abroch McGregour, Johne Dowe McAllister McGregour, Callum McGregour of Coull, Duelchay McGregour and McRobert McGregour his bruther or ony utheris of the rest of that race, That everie suche persone slayar of ony of the personis particularlie abone-written or ony utheris of that race sall haif ane reward in money presentlie payit and delyverit unto thame according to the qualitie of the persone to be slayde, and the least soume salbe ane hundreth merkis, and for the chiftanes and ringleidaris of thir M'gregouris ane thousand pundes apiece." Proclamation of this to be made at the Market Crosses of Dumbarton, Stirling, Doune in Monteith, Glasgow, and Auchterarder. All the inhabitants of the three first-mentioned places between the ages of sixteen and sixty were thereupon summoned:—"That thay and euery one of thame weele bodin in feir of weir for thair awne defence and suirtie convene and mete at the heid of Lochlowmond vpoun the xij day of Februair now approaching and to transport and carye fra the said yle, the haill boitis and birlingis being upoun the same to the said loche of Lochketterine, wherby his Majesties forceis appointed for persute and hunting of the saidis woulffs and thevis may be transportit into the yle within the saide loiche vnder the pane of tinsall of lyffe landis and goodis." On the 23rd May, 1611, the Lords of Council ordained that "The haill bairns that are past xij yearis auld to be sent to Ireland be your lordships warrant to sic Scotchmen as your lordships thinks metest that dwells thair, be whose advyce thair name be changit and maid hindes, and thair to remain under pain of dede.

"As anent those that ar wythin xij yearis auld that they be your lordships warrant be transplanted besouth the waters of Forth and Clyde, conform to his Majesties will to Justices of Peace of these boundis at thair next general meeting whilk is the fyrst Tyesday of Feb.; and be thair advyce to be placed and assigned in tounes and parochinis and thair name changit, and thair to remain vnder pain of dede; with power to the said Justices of Peace to give and allow ane fyne to everi ilk ane of these for the help of thair sustenance; and when they come to xij yearis, that they be transplanted to Ireland."

Two years later the Chancellor (Alexander Fyvie, Earl of Dunfermline) requires the presence of the Laird of Luss on the occasion of a report being presented as to the proceedings against the Clangregor. About this time several of the unhappy fugitives seem to have fallen into the toils prepared for them by the Council. In a document among the Luss papers, bearing to be "The namis of the Clangregours that ar outlawis, and hes nocht fund cautioun," there is marked against four of them the expressive memorandum, "hangit the xxij. of June, 1613." Their names were Eune Cowbroche, Allister (bastard son to John Grahame), Duncan M'Phatrick, and John Dow M'Condochie. On the last day of November, 1613, the Council arranged that the landlords should not be called upon to pay any contribution, provided they took the Clangregor bairns according to the proportion of their lands, and made them forthcoming when called for until eighteen years of age, when they were to be exhibited to the Privy Council, and their subsequent fate decided upon. If any of these unfortunate captives happened to escape from his keeper and be recaptured, the child so escaping, if under fourteen, was to be scourged and burnt on the cheek for the first attempt, and hanged for the second. If above fourteen, they were to be hanged at once without further ceremony. Seven years later—after Shakespeare, during the life of Lord Bacon, in the country of Buchanan—the Lords of His Majesty's Council are again engaged in the barbarous work of exterminating the hapless children Clan Alpin :—

"Quhairas (it is recorded, August 29, 1621) thair is a new broode and generatioun of this clan rissin up quhilk daylie incressis in nomber and force and ar begun to haif thair meitingis and gois in troupis athorte the cuntrey armed with all offensive weaponis, and some of the ringleaderis of thame who anes gave thair obedyence and fund cautioun ar brokin louse and hes committit sundrie disordouris in the cuntrey, as namelie upoun the Duke of Lennox and Laird of Craigcrosten, That thairfoir the former Act maid aganis suche of the Clangregour as wer at Glenfroone and at the hershippis and burning of the landis pertening to the Lairdis of Glenurquhy and Luss and Coline Campbell of Abirurquhill, *That they sould weare no armoure but a pointles knyffe to cutt thair meate*, be renewit, with this addition, THAT THE SAID ACT BE EXTENDIT AGANIS THE WHOLE NAME."

With enactments of this kind in even partial operation, the existence not of one "Rob Roy," but of scores, was less a wonder to our ancestors than to us. Such legislation continued to disgrace constitutional law till the reign of Charles II., when, in consequence of the uniform attachment the Macgregors had exhibited to the cause of a misguided father, his first Parliament passed an Act restoring to them the full use of their family name and all the other privileges of liege subjects. In 1693, however—a year after Glencoe, and a part of the same policy it was thought—the penal Acts against the Macgregors were renewed, without any special reason being assigned; and though put into execution only on rare occasions, they were not finally swept from the statute book till a British Parliament interfered in the reign of George III., 1784.

THE GREAT DOUGLAS CAUSE.

EARL HOME'S somewhat sudden death (summer of 1881), naturally directed renewed attention to the relation in which he stood to the successful litigant in the great legal contest of last century, between the houses of Douglas and Hamilton—a contest not only of unsurpassed magnitude so far as the estates in dispute were concerned, but which created an amount of excitement in Scotland, and even on the Continent, altogether unparalleled. Raised in the dry technical form of an action for "reduction of service" the inquiry revealed many features of romantic interest, and engaged for eight years the highest legal talent at both the Scotch and English Bars. Without searching amid the mists of antiquity for matter to illustrate the annals of the renowned house of Douglas, the "Cause" may be briefly mentioned as originating in events connected with the life of William, eleventh Earl of Angus, created Marquis of Douglas by Charles I., June, 1633. As King's Lieutenant on the Borders the Marquis kept up a princely hospitality at Douglas Castle, and during the Civil War supported the cause of the King equally against Cromwell and the Covenanters. He was twice married—first to Margaret Hamilton, sister of the first Earl of Abercorn, and, secondly, to Lady Mary Gordon, daughter of the first Marquis of Huntly, whose descendants came to represent the Hamilton party in the Douglas plea. By his first wife the Marquis had, among other issue, a son, Archibald, Earl of Angus, who died before his father, but left a son, James, who became second Marquis, and father of Archibald, third Marquis, first and only Duke of Douglas, born in 1694, and Lady Jane Douglas, born in Douglas Castle, 17th March, 1698. With the Duke and his sister this narrative is more immediately concerned. The second Marquis died in 1700, leaving a son and heir, six years, and a daughter, two years old. In consideration of his illustrious descent and the signal services rendered to the Crown by his ancestors, Archibald, third Marquis, was created a Duke in 1703, when he was yet a minor, and signalised his adherence to the Hanoverian Government by engaging as a Volunteer at Sheriffmuir, 1715. This, however, was almost the only appearance he ever made in public. An unfortunate and fatal encounter with a distant kinsman of his mother, named Kerr, led to his withdrawing to the Continent, and, after remaining in hiding there for some years, he secretly returned—a morbid, melancholy misanthrope—to shut himself up in gloomy seclusion at Douglas Castle, seeing no one except a few greedy interested dependents. His sister, Lady Jane, by this time grown up to be a handsome accomplished woman, he systematically refused to see, and she was more than once turned ignominiously away from the doors of the castle in which she was born. Disappointed in a matrimonial alliance with Francis, Earl of Dalkeith, afterwards second Duke of Buccleuch, Lady Jane rambled in an unsettled way over the Continent for several years; but in August, 1746, when she had reached the mature age of forty-eight, and was getting considered by society as a somewhat fantastic and faded beauty, privately married Captain John Stewart, younger brother of Sir George of Grandtully, the Captain at the time being a widower of fifty-eight, with a grown-up son. The marriage took place in Edinburgh, and a few days afterwards Lady Jane, accompanied by her companion, Mrs. Hewitt, and two maids, again set out for the Continent, where she was afterwards joined by her husband. In the spring of 1748 the marriage, hitherto kept secret, was communicated to several persons on account of Lady Jane's condition, which, it was said, could no longer be concealed. The family party left Aix-la-Chapelle for Paris, and, always in poverty, moved about from one obscure lodging to another till they landed at the house of one La Brunne, where, on the sixth day after her arrival, and when she was fifty years of age, Lady Jane gave birth, or, as the Hamilton party afterwards pleaded, was alleged to have given birth to twins. Her recovery was certainly rapid, for nine days after her confinement the lodgings were again changed to the Hotel d'Anjou. There may have been no connection between the two circumstances, but the Hamilton executors afterwards established in evidence that about the period in question two male children, answering to the description of Lady Jane's, were stolen from their parents in Paris. One of the twins was strong and healthy, and accompanied Lady Jane and the Captain to Rheims, where he was baptized in August, by the name of Archibald. The other twin, being weak and sickly, was said to have been left at nurse in the neighbourhood of Paris, under the charge of Pierre La Marre, the accoucher, who thought it necessary as soon as he was born to baptize him Sholto, according to a form used in such cases by midwives in France. Both the children were invariably acknowledged by Lady Jane and Captain Stewart as theirs, and presented as such to all their friends. On returning to London in December, 1749, the unfortunate couple became plunged in even deeper poverty than before. The Duke, who had always behaved with great indifference to his sister, now withdrew even the small pension he had hitherto allowed. Mr. Stewart was overwhelmed with debt, prosecuted by his creditors and cast into prison. He has been described as a reckless, light-hearted "bon vivant," who had no objections to indulge his own selfish tastes at the expense of the narrow means possible to be scraped together by his self-denying wife. As is shown by a correspondence carried on between them, and which it is impossible to read without compassion, Lady Jane in her shabby lodgings at Chelsea was reduced to such straits as to sell her clothes and any trifling ornaments she possessed in order to buy bread for her children and supply her imprisoned husband with pocket money. Among those who interested themselves in her behalf were General the Earl of Crawford and Lindsay and Lady Shaw, widow of Sir John Shaw, of Greenock. They failed to mollify in any way the feelings of her brother the Duke, but obtained from the Government of the day a small pension. Sholto, the weaker twin, died in May, 1753, the sorely-tried mother herself dying, November following, in Edinburgh. Help for the family soon came from an unexpected quarter. To the surprise of anybody who interested themselves in the affairs of the recluse at Douglas Castle, the Duke in March, 1758, married Miss Margaret Douglas of Mains. Nettled, it was given out, at some slight put upon her by the Duke, the new Duchess became a warm partizan of the cause of young Archibald Douglas as heir of her childless husband, and, in course of time, materially aided him with means to carry on his expensive contest. The Duchess, indeed, became only too keen in her patronage of the friendless boy. She offended the Duke, and a temporary separation took place. However, they were soon brought together again, and in the year 1759, the Duke devised his whole estate "to his own nearest heirs whatever," without making any exception as to Lady Jane's son. In 1760 the Duke cancelled certain deeds in favour of the Hamilton family, and a short time before his death in July, 1761, he entailed his whole estate in favour of the heirs of the body of his father, and executed at the same time a deed setting forth that as his sister's (Lady Jane) son Archibald would be his heir, he appointed his Duchess, as well as the Duke of Queensberry and several other persons, to be his guardians. In 1759 the youth's reputed father, after years of poverty and misery in jail, succeeded to the family estate of Grandtully, and became Sir John Stewart. He lived about five years after, and married a third wife, a daughter of Lord Elibank. Sir John made a suitable provision for his son by Lady Jane Douglas, and in 1764, on the eve of death, made a solemn declaration that the twins were the children of his lawful wife. Lady Jane's companion, Mrs. Hewitt, made a similar declaration.

Upon the death of the Duke of Douglas in Queensberry House, Edinburgh, July, 1761, the guardians of Archibald Stewart (now Douglas) proceeded without delay to vest him in the feudal right of his uncle's estates by getting him served heir of entail and provision before a jury of competent witnesses. Being a case of exceptional delicacy and importance, proof much fuller than usual was entered upon, and the whole appeared so satisfactory that the jury served Archibald heir to the Duke, or, in other words, found by their verdict, from evidence documentary and oral, that Archibald Douglas was the son of Lady Jane. Mr. Douglas soon after completed his title by a charter from the Crown, and thereupon entered formally into possession of the immense Douglas estates in Lanarkshire, Renfrewshire, and other counties. Unsatisfied with the verdict of the jury, the guardians of the Duke of Hamilton resolved to investigate the matter thoroughly in his interest, as also in that of his brother, Lord Douglas Hamilton, as heirs-male of the Duke of Douglas through their great-great-grandfather, Lord Selkirk. An active guardian and a powerful agent was found in the person of Andrew Stewart of Castlemilk and Torrance, the accomplished historian of the Royal House of Stuart. His discoveries appeared to himself and his colleagues to amount to nothing short of a proof that the whole story of the pretended birth, as set forth in the service of Mr. Douglas, was an absolute fraud, and in December, 1762, an action was raised in the Criminal Department of the Parliament of Paris accusing Sir John Stewart and Mrs. Hewitt of the crime of *partus suppositio*, or procuring false children. (See "Torrance.") This action was taken secretly against Sir John, and the witnesses bound over to give evidence in Scotland; while the charge, being of a criminal nature, precluded him from interfering in favour of his son. The doubtful or weak points connected with this puzzling case are so apparent that it is only necessary to mention briefly the contentions of the pursuers—that Lady Jane was never confined at all, and, in particular, that she was not confined in the house or in the presence of Madame La Brune, inasmuch as no such person existed; and that there was imposture, mystery, and concealment in the movements of all the principal parties in and around Paris during the July of 1748. The discovery of the two stolen children has already been mentioned. In due course the great "Douglas Cause" came before the Court of Session, and on July 15, 1767, a decision was given in favour of the Hamilton plea for "reducing the service" by the casting vote of Lord-President Dundas. The voting stood:—For the Duke of Hamilton—James Erskine, Lord Barjarg; Andrew Pringle, Lord Alemare; James Veitch, Lord Elliock; John Campbell, Lord Stonefield; Robert Bruce, Lord Kennet; Sir David Dalrymple, Lord Hailes; and Sir Thomas Miller of Glenlee, Lord Justice-Clerk—seven in all. For Mr. Douglas—Alex. Frazer, Lord Strichen; Henry Home, Lord Kames; Alexander Boswell, Lord Auchinleck (father of Dr. Johnson's friend); George Brown, Lord Coalston; James Fergusson, Lord Pitfour; Francis Gardine, Lord Gardenstone; and James Burnett, Lord Monboddo—seven in all. Between July 7 and 14 each Judge spoke in the order of seniority. The interlocutor formally declaring the decision of the Court in favour of reduction was dated 15th July. Among the lawyers engaged at one time or another in the case, besides many elevated to the Bench during its progress, were—Andrew Crosbie, the reputed original of Scott's "Counsellor Pleydell;" Alexander Wedderburn, afterwards first Earl of Rosslyn and Lord Chancellor of England; Robert Macqueen, afterwards Lord Braxfield; and James Boswell, friend of Johnson, a contributor to the prolific literature of the case in the form of what he called "The Essence of the Douglas Cause." Another busy writer of the time in favour of Archibald Douglas was a distant north-country kinsman, Francis Douglas, farmer and journalist, and afterwards rewarded with a life-rent of the Douglas farm of Abbotsinch, near Paisley. Popular sympathy running strongly in favour of Mr. Douglas, several threatening letters were received by the Lord-President, to which he simply drew the attention of the Court, but rewards for discovering the authors of which were offered by each of the parties concerned in the suit.

On the failure of Mr. Douglas's case before the Court of Session in Scotland there was an immediate appeal to the House of Lords, and two years afterwards (February 27, 1769) a decision was pronounced in favour of Mr. Douglas which secured him the estates as lineal heir of Duke Archibald. The decision was received in Edinburgh with much rejoicing and some tumult. The counsel who spoke before the Lords were, for the appellant (Douglas)—the Lord-Advocate and Sir Fletcher Morton; for the respondents (Yarke)—Wedderburn and Dunning. The Lord-Chancellor (Camden) and Chief-Justice Mansfield spoke with weighty eloquence in favour of Mr. Douglas. A man of quiet, retired habits, and an excellent landlord, he was raised to the peerage as Lord Douglas of Douglas, 1790, and died universally respected, December, 1827. His friend the Duchess died at Bothwell Castle, October, 1774.

Lord Douglas married (1) in 1771 Lady Lucy Graham, sister of the Duke of Montrose, by whom he had Archibald, who succeeded as second Lord Douglas, and died unmarried January, 1844; and Charles, who also succeeded as third Lord Douglas, and died September, 1848; also Jane-Margaret, Lady Montague; (2) in 1785, Lady Francis, sister of Henry, third Duke of Buccleuch, and had with other sons and daughters, James, who of all the second family alone survived to succeed to the honours of this ancient and distinguished family. The Rev. James, fourth and last Lord Douglas, half-brother of two preceding Lords, and eldest son by second marriage of Archibald, first Lord Douglas. Taking holy orders, he became Rector of Marsh Gibbon, Buckinghamshire, 1819; Rector of Broughton, Northamptonshire, 1825; succeeded his half-brother, Charles, as fourth Lord Douglas, September, 1848; married, 1813, Wilhelmina, daughter of the Hon. General James Murray, and died at Bothwell Castle without issue in April, 1857, aged sixty. This was the last male descendant of the Douglases of Douglasdale, the title becoming extinct, and the wide estates devolving on Jane-Margaret, widow of the second Lord Montague, and on her death in 1858, on her daughter, Lucy-Elizabeth, who, in 1832, married Alexander, tenth Earl of Home, descended from the old Northumbrian line of Cospatrick, the parents of Alexander, eleventh Earl, whose sudden death within his grounds of The Hirsel, Coldstream, in the summer of 1881, was lamented by friends and tenants. The deceased Earl was succeeded in the family honours by his eldest son, Charles Alexander Douglas, Lord Dunglas, born in 1834, and educated at Eton and Cambridge.

MONTROSE FAMILY DESCENT AND POSSESSIONS.

SOME misapprehension existing as to the position occupied by the present Duke, or fifth in the line of descent, the marriage of his Grace to a lady of his own name (1876), presents a favourable opportunity for mentioning a few facts connected with a family not more distinguished for activity in public affairs than the private merits of some of those who in modern times have borne the honours of the ancient house of Montrose. Passing lightly over such occurrences as may have happened within the fabulous period of Scottish history, extending from King Eugene in the fifth to Malcolm Canmore in the eleventh century, a firm footing within a time of law and record is reached in the reign of Bruce. In exchange for lands in Cardross, the lands, it may be presumed, where the great King ended his days, as described by Froissart, Sir David Graham of Kincardine obtained the property of Old Montrose, Forfar, and was succeeded by his son, another Sir David, made prisoner at the battle of Durham in 1346. A grandson, Sir Patrick of Dunduff and Kincardine, was one of the hostages through which the release of King David II. was ultimately obtained. By his first wife, Matilda, Sir Patrick had issue, among others, William, his successor; and by his second, Edgidia Stewart of Ralston, he had Patrick, who became Earl of Stratherne in virtue of his marriage with Euphame, Countess Palatine. By his first wife, a daughter of the house of Oliphant, Sir William Graham had a son, Alexander, who predeceased his father, leaving Patrick to succeed to the honours of the house; and by his second marriage with Lady Mary Stewart, daughter of King Robert III. (who had been twice a widow before, and afterwards married a fourth time), there was issue among others two sons, founders of branches famous in the history of the family. The eldest, Robert, was ancestor of the Grahams of Fintry and Claverhouse; the latter, in the person of James, created Viscount Dundee in 1688, about a year before his death on the field of Killiecrankie. A younger brother, William, founded the house of Garvock, from which descended in due course Sir Thomas Graham, Lord Lyndoch, the renowned hero of Barossa. Patrick Graham of Kincardine, above referred to, one of the Lords of the Regency during the minority of James II., was elevated to the dignity of a Lord of Parliament, with the title of Lord Graham, in 1445. Patrick left William, who, by his marriage with

Lady Anne Douglas, daughter of the Earl of Angus, left another William, third Lord Graham and first Earl of Montrose. The additional honour was conferred for gallantry shown on the field of Sauchieburn, where his Royal master, James III., lost his life; and, in fitting harmony with the loyal traditions of his house, Earl William fell at Flodden with King James IV. and the flower of the Scottish nobility. He was twice married—first to Annabella, daughter of Lord Drummond, by whom he had William, the second Earl in succession; and second, to Janet, daughter of Sir Archibald Edmonstone, by whom he had Patrick, ancestor of the Graham of Inchbraikie. From Mungo, youngest son of William, second Earl, descended the house of Killearn. John, third Earl, posthumous son of Lord Graham, who fell at Pinkie in 1547, was first Chancellor and then Viceroy of the Kingdom of Scotland. His son John, fourth Earl, was appointed President of the Council in 1626, but dying the same year was succeeded by James, the only son of his wife, Lady Margaret Ruthven, eldest daughter of William, first Earl of Gowrie.

The career of this James, fifth Earl and first Marquis, known in history as the great Marquis of Montrose, falls rather within the history of Scotland than the annals of a single family, even though it be as illustrious as the house of Graham. A very few sentences, therefore, must serve to indicate the part he took in the affairs of the nation during what was probably the most troubled period of its history. Coldly received, as he imagined, at the Court of Charles I., Earl James, afterwards Marquis, threw himself with characteristic ardour into the cause of the Covenanting party, and in company with Argyll assisted to keep in check movements made by the more active Royalists in the north. In this way he came to be mixed up with the attack on the house of Ogilvie, famous in song as "The Bonnie House of Airlie," and referred to by the "great Argyll" himself in presence of the late Duke of Montrose so late as 1864, the occasion being a dinner at Stirling in connection with the Highland and Agricultural Society's show. "You will go (so ran the instructions of Argyll to one Dugald, with so many hundred men) into the country of my Lord Ogilvie, and you will lift his cattle, and you will drive them to Straanmare; and you will proceed to the house of my Lord Ogilvie, and you will destroy the said house, and you will pull down the yetts and windows, and gin it be langsome ye will fire the house." Castle Campbell suffered for this in after days. Suspicious of the sincerity of the Covenanting party, annoyed it has been said at their excesses, and anxious it may be concerning the ultimate fate of Monarchy in the strife, Montrose, after a second audience of the King, passed over to the Royalist party about the close of 1639. "Division (writes Principal Baillie in October of that year) is much laboured for in all our estate. They speak of great prevailing with our nobles—Home evidently fallen off, Montrose not unlikely to be ensnared with fair promises of advancement." During a lull in the military operations of 1640 there was offered for signature to Montrose a new covenant or bond, suggesting that Argyll should be named Captain-General, with arbitrary powers north of the Forth. Stung at the proposal, the Marquis suddenly quitted his division of Alexander Leslie's army on Dunse Moor, and took horse for Cumbernauld, the house of the Earl of Wigtown, where he met Home, Athole, Mar, and other friends. A new bond was then drawn out, acknowledging obligation to the covenant already signed, but stipulating for their mutual aid and defence in case of need. For five years Montrose continued to be the most prominent and successful leader on the King's side. In six well-disputed conflicts against superior armies—at Tippermuir, Bridge of Dee, Castle of Fyvie, Inverlochy, Aulderne, and Alford—the gallantry and military genius of the great Marquis prevailed. "Tell," it has been written, "those traitors of proud London town that the spears of the North have encircled the Crown." But for Naseby all might have gone well with the King. At Kilsyth, the last and crowning victory, Montrose appeared to be master of all Scotland. His troops, according to Earl Stanhope, spread over the low country like a torrent, and only such castled crags as Edinburgh, Stirling, and Dumbarton could lift themselves above the general inundation. Argyll and the other leaders of the Covenant fled for safety to

Berwick. Montrose himself entered Glasgow in triumph, while young Napier, pushing forward to Linlithgow and Edinburgh, had the delight of freeing from captivity his father, wife, sisters, and uncle, Stirling of Keir. John Lord Graham, only surviving son of the Marquis, was still held a prisoner by the chiefs of the Covenant. After these brilliant victories, Montrose was surprised and defeated in September, 1645, by General David Leslie. Detention at Oxford appearing irksome to the King, he adopted the foolish plan of entrusting his person to the Scots army at Newark, then negotiating with the leaders of the English Parliament for their arrears of pay. The Scots in turn delivered their Sovereign up to his English adversaries at Newcastle. Royal instructions were thereafter issued that Montrose should lay down his arms and leave Scotland. He was absent about two years. On the execution of the King, in 1649, the Marquis tendered his allegiance to Charles II., and took an early opportunity of presenting himself in the midst of the exiled Court at The Hague. There is still extant in the charter-chest at Buchanan House Montrose's key for secret correspondence with friends at home at this time. The Earl of Roxburghe, whom the Marquis suspected of double-dealing with David Leslie, is designated "The Fox;" David Leslie himself is "The Executioner," from his cruelties after the day of Philiphaugh; the Marquis of Huntly is "The Moor Game," from his having lurked so long in the northern hills; Argyll is "Ruling Elder," and sometimes "The Merchant of Middleburgh." In an unfortunate attempt to draw the Highlanders once more to the Royal standard during the spring of 1650, Montrose was taken prisoner by MacLeod of Assynt, and conveyed under secure guard to Edinburgh. Exposed to many insults by the way, it was only when he reached Dundee —where great suffering was yet felt from his army—that clothing and other necessaries suited to his rank were provided. At Edinburgh the Covenanting magistrates received him in mock solemnity, and with all the indignity which triumphant malice might be supposed to suggest, conveyed him from the Water-gate to the Tolbooth.

> "By sorry steeds in servile cart
> A high-backed chair is borne—
> The sitter he has turned his face—
> Why start you, young Lord Lorne?

> "Good sooth in yon poor captive dies
> The dreadest of your foes;
> But chained and tied to hangman's cart
> Ye dare not meet Montrose!"

From the Tolbooth Montrose was taken on Monday to the Parliament House, and there, "in the place of delinquents, on his knees, received sentence to be hanged on a gibbet at the Cross of Edinburgh, with his book and Declaration tied on a rope about his neck, there to hang for the space of three hours until he be dead; and thereafter to be cut down by the hangman, his head, hands, and legs to be cut off and distributed as follows:—viz., his head to be affixed on an iron pin, and set on the pinnacle of the west gavel of the new prison of Edinburgh; one hand to be set on the port of Perth, the other on the port of Stirling; one leg and foot on the port of Aberdeen, the other on the port of Glasgow. If at his death penitent, and relaxed from excommunication, then the trunk of his body to be interred by pioneers in the Greyfriars: otherwise, to be interred in the boroughmoor, by the hangman's men under the gallows." The sentence was carried out in all its revolting details, the head remaining for ten years a ghastly spectacle on the top of the Tolbooth. By the adventurous spirit of Lady Napier the heart was recovered, embalmed in the most costly manner, and was last heard of in India. Thus died James, first Marquis of Montrose, a nobleman described as the only person in modern times who recalled the heroes described by Plutarch. This was said by Cardinal de Retz, and he knew Turenne and Conde. Being an only son, he appears to have married early, as he had by his wife Margaret Carnegie, daughter of the Earl of Southesk, two sons when twenty-one years of age.

James, second Marquis, recovered the family estates on the Restoration of

MONTROSE FAMILY DESCENT AND POSSESSIONS. 173

Charles II., and was made a Privy Councillor. By his wife, Isabel, daughter of William, second Earl of Morton, and widow of Robert, first Earl of Roxburghe, he had a son, James, who succeeded as third Marquis of Montrose, and married Christian, daughter of John, Duke of Rothes. Their son, James, fourth Marquis, filled the office of Lord-President of the Council previous to the Union, and on the accession of George I. was appointed one of His Majesty's principal Secretaries of State. He was installed as Knight of the Garter in 1706, and on 24th April, 1707, created Duke of Montrose. By his wife, Christian, daughter of the Earl of Northesk, he had David created a Peer of Great Britian, with the title Earl Graham of Belford, Northumberland, but who died unmarried during the lifetime of his father; William, who succeeded as second Duke, and George, a Captain in the Royal Navy, who died unmarried, 1747. Duke William married Lucy, daughter of second Duke of Rutland, and had issue, James, who succeeded, and Lucy, married to Archibald, Lord Douglas. James, third Duke, married first Jemima-Elizabeth, daughter of Earl Ashburnham, by whom he had an only son who died in infancy, and second Caroline-Maria, daughter of fourth Duke of Manchester, by whom he had issue:—James, who succeeded; Montague William, M.P., Captain in the Coldstream Guards; Georgiana-Charlotte Caroline Lucy, married Edward Earl Powis, with issue; and Emily, married to E. T. Foley, Hereford. James, third Duke of Montrose, was a K.G., Lord-Justice General of Scotland, and Chancellor of the University of Glasgow. He died 30th December, 1836, and was succeeded by his elder son, James, the late Duke. Born 16th July, 1790, he married, 15th October, 1836, Caroline Agnes, youngest daughter of John, second Lord Decies, and had issue, James, Marquis of Graham, born 7th Feb., 1845, died 31st January, 1846; James, also Marquis of Graham, Lieutenant First Life Guards, born 22nd June, 1847, died unmarried, 3rd April, 1872; Douglas Beresford Malise Ronald, present Duke, born 7th November, 1852; Agnes Caroline, married, 1859, Lieut.-Col. Murray Polmaise; Beatrice-Violet, married, 1863, Algernon W. F. Greville, son of Lord Greville, with issue; and Alma-Carlotta, married, 1872, to Earl of Breadalbane. The late Duke succeeded his father as

Chancellor of Glasgow University, and was made a K.T. He acted as a Commissioner of the Board of Control from February, 1828, to December, 1830; Lord Steward of Her Majesty's Household, from February to December, 1852; Chancellor of the Duchy of Lancaster, from Feb., 1858, to June, 1859; and Postmaster-General in Earl Derby's second Ministry, 1858, and again 1866–68. Some incidents, arising out of his famous contest with the Earl of Crawford and Balcarres, concerning the Dukedom of Montrose, may be more appropriately mentioned in another page. The late Duke was known to be a considerate yet improving landlord, courteous and easy of access with all whom his varied relations brought him into contact, and his death, 30th December, 1874, was regretted all the more that a little over two years previously he had the affliction to see his son and heir, then a young man of high promise, laid before him in the burying place of his house. The present Duke married Violet Hermoine, daughter of Sir Frederick Ulric Graham, of Netherby, by Lady Jane Hermoine St. Maur, eldest daughter of Edward Adolphus, Duke of Somerset, K.G. The father of the present Baronet of Netherby, the second in descent, was Sir James Graham, the eminent statesman and Cabinet minister, and his mother Fanny, daughter of Colonel Callander, Craigforth.

The lands of the Montrose family lie principally within the counties of Stirling and the adjacent borders of the neighbouring counties, Dumbarton and Lanark. The lands of Buchanan parish surrounding the family mansion were purchased from the trustees of the last Buchanan of that Ilk in 1682, and the lands of the Dukedom and Regality of Lennox from Charles Duke of Lennox and Richmond in 1702. Among other Lochlomond islands now included within these lands are Inchmurren and Inchcalleoch. The former, now used as the Montrose deer park, is full of historical associations connected with the Lennox family, here being the old stronghold of the house to which the Duchess Isabella repaired to spend the close of her days in acts of piety and munificence, after the cruel wrath of James I. had sent her father with her husband and two sons to the scaffold at Stirling. In this lonely retreat the Duchess lived long enough to hear the dreadful fate of a king who had cut her off from all living kindred. It was to her piety and munificence Dumbarton was indebted for its old Collegiate Church, of which only a solitary arch now remains, and among the last of her kind deeds was the gift of certain lands in Kilmaronock parish to the Preaching Friars of Glasgow to secure prayers for the welfare of her soul and the souls of her kindred. This island was repeatedly visited by James VI. for hunting purposes. "These are to give you notice (it was written on one occasion) that His Majesty has concluded to dine at Inchmurren, where his dinner shall be sent, and there are tents to be provided for that effect, and you must expect a good number of sharp stomachs." Inchcalleoch, or "Old Woman's Isle," was the site of the parish church, and in an adjoining graveyard lie the remains of several members of the clan Gregor:

> "And answering Lomond's breezes deep,
> Soothe many a chieftain's endless sleep."

As is shown by a report of the Historical Commission, the Lennox papers at Buchanan House are numerous and curious, one among others of extreme interest being a grant by King Robert Bruce to Malcolm, Earl of Lennox, of a right of girth or sanctuary for three miles round the Church of Luss, in honour of the blessed Saint Kessog. Other lands of the Montrose family are situated within the parish of Strathblane, where they had as a residence the old Castle of Mugdock, from which many Lennox and Graham charters are dated. On the forfeiture of the great Marquis, in 1644, Mugdock barony fell in the way of compensation to Archibald, Earl of Argyll, but it was restored to the Graham family in 1656. Mugdock appears to have been their first residence in the west, after disposing of the original Kincardine property. From an inventory of "stuffe," preserved at Buchanan House, the removal would appear to have taken place in 1666. Arras hangings are described as being brought from Kincardine, and other furnishings from Angus and Strathern. At Catter, now the factor's seat, are the remains of a moothill or seat of judgment. Donald, sixth Earl of Lennox, in granting a charter to Maurice of the lands of Buchanan, allowed him the privilege of holding courts of life and limb within his territory, only on the condition, however, that everyone sentenced to death should be executed on the Earl's own gallows at Catter. In the return of owners of lands and heritages (Scotland) the area of such of the Montrose estates as are referred to above is set down:—Buchanan House, Drymen, 2,588 acres; Stirlingshire, 68,878 acres. It has been found that figures in this return are liable to correction.

In immediate connection with the descent of Montrose honours, it may be judged appropriate to mention a few details regarding a famous contest for the honour of a title borne by some of the most illustrious statesmen and soldiers who have figured in the stormy scenes of Scottish history. Rather less than thirty years since, and after a contest in which various members of the "lichtsome Lindsay" family were concerned, the House of Lords confirmed the Earldom of Crawford to James Lindsay, Earl of Balcarres, afterwards known as the Earl of Crawford and Balcarres. Following up this success, and having at the same time a certain relation to well-known incidents in the history of the Crawford family, the Earl, in February 1850, presented a petition to Her Majesty claiming the Dukedom of Montrose conferred upon his predecessor David, fifth Earl of Crawford, by James III. in 1488. This petition was as usual referred to the House of Lords, and a "Case" containing the evidence with arguments founded upon it in support of the claim came in due course to be laid on the table. The Earl, known throughout the subsequent proceedings generally as the Claimant (the Duke being the Petitioner in opposition) affirmed in the first instance—(1) That the patent of the Dukedom of Montrose, 18th May, 1488, still subsisted, and was valid and effectual in law; (2) That the limitation to "heirs"—a term, he held, of confessed flexibility in Scottish law and practice, denoted and signified "heirs-male;" and (3) That he, the Claimant, was heir-male of the first grantee. The reader will observe that the title only was claimed. James, late Duke of Montrose, thereupon presented a counter petition, praying that he might be heard before the Committee of Privileges, through counsel or agents, that he might have liberty to submit a Case on his own behalf; and in order to permit himself and all other peers interested to make the necessary investigations, that all proceedings in the claim be stayed till the following session of Parliament. The claim, it was urged, if successful, though it did not challenge the honours and dignities enjoyed by the noble petitioner, would manifestly be a matter of inconvenience and injustice to him in different ways, and would at the same time alter the whole rights of precedency of that order of the peerage in Scotland to which the petitioner belonged. During the recess the claimant discovered what he called new evidence, proving the Dukedom of Montrose, which he claimed, to be entirely different in style, designation, and derivation from that held by the noble petitioner, and precluding him, it was urged, from being admitted as a party in the case. On this crucial point the claimant contended (1) That the Dukedom of Montrose conferred in 1488 was derived exclusively from the royal burgh of Montrose, created and incorporated by the patent into a Dukedom with free regality in favour of David, Earl of Crawford, and his heirs, who thereupon added to their escutcheon a single red rose, the arms of the burgh, to denote derivation of the honours. But he contended (2), That the Graham Earldom, Marquisate, and Dukedom were derived, not from the royal burgh of Montrose, but from the private estate of the family called "Auld" or Old Montrose, some miles from the burgh, with which it had no connection whatever, and was held by quite a different tenure. James IV., it was yet urged, by charter 3rd March, 1514, created and incorporated the "terras de Ald Montross," solely "in liberam baroniam et comitatum perpetuis futuris temporibus baroniam et comitatum de Montross nuncupandum." This, urged the claimant, was the original written constitution of the title of Earl of Montrose, in the family of Graham, and it was exclusively founded upon at the ranking of the nobility in 1606, by John, Earl of Montrose, direct male descendant and representative of the grantee, in order to prove the antiquity of his earldom. Moreover, William, the original grantee, is expressly styled in two public deeds executed by the burgh of Montrose as "William, Earll of Ald Montross;" and lastly (3), That the grants and patents of the Marquisate and Dukedom of Montrose in the Grahams are mere repetitions or elevations of the original or comital fief (as it stood) into the higher titles or designations of Marquis and Duke of Montrose. The charter or patent the claimant held, obtained by Earl David from James III. in May, 1488, elevated the Earldom of Crawford into the hereditary Dukedom of Montrose, and conveyed other subjects to be held "in libera regalitate" under a general limitation to himself "et heredibus suis." The King was then in arms against a rebellion of the barons headed by his eldest son, afterwards James IV., and the advance in honour was understood to be in acknowledgment of a force of eight thousand horse and foot brought by the Duke and his family in support of the Royal standard. No charter of the Dukedom was extant, but there was an entry in the Register of the Great Seal of a charter of the date referred to. In June following, the King was slain at Sauchieburn, or "The Field of Stirling," as it was sometimes called, and on the coronation of his successor a proclamation was issued annulling all recent grants made by the late King to his adherents. In October of the same year (1488) Parliament passed an Act known as the Act Rescissory, annulling all alienations of lands and creations of new dignities granted since the preceding February by the late King, which might be prejudicial to the young King, because, in the judgment of Parliament, such alienations, gifts, and privileges were granted in aid of perverse counsels, and contrary to the good of the realm as causing the slaughter of the King's father. The Earl of Crawford was removed from certain high offices, yet allowed to retain his estates, and ultimately, as the petitioner admitted, was so far restored to royal favour as to obtain a renewed grant of the honour of the Dukedom of Montrose—for life only—"pro toto tempore vitæ suæ"—with the burgh of Montrose, its rents and customs, and the lordship and castle of Kinclevin. The original charter was not extant, but the Act of Parliament and Register of the Great Seal were held to prove its terms with sufficient accuracy. The late Duke of Montrose, therefore, as petitioner against the claim, undertook in his first case to establish two fundamental propositions: That the charter of 1488 did not subsist, or was not valid in law; and that even if it could be held as subsisting, the claimant was not the heir under the limitations of the patent. In seeking to establish the first point, the petitioner contended—(1), That there was reason for doubting whether the charter of May, 1488, was ever completed; (2), that if ever effectual it was annulled by the Act Rescissory; (3), that David, Earl of Crawford, was not recognised as Duke of Montrose until after a new grant in Parliament and relative patent of Dukedom; (4), that the Act Rescissory was not inoperative, as the claimant held, and in particular that it cut down the charter of the Dukedom of Montrose of 1488; (5), that the same Act was effectual in annulling the Earldom of Glencairn, an honour granted in similar circumstances; (6), that the Act was effectual against other grants; (7), that a statute alleged to have revoked the Act was not intended to affect it; (8), that the new patent for life was the only valid creation; and (9), that the other proofs of the Dukedom being a grant for life only are corroborated by the fact that the Duke's son and subsequent heirs never assumed the title nor asserted any claim to it, or the possessions which accompanied the honour. The Duke's son, John, it was said, was a prosperous person, and married to a daughter of Home, the Chamberlain, among the most influential Scotsmen of his age. He was employed in many offices of trust, and on good terms with James IV., whose side he had taken in the struggle against his father. To this the claimant answered that Earl John was all his life in a situation encouraging the Government to tyrannise over and oppress him. Independently of prodigality and recklessness, he had murdered his elder brother, Alexander, Master of Crawford, whereby the succession opened up to him, and the legal consequences of the crime hung suspended over his head till his death on the Field of Flodden. David Edzell, ninth Earl of Crawford, restored the honour and estates to the son of the "Wicked Master;" but from his time the family retrograded till their fortunes were shipwrecked in the person of David, the twelfth or "Prodigal Earl," confined in Edinburgh Castle so long as to obtain for him the title of the "Comes Incarceratus." Succeeding Earls again were soldiers of fortune in Spain, Flanders, and Germany. The question of "heirs" *heredibus suis*, gave rise to a lengthy and intricate argument on the law of Scotland touching the descent of dignities, but which it would be difficult to make interesting to ordinary readers. The claimant contended that the words carried the honours to him—a collateral heir-male, descended from the uncle of the patentee; while the petitioner held on the other hand that for anything submitted heirs of the body of the patentee might still exist, and in particular that the practice of describing "heirs" only as "heirs-male," and not as "heirs general," by which the succession opened up to females, was confined almost exclusively to the family of Crawford. So far as concerned the confusion likely to arise from the use of similar titles, though even this was not without precedent, the claimant expressed his intention, in the event of the claim being admitted, to continue the title of "Crawford," borne by his predecessors for 700 years, and thereby avoiding even the appearance of infringing "upon a title consecrated by history to the gallant race represented by the noble petitioner." This was put aside by the latter, who also insisted upon the connection of his family not only with the lands of Old Montrose, but with the Burgh of Montrose. The case came before the Committee of Privileges, 14th April, 1851, on which day the Duke of Montrose was permitted to appear in opposition. Mr. Rolt, Mr. Hope Scott, and Mr. Cosmo Innes appeared for His Grace as petitioner; Sir Fitzroy Kelly, Mr. Bethell, and Mr. Wortley, with Mr. Riddell, appeared for the Earl of Crawford and Balcarres as claimant. The Attorney-General and Solicitor-General watched the case for the Crown. Arguments on the merits were heard between 18th and 23rd July, 1853. Documentary evidence—consisting of charters, precepts, sasines, and accounts—was also submitted during the month, the documents being for the most part spoken to by Mr. G. Melville, writer, Edinburgh, and Mr. W. Fraser, Register House. Sir Fitzroy Kelly was heard two days at the close in reply for the claimant. On 5th August, with Lord Redesdale, as usual, in the chair, the committee came to the resolution, "that the charter bearing date 18th May, 1488, by which James III. of Scotland granted the Dukedom of Montrose to David, Earl of Crawford, *et heredibus suis,* was annulled and made void by the Act of the first year of the reign of King James IV. of Scotland, called the Act Rescissory; that the grant of the Dukedom made by King James IV. to the said David, Earl of Crawford, in 1489, was a grant for the term of his life only; and that the petitioner (claimant), James, Earl of Crawford and Balcarres, has not established any title to the Dukedom of Montrose created in 1488." This resolution was reported in due form to the House, and so the ingenious claim fell to the ground. The then Earl of Crawford and Balcarres was succeeded December, 1869, by his son, Alexander William Crawford, Lord Lindsay, eighth and late Earl, the accomplished author of "Lives of the Lindsays," and of the "History of Christian Art." The Duke of Montrose died 30th Dec., 1874, and was succeeded by his only surviving son, Douglas-Beresford-Malise-Ronald Graham, the fifth and present duke, born November, 1852, Lieutenant 5th Lancers. The Montrose Dukedom dates from 1707, the Marquisate from 1684, and the Earldom from 1504. The knightage goes back to the earliest period of our national history. Other titles carried by the present Duke are—Marquis of Graham and Buchanan, Earl and Marquis of Montrose, Earl of Kincardine, Viscount Dundaff, Lord Graham, Aberuthven, Mugdock, and Fintry, in the peerage of Scotland; Earl and Baron Graham, of Belford, Northumberland, in the peerage of Great Britain.

CUMBERNAULD HOUSE AND THE FLEMINGS.

BUILT in 1731, and occupied for only a short period by chiefs of the Fleming family, the mansion destroyed in March, 1877, came to be associated in an indirect way with many stirring events—national as well as domestic—in the history of a once powerful house. Originally from the Low Countries, Baldwin, the first recorded Fleming, appears as settled at Biggar in the reign of William the Lion, while a Sir Malcolm of the name was appointed Sheriff of Dumbarton in the reign of Alexander III. The family came strongly to the front as adherents of Bruce in the early struggles for national independence, and rose in a great measure on the ruin of Bruce's powerful rival, Comyn of Buchan. The Sir Malcolm of the day is said to have witnessed the slaughter of the Red Comyn at the altar of the Minorite Friars, Dumfries, and to have so thoroughly identified himself with the cause as to follow Bruce in his flight to Glasgow, and witness the absolution in the Cathedral, while the blood of his rival was scarcely dry upon the dagger. Even earlier than this the Comyns of Cumbernauld had smarted under the resentment of Bruce's party. Bishop Robert Wischart, ghostly confessor to the young patriot, begged timber for the spire of our Cathedral from Edward I., then ruling in Scotland as Overlord, and received forty oaks from Darnaway, sixty from Ettrick, and twenty stags for his own table. But, as Dr. J. Robertson shows, the spire of St. Kentigern was not yet to be built. The faithless prelate had scarcely digested the last of King Edward's venison before he turned the oaks into catapults and mangonels, and with them laid siege to the garrison which kept the Comyn's Castle of Kirkintilloch. The barony of Kirkintilloch, known in later times as the Lenzies, and including all the lands of Cumbernauld, passed from Bruce's opponent to Bruce's friend, King Robert granting a charter conveying to Malcolm Fleming that barony formerly held by John Comyn. This Malcolm was also created Earl of Wigtown; but in 1371 this title passed by a formal deed to Archibald, Earl of Galloway, a branch of the Royal Family of Scotland. The title was, however, revived in later days in favour of the Flemings of Cumbernauld. A second Sir Malcolm, son of the above, was present at the disastrous battle of Halidon Hill, 19th July, 1333. Making a skilful retreat from the fatal field, Sir Malcolm secured the person of the young Prince David, with his consort Joanna, and hurrying with them to Dumbarton Castle, of which he was governor, fortified the place against all attack. From this fortress the young couple were removed in safety to France, where they remained between seven and eight years. A descendant, Sir David, of Cumbernauld, distinguished himself at the battle of Otterburn, and was one of a Commission appointed to treat for peace with England in 1405. Having seen Prince James, son of Robert III., set sail on what was understood to be a voyage to France for liberty, but which turned out in reality a long captivity in England, Sir David was murdered on returning by Douglas of Balveny, at Hermandstone, near Edinburgh, and buried in the chapel of Holyrood. The Cumbernauld family appear to have been ennobled about 1460, Robert Lord Fleming appearing in the records of Parliament, 1466. As a diplomatist in the stormy time which succeeded the death of James IV., few sustained a more conspicuous part than John Lord Fleming of Cumbernauld. In the spring of 1520 he was appointed ambassador to the Court of France to secure the return of Albany to Scotland as Regent, and to accomplish, if possible, the still more delicate task of undermining the friendly sentiments which it was thought Francis I. then entertained for Henry VIII., and with whom he had afterwards a romantic interview on the "Field of the Cloth of Gold." A daughter, Mary Fleming, who became the wife of Maitland of Lethington, was said to have been in her youth one of the Queen's celebrated "Four Marys," although one version of the popular ballad describes the enticing group as made up from the families of Hamilton, "May Hamilton," Seaton, Beaton, and Carmichael. In 1526 James V. ratified and approved "a charter of new infeftment maid to Malcolm Lord Fleming, making the touns of Biggar and Kerkentulloch burghis of barony, with the mercat dais, in all punctis" as other burghs of barony. Soon after the imprisonment of Queen Mary in Lochleven, a party professing adherence to her cause, and known as the "Queen's Lords," finding themselves removed from all offices of importance under the new Government, betook themselves to the Castle of Dumbarton, then held by Lord Fleming, zealous in the Queen's support, and there entered into a bond to release and protect their captive sovereign, and, if possible, bring to punishment the murderers of her husband, King Henry, Lord Darnley.

After the defeat at Langside, and when the unfortunate Queen had so far carried out the doubtful scheme of submitting her case to her sister of England, Mary writes to Elizabeth regarding Lord Fleming of Cumbernauld :— " As for my Lord Fleming, seeing that upon my credit you have suffered him to go home to his house, I warrant you he shall pass no further, but shall return when it pleases you. But for Dumbarton I answer not when my Lord Fleming shall be in the Tower. For they which are within it, will not forbear to receive succour if I don't assure them of yours; no, though you should charge me withal, for I have left them in charge, to have more respect unto my servants and to my estate than to my life." The confidence reposed by the Queen in Lord Fleming is further brought out during an interview, when it was proposed to remove her from Carlisle to Bolton Castle, this being the first decisive step taken by the English Court to dispose of her person against her will. " I require " (said the fugitive Queen in anger), " I require the Queen, my good sister, either that she will let me go into France, or that she will put me into Dumbarton, unless she will hold me as a prisoner, for I am sure that her Highness will not of her honour put me into my Lord of Murray's hands." Straitly besieged by the Regent Lennox, Fleming ventured to bring under notice of the Queen's Commissioners the persecution he was being subjected to, and the destruction to which his private property was exposed. Among other enormities perpetrated by Lennox, particular stress is laid upon the slaughter of the white kye in the forest of Cumbernauld "as the lyke was not manteint in ony uther pairt of this Ile of Albion." When the Castle of Dumbarton was surprised by the intrepid daring of Crawford of Jordanhill, Lord Fleming made his escape to the Clyde, and afterwards got on board a vessel proceeding to France. Lady Fleming was captured, but dismissed with many marks of the Regent's favour. Hamilton, Bishop of St. Andrews, deeply implicated in the murder of Darnley, was taken to Stirling and executed. During the civil war the Cumbernauld family threw in their lot with the King and served loyally under Montrose. It was in the old Castle of Cumbernauld that Montrose and his party in August, 1640, entered into that bond which first brought them into direct hostility with the Covenanting party they had up to that time supported. In September, 1650, the Committee of Estates, considering the Castle of Cumbernauld to be a place of great importance, ordered it to be victualled and garrisoned. Sir William Fleming, then with Charles II. at Breda, was, as appears from the Wigtown family papers, despatched on a special mission to Scotland, the King's instructions being of this tenor :—"In case my friends in Scotland do not think fit that Montrose lay down arms, then as many as can may repair to him. You shall see if Montrose have a considerable number of men; and if he have you must use your best endeavours to get them not to be disbanded; but if he be weak then he should disband, for it will do me more harm for a small body to keep together than it can do me good." Some days before the date of the "instructions" Montrose had fallen into the hands of his enemies, and Fleming arrived in Edinburgh only to learn that the Marquis had terminated his career on the gallows. The old castle, it may be remarked, after being deserted by the Cumbernauld family in favour of the spacious new mansion, was set fire to by a party of Highlanders during the rebellion of 1745 and burned to the ground. The parish of Cumbernauld was detached from Kirkintilloch about 1649. The first minister, Thomas Stewart, was ejected for non-conformity in 1662, and his successor, Gilbert Muschett, seems to have been much troubled by the predilection his parishioners manifested for conventicles. Even after the Revolution had transformed the Episcopalian rebel into a Presbyterian Dissenter, the spirit of hostility continued as strong and active as ever. Thus, in July, 1688, after denouncing twelve persons as fugitives, the parish clergyman thought proper to enter in the session-book that "the meeting-house preacher is ane rebell, and not pardonded; excommunicate, and not relaxed; and ane slander and leising-making, alienating the hearts of His Majesty's subjects by not keeping the three late thanksgivings." The ancient dignity of the family, it may be mentioned, was revived in 1606 by James VI., John Lord Fleming, successor of the Governor of Dumbarton Castle, being then created Earl of Wigtown and Lord Fleming of Biggar and Cumbernauld. John, sixth Earl, following the loyal traditions of his house, passed with James II. to St. Germains at the Revolution, but returned to Scotland and took an active part in opposition to the Union negotiations. Suspected of complicity in Jacobite plots, he was committed prisoner to Edinburgh Castle in 1715, but was afterwards liberated by order of the High Court of Justiciary, and took up his residence at Cumbernauld, where, in 1731, he erected the fine mansion—the destruction of which in 1877 was so much regretted. Earl John died in 1744, and was succeeded in his titles and estates by a brother Charles, who died unmarried 26th May, 1747. The estates thereupon devolved on a niece, only daughter of Earl John, the Lady Clementina Fleming, who in 1735 had married Charles, afterwards tenth Lord Elphinstone. One or two of the descendants of Lady Clementina merit special notice. Her eldest son, John, succeeded to the Elphinstone honours; Charles, R.N., was lost in the "Prince George," burnt at sea in 1758 when proceeding to the Mediterranean, the loss by this calamity being 485 out of a total of 745 on board Admiral Broderick's war-ship; a third son, William, had a son, Charles, lost in the "Blenheim," 1707, the mysterious fate of this war vessel forming the subject of a once popular ballad by James Montgomery. The fourth and youngest son of the Lady Clementina was George Keith Elphinstone, Admiral of the Blue, a naval officer of very high reputation, created Lord and afterwards Viscount Keith. By his first wife, only daughter and heiress of William Mercer of Aldie, Viscount Keith left one daughter, Margaret Mercer, married to the Count de Flauhault, French Ambassador at the Court of St. James'. Viscount Keith married secondly Hester Marie Thrale, who survived till 31st March, 1857, when she passed away at the great age of ninety-three, the last surviving member of the once renowned Johnsonian circle at Streatham. (See also pp. 187–191.) The mansion of Cumbernauld had been only partly tenanted during the last seventeen years. In 1875 the estate was sold by the Hon. Cornwallis Fleming, nephew of Admiral Fleming, to

Mr. John William Burns of Kilmahew, Dumbartonshire, for £165,000. The property was then described as consisting of 3,807 imperial acres, whereof 2,833 were arable, and the remainder as plantation or rough pasture. The gross rental was then set down at £4,692, and the public burdens at £421.

Making a pleasing addition to personal as well as family history, the "Memoir of Admiral Lord Keith," completed by Mr. Allardyce, was an altogether fresh work in biographical literature, and bore at the same time not remotely on the stirring events occurring in Egypt. The closing scene of Admiral Keith's official life was intimately associated with the memorable surrender of Buonaparte to Captain Maitland, of the "Bellerophon," during the command of the Channel Fleet by the gallant Viscount. On his shoulders rested the responsibility of transferring the fallen monarch on board Sir George Cockburn's ship, the "Northumberland," preparatory to being despatched, with a few chosen attendants, to his lonely banishment on St. Helena. It cannot be forgotten, however, by students of the great Revolutionary war, that some fifteen years before the "Surrender" Keith-Elphinstone commanded the fleet which carried out Sir Ralph Abercromby with a British force to Aboukir, when the French power in Egypt was broken for the time, and where Sir Ralph fell mortally wounded as the enemy retreated to Alexandria, preparatory to a full capitulation within a few months. In announcing the accomplishment of the expedition to Egypt, General Hutchinson, who succeeded the brave and popular Abercromby, wrote to the Secretary of State:—"I cannot conclude this letter without stating to your Lordship the many obligations I have to Lord Keith and the navy, for the great exertions they have used in forwarding us the necessary supplies, and from the fatigue they have undergone in the late embarkation of a considerable number of troops and stores, who were embarked on the new lake, and proceeded to the westward under the orders of Major-General Coote. The utmost despatch has also been used in sending the French troops lately captured to France, which in our present position was a service of the most essential consequence." The despatch of French prisoners would appear to have been not the least of the troublesome duties laid on Admiral Keith, during his command on the coast of Egypt. While the troops from Cairo were on their way down to Rosetta, Menou made an offer to get rid of a number of his non-combatants in Alexandria, and sent a brig out of the harbour, under cartel flags, with a large company of "savants," members of the Institute and of the Commission des Sciences et des Arts, who wished to get home with their archæological booty. "But as I did not consider it proper," says Lord Keith, in his report to the Admiralty, "to allow any person whatever to depart from a town long since blockaded, and, I hope, immediately to be besieged, I have advised them all to return, and acquainted General Menou that I shall observe a similar conduct towards the invalids and blind if he sends them out, as proposed in his despatches." With grim humour the Admiral offered to surrender to him a company of French comedians who, sent by the French Government to enliven the garrison of Alexandria, had been captured by the British cruisers; but Menou obstinately refused to accept this addition to his garrison. So actively, however, did his Lordship expedite matters for the despatch of the garrison of Cairo, that he was able to announce to the Admiralty on 21st July—"The transports for the reception of the French corps from Cairo are far advanced in preparation, and will be ready before they arrive at Rosetta; notwithstanding we suffer much interruption by the almost constant swell and impracticability of the bar." The embarkation began on 1st August, and was completed, in spite of the enormous quantity of baggage, within eight days; and the convoy, consisting of six of His Majesty's ships and nearly 50 British and Turkish transports, was despatched without delay. Fifth son of Charles, tenth Lord Elphinstone, George Keith, whom history has ranked among the first of British naval commanders, was born in his father's old tower of Airth, Stirlingshire, early in January, 1746, a critical period in the history of Scotland, for only a few miles off the remains of Prince Charles's retreating expedition were intensifying, if possible, the terror and distress of civil war by a final desperate effort to reduce Stirling Castle. His mother, Lady Clementina Fleming, one of the beauties and toasts of Edinburgh society in her youth, was strongly imbued with Jacobite principles, and in addition to the extinct earldom of Wigtown, came to unite in herself the two attainted honours of Marischal and Perth. Young Keith was named after his grand-uncle, the Earl Marischal, who had taken part in Mar's rebellion, and was then living in exile at the Court of Prussia, sharing in the favour which Frederick the Great had extended to his illustrious brother, Marshal Keith. Encouraged by the advice of his grand-uncle, Keith Elphinstone followed the example of his brothers, Charles and William, by entering the navy in his fifteenth year, being received as midshipman on board the "Gosport" at Portsmouth, with but slender thought that a peerage and the baton of commander awaited him in the profession he had selected. The commander of the "Gosport" was Captain John Jervis, afterwards ennobled as Earl of St. Vincent, for his memorable defeat of the Spanish fleet. The naval service becoming unsettled by the reduction of the fleet after the peace of Fontainbleau in 1763, Elphinstone served for a short time on board his brother's vessel, under the flag of the East India Company, but again, through the friendly influence of the Earl Marischal, whose attainder had been reversed in consideration of services rendered to England at the Court of Spain, Keith rejoined the Royal Navy as second lieutenant on board the "Trident," from which he passed in 1772 with his first commission as commander of the "Scorpion," of 14 guns, employed on the coast of Minorca and in the Gulf of Genoa. From 1776, when Elphinstone entered upon his first duties on the American station, his career becomes associated with all that is most memorable in the naval history of England, and can only be glanced at here in the briefest manner. He commanded a detachment of seamen on shore in the reduction of Charleston, was present at the attack of Mud Island, November, 1777, and being sent home with despatches from Admiral Arbuthnot, was appointed to command the "Warwick," of 50 guns. On the conclusion of the American war in 1793, Captain Elphinstone returned home, and was elected M.P. for Stirlingshire, having previously sat for Dumbartonshire, after a contest of uncommon closeness carried on during his absence on the American station with Lord Frederick Campbell, brother of the Duke of Argyll. When the war of the

Revolution broke out with France, Elphinstone was again on active service, joining Lord Hood in the Mediterranean, and rendering services worthy of official recognition in the famous descent on Toulon, August, 1793. Rather more than a year later, on hostilities occurring between England and the Batavian Republic, Elphinstone, then Rear-Admiral of the "White," sailed to the Cape of Good Hope, and in conjunction with General Clarke compelled the Dutch, who advanced to the relief of the colony, to surrender at discretion without firing a gun. Pursuant to instructions received from the Admiralty before sailing, Admiral Elphinstone next entered the Indian Ocean, where he first secured to the British Crown the important possessions of Ceylon, Cochia, Malacca, and Molucca; but, on returning to the Cape, captured the entire Dutch fleet, which had been sent out under Lucas, and taken up a position in Saldanha Bay with the view of striking a decisive blow for the recovery of the colony. In 1779 the mutiny at the Nore called out the Admiral's highest qualities in the way of gentle persuasion and concession, coupled with a judicious firmness, necessary to be directed towards the leaders of the revolt. The mutiny was ultimately found to spring from two very different causes—one a well-founded disaffection with pay, provisions, and pensions; second, a dangerous spirit of Republicanism springing directly from the principles and examples of the French Revolution. Scarcely was subordination restored at the Nore, when the Admiral (now Lord Keith) was hurried off to Portsmouth to procure a ship and act as second in command of the Channel Fleet under Lord Bridport, the distrust which had been excited by the conduct of the seamen, as well as the numerous services which were to be performed in the Channel, making the Admiralty anxious to strengthen Lord Bridport's hands. He was ordered to hoist his flag on the "Queen Charlotte," which had been the chief centre of the Spithead mutiny. At the close of 1799 Lord Keith took command in the Mediterranean, which ill-health had compelled Lord St. Vincent to resign. In March he blockaded the harbour of Leghorn in co-operation with the Austrians, and was mainly instrumental, by the rigid blockade maintained, in reducing the French troops under Massena to such straits as resulted in his surrender. Engaged successfully in restoring order throughout the islands of the Mediterranean, Lord Keith experienced the keen distress of seeing from shore the burning of his noble flag-ship off Capraja, when no fewer than 673 perished in the water or by the flames, and only 156 were saved from the burning wreck. Prominent services discharged later in life were connected with the operations of Abercromby in Egypt, and the command of the Channel Fleet when Napoleon surrendered in 1815. On being transferred from the "Bellerophon" to the "Northumberland," the ex-Emperor repeated his former protestations against being sent to St. Helena, or being treated in any other way than as a distinguished prisoner of war. "I do not (he said to Admiral Keith) voluntarily go from this ship or from England. It is you, Admiral, who take me." To this the Admiral replied, "I hope, Sir, that you will not reduce an officer like me to do so disagreeable an act as to use force towards your person." He answered, "Oh, no; you shall order me." I replied, "I shall attend you at your convenience in my barge. I beg not to hurry you." This, writes his biographer, Mr. Allardyce, was the last important service that Lord Keith was to perform for his country, and he doubtless felt proud that his public career should be wound up by so memorable an incident. Seventy years of age when he quitted the service, Lord Keith spent other seven active years in improving his estates, and, dying at Tulliallan Castle in March, 1822, was buried in the old church of Overnewton, in his own parish, which he had selected as a mausoleum for his family. Created an Irish Baron in 1797, Admiral Keith was four years afterwards created a Peer of the United Kingdom, as Baron Keith of Barrheath, Dumbartonshire, and presented at the same time with the freedom of the City of London and a magnificent sword by the Directors of the East India Company. Lord Keith was twice married—first to Miss Mercer, of Aldie, Perthshire, in the line of succession to the attainted Barony of Nairne, by whom he had an only child, a daughter, Margaret, who in 1817 married the Count de Flahault, aide-de-camp to her father's last distinguished captive, and in after days attached to the Court of Louis Philippe, as well as of Louis Napoleon. The Countess Flahault died in 1867, three years before her husband, when the Barony of Nairne, to which she had succeeded, descended to her daughter, the Dowager-Marchioness of Lansdowne. The second Lady Keith was the daughter of Dr. Johnson's friends, Mr. and Mrs. Thrale, the latter afterwards, to the Doctor's distress, Mrs. Piozzi. Born in 1764, she had been dandled, and even partly educated, by Johnson, had, it has been affirmed, refused the hand of Samuel Rogers, and died in Piccadilly, London, so late as 1857, when she had reached the extraordinary age of ninety-three, the last survivor, and in her youth an adored member, of the once brilliant Streatham circle. The materials for Mr. Allardyce's delightful memoir were chiefly taken from the journals, despatches, and official letters of Lord Keith preserved in the charter-room of Tulliallan Castle, Perthshire.

GLASGOW BURGH RECORDS.

APART altogether from his official connection with Glasgow as Town-Clerk, there was good ground for expecting that the attention of Mr. Marwick, as Secretary to the useful Burgh Record Society, would soon be turned in the direction of that pile of old deeds and minutes gathered together for centuries by the different law advisers of the Corporation. Their existence was known to many far removed from the circle of immediate official connection. In November, 1832, Mr. John Smith, youngest, presented to members of the Maitland Club a volume composed of selections from the Records between the years 1572 and 1581. Owing to the local interest excited by the information contained in that collection, further investigation was prosecuted, and the result given to another select circle in the shape of a dumpy, but now scarce quarto volume, entitled, "Memorabilia," giving (with the exception of a score of pages at the commencement relating to Ayr burgh) a series of Glasgow notices extending somewhat irregularly from 1588 to 1750. Previous to being printed off in a book form, this latter volume of selections from the minute-books had appeared in the "Courier" newspaper, conducted by

Mr. Motherwell till his death in 1835. In 1868 Mr. West Watson, City Chamberlain, printed for private circulation a similar series of "Memorabilia" from the minutes, commencing also in 1588, but continued down so late as June, 1749. Volumes earlier than 1573 are thought to have been in existence about the middle of last century, but recent inquiry for recovery has been unavailing, and the reference in Gibson's History, published 1777, appears to be all that is known regarding them. Mr. Marwick's diligent search, however, has been rewarded in a way not more interesting to his readers than we are sure pleasant to himself. He has discovered four volumes unknown in modern times to predecessors in office. One extends from May, 1581, to April, 1586; a second from October, 1594, to May, 1597; a third from November, 1598, to October, 1601; and the fourth from June, 1605, to June, 1610. The handsome volume now issued by the Scottish Burgh Record Society, under the care of Mr. Marwick, embraces the period between January, 1573, and September, 1642; but, even with his good luck in bringing the four lost volumes to light, there are still five provoking breaks within the period, one of them indicating so long a time as ten years—from 1613 to 1623. Still, the selection is as complete as can at present be made, and contains, the editor writes, everything to be found in that series of local records illustrative of the constitution of the burgh, its municipal government, and the social life of the people. Although some of the matter inserted has only a limited or technical interest, Mr. Marwick wisely resolved that in a case of this kind, where the original records were frail and practically inaccessible, it was expedient to err on the side of too much rather than too little. Modern in date compared with the fine series of Aberdeen minutes issued by the Spalding Club, this new volume presents a more enticing and accurate picture of Glasgow growth and daily life of the burgesses than any smooth-written history or compilation, however comprehensive may be its pretensions. For such special excellence, indeed, the reader is inclined to feel a personal regret that the record does not open a few years earlier than 1573. One single volume would have let us see how Glasgow received the Regent Murray and his troops before the swift advance to Langside in the summer of 1568, and might even have described the welcome given to the hapless Mary herself when she arrived to visit her sick husband before his suspicious removal to the Kirk-of-Field. Crawford of Jordanhill, afterwards Chief Magistrate of the City, heard Darnley say to the Queen in his lodging, "If you promise me on your honour to live with me as my wife, and not to leave me any more, I will go with you to the end of the world and care for nothing; if not, I will stay where I am." "It shall be as you have spoken," she replied; and thereupon she gave him her hand and faith. This was in Glasgow on the 27th January. The tragedy of the Kirk-of-Field took place on 9th February following. Mr. Marwick's volume is just sufficiently near the time to let us hear an after-clap or two of the great Reformation struggle in 1560. We do not see, it is true, that gallant defence of the Cathedral by the crafts with Deacon Rabat at their head, when the commons of Renfrew, Barony, and Gorbals marched in one fair morning to purge the old fabric of Popish nick-nackets, and actually succeeded in removing the images from the shrines, breaking them afterwards, as they said, by Scripture warrant, and flinging the pieces into what was then the silvery Molendinar. Yet we see early in the work that the Church was cared for, even though it might be in desolation —" with dust on her forehead, and chains round her feet." Here is a portion of a resolution come to, 21st August, 1574, avoiding, for the comfort of the reader, as much as possible the antiquated spelling :—The Provost, Bailies, and Council, with the deacons of crafts, and divers other honest men of the town, convened in the Council-house, and having respect and consideration into the great decay and ruin that the High Kirk of Glasgow is come to through taking away of the lead, slate, "and uter grayth thairof, in this trublus tyme bygane," so that such a great monument will utterly fall down and decay, without it be remedied; and because the helping thereof is so great and would extend to more than they might spare; and that they are not indebted to the upholding and repair thereof by law, yet of their own free-will, uncompelled, and for the zeal they bear to the kirk, of mere awms and liberality, have consented to a tax and imposition of two hundred pounds money for helping to repair the said kirk and holding it waterfast.

Among other encouragements given to the labours of the Record Society, Mr. Marwick mentions that the present Provost, Magistrates, and Council have authorised the translation and printing of a volume of charters and kindred documents relating to Glasgow, from its erection as a burgh about 1175 till the middle of the seventeenth century. This will tend greatly to complete a view of our City in the old days, and be highly useful for general historic purposes. A little over forty years since, when the Royal Commissioners were busy with their Reports on Municipal Corporations in Scotland, it was remarked of Glasgow that it did not appear when the inhabitants first began to enjoy any peculiar rights or privileges under the protection of the bishops; but, as they were not tenants or vassals of the Crown, they could originally have had no such political existence as belonged to the burghal vassalage of the king, and there even seemed good ground for supposing that the whole territory of Glasgow was originally included within the bounds of the royal burgh of Rutherglen, erected by David I. Under the powerful patronage of the Church, however, the people of Glasgow were at an early period enabled, by royal authority, to exercise some of the more limited rights of traffic, and about 1172 King William the Lion granted to Bishop Joceline permission to hold a weekly market, and gave a general protection at the same time to the persons and chattels of the bishop and burgesses. About 1197, and, as Dr. J. Robertson thinks, in immediate connection with the consecration of the Cathedral crypt, the privilege was conceded of holding an annual fair, often referred to in Mr. Marwick's volume, and still kept up with stinted show, of eight days' duration, at the octave of the feast of St. Peter and St. Paul. In virtue of these early charters Glasgow became what has been called a free burgh, but the Reports describe it as a mistake to suppose that it was thereby erected into a burgh royal. It was then on the contrary what came to be described in later days simply a burgh of barony. It was afterwards erected into a burgh of regality, but in this as in all analogous cases there was an interposed or mid-superior between the Crown and the burgesses; and their rents or mails (census burgales), whatever they may have been, were due, not to the Crown, but to the Bishop.

The presumed inferiority of the early burgesses became so intolerable that in 1226 Alexander II. granted a charter prohibiting the people of Rutherglen from taking toll or custom in the town of Glasgow, or nearer than the Cross of Schetelston. Dumbarton was also unwearied in its opposition, so far especially as Clyde trade was concerned; and even so late as the period embraced by the new record volume, scores of entries are taken up with the contention of the two burghs. In 1242, twenty years after Dumbarton had been erected into a Royal burgh, Alexander II. granted a charter declaring that the burgesses of Glasgow, Argyll, and Lennox, and throughout the whole kingdom, might go and buy or sell all kinds of merchandise as freely, quietly, fully, and honourably, without any impediment from the Bailie of Dumbarton, as the burgesses and men of Glasgow were able to do before any town or burgh was erected at Dumbarton. The charter of regality in favour of Glasgow was obtained by Bishop Turnbull from James II. In the exercise of their high prerogative the Bishops continued for about a century to nominate the Provost and Magistrates. This came to be modified in 1554 by the introduction of a leet of names suggested to the Bishop apparently by the burgesses as a whole; and for a year or two at the Reformation they exercised the privilege of electing their own Magistrates. Shortly before the abdication of the See by Archbishop James Beaton in 1559, he had appointed the Earl of Arran and his heirs to be bailies of the regality, they, on the other hand, becoming bound to protect the See in all its rights and privileges; but, in spite of this precaution, the opportunity was seized by the citizens of electing their own Magistrates, and the contending rights of the See and the burgh can hardly be said to have been adjusted till the abolition of Episcopacy under the Revolution Settlement. The system of leets is in operation at the commencement of Mr. Marwick's volume, the first Provost mentioned being Robert, Lord Boyd, elected October, 1574, on the recommendation of Archbishop James Boyd. Robert, Earl of Lennox, Lord Darnley, was nominated and appointed in like manner in 1579.

Another event of more than local interest, illustrated by this Record volume, is the famous Assembly of 1638, presided over by Alexander Henderson, and commonly described by Presbyterians as the Second Reformation. Buchanan's pupil—Andrew Melville—had clamoured among others for the instant destruction of the Cathedral as a monument of idolatry, whither superstitious people resorted for devotion, but which by its vastness was all unsuited for the simplicity of orthodox rites. But large as the building was, it was too small for the crowd described as surging round it in December of that year, "while within Covenanted Ministers and nobles gorged with Church plunder were defying their King and excommunicating their Bishops." Burnet says, "It was perhaps the greatest confluence of people which ever met in these parts of Europe—yet a sad sight to see, for not a gown was among them all, but many had swords and daggers." Great excitement is said to have been manifested as the "Jericho of Prelacy was smitten down, and the curse of Hiel the Bethelite pronounced against all who should attempt to rebuild it." The High Church was put in order for the occasion, and, as appears from a minute of date November 3, a special guard was appointed to watch the town night and day. Acting on instructions received from the Council, Commissioner Provost Bell was among those who voted for continuing to sit in judgment on the Bishops after the formal dissolution of the Assembly, and for repealing the Five Articles of Perth as "unfree, unlawful, and null." During the sittings the poor were kept off the street and maintained in their own houses. There is much also in the volume concerning the arming and maintenance of the men sent from the West to support the cause of the Covenant under General Alexander Leslie at Dunse Law; and about all local institutions and topography—college, schools, churches, and hospitals—wells, streets, and marches—old customs and old trade regulations—unfailing information will be found. The volume concludes with about forty pages of extracts from the Burgh Accounts, extending over a period similar to that embraced by the Minutes of Council. There is here room for only a sample of the "Items." The sums must be understood in each case as of Scots currency:—

"1575, Jan. 6. Item on Fastrinis ewin, to ane fule with the treyn suerd xviijd.—Item to the pyper callit Ryall Dayis for playing xviijd.—Sept. 8. Item to Malcolm Hammiltoun, for scurgeing of ane wod hussy throw the toune vs.— 1576, Jan. 3. Item to ane boy to rin in the nicht to Dumbartan to caus the baillies and thair clerk cum on the morn iijs.—June 16. Item to Eufame Campbell, spous to Andro Baillie, for xvj quartis wyne propynit to my Lord Boyd, prouest, sen Vitsondaye last iiij lb. xvjs.—July 24. Gewin to David Kaye for the price of the knok and vpsetting of hir in the tolbuyth quhilk wes borrowit fra Thomas Garne jc lib.—1582, June 2. Item for ane lok to put on the theif that brunt the wyfe of the Cowcadennis, xxs.—1583, June 18. Item gewin to James Lyoun for denneris, afternoonis drink to the proveist, bailleis, counsell and deacones the tyme the proveist remanit in this town for pacifeing of thee trublis betuix the merchandis and craftismen, xlviij. li. iiijs.—1584, Oct. 9. Item, gewin to Barbara Ramsaye, ane pure wowman with mony barnis, in almous, xxs.—1610, Sept. 27. Item to Margret Young for candill furnist be hir that nycht the fyre was in Salt Mercat, xxs.—1612, Feb. 15. Item gifin to ane young man quha was rubbit of his pak xls.—1628. Item to Johne Clydsdaill for carying of ane crippill mane to Pasley xxvjs.—1638. Item, debursit for particularis when his Majesties commissioner the Marqueis of Hamiltoun was in the tolbuithe xxxiiij. li. xvijs. iiijd.—Item to Quintein Muir for instructing of the young men to handill thair armes xl. li.—1640. Item for outreiking of xj sojoris that went in the commoun caus with Colonell Monro lxxxv. li. ixs. jd.— Item to maister Zacharias Boyd for ane termes annuall of 3 markis, lxxx. li.— 1641. Item to ane blind minister xxvij. li.—Item to George Andersone, prenter, for his yeirs pensioune, lxvj. li. xiijs. iiijd."

Mr. Marwick's volume is illustrated by a Plan of the City in 1773; and, better still, has a Table of Contents and Index so minute as to allow of the book being easily consulted by the most inexperienced reader. For much of its completeness in this respect a graceful and appropriate reference is made to Mr. Renwick, who copied the records for press, collated the proof-sheets, and prepared the Index of this interesting City volume.

Dry as record study may appear at first sight to the student who knows how to work in the mine and how to employ the discoveries certain to reward patient, intelligent labour, it is not only an informing but a delightful pursuit. Portions of what may be called history, touching at one point or other almost the entire domain of human knowledge, no historical research worthy of the name can be conducted without a careful study of the records pertaining to the period, or the subject, it may be, under investigation. This is true of all history, but true in an especial manner of local or municipal history. In this way books like Dr. Marwick's "Extracts from the Records of the Burgh of Glasgow" come to have a double value—they suggest and they authenticate; they suggest new lines of inquiry, and authenticate what may have been only imperfectly known before. Even more than this often happens. Attention in the study of known records leads to the discovery of kindred records not known to exist, or which may have been removed from their proper resting-place. In rewards of this kind Dr. Marwick has been more than usually lucky. While directing the preparation of the first Glasgow record volume the Town-Clerk was fortunate enough to bring to light four MS. volumes of Council minutes unknown to predecessors in office, one extending from May, 1581, to April, 1586; a second from October, 1594, to May, 1597; a third from Nov., 1598, to October, 1601; and the fourth from June, 1605, to June, 1610. This first volume, printed for the Scottish Burgh Record Society about seven years since (see p. 193), embraced the period between Jan., 1573, and Sept., 1642; but, even with Dr. Marwick's good fortune in bringing the four lost volumes to light, there were still five provoking breaks within the period, one of them extending from December, 1630, till May, 1636. But this MS. was also found after the first was printed, and is now included in the new volume, which otherwise covers the period between May, 1641, and December, 1662. Like the first volume, the second contains everything to be found in the Council records within that period illustrative of the constitution of the burgh, its municipal government, its relation to other local bodies, and many glimpses, to be had nowhere else, of the social life of the people in those days. This arises, no doubt, partly from the meddlesome over-legislation by local Magistrates in the sixteenth century—a meddlesomeness which would be now felt as intolerable—but which yet permits the present generation to see ancestors in the manner as they lived. The reader may learn from these records "how offences against the law were created and how they were dealt with; how civil war originated and how it was conducted; how property was acquired and how it was protected; he may see the people worshipping in the church and trading in the market-place; how they dressed, how they lived, and how they talked; and he may learn if he pleases what calamities saddened and what festivals rejoiced the hearts of the old burgesses who live again in the pages of their own records." When not otherwise mentioned money value is to be calculated in Scots currency, or one twelfth sterling. The first entry in the volume (December 18, 1630) is suggestive enough of the motto, "Let Glasgow Flourish by the Preaching of the Word," the treasurer on that date receiving "ane warrand for fourtie pund gevin be him to Maister Andro Stewart for preitching Godis Word, as helper to Maister John Maxwell quhill he transportit his wyff, bairns, and familie to this burghe, and that be the space of fyftein weikis or thairby, as was promeist to the said Maister John for his supplie." The second entry, on the same date, has reference to the building of the now familiar Tron steeple, five pounds (Scots) being then paid to Gabriel Smith "for scharping of the measoun irnes for the wark." Many following entries relate to this erection, one in May, 1630, ordaining the treasurer to "have ane warrand for fourtie pund gevin be him to Mungo Huitschaw for gilting of the cok, glob, and vaines of the stipill in the Trongait, as the Proveist and Deacone of Gild agreit with him." A laudable desire for the repair and preservation of the Cathedral, or "Metropolitane Kirk," as it is called, is shown by many entries relating to payments for lead, woodwork, and painting. On 4th July, 1635, Matthew Colquhoun undertakes the glass windows of Outer Kirk and Quire, and "to sweip and keip clein the haill battilingis and spoutis, and to sweip and keip clein the haill turnpykis and pillar heidis of baith kirkis, and speciallie the pend heidis and pillar heidis abone the Counsall sait, and all uther placis neidfull, quhair the kirk officeris cannot win to." Some notion of the extent, and even an outline, of the streets may be had from the election of constables for the year 1631. The proportion was arranged as follows:—"Abone the Wynd heid, 5; fra the Wynd heid to the Cros, on baith sydis of the gait, 7; Gallowgait, on baith the sydis and outwith the port, 5; Trongait on baith the sydis, 3; out of the West Port, on baith sydis, 3; Stockwallgait, 3; Briggait, 3; Saltmercat, 4; Waster Wynd, 2; New Wynd and Maynis Wynd, 2."

Regarding national events, the first low breathings of the coming storm with the King may be traced in an order regarding drilling of 24th August, 1633, a few weeks after Charles had paid his ill-starred visit to Edinburgh in company with Laud. On that date the treasurer is instructed to give "to James Aitchisoun, dreil maister, for allevin scoir buikes, ane less, send be him to this burghe, beiring the forme of dreilling, fourtie pund; and ordanes ilk young man of ane mid and guid qualitie that hapins to be ressavit burgessis heirefter ressave ane of them for four schilling to the treasurer, and he to be compatabill theirfoir." The day after the King's execution the Magistrates were busy negotiating with Sir Robert Douglas for the purchase of Gorbals, at the price of 110,000 merks, "with some little moir befoir the bargane give up." On 15th July, 1650, the day when Charles II., having previously accepted the Covenants, was proclaimed King at Edinburgh, it was appointed that a levy of 150 men be "presentlie outreikit," and public intimation made that "quhasoever hes ane mind willinglie to offer themselfis for defence and saftie of the Covenantis, King and Kingdomes, to go out, aither upone horse or fitt, that they wuld come presentlie to the laich Tolbaithe, and give up their names, certifieing all suche quha sall not come betwixt and twa efternoone that besyde they will be layable to the fynes contenit in the Actis of Parliament that they will be appoyntit to goe out and to furneis men in thair rowmes with thirittie dayes provisioun. Lykas, it is heirby declarit that quha so offeris themselfis to go out that they sall be frie of the putting out of the proportioune of the 150 futt appoynted presentlie to goe out." On 12th August, 1650, when Cromwell was moving northward by way of Berwick, "it being showne the danger that the countrey stands in fra the Inglis, and that thair is ane ongoeing of the shyres of Air, Lanerick, Galloway, and Ranfrew to associat thair forces for thair continuall saiftie, it was thairfor resolvit to joyne with them thairin, and that the Proveist (George Porterfield) and the Clerk goe the morne to attend the meiting at Kilmarnock for that effect, with ample commissioune." September 2 (same year, and the day before the cause of the Covenant was shattered by Cromwell's Ironsides at Dunbar), it was appointed that 1200 "bisket breid be sent east to the sojouris that were outreikit be the toune," and then serving under General David Leslie. Towards the close of the month, when Cromwell was advancing on Glasgow, one portion of the town's bonds and Hutcheson Hospital bonds were sent for safety to Avondale Castle, and later in the year another portion were conveyed to Carrick Castle. When the English garrisoned Hamilton in December a weekly cess was fixed on Glasgow of "threttie bollis meill, threttie bollis horse corne, ten bollis malt, and that by and besyde great quantiteis of cheis, candlle, salt, and breid, certefeing that if they wer not thankfullie payed and readilie answerit therof they wuld plunder the toune and give it over to the mercie of insolent sojouris; and these wha were Magistratis and Counsellouris of the poore toune for that tyme haveing left and desarted the same in so sad condition, and many poore and uther honest people wha remained crying out for help in so distressed estate and condition, it pleased God of His goodness to stir upe the harts of ane certane number of young men, burgessis and burgessis sones, wha teuk upone them in name of the communalitie to find out meanes and wayes to get the Inglisch satisfeit, and so the toune thairby preservit from outer ruine, and haveing nothing quhairwith to do the same bot ane voluntary collection quhilk was uplifted weiklie be their severall mylnes," &c., &c. Account of charge and discharge to be entered. Pressed on by the King for supplies, the Provost, on April, 1651, read a new demand of another kind, contained in letters from the Lieutenant-General and Major Montgomery, with two Acts, "one appoynting to give the publict quhat pistollis the towne hes, and the other to give Ritmaster Buntein ane thowsand merkis. To the first it was desyret to wryt that the towne knew not of ony pistollis in the place, and for the nixt it was fund that the towne had no money to give, but committit to the magistrates to doe their best with the Ritmaster to put him by, on easie terms if possible." In May, King Charles writes from his Court at Stirling, desiring that the Magistrates, Council, and community of Glasgow would advance in loan £500 sterling, a portion of which was raised from the teinds and by advances from four private burgesses—William Home, James Armour, Thomas Campbell, and James Kincaid. The sad shifts to which the burgh was reduced between the exactions of Charles and Cromwell is brought out with much simple pathos in a resolution come to, we may well believe, reluctantly, to close Hutchesons' Hospital, completed only two years previously, "for the entertainment of poor, aged, and decripit men to be placed therein." On June 3, 1652, "the Proveist, Balyeis, and Counsell, haveing seriouslie takine to their consideratioune the present estaite and conditioune of the foiresaid Hospitall, and finding that the haill sowmes of money now awine to the house will scairce pay the debt awine for its pairt of the Gorballis boght, and that there is no rent quhairwith to keep the boyes in the house or to hold the scoolmaister as he hes bein heirtofoir, seeing the haill rent, almost that the said Hospitoll hes to susteine any of these consistis most of the lands of Gorballis, quhilk has now beine eattine upe and destroyed these twa yeiris bygane. . . . . It is thairfor resolvit that the fyve poor boyes that is presentlie in the house be put home to thair parentis, and the maister of the hous to pay thair parents for thair enterteinment as he and they best can agree." In like manner the Deacon-Convener of the Trades' House, Manasses Lyle, made an appeal to the Council in November of the same year regarding the "poore decayit brethrein" impoverished through the wasting of Gorbals lands belonging to the Crafts. On Christmas Day certain skilled men were instructed to be chosen to divide the Gorbals barony among the three purchasing bodies—the Council, the Hospital, and the Trades House. Matters would appear to have mended with the town a little before the

Restoration, as in June, 1660, high public rejoicings were held in celebration of the event, and two hogsheads of wine provided for the use of the soldiers in town.

Next to exactions by Cromwell, Glasgow suffered grievously from pestilence and fire during the period embraced in the new volume of "Minutes," and referred to in many common histories of the City. The pestilence would appear to have been most virulent in the summer of 1648, quartermasters being appointed on 22nd July to inspect the town, to discharge the inhabitants from repairing to wine or alehouses, and to refrain from wandering about the streets. On 5th August the pestilence is described as "growne hotter nor hes beine seene heirtofoire," and ten new persons were appointed special inspectors, with magisterial power. Seven days later, when travelling to Edinburgh was prohibited, the disease is described as still increasing "in ane more hot maner than hes beine seene and knowne heirtofor to any now liveing, quhairby manie familees are removeit out to the Muir." Two thousand merks were at this time voted by the Council for relief of the poor sufferers. Later in the season an additional surgeon was introduced into the City, " Becaus of the neid the towne stands in of some qualified chirurgeonne, and that thair is ain large commendatioune gevine to Arthour Tempill, ane of that professione, tharfor ordaines the Deene of Gild and his brethrein to receave him burges and gild brother in hopes of his good service." Under date 22nd June, 1652, it is recorded, "Forsameikill as it has pleased God to raise on Thuirsday last was the 17 of this instant, ane suddent fyre in the house of Mr. James Hamiltoune above the Croce, quhilk has consumet that close, the haill close on both sydes belonging to William Stewart, Thomas Norvell, and others, ... the haill housis bak and foir upon bothe syds of the Saltmercat," with houses on the west of Gallowgate and north side of Briggate, "quhairby efter compt it is fund that thair will be neir four scoir closses all burnt, estimat to about ane thowsand punds, so that unless spedie remidie be useit and help sought out fra such as hes power and whois hartis God sall move, it is lyklie that the towne sall come to outer ruein." Commissioners were at once sent over the country for contributions in aid of the distressed; tradesmen were permitted to be drawn from any quarter they could be got, and in September Parliament made the welcome grant of £1,000 sterling, from the treasury of sequestrations in Scotland, for relief of the sufferers.

Among the more miscellaneous entries, several of great interest (only to be mentioned briefly here) will be found, relating to Hutchesons' Hospital and School, to Zachray Boyd and his "Mortifications," to the University, to Principal Robert Baillie, translated from Kilwinning to Glasgow, and to nearly every craft incorporated within the burgh, the latter frequently complaining of the interference of non-freemen, and the injury of their patrimony by the English. Some notices also occur of the Grammar-school and Library-house, James Colquhoun receiving on 3rd January, 1634, one hundred and ten pounds for completing the latter, "casting the town's arms thairon, gilting of the Bischop's armis, for the pains taken be him at Robiestoun Loche, and in making ane of the lyoun's mouthis at the spoutis of the Tolbuith." Sharp steps would appear to have been taken November, 1635, for raising the status of the Water Bailie, the Council having then considered "the great contempt the place of watter bailyearie within this burgh is fallen in be the admissioun thairto of divers decayed and depauperat persounes, quhilk tendis greatly to the prejudice of the haill inhabitants of this burgh and river, and thairfor they being most willeing to raise the same into the old worthie and laudable estait quhairin it once wes, they haif concluidet ane of the best sort and rank of the Counsell to be electit and choysen for dischargeing of the said place, and his electione, with the forme thairof, and his jurisdictionn to be set down on Settirday next." The Fleshers are censured July, 1647, in so far as they had slighted the town by sending in no flesh to the market, and "becaus it is verie needfull that the towne be servit with vivers," it is ordained, &c., "to grant licence and libertie to all men in the countrey to bring in flesche, or beif and muttonne, and all other sort of flesche, all the dayes in the weik, and they sall have libertie to sell the same at all occasionnes frie of payment of any excyis till Lambes nixt." In January, 1651, attendance at Council came to be regulated with greater strictness than formerly. It was then appointed that "all quha comes not in tymeouslie without lawfull reasone shall pay sax shillings, to be immediatlie put in the poores box."

GLASGOW CHAMBER OF COMMERCE.

UNDER the somewhat unpromising title of "Curiosities," a contribution of great and permanent interest to local literature has just (1881) been made by Mr. George Stewart, librarian of the Chamber of Commerce, now within a short time of completing the hundredth year of its useful existence. "Curiosities of Citizenship" is not only apt by itself to convey an erroneous notion of Mr. Stewart's labours, but the phrase falls much short of doing justice to the contents of his book. It is in only a very remote sense a collection of "Curiosities" at all, whether the word is taken as applicable to individuals or to the manner in which they become vested with citizenship. Our early Buchanans, Glassfords, Stirlings, Monteiths, and Finlays were nothing of the nature of "Curiosities," and might rather have been inclined to resent the application to themselves of such a term. "Bob Dragon" was certainly a typical Glasgow "Curiosity" in person as well as in habits, but to run the risk of including such a character in a history devoted to men like David Dale, or the Tennants, or Orrs, besides those already mentioned, is apt to lead to serious misapprehension. It can only now be hoped that Mr. Stewart's work will not be judged by its title-page exclusively. Our early merchants, no less than the Chamber they had the far-seeing wisdom to establish, well deserved such a full, accurate, and appreciative record as has been put together by Mr. Stewart concerning them. If their rise was not curious in the sense of being odd, it must always remain wonderful; and yet, apart from their exceptionally humble beginnings, their enterprise, thrift, and industry only secured the reward still daily reaped in the shape of affluence, position, and power. Mr. Stewart has arranged his book on the most simple and obvious lines, admirably fitted to carry out the design contemplated in publication. Some time ago, he writes, the directors of the Chamber of Commerce suggested the preparation of a few notes descriptive of the circumstances giving rise to the Chamber, and of the early transactions forming subjects of deliberation and discussion. Mr. Stewart readily acted upon the suggestion, and confesses that he found the study one of great interest. It occurred to him, however, that many curious and complicated details might be rendered more attractive and interesting if, instead of being presented in a dry historical or statistical form, they could in some way be associated with the lives and labours of the most notable of those men who were the early directors and members of the Chamber, and to whom, it is no exaggeration to say, modern Glasgow owes a debt of honour and gratitude she can never pay. Preceded by a chapter on the condition of Glasgow at the Union of the Parliaments, there falls to be noticed in this way at considerable length the Buchanans of Drumpeller and Mount Vernon in connection with the great Virginia trade, Charles Tennant of St. Rollox, with the Macraes of Ayrshire, and bleaching chemicals; David Dale of Rosebank, and the rise of the cotton industry; George Macintosh of Dunchattan, and his cudbear works at the Craigs Park, Ark Lane; John Monteith of Anderston, and early weaving; the Stirlings of Cordale and Dalquhurn, famous for their calico printing and dyeing; Henry Riddell, Virginia merchant, deeply concerned in the extension of the City westwards to George Square. J. C. Campbell of Clathick, John Robertson of Plantation, and Robert Carrick may be confidently accepted in illustration of such commercial enterprises as were represented in their day by the Thistle Bank, the Glasgow Arms Bank, and the Ship Bank. Following these, Mr. Stewart presents a facsimile list of the original subscribers to the Glasgow Chamber of Commerce, and a historical sketch, which might have been much enlarged to the advantage of the reader, concerning the origin and objects of the Chamber, followed up by a notice more or less minute of almost every merchant connected with it in early days resident in Glasgow, Greenock, or Paisley. Mr. Stewart describes the commercial prospects of Glasgow at the close of the American War in 1782 as of the most gloomy kind. The great Virginia trade, he writes, which for a long series of years employed the largest share of the city capital, was then lost. Cotton-spinning, with its accompanying industries, was yet unknown; in fact, except a growing traffic with the West Indies and the manufacture of a few domestic fabrics, the trade of the town was extremely limited. It therefore became apparent that a means of combined action for opening up new sources of trade and commerce, and of organising a method whereby direct and efficient communication between the trade of the West and the Government and Legislature could be established, was a pressing necessity. The result of much eager discussion was the formation of the Glasgow Chamber of Commerce, the first institution of its kind in the kingdom, the Edinburgh Chamber, not being established till nearly three years later (December, 1785).

Guided by strictly official records, Mr. Stewart is no doubt correct in mentioning that the first formal meeting of the Chamber was held early in January (most likely Thursday the 2nd), 1783; but, as appears from the newspapers of the day, the scheme had been wrought into practical shape a month or two earlier. In November, 1782, intimation was made that a plan for establishing a Chamber of Commerce and Manufactures in Glasgow, comprehending the towns of Paisley, Greenock, Port-Glasgow, and places adjacent, had been submitted by the Lord Provost to the consideration of the merchants, traders, and manufacturers in these towns. In November, 1782, many merchants had concurred in what came to be the real, practical objects of the Chamber as more minutely defined at a later date—viz., to promote such branches of trade as are more peculiar to this country; to establish local rules for the convenience and assistance of foreign and inland traders and manufacturers; to discuss all memorials and representations from members of the Chamber in matters regarding trade; to afford them assistance and relief in negotiating public business; to assist in procuring redress of any grievance, hardship, or oppression affecting any particular branch of trade or manufacture; to consider all matters affecting the Corn Laws in this part of the United Kingdom, for the purpose of supporting the industrious poor; and, in general, to take cognisance of every matter and thing in the least degree connected with the interests of commerce or manufactures. It was agreed at this preliminary meeting in November, 1782, that the care of the Chamber should be committed to the thirty Directors, chosen from the most intelligent class of merchants and manufacturers. The names of those selected at the first formal meeting in January following may recall some of the then important Glasgow houses to our older readers:—Patrick Colquhoun, Lord Provost (afterwards the well-known London Magistrate), chairman; James M'Gregor, deputy-chairman; John Glassford, James Dennistoun, sen., Wm. Cunningham, J. Campbell (Clathick), Wm. French, James Somervill, Henry Riddell, Robert Dunmore, John Robertson, Wm. Coates, John Lawrie, George Bogle, Robert Cowan, Gilbert Hamilton, Archibald Graham, James Gemmell, Hugh Moody, John Stirling, John Brown, jun., Walter Stirling, James Finlay, William Lang, David Dale, Dugald Bannatyne, Alex. M'Alpine—nearly all of Glasgow; Robert Fulton, John Wilson (father of "Christopher North"), and William Carlile, Paisley. At an adjourned meeting held on the 8th January in the Assembly Room, Gilbert Hamilton, merchant, was appointed secretary, and John Maxwell of Dargavel, writer, clerk of submissions to the Chamber. Early in August members held their first meeting under the Royal Charter obtained 31st July, when a vote of thanks and presentation of plate was resolved on to Lord Provost Colquhoun, LL.D., "for the uncommon attention and pains bestowed by him upon the business of the society." Dr. Colquhoun, engaged from youth in the Virginia trade, purchased part of the estate of Woodcroft, now Kelvingrove, but removed in 1792 to London, where, as police magistrate, he wrought out a variety of important reforms in the police system of the Metropolis. At present (1881) the oldest living members of the Chamber are Mr. Walter Buchanan, ex-M.P. (chairman in 1836), with W. F. Burnley and W. H. Dobbie—the latter now of Edinburgh.

The Chamber was not long in setting to the serious work before it in connection with the shipping, manufacturing, and general commercial enterprise of the time. In 1668, with the view of overcoming the difficulties of the river, then in a state of nature, the Magistrates of the City purchased sixty acres of ground at Newark for the purpose of building New, or, as it afterwards came to be called, Port, Glasgow. As certain traders sought systematically to evade the dues levied at that port by landing their goods at other places on the Clyde, the Merchants' House in 1705 went as far as it could in passing a resolution ordaining, under severe penalties, that all vessels bound for that river should land the cargo at Port-Glasgow, except in cases of necessity. At the second annual meeting of the Chamber of Commerce held in the Town Hall, January, 1784, it was resolved to apply to the Commissioners of Customs and Exchequer for an establishment in Glasgow for "proving" merchandise, as in London, whereby the necessity of opening debenture and bounty goods at the ports of exportation might be rendered unnecessary in future. The Chamber naturally contended that if their desire was carried out many existing abuses would be prevented, while it would tend at the same time to remove the prejudices against local manufactures, "which, by being opened, exposed to the weather, and improperly repacked, often occasioned them to be found in bad order when landed at a foreign market." Another serious matter engaged the attention of the same meeting, representations being then made that certain traders between Greenock and America, had been in the habit of plundering the revenue and defrauding the underwriters, by first landing their goods surreptitiously and then wilfully destroying their vessels. The Chamber therefore resolved to use every effort for the purpose of bringing such persons to justice, and in addition pressed upon shipowners the necessity of exercising increased precaution in the engagement of seamen. That the action of the Chamber in this grave question was not premature, may be inferred with certainty from criminal proceedings which took place at Edinburgh on the 23rd April following. On that day, and at the instance of Robert Hunter and others, underwriters in London, James

Herdman, John M'Iver, and Archibald Macallum, merchants in Greenock, and jointly concerned in the ownership of the brigantines "Endeavour" and "New York," were committed to the Tolbooth, charged with feloniously sinking ships at sea with intent to defraud the underwriters. Application for their imprisonment on the capital charge was made before the Judge of the High Court of Admiralty, but an additional reason for the prisoners being then in Edinburgh arose from an apprehended attempt at escape, through the bad condition of the prison in Paisley, and the overcrowded state of that of Glasgow, in which jails they had been confined for some time past. , The trial came on before Judge Pringle, 19th May following, when, after an argument on the statutes dealing with capital and arbitrary punishments for the offences charged, the Crown restricted the indictment, and the jury found the panels guilty. The sentence was—"That they shall stand at the pillory in Glasgow, July 28 (Wednesday), for the space of one hour with a rope about each of their necks, and bare-headed," with the following label affixed to their breasts:—"Here stands John M'Iver and Archibald Macallum, infamous persons, who did wickedly procure holes to be bored in the ship 'Endeavour,' in order to sink the same and thereby defraud the underwriters." They were also banished Scotland for life, and, in case of their return, were to be imprisoned for one year, and to be publicly whipped on the first Wednesday of every month during such imprisonment. A Bill of Suspension was presented to the Court of Justiciary, but the Judges repelled the reasons, and, finding no just cause for mitigation of punishment, the panels were duly pilloried, agreeable to their sentence. The prisoner Herdman was tried 28th July, and being found guilty was sentenced, like his companions in guilt, to stand in the Glasgow pillory, and be thereafter banished the kingdom.

Although the "Wealth of Nations" was not published till 1776, twelve years after Adam Smith resigned his professorial chair in Glasgow University, yet his teaching had begun to exercise a strong influence in his lifetime among members of the Glasgow Chamber of Commerce, as may be gathered from the proceedings at a meeting of cotton and muslin manufacturers called in August,

1784, for the purpose of protesting against the new scale of duties then imposed upon their goods. The minutes set forth that when the first class of cottons and muslins peculiar to the West Country trade were taken at a fair average, the new tax would be about 5 per cent. of the value, but as the second class would chiefly include the kind of goods known as 6-4ths muslins, the tax of 2d. 6-20ths per yard would amount on an average to 7 or 8 per cent. of value. Expressing a hearty willingness to share in the general burdens of the country, the Glasgow manufacturers yet considered themselves unfairly matched against the East India Company, in so far as their home produce was selected for taxation at a time when the Company was supported at the public expense with little short of one million of money, free of interest, which would nearly equal the whole produce of the tax on cottons. The manufacturers therefore concluded by protesting against the competition as unfair, partial, and unwise, at least so long as the Company enjoyed its English monopoly and pecuniary aid from the State. Many readers still engaged in business will recollect that one of Kirkman Finlay's great services was the assistance he gave to break up this monopoly, and the example he set in opening up the extensive Indian trade. The first ship direct from the Clyde to India—the van of a vast fleet, Mr. Stewart justly remarks—was freighted by Kirkman Finlay, the "Buckinghamshire," of 600 tons, being sent out for Calcutta direct.

Organised mainly for the purpose of serving commerce, the Chamber has occasionally unbended from its high duties and gracefully acknowledged services rendered indirectly to merchants, forgetting even for a moment that her symbols are those of peace and not of war. In the course of the great struggle for independence by the American Colonies, aided by France, a number of the more important West India Islands—Tobago and St. Christopher among the rest—was seized on behalf of his Most Christian Majesty by General the Marquis Bouillé, famous in many lands before that for magnanimity no less than bravery, and destined to high command afterwards in the unhappy contest carried on by his brother nobles against the Republic. Having done all that was possible to protect property in the islands—and in much of it Glasgow merchants had a deep interest—the Chamber of Commerce in the first year of its corporate existence, agreed to present a sword to the gallant Marquis, in testimony of their appreciation of the high qualities manifested in his late command, when, in the career of victory, "he softened the horrors of war in a manner hitherto unknown, and protected the property of individuals in those moments of distress, when the vanquished were accustomed to experience devastation and ruin." The sword, made after an ancient Scottish pattern, and reputed at the time as the finest ever made in the country, was conveyed by General Melvill to the Marquis, who duly acknowledged the gift with expressions of esteem for Great Britain, and the most lively sentiments of gratitude to "the gentlemen of the Chamber of Commerce."

The above incident, taken almost at random from the first year in the history of the Chamber, may indicate to Mr. Stewart in what manner, if not to what extent, he might have usefully shown, with more minuteness than he has done, the more important questions taken up from time to time by the Chamber, as well as the influence it may be presumed to have exercised in their settlement. With this exception, no words except words of praise need be used in describing his labour. The merchant, the historian, the genealogist, will all find it full of excellent matter fitly arranged. Even those curious on the subject of street nomenclature will find it of much use, for many an important thoroughfare, many a street, lane, and square owes its name to members of the Chamber described by Mr. Stewart.

OLD GLASGOW HOUSES.

SOME years since there was issued a handsome folio volume filled with 100 highly-finished photographs of mansions in and around Glasgow, historically interesting, as being associated with the names of old City merchants, or with the families of landed proprietors. In addition to the excellent pictures by Annan, each mansion had devoted to it a few pages of letterpress, descriptive of its age and history, with some account of the families, past and present, reared within its walls. When it is mentioned that many of these sketches came from the pen of our amiable and accomplished friend, the late John Buchanan, LL.D., assurance was given that the duty of preparing the text had been committed to most competent writers, familiar alike with the details of burghal life and property, as well as trained in the somewhat special pursuit of genealogical investigation. The impression was limited to a little over 100 copies, almost instantly taken up by subscribers. Since the date of publication the chance of obtaining the volume has only rarely been afforded by sales when libraries were being broken up, and when nobody thought of grudging a very large advance on the original cost. The book was a rarity, and it was besides—what is not always the case with book rarities—a substantial and valuable addition to local historical literature. There was room at any time for a new impression. Under these circumstances, and as applications for the work were much increased of late (1882), Mr. Maclehose issued a new edition of 225 copies, fully subscribed for, in like manner to the first. It is, indeed, in some respects rather a preferable volume, the opportunity of reprinting the sheets having been taken advantage of to correct a few unavoidable slips in names and dates, as well as to bring in a general way the family records to a point nearer the present day. Annan's photographs are still perfectly fresh and lustrous. They have been taken in almost every instance from such a point of view as gives a fair notion of the fabric, with the exception probably of Garscube, where we miss the fine old English manor front, designed with so much taste by Mr. Burn. In a book otherwise handsome, entertaining, and useful—a book, besides, which hardly makes any appeal to the general public for patronage, it may appear ungracious even to refer to apparent defects; but one or two will be noticed in turning over the leaves. The photographs, though strictly speaking correct and bright, are yet cold and stiff—a result largely due to the fact of many of them having been taken in the winter season, when trees stand bare of foliage, and produce startling pictorial effects with their skeleton branches. In many cases the bleak aspect outside contrasts strongly with the comfort and good cheer which it may be presumed was enjoyed within. Then the two maps of Glasgow, showing the City at different dates, are on much too small a scale to permit of tracing out streets or properties referred to in the text. A full-page, or even a double-page, map of the dates given would have been of considerable service to the reader. Lastly, we miss one or two mansions interesting on their own account, or as being associated with Glasgow merchants. There is Cordale, with its memories of the elder Stirlings, Campbell, Sir William Hamilton, and "Cyril Thornton;" there is the stately pile of Tillichewan, acquired by one who was in many respects a typical merchant of the early years of the present century; and there is the fine old house of Gartshore, now absorbed in the Gartsherrie connection.

The rise of the great industries of Glasgow not dating much beyond the latter quarter of last century, the history of these old merchants comes to be really a history of the commercial enterprise of the period read in the light of their daily experience and domestic usages. Would we know the facts about the tobacco or wine trade, about coal or iron, about spinning or weaving, where need we look with more confidence than in the family records of citizens so prominent as the Buchanans, the Bogles, and the Glassfords, the Hamiltons, Douglasses, and Dunlops? It is only a pity the labour was not undertaken earlier. Between improvement schemes and railway operations the City has become a new place to citizens who might be offended if they were called elderly. The Cathedral, to be sure, St. Andrew's, and the Tron Steeple still remain; there is a Gallowgate and a High Street in name, though the first is changed to a broad and well-built thoroughfare, and the last pulled down in many quarters beyond hope of identification with old land-marks, but no assurance can be given for the preservation even in name of old buildings in the outskirts. Of the 100 mansions figured in the work, ten have gone since it was first issued. North Woodside and Camplefield were spared just long enough to have their features taken in 1870; since then Annfield, Gilmorehill, Kelvinbank, Kelvinside, Meadow Park, Possil, Stobcross, and Whitehill have all disappeared. It is appropriately remarked in the introduction that those whom people here used to own as their natural leaders were "kent folk," who made no pretence to count them their equals, but who shared their feelings, opinions, and prejudices—who spent their lives within hearing of the Tolbooth chimes—who found in Glasgow, kirk and market, the centre of their interests in business and out of business. Every year the notables of our day grow more of strangers to the place that they live by—spend fewer hours in its smoke and din; outside their own little circle are more and more unknown even by face, till it has come to this, that a man may be in the foremost rank on 'Change, may by all who know him be looked up to and recognised as exceptionally fitted by talent, knowledge, and force of character for the highest post in the gift of citizens, and may yet to the bulk of these be so unknown that his candidature is resented as the intrusion of a stranger.

Mention has already been made of the important services rendered to the volume by the late John Buchanan, LL.D. Availing themselves of his account of Slatefield, where his mother, Catherine Miller, was born, the editor of the new issue takes occasion to refer in a few graceful and appropriate lines to some of his many merits. It is mentioned of him that he was well read in general literature, and in history, especially Scottish history; but his favourite study was archæology, and most of all the archæology of his native City. "He loved old Glasgow with a lover's love, and he made it such a study from boyhood that a knowledge of it died with him, never to be replaced. A diligent student may recover as much of the past as lies buried in books and cartularies, and there is some hope that this work may erelong be done by one every way fitted for it. But John Buchanan had a minute personal knowledge of those who once lived here that records cannot give. The Glasgow of a hundred years ago he knew as few know the Glasgow of to-day. Its old merchants and bankers, its ministers and professors, its beaux and its belles, still lived for him; he had known them from their cradles, and their fathers and mothers before them ; he knew where they had been trained, and the use they made of their training; whom they had married, and whom they had tried to marry; where they lived, and how they lived; where they died, and where they lie. And he had the rare art to make them live again for our benefit. At his bidding they rose from the Ramshorn or the High Kirkyard, and once more paced the planestanes in red cloak and cocked hat, or tramped the Trongate in pattens and caléche." In the "Mansions" his help was invaluable. No one but himself could have written "Kelvingrove," "Stobcross," and other papers readily recognised. It was hoped he would have given his help to the new issue, but his final illness prevented him from doing more than making a few verbal alterations on what he had already written. Dr. John Buchanan died (June, 1878) as the "Country Houses" was being finished. In a brief introductory advertisement, the publisher, Mr. Maclehose, expresses warm thanks to his friends, John Guthrie Smith and John Oswald Mitchell, for the unwearied labour they also have bestowed on the new volume. The papers, it is mentioned, have been not only revised and enlarged, but in many cases entirely re-written by them. Only those who have tried this kind of work can have any idea of the amount of research and patience that is necessary to secure accuracy; and none but those who have been associated with Glasgow and its history could have accomplished the task. The result is a work which the publisher may well describe as rare in character, if it be not indeed the solitary example of its class.

A GLASGOW CATHEDRAL RELIC.

A SCULPTURED memorial, suggestive in the highest degree of the ancient ecclesiastical dignity of Glasgow, was removed in 1878 under circumstances somewhat unusual, yet at the same time extremely interesting and appropriate.

While the Cathedral itself was saved from destruction at the Reformation by the energetic action of the City trades, the adjoining Archiepiscopal Castle or Palace was allowed to fall gradually into decay. So late, comparatively, as 1715 it was hastily fitted up as a prison for 300 Highland rebels, but for all really useful or permanent purposes it may be set down as having been in ruins. In 1720, a Robert Thomson, merchant, who lived near the fabric, represented to the Barons of Exchequer that the Palace, not having been inhabited for many years, was then in ruins, and men were getting so barbarous and unjust as to carry off stones and timber for their own use "to the shame and disgrace of the Christian religion." Nothing, or rather worse than nothing, was then done to arrest decay, and in 1755 the Magistrates (George Murdoch being Provost at the time) gave formal permission that Robert Tennant, builder, might use the castle as a quarry, wherein stones might be obtained for the purpose of building the old Saracen's Head Inn. Not far from the castle, and giving direct access to its chief entrance-hall, was the gate-house and arched gateway, erected by Archbishop Gavin Dunbar, 1524–47, and adorned with what must have been at the time a most effective sculptured emblazon of his own family armorial bearings, surmounted by the Royal Arms of Scotland. When the work of spoliation was going on at the palace, this portion of the plunder would appear to have fallen into the hands of one, Charles Selkirk, who, being a man of some little taste, as it was understood in those days, and actuated probably by some feeling of compunction regarding the abuse of ecclesiastical ornaments, saved the armorial, and afterwards inserted it high up in the back part of a tenement erected by him near the foot of High Street in 1760. This building now forms part of the premises known as No. 22 (east side), owned by Messrs. John Millar & Sons, drapers, as figured and described in "Glasgow, Ancient and Modern." This interesting memorial of Archbishop Dunbar may be described as consisting of three portions, measuring in all 7 feet by 3 feet 3 inches—(1) The Royal Arms of Scotland, a lion rampant within the double tressure, and unicorn supporters bearing the letter I, and figure 5, most likely by permission of King James V. himself, who had in early life been the pupil, and to its sad close at Solway Moss, continued to be the friend and patron of the archbishop; (2) The armorial bearings of that branch of the Dunbar family to which the arch-prelate belonged, viz., Dunbar of Mochrum, Wigtownshire, three cushions within the double tressure of Scotland, being the arms of Randolph, Earl of Moray, assumed by the family of Dunbar, subsequent to the marriage of the son of the Earl of March to a daughter of the former house. It is possible there may have been a mallet or some such ornament occupying the space between the three cushions, but now mouldered away. The third or lowest division in the group is made up by the armorial bearings of James Marshal, Sub-Dean of the Cathedral, friend and executor to the archbishop—viz., a chevron cheque, between two martlets in chief and one in case, a rose occupying the middle chief point. Under each shield is a scroll which may have borne an inscription or motto not now to be traced. On either side are two ornamented pillars, the dexter, or right, now slightly broken. A line or two regarding the archbishop's career will best explain the story of the removal of this interesting memorial. A younger brother of Sir John Dunbar of Mochrum, by Dame Jannet Stewart, of the house of Garlies, Gavin was educated at the University of Glasgow, became Dean of Moray, tutor, as has been already mentioned, to the young Prince James, and was also raised to the dignity of Prior of Whithorn, a religious foundation in his native county, reared in commemoration of the labours of St. Ninian. By a curious coincidence this earliest of Christian missionaries in the north had fully a thousand years before Dunbar's date consecrated for Christian burial the ground by the Molendinar, where St. Mungo reared his first cathedral, and then passed to Galloway, where he laid the foundation of that religious establishment governed in later days by one who was also destined to fill a chief seat among the hierarchy of the West. On the removal of Beatoun to the Primatal See of St. Andrews in 1524, Gavin Dunbar was made Archbishop of Glasgow, and filled the See till his death in 1547, when his body was placed within a tomb prepared by himself in the Cathedral chancel. No portion of it is now to be seen, but some traces of the erection and also of the remains were thought to have been discovered in the course of repairs made in May, 1856. As Dunbar had succeeded one Beatoun, so he in turn was to be succeeded by another James Beatoun, the Cardinal's nephew, and who proved to be the last of the pre-Reformation Archbishops. Dunbar was elevated to the dignity of Lord Chancellor in 1528, and was made a Lord of the Articles in 1532, the year when the College of Justice was instituted. The present (1878) lineal representative of the Dunbars of Mochrum is Sir William Dunbar, eldest son of James, second son of the fifth Baronet. Sir William sat for the Wigtown district of burghs from 1859 to 1865, and was during the same period a Lord of the Treasury and Keeper of the Great Seal for Scotland to His Royal Highness the Prince of Wales. He also represents the Dunbars, hereditary Sheriffs of Morayshire, one of whom, it may be mentioned, was killed at Donibristle Castle by Huntly and his party, along with "the Bonnie Earl of Murray" of ballad fame. Engaged in the erection of a new mansion on his Wigtownshire property, and hearing through ex-Bailie Salmon that the memorial stone from the Archbishop's gateway was still where it was placed, in much the same condition as in 1760, Sir William indicated a desire to rescue it from obscurity, and give it a place of honour in the new residence of the family to which the great churchman belonged. Coming to hear of the wish, Bailie Millar, proprietor of the premises in High Street, readily placed the old armorial stone at the disposal of Sir William. The offer being accepted in the same courteous spirit in which it was made, the stone was withdrawn from its secluded and all but inaccessible niche to adorn the family pile of the Archbishop's home, and to revive his fame within a few miles of the priory where he bore rule.

THE SPREULLS OF GLASGOW.

REPRESENTING through his mother the old Glasgow family of Spreull, and in possession besides of several curious memorials relating to "Bass John," Mr. J. W. Burns of Kilmahew and Cumbernauld, rendered a service to general as well as local history by gathering together and printing in a neat form the miscellaneous papers concerning one who was at once an intelligent advocate of the truth and a sharp sufferer in its behalf. Born in the year of King Charles's surrender to the Scottish army at Newark, John Spreull was nearly old enough to remember the execution at Whitehall, and is almost certain to have been engaged in business soon after the Restoration. Seized during the "killing" time which set in after the affair at Bothwell Brig, and declining to give any information to the Privy Council, either as to his connection with Cargill or knowledge of the pretended plot against the Duke of York, John Spreull was first subjected to the cruel torture of the "boot," fined £500 sterling, and then thrown into the noisome Bass Prison, where he lay with other sufferers for over six years, when he was released unconditionally. The story will be found told at considerable length in Woodrow's "Sufferings," the historian, who appears to have been acquainted with Spruell, making special mention of the different examinations before and after torture, and of the public indignation excited by the cruelty manifested throughout the proceedings against this unoffending victim of tyranny. From his long imprisonment Spreull acquired the name of "Bass John," whereof (writes Woodrow) "he needs not be ashamed." In later and happier days the sufferings in and out of the Bass suggested a family crest of a palm-tree held down by two weights on either side, with the motto, "*Sub pondere cresco*." Although connected with a long line of Glasgow Spreulls, "Bass John" was of Paisley birth. His father was a bailie and merchant of that burgh, connected with the Cowden family, suffering, like his son, for refusing to accept the ensnaring oaths of the day, but of high repute among his townsfolk for having purchased from the Dundonald family the right of electing their own magistrates. His wife was Janet, daughter of James Alexander, Paisley, and Janet Maxwell of Pollok. Failing issue from any of his three sons or four daughters, "Bass John's" position as head of the family passed to James Spreull, surgeon, Paisley, who married his cousin Ann, only child of John Spreull or Shortridge, town-clerk, Glasgow, author of "Some Remarkable Passages of the Lord's Providence." From this marriage came an only daughter, who, in 1700, married James Shortridge, and carried with her as "tocher" the property adjoining the old Hutcheson Hospital, north side of Trongate, on which site came to be built the entailed property long familiar to readers of the "Herald" as "Spreull's Court." In "Glasgow Past and Present" mention is made of the town-clerk's name as being originally Shortridge, but changed under the conditions of a legacy left by Miss Spreull. The descent is not so clear at this point as a genealogist would like, but from William Shortridge, of Messrs Todd & Shortridge, of Levenfield Printworks, came Mrs. Burns, wife of the late James of Bloomhill, Cardross, and mother of the present John William Burns of Kilmahew and Cumbernauld. After the Revolution Settlement "Bass John" would appear to have taken an active part in the politics of his day, and, as a prosperous Glasgow merchant, subscribed what was then the large sum of £1,000 towards the Darien scheme of his friend Paterson, whom he a good deal resembled for knowledge and enterprise in commercial affairs. Woodrow describes John Spreull in general terms as an apothecary, but long before the Union he would seem to have been engaged in an extensive foreign trade, as he mentions in the "Account current betwixt Scotland and England," published in 1705, that he had dealt in pearls for forty years and more, "and yet, to this day, I could never sell a necklace of fine Scots pearl in Scotland, nor yet fine pendants, the generality seeking for Oriental pearl, because farther fetcht; yet, for commendation of our own pearl, at this very day I can show some of our own Scots pearl as fine, lucid, and more transparent than any Oriental; it's true the Oriental can be easier matcht, because they are all of a yellow water, yet foreigners covet Scots pearl." Another personal glimpse of John Spreull is presented through a "Representation" in reference to a seat in the Tron Church, wherein mention is made that "in or about anno 1686, sometime before the late glorious Revolution, I was, in God's good time and providence, delivered out of my prison in the Bass, and then had my abode and dwelling-house in Provost Gilson's land, and so consequently I was a parishioner in the Outer High Church, in which I could never procure a seat for myself and family until Provost Pedie gave one in anno 1693, for which I willingly and duely paid the rent, and kept my own Parish Church, under the Rev. Mr. Alexander Hastie's ministry, in obedience to the comely Order of Christ's Church until anno 1700; when I had built my house in the Trongate, by which I became a parishioner in the late Rev. Mr. Neil Gillies' quarter in the Tron Church; after which I tryed for a seat in that church, and often regrated my want of a seat to my minister, the said Mr. Neil Gillies, while alive, and he desired me to delay a little till the new church was finished, and then it would be endeavoured, by the help of the Lord, to amend, rectifie the disorders and inconveniences in the seats of the kirks, that had been given promiscuously, to persons of different parishes, contrary to the rule of God's Word, the practice of purest churches, and contrary to the Acts of our General Assembly." These "Miscellaneous Writings," by John Spreull, were admirably printed at the University Press by Mr. Maclehose, illustrated with a number of facsimiles of documents relating to the imprisonment in the Bass, and a characteristic portrait of the old merchant, from an original by Sir Godfrey Kneller. Mr. Burns deserves thanks for his pleasant, dainty little quarto volume.

ANDREW MELVILLE IN GLASGOW.

GRAVE as the subject is, and scholarly as should be the treatment, it is not easy to repress a smile when remembering that fuss and folly have before now paid an unconscious tribute to wisdom by directing the attention of thinking people to some fact or circumstance liable to be overlooked even by those who make ecclesiastical history a special study. Neither the time, place, nor manner of bringing such things up may have any sort of appropriateness—it is on most occasions far otherwise—but none the less a good end through time comes to be secured. The discussion (1884) on Andrew Melville's alleged advice to pull down the Cathedral as a seat of idolatry may well be lifted from the dusty area of the Tron Kirk, and looked at in connection with the presence in our City of a University dignitary rivalled by Buchanan alone among scholars of the Reformation period for learning and courage. Historically inaccurate as we judge Dr. Burns to be in his general statement—based on Spottiswood—the assumption prefacing the statement is still more liable to objection. So far from their being "little doubt" about the imputed vandalism, it has been disputed over and over again since Dr. M'Crie's Memoir of Melville appeared; nor even yet, with all the busy search made among ancient documents, has anything been found corroborative of a statement, not probably extraordinary in itself, considering the circumstances of the times, but made, it must be remembered, so far as known, on the single authority of a keen and active ecclesiastical opponent—an opponent none the less keen and active because he had himself been a pupil of Melville's in Glasgow, and undertook various repairs on the fabric of the Cathedral during his occupancy of the See. The harshness and even unfairness of Spottiswood to Melville has been frequently commented upon by historians and critics, some of his own communion, like Zouch, going the length of saying that the Archbishop was uniformly unfriendly to the memory of the great Presbyterian who, more than any other of his later days, combined the rarest gifts of learning with a spirit of independence, scorning danger however near, and hostility however powerful. Melville's valiant battle for the independence of the Kirk as against the State, bigoted and even mistaken as it may now appear in peaceful times, recalled to his contemporaries in no remote manner the mighty pretensions of Hildebrand and Becket. In answer to the charge made by Archbishop Spottiswood—a charge, it should always be remembered, otherwise unsupported, and, even if correctly stated, should no more be measured by present-day feelings or sentiments than the Cathedral itself should be confounded in its decay during Melville's time with its noble restoration in our own—the answer to the otherwise unsupported charge is of necessity based mainly on a kind of negative evidence, but, as will be shown below, on negative evidence not to be put lightly aside. Born 1545, only three years after Queen Mary, and one year before the martyrdom of George Wishart at St. Andrews, Melville was close on thirty years of age when he accepted an invitation from the General Assembly, backed by his preceptor Beza, to become Principal of Glasgow University, an office vacant through the death of Principal Davidson, who had struggled manfully, but with indifferent success, to save a remnant for learning from the remorseless plunderers of the old Church. As the professors of the higher branches had no salaries, but depended on their Church livings for support, the classes accustomed to gather round such chairs as then existed were broken up in the strife and well-nigh scattered abroad when Melville arrived at Glasgow in the autumn of 1574—only two years after the first Presbyterian minister obtained a footing in the City. Willocks had previously officiated as a Protestant, but Lauder, described as the last Roman Catholic "parson of Glasgow," was allowed to retain the benefice till his death. Roused into action through his natural zeal for Reformation principles, Melville selected a number of young men fairly grounded in the Latin language and introduced them to the knowledge of Greek, logic, rhetoric, mathematics, and geography, moral and natural philosophy, history and chronology, Hebrew, Chaldee, and divinity—a course of study designed to be completed in six years. James Melville, son of Richard, of Baldovy, and nephew of the Principal, was appointed to the office of "Regent" or Professor; but, in the course of a year or two, branches of learning were apportioned to other scholars, and ere the time arrived for closing the second session the drooping fortunes of the University founded by Bishop Turnbull were so far restored that students were preparing for attendance in all parts of the kingdom. In 1577 a new foundation by Royal Charter was obtained, and a gift made of the valuable living of Govan—a gift valuable to the Principal—less in a money point of view than because it gave him a status in the Church Courts to deliberate upon, advise, and direct the settlement of various ecclesiastical questions pressing for settlement in his time. Melville was—from deliberate conviction, it may be assumed—hostile to every modification of Prelacy, and in the Assembly held at Edinburgh, March, 1575—the first which had occurred since his admission to Glasgow—not only spoke as a Professor of Divinity against that mode of ecclesiastical government, but became a member of a committee appointed to prepare the Second Book of Discipline. Amid the discussions relating to the new Constitution for the Church, University education received a fair share of the Assembly's attention, and the resolution to erect a theological seminary within St. Andrews led to the removal of Melville from Glasgow. His office of Principal was formally resigned towards the end of November, 1580, " with infinite tears on both sides, those who had at first misliked and opposed him being forward to testify their regret at his departure." Isaac Walton, in like manner, although displeased with the freedom which Melville took with his favourite Church, does justice to his talents, judging him as second only to Buchanan, who may be said to belong to an earlier period, although he died advanced in age two years after Melville took up his residence in St. Andrews. The time spent in Glasgow, it will thus be seen, was a few months over six years. The only writing he is known to have published within that period was his "Carmen Mosis," a poetical paraphrase of the song of Moses, and a chapter of the book of Job, printed in Latin at Basle, 1573.

So far as the serious statement made by Archbishop Spottiswood is concerned, if the advice to pull down the Cathedral was ever given at all, it must have been among the last years of Melville's residence here—probably 1579—as King James, born May, 1567, is incidentally spoken of as not quite thirteen years of age. The Archbishop's narrative, written it may be partly when he filled the See of Glasgow, to which he was elevated on the death of Archbishop Bethune, 1603, thus proceeds :—" In Glasgow the next spring there happened a little disturbance by this occasion—The Magistrates of the City, by the earnest dealing of Mr. Andrew

Melvil and other ministers, had condescended to demolish the Cathedral, and build, with the material thereof, some little churches in other parts for the ease of the citizens. Divers reasons were given for it, such as the resort of superstitious people to do their devotion in that place; the huge vastness of the church, and that the voice of a preacher could not be heard by the multitudes that convened to sermon; the more commodious service of the people; and the removing of that idolatrous monument (so they called it) which was, of all the cathedrals in the country, only left unruined and in a possibility to be repaired. To do this work a number of quarriers, masons, and other workmen were conducted, and the day assigned when it should take beginning. Intimation being given thereof, and the workmen, by sound of a drum, warned to go into their work, the crafts of the City, in a tumult, took armes, swearing, with many oaths, that he who did cast down the first stone should be buried under it. Neither could they be pacified till the workmen were discharged by the Magistrates. A complaint was hereupon made and the principals cited before the Council for insurrection; where the King, not as then thirteen years of age, taking the protection of the crafts did allow the opposition they had made, and inhibited the ministers (for they were the complainers) to meddle any more in that business, saying 'that too many churches had been already destroyed, and that he would not tolerate more abuses in that kind.'" So far Spottiswood, as printed in the "Church and State of Scotland" by Spottiswood Society, vol. ii., p. 258. The reader must remember that the above tumult, from whatever cause it may have arisen, is not to be confounded with any excitement which may have been caused by the action of the Royal Commissioners under the somewhat drastic minute for "purification" of such edifices, passed by the Reformers in the summer of 1560. It is this earlier throwing out of the "idolatrous statues of saints" Scott is understood to have made Andrew Fairservice describe with such graphic force rather than an occurrence of twenty years later, when the images had been broken, the shrines rifled, and the fabric itself, much as it was prized by the City authorities, was fast hastening to decay, apparently through the poverty rather than the apathy of the people. Spared as the bare walls were at the time through the earnest intercession of the inhabitants, the architectural glory of the West had, as Sir Walter mentions, nearly "slipped the girths in gaun through siccan rough physic." Indeed the veneration entertained for the old fabric furnishes the best possible indirect answer to the charge brought against Melville and the City authorities of his day. Amid all the troubles which beset our local magistrates at and for years after the Reformation, few are more creditable to their enlightened zeal than those relating to watching and maintaining the Cathedral, of which they then became custodiers. Broken as the very earliest records are in sequence, those relating to this period are happily preserved in fair condition, and have been printed quite recently (1883) for the Burgh Records Society. Entries of the kind referred to regarding the Cathedral are so numerous that it is not easy to accept any statement regarding its proposed demolition in Melville's time, whether coming from friendly or hostile sources, without having corroborative evidence either from Council Minutes or Treasurer's Accounts, both of which are in existence, so far as known, in a complete form. But no entry, direct or indirect, lends any colour to such a charge. There are, on the other hand, as has been said, many tending to disprove it. With a circumstantiality hardly, it must be admitted, in keeping with pure invention, Archbishop Spottiswood makes mention of an appeal being made to the Council—presumably the Scottish Privy Council, although this need not be rashly accepted, the "Council of the King" continuing to be a term of varying import during the reign of James VI., as it had ever been from its first appearance in constitutional history. Sometimes it was subordinate to, and sometimes it overawed, three very distinct bodies concerned in the administration of justice—the Lords of the Articles, the Lords Auditors for Complaints, and the Court of Session. But if the Archbishop's reference is to the Council, as generally understood, here also the Records are silent as to any such complaint, or any other proceedings connected with the proposed destruction of the Cathedral. A recent volume of the series of Privy Council Records, edited under the authority of the Lord Clerk-Register by Professor Masson, embraces a period long anterior and subsequent to that in dispute (1579), and no such case is found recorded. Nor is there, so far as known, any corroboration to be had from other ecclesiastical historians—say Bishop Keith or Calderwood, or from any letter or memoir of the time. However frequently it may have been repeated, the whole story rests on Spottiswood, and for reasons above suggested, needs clear confirmation from other sources, especially as the Archbishop himself is known to have interfered without much ceremony in the election of Glasgow Magistrates.

LORD PROVOST PATRICK COLQUHOUN, LL.D.

CENTENNIAL celebrations have now become so common in connection with events as well as with individuals, that a fresh occurrence of the kind hardly calls for more than a passing notice, even although it may combine features peculiar to both. And yet the presentation to our Chamber of Commerce of a portrait so suggestive of by-gone days as that of Lord Provost Colquhoun, LL.D., is of more than ordinary interest, because such events in the nature of things must be of rare occurrence. The present year (1883) is the centenary of the Doctor's magisterial reign, and the centenary also of some of the useful local institutions originated by him in the course of his long and active public life. Then Patrick Colquhoun was something more than even a Glasgow Magistrate, important as such an honour is justly considered. Serving his own City well in early life, and held in high esteem by all classes, he removed to London about middle life, and exercised a power in the police administration of the Metropolis as salutary at the time as it is likely to be of long continuance. Faithful and painstaking in discharging the onerous duties of a police magistrate, Patrick Colquhoun yet found time through his rare gifts of method and application to make such contributions to the social, educational, and commercial questions of his day as might have made a lasting reputation for any writer, devoting his whole time to a single branch of such studies. This latest addition to the Chamber Gallery has therefore a double interest, attaching in the first place to the character of an enlightened philanthropist as represented by the artist, and to citizens who may worthily desire to emulate his usefulness. Patrick Colquhoun started in the race of life with no gifts of fortune beyond what all may acquire through a moderate education joined to unflagging perseverance. He was born, it may be mentioned, in that year of turmoil and peril, 1745, in the west end of Old Kilpatrick parish, and therefore almost within the family inheritance of the ancient Colquhoun race. His father, who died at the early age of forty-four, while holding the office of Keeper of Sasines for the county of Dumbarton, had been a class-fellow of Tobias Smollett in the Burgh School, and it was there young Patrick received the first part of his education. He went to America early in life, pretty much, it may be surmised, on his own account, being an orphan, and, settling in Virginia, conducted affairs so successfully as to be able to return to Glasgow in a position for carrying on the business of a merchant when only twenty-one years of age. Mr. Colquhoun's residence (long since removed) was on the north side of Argyll Street, nearly opposite the Buck's Head Hotel, and here in 1775 he took home his young wife, a namesake of his own, and daughter of James Colquhoun of Newlands, Provost of Dumbarton, 1783-89. Patrick Colquhoun was elected Provost of Glasgow on the death of Hugh Wylie, February, 1782, and about the same time he was appointed to take a general superintendence of the Tontine Buildings at the Cross, a project which the Chief Magistrate is thought to have originated, and certainly promoted with his customary vigour. The name of Patrick Colquhoun stands first on the list of proprietors for two shares, in name of his sons, Adam and James, followed by Walter Stirling, Campbell of Clathick, and other well-known Glasgow merchants. In the year of his Provostship he also obtained a Royal Charter for the present Chamber of Commerce, originated by him to promote and improve such branches of trade as are peculiar to this country, to establish rules for the convenience and assistance of foreign and inland traders and manufacturers, to discuss memorials regarding trade, to assist in procuring redress for trade grievances, to consider the Corn Laws in so far as they affected the industrious poor, and, in general, to take cognisance of everything in the least degree connected with commerce or manufactures. In November, 1789, Mr. Colquhoun removed with his family to London, mainly for the purpose of promoting a Scottish trade there. Having, however, composed several popular treatises on the subject of Police Government, he was, in 1792, when seven police offices were established, appointed to one of them through the influence of his friend, Henry Dundas, afterwards Viscount Melville. Three years later he published a treatise on the Police of the Metropolis, which passed through six editions, and brought him the honorary degree of LL.D. from Glasgow University. He was also appointed by the local legislature of the Virgin Islands, in the West Indies, agent for the colony in Great Britain. In 1800, Mr. Colquhoun published his important work on the Police of the River Thames, containing an historical account of the trade of the port of London, and suggesting means for the protection of the River and adjacent wharves and warehouses. His plan was afterwards adopted, and a new police office erected at Wapping. As some acknowledgment of the success of his endeavours to promote the safe navigation of the Thames, it is mentioned by his biographer that the West India merchants presented him with £500, while the Russian Company voted him a piece of plate valued at 100 guineas. Mr. Colquhoun's early publications in Glasgow, at least eight in number, had chiefly reference to the cotton trade and the exchange of home manufactures with foreign countries. While on the Police Bench in the Metropolis he issued "Friendly Advice to the Labouring Poor" (1799); "Police of the River Thames," already referred to (1800); "Suggestions, drawn up at the desire of the Lords of Council, for the Encouragement of Soup Establishments" (1800); "The Duties of a Constable" (1803); "A New System of Education" (1806); "Indigence," exhibiting a general view of the national resources for productive labour (1806); and finally, his largest, if not most important work, on "The Population, Wealth, Power, and Resources of the British Empire in every quarter of the World, including the East Indies" (4to, 1814). The career of this active, practical philanthropist was closed in London in April, 1820, when it was found he had bequeathed the interest of £200 for division yearly among poor people of the name of Colquhoun, residing in the parishes of Dumbarton, Cardross, Bonhill, and Old Kilpatrick, not in receipt of parochial relief. Dr. Colquhoun died at his residence, St. James' Street, Pimlico, and was buried in the Churchyard of St. Margaret's, Westminster, adjoining the Abbey. A memorial tablet near the west door of the church (the old parish church of Westminster) makes lengthy mention of Dr. Colquhoun's varied labours and attainments, the well-merited eulogium concluding by making mention of his mind as "fertile in conception, kind and benevolent in disposition, bold and persevering in execution."

SHERIFF ALISON.

TIME, exercising its usual influence, has smoothed down many asperities arising out of controversies in which Sir Archibald Alison was concerned as a politician or historian. Dead now (Dec., 1882) for over fifteen years, it is pleasant to brush aside opinions on social questions, erroneous as we thought them at the time, although held with unflinching sincerity, and think only of the impartial painstaking judge, the industrious author, the high-minded accomplished gentleman. Parliamentary Reform, the Currency, the Corn Laws, and even Education, have all moved from the lines for which Sir Archibald battled with unwearied persistence, but years as they roll on have in no way lessened the justly high reputation of the courageous magistrate whom neither conspirators nor rioters could intimidate. The two new handsome volumes, modestly styled "Some Account of my Life and Writings," edited with much intelligent discretion by the present Lady Alison, proceeds on the principle now widely recognised, that an author who has met with any degree of success owes a brief account of his career, on private as well as public grounds—to the family, that his memory may not be injured after death, as happened on a recent memorable occasion, by the indiscreet zeal of surviving friends or the injudicious disclosures of partial biographers; to his country, that readers may know by what means success was obtained, and how often it falls to those who apply themselves with industry to such task as they undertake. Sir Archibald Alison would appear never to have kept a "Journal," in the ordinary sense of the term, but when he died in May, 1867, he left in manuscript an Autobiography written at various times of leisure from 1851, and which was complete from his earliest years to the close of his literary career in 1862. Avoiding all appearance of vanity, no part of the "Autobiography" was to be published or even to be shown to any one during Sir Archibald's life. His primary object, as explained by himself, was to convey to future times, if the work should live so long, a faithful portrait of the eventful period in which he lived and of the many eminent persons he had met during a long and varied life. By his will the Sheriff constituted his eldest son, now famous as General Sir Archibald Alison, his literary executor, and expressed a wish that the work should be printed at as early a period as might be deemed advisable. A few years ago it was thought the time had arrived when this might be done, but the nature of the younger Sir Archibald's military profession would appear never to have left him the quiet and leisure necessary to revise the manuscript. The task was therefore undertaken by his wife, Lady Alison, and executed with much fidelity, as a labour of love. Son of the Rev. Archibald, a clergyman of the Church of England, author of two volumes of Sermons, but still more widely known for his finished "Essay on Taste," and connected through his mother with the memorable Edinburgh family of Gregory, the Sheriff's very early days, or from his birth in 1792 till 1800, were passed in the parsonage of Kenley, Shropshire. Chiefly for the purpose of securing a sound education for the family, his father, during the last-mentioned year, accepted the post of senior minister in the Episcopal Chapel, Cowgate, Edinburgh, and at the University there some years later study for the law was carried on till he passed as advocate in December, 1814. In the spring of that year the future historian made his first Continental trip, in company with P. F. Tytler and David Anderson of Moredun, and, although many years was to elapse before publication, it was the military displays in Paris during its occupation by the Allies which suggested the voluminous "History of Europe during the French Revolution." Earlier works were an anti-Malthusian Treatise on the Law of Population, and a useful book on the Criminal Law of Scotland, published in 1832. With a fair professional connection from the commencement of his career, official promotion naturally followed, his friend Sir William Rae, the Tory Lord-Advocate, bestowing on Alison in 1822 a Deputeship, which he held till 1830, when the Wellington Ministry was defeated on a division regarding the Civil List. The connection with "Blackwood" began with the first of a series of papers on the French Revolution, January, 1831. The appointment to the Sheriffship of Lanarkshire was made in 1834, during the period of Sir Robert Peel's first but short-lived Ministry.

A domestic interest surpassing anything connected with either the Sheriffship or the Baronetcy centered in two sons while on their first active service in the Crimea with the 72nd Highlanders, under Sir Colin Campbell as General of Division. The first interview of Captain, now General Sir Archibald, with Sir Colin is told graphically enough. Uncertain one night where to place his men in the trenches, he politely solicited instructions from his General, who was met by accident. "Don't ask me," replied Sir Colin; "I don't even know where I am." "Oh," resumed Captain Alison, "I think I can show you where you are," and with these words he drew from his breast a drawing of the trenches which he had copied in the inside of an envelope. Having pointed out the locality and placed his men, Sir Colin, after a little further conversation, said—"Well, Sir, you seem to be a sensible fellow; come to my chateau at two in the morning, when all is quiet, and we will have some talk." Captain Alison naturally complied, and found the General's chateau to be a little hollow in the earth, just capable of holding two or three persons, in the middle of the trenches occupied by the Highlanders. They remained there for a short time in the dark, talking of the siege, and then separated to return to their respective duties. Captain, soon after to be Major Alison, accompanied Lord Clyde as military secretary during the Indian Mutiny, and was present at the relief of Lucknow, where he lost his left arm.

Projected, as has been mentioned, so early as 1814, it was not till fifteen years later that the composition of the "History," the great literary labour of Sir Archibald's life, was seriously begun. The first volumes appeared in 1839, the last of the Revolution set in 1842, the planning and writing thus extending over twenty-eight years, or five years longer than Gibbon devoted to his "Roman Empire." When Sir Archibald had completed his last page, far into a summer morning at Possil, the words of Gibbon on a similar occasion, in the summer-house at Lausanne, naturally enough recurred to his mind—not that the books were to be compared with each other, but he felt that his labour had been pursued with as much perseverance, and had been the source of at least equal pleasure. Sir Archibald's work was generally accepted as upon the whole a valuable addition to European literature, such defects as were manifested being rather matters of taste and political opinion than literal inaccuracies, although there was no lack of these in the early editions. So far as the expression of political opinion was concerned, some readers approved, others overlooked them, and even the most fastidious admitted that it did not materially interfere with the great plan of the work. Its merits were admitted for minuteness and honesty—qualities which were accepted as a reasonable excuse for even a faulty style, strong political prejudices, and exaggerated declamation. His narrative of war operations especially were admitted to be not only minute and spirited, but to display considerable scientific knowledge. The different battlefields, it was remarked, had been surveyed with the feeling of an artist and the precision of a tactician. A strong and manly sympathy with military devotion never blinded Sir Archibald to the sufferings inflicted by war, but permitted him always to give warm and impartial praise to every brave action on whatever side.

Wordy the "History" was no doubt found to be, and wordy, too, many wondered, with less variety in expression than might have been expected from Sir Archibald's long literary experience. The same defect frequently crops up in the "Autobiography." In the "Continuation" almost every statesman referred to is somewhat unnecessarily described as a "remarkable man." Thus, "Lord Grey was beyond all doubt a most remarkable man." Daniel O'Connell is "a very remarkable man." Lord Eldon is "one of the most remarkable men who ever sat on the woolsack." Thiers is "undoubtedly a very remarkable man." Louis XVIII. is "undoubtedly a very remarkable man." Then Canning's talents for business and debate "were of the very first order." Palmerston's talents for diplomacy and administration "are unquestionably of a very high order." And so fond had the historian become of the phrase, or so expressive did he deem it, that it is used with reference to the same statesman a second time on the same page. Lord Melbourne alone hardly comes up to Sir Archibald's standard, or at least only in a hypothetical sense, as "if his talents were not of a very high order." In like manner the "Autobiography" sets down what is no doubt quite true, but not needing expression, that the Marchioness of Londonderry was "a very remarkable woman." Dr. Whewell was "a man of very great abilities." Sir Henry Rawlinson is "a very remarkable man." Monckton Milnes, only a page or two onward, is also "a remarkable man." Lord Palmerston turns up again as "one of the most remarkable men of the age." Mr. Secretary Walpole is also "a superior man." A conversation with the Princess Mary of Cambridge was "very remarkable." Lord Provost Clouston is another man of "remarkable intelligence." The Hon. Mr. Vernon and the late Colin Campbell, Colgrain, are each simply "superior" men.

But John Hope was a "remarkable man," as was also Professor Wilson and Duncan M'Neill; and so on through both volumes, till we come to poor Lord Elgin, "although not a man of very remarkable talents."

Apart from Interlocutors, and some were so elaborate and interesting as almost to reach the dignity of literature, the chief book-work engaged in by Sir Archibald in his later years is represented by the volumes making up the "Continuation" of the "History" from the battle of Waterloo to the accession of the Emperor Napoleon III., the early volumes of which were issued in 1852; and the lives of the half-brothers, Castlereagh and Londonderry, completed in 1861. The first added little or nothing to his fame as historian of the "Wars of the Revolution," being, indeed, frequently spoken of as a "Book of Fallacies" and exploded political crotchets. Nor did the second fare much better, Castlereagh himself being an unpopular subject since the power of the people has become a fact. The Marquis, in his prime one of the most dashing cavalry officers who ever served under Wellington, was latterly known as an unsuccessful diplomatist, a vain, fussy statesman, and might have been forgotten altogether had it not been for Seaham harbour, docks, and railway, in which the Murat of the British army exhibited all the enterprise and shrewdness of a Sunderland skipper. The preparation of the Londonderry volumes led Sir Archibald on more than one occasion to Wynard and Seaham, the first, in addition to its famous Ghost Story, having suffered more from fire in recent days than any mansion of its kind; the second, purchased from Mr. Milbanke, father of Lady Byron, the marriage of the poet having taken place within the modest mansion on the estate. Although the Marchioness of Londonderry was, as Sir Archibald records, a "remarkable" woman, even when she was an "infant" but wealthy ward in Chancery, he admits that he never was able to divest himself of a certain degree of awe, or feel altogether at ease in her company. While there is much—rather too much—in the "Autobiography" regarding visits to great people and great houses, all readers will peruse with pleasure the graphic details given by one who not only saw but took part in suppressing the Cotton-spinners' Combination, the Glasgow riots of 1848, the lesser Briggate rising concerning the Stone Pulpit, and, indeed, who was familiar with all the ups and downs of Glasgow life, from the passing of the Reform Bill to a period even beyond the trial of Mrs. M'Lachlan, in which he was concerned, and describes. Every reader of the "Autobiography" will turn over its pages with pleasure, not only because it records the opinion and the experience of a careful observer, or even because he was a painstaking and intelligent Judge, but because they will see therein reflected a generous appreciation of politicians who differed from him in thought, as his fine review of Macaulay's "History" still bears witness.

GRAHAM OF THE MINT.

LATEST and, to all present appearances, last scientific Master of the Mint, Thomas Graham was also the last of that brilliant group of inquirers who did so much to reveal the wonders of chemical science during the first half of the present century. Berzelius, given to Sweden in 1779, one year after the death of his illustrious countryman, Linnæus, was spared to carry on his researches till Graham had established for himself a world-wide reputation, first in the Andersonian Institution here, as successor to Ure, and afterwards in University College, London, as the successor of Professor Edward Turner. Born in 1805, Graham was busy with experiments when Davy was called away in 1829 at the early age of fifty-one. Dalton, born in 1766, was spared till he reached seventy-eight; while Faraday was only five years younger when he died in 1867, two years before his friend Graham, then Master of the Mint in succession to Sir John Herschel. Clerk-Maxwell, a friend and favourite with all the scientific men of his day, was cut off Nov., 1879, at the early age of forty-eight, while his successor in the new

Laboratory at Cambridge, Lord Rayleigh, president of the British Association, was born so recently as 1842. Graham's friend and pupil, Dr. Young of Kelly, who died only last year (1883), was spared till he had reached seventy-two. Without making any pretensions to having been a discoverer herself, but justly esteemed as a profound interpreter of researches made by others, the case of Mary Somerville, who showed so wisely the "Connection of the Physical Sciences," remains still without a parallel so far as age and mental activity is concerned. This good lady, known in youth as "The Rose of Jedwood," did not commence publishing till she was near fifty, when Brougham induced her to undertake a translation of Laplace's "Mecanique Celeste." Mrs. Somerville lived till she was ninety-two, her brilliant intellect remaining so vigorous that at the age of eighty she sent out her famous treatise on that science of molecules which Graham had evolved with so much patience and ingenuity. Fascinating beyond the dreams of romance as have been the discoveries made during the present century by Graham and his brother scientists, it must be remembered at the same time that they had a long line of predecessors, and are certain to have many after them fitted by careful training to pass on the torch of knowledge. As it is impossible to eliminate altogether some notice of astrology in the history of astronomy, so the early alchemists must be accepted as in some way preparing the ground for our modern Wollastons, Stahls, Liebigs, and Lavoisiers. Earlier even than the alchemists of the Middle Ages, earlier even than the introduction of the Christian Era, Lucretius was speculating with much ingenuity and accuracy concerning that atomic theory with which Graham's name is now so closely associated. "Sunt igitur solida primardia simplicitate," &c., writes the poet in his first book of Nature—all primordial bodies are solid in their simplicity, and consist of the smallest parts closely united, not combined by a union of others, but rather endowed with eternal simplicity.

Younger than Graham by twelve years, one of his most distinguished followers was the late Dr. Angus Smith of alkali fame, who shortly before his death in the spring of 1883 put together for the Graham Lecture Committee of the Glasgow Philosophical Society a brief memoir of his friend, full of suggestive matter concerning investigations pursued by the Master of the Mint. Engaged in preparing the paper as a lecture to be delivered by himself before the Philosophical Society, Dr. Angus Smith was seized with his fatal illness, but contrived amid much feebleness and effort to get the manuscript sent on here, where it was read to members by Professor Ferguson. The title, "Life and Works," is only correct in a modified sense. The "Life" is admitted to be but fragmentary in character, while "Works" rather indicate work accomplished than present Graham's researches at length. The special value of the memoir centres in the sixty-four letters hitherto unpublished, furnished by Dr. Smith, and addressed by Graham for the most part to relatives at home—his mother, sisters, and brother—although one or two of exceptional interest connect themselves with Liebig and Professor Johnston of Durham University. Here is a pleasant glimpse flashed to his sister Margaret, from Köchlin's Laboratory, at Mulhausen, Alsace—"We found here the excellent chemist Schlomberger, who has written the best papers on madder. The chemist was throng at work in his blouse coat and wooden clogs. Köchlin is himself a most interesting person. By the way, C. Thomson is studying with him; he has a high opinion of Walter Crum, and pronounces him, now that James Thomson is getting old, the most accomplished printer we have in England. The afternoon we devoted to Mr. Hoffer's own establishment; John finds them exceedingly communicative, and they seem to show us everything without reserve. He thinks that he has already attained the most important objects of his mission, and that he will be able on returning to produce the beautiful madder rose-reds for which Alsace is famed, so that the journey will not be lost." Again, and also to his sister, a few years earlier, when in Edinburgh—"The gingerbread was excellent. Mr. Johnston got away the last of it as a supply for his Durham journey, thinking greatly of it from the scientific principles upon which it had been baked." A prince of chemists in his laboratory, out of it Graham's life glided on in the most uneventful manner, and may be condensed within the compass of a few lines. Born in Glasgow, December, 1805, he passed first to a preparatory school, then to the High School, when he was nine years of age, and in 1819 to the University, where he remained seven years, taking his M.A. degree in 1826. Graham was originally intended for the Church, but strong predilections for a scientific career, especially as a chemist, caused him to shape out a path for himself, much to the grief of his father, a merchant of good position, who, not knowing much about the aims or scope of science, may have been prejudiced in his judgment. From Glasgow the young student proceeded to Edinburgh, where his scientific inquiries were carried on under Dr. Hope.

Graham's progress afterwards may be thus indicated:—Lecturer on Chemistry in the Mechanics' Institute; Professor in Andersonian Institution, 1830; succeeded Dr. Turner in Chemical Chair of University College, London, 1837; Chairman of Chemical Section, British Association (Birmingham), 1839; first President of Chemical Society of London, 1841; Master of the Mint, 1855. It was in Glasgow under the skilful teaching of Dr. Thomson, that Graham first applied himself to chemistry as a science, for, however much his boyish mind may have been attracted by the wonders of experiment, Dr. Smith believes that it was at a very early age Graham began seriously to consider the recondite laws of matter. In 1826 a paper was prepared by him on the absorption of gases by liquids, and his shrewdness and calm mode of speculation were as apparent at twenty-one as at any time of his after life. He supposed, for example, that absorption and liquefaction of gases are regulated by the same fundamental properties. Three years later (1829), he succeeded in demonstrating what has come to be known as Graham's Law—that the diffusion of gases is inversely as the square root of their density. Other rapid discoveries regarding the nature and movement of gases and liquids soon placed Graham alongside the foremost chemists of his day. In addition to many delicate experiments connected with the gold coinage, much time was devoted by the new Master of the Mint to the issue of a bronze coinage as a substitute for the once familiar copper pieces. When Graham died in September, 1869, the Mastership of the Mint was not filled up, the coinage Act of next year providing for the title passing to the Chancellor of the Exchequer for the time being, the practical duties connected with the office falling to be discharged by the Deputy-Master. In this way an end came to be put to an office which had been filled by the most illustrious men of science from the days of Sir Isaac Newton, who called in the vitiated coinage of his time, till Thomas Graham, who, in his own department of physics, was no way overshadowed by the universal fame of even the great astronomer. In addition to the text of the "Life," made up as indicated, there is an appendix in the shape of "Critical Remarks," written by Dr. Smith, and originally prefixed to the "Physical Researches of Thomas Graham," printed for private circulation eight years since by himself and Dr. James Young of Kelly. A photographic portrait conveys a pleasing impression of Graham's mild and retiring yet happy disposition, although even in these points it does not surpass Brodie's fine statue in our Square, where the seated figure of the great chemist (presented to the City by Mr. Young), and almost within earshot of that useful Institution where he filled his first professorial chair, fitly matches with Chantrey's wonderful delineation of the great engineer on the opposite or western corner.

GENERAL ROY OF CARLUKE.

FORMING, as it now does, the basis for most surveys within Great Britain and the foundation also for all reliable maps, whatever scale it may be found necessary to use, the Annual Official Survey Report just sent out in the form of a Parliamentary Blue-book, suggests matter for reflection involving wider issues than the usual duty of simply noting what progress has been made with this great national undertaking. A hundred years (in 1884) has just run out since General Roy, then a Colonel of Engineers, took the first real scientific step in the enterprise; by laying down, under command of His Majesty, the famous basis line of triangulation on Hounslow Heath. Little being known of General Roy earlier than what touches the busy middle-age portion of his life, time may not be thought lost in setting down a few words concerning an officer who was at once the foremost surveyor of his day, eminent beyond most in mathematical studies, and, so far as Scotland was concerned, the father of geodetic science. Our West Country has special reason for feeling proud of its connection with a scholar who would have been great had he done nothing more than initiate the Ordnance Survey and write "The Military Antiquities of the Romans in Britain." The son of an intelligent grieve, who combined the duties of factor with that of gardener on the estate of Hamilton of Hallcraig, Carluke parish, William Roy was born at Milton-head, 4th May, 1726. Carluke village at the time was in a state of chronic decay. Small as the place was in the early days of Charles II., a charter was obtained in the second year after the Restoration, erecting it into a burgh of barony under the name of Kirkstyle. Any improving influences that might be supposed likely to spring from such an increase of dignity would appear to have operated for only a short time, as at the birth of Roy the burgh comprised little more than the parish church, the manse, and a very few cottages. The population of the entire parish, ministered to in things spiritual by the Rev. James Dick, was not much, if anything, over 1,460. The latest census return (1881) gives the parish population at 8,552. In Roy's early days the working of iron and coal which has made the district so prosperous, and it may be even said famous, in the annals of industry was on the most limited scale. Even cotton weaving, which first raised the drooping fortunes of the place, was all but unknown. Only a very little is known concerning Roy's early education or pursuits. It may be surmised, however, in a general way that he devoted considerable attention to engineering studies before obtaining a commission in the army as lieutenant in or about 1741. His brother, Dr. Roy, was born in the same parish.

The Rebellion of 1745 first brought Roy into notice as an engineer and surveyor. After the "rising" had been stamped out in blood by Cumberland, at Culloden, in April of the following year, Government became more alive than before as to the necessity of exploring and laying open a country so difficult of access as the Highlands of Scotland. It was determined, therefore, to carry roads through the most remote recesses, and establish efficient military posts along the entire line. In this way it came about that the first methodical operations for a military survey of Great Britain took place at the distant point of Fort Augustus, in 1747. General Watson, Quartermaster-General to Lord Blakeney, was encamped in the fort at the time, and by this officer the Highland survey, afterwards known as "Cumberland's Map," was entrusted to his junior officer, Colonel Roy. Although the original intention would not appear to have embraced more than the Highlands, yet the surveyor gradually found his way into the Lowlands, and even along the more important coast lines. The field work was carried on in summer, and the drawings, on the scale of one inch and three-quarters to a mile, prepared during the winter in Edinburgh Castle. At the end of eight years the undertaking was advancing, but far from finished; and when it was then suspended, Colonel Roy admitted that the survey, having been carried on with inferior instruments, and the sum allowed very inadequate for its proper execution, it ought rather to be looked on as a fair military sketch than an accurate map of the country. The breaking out of the war in 1756—a war waged against France in America, in India, and on the high seas—scattered the surveyors, and called away from Scotland such engineers and foot soldiers as could be spared. The Highlands for the time being crushed into peace, the survey drawings were consigned to the Royal Library, unusually rich in such collections, as any one may see by a glance at the formidable row of cases in the British Museum, and there they lay, almost neglected, while geographers like Ainslie were making private independent surveys, instead of perfecting, as they might have done, the work of Roy. Even in the face of colonial troubles the scheme of a national survey was brought up in Parliament from time to time; and at length, in 1763, Government undertook to propose a money vote in aid. Yet even preliminaries were not finally settled for twenty years, or in 1783, when Roy was engaged in measuring on his own account a base of 7744·3 feet across the fields between the Jewsharp, Marybone, and Black Lane, near St. Pancras, as a foundation for a series of triangles carried on at the same time, for determining the relative situations of the most remarkable steeples, and other places in and about London, with regard to each other and the Royal Observatory at Greenwich. Some little time before this a correspondence had been going on between the Count d'Adhemar and Mr. Fox as to the advantage which would accrue to astronomical science by carrying a series of triangles from the neighbourhood of London to Dover, there to be connected with the triangulation already executed in France. The King approved of the design, and agreed to share the cost with the Royal Society, that body having taken a lively interest from the first in all the proceedings. Roy was thereupon summoned to Windsor, and instructed by the King to commence the survey. His first step was the measurement of that now historical base-line on Hounslow Heath (5·19 miles) —measurements, it has been found, so careful that no essential error has been discovered by the most rigid scrutiny of modern surveyors. The great three-foot theodolite, constructed for the occasion by the optician Ramsden, after being carried up the highest mountains, placed on the pinnacles of our loftiest churches, and shipped to distant islands, is still in daily use, and as perfect as when it left the hands of its cunning constructor. Ramsden, indeed, made his instrument something more than a theodolite. It is also a quadrant and transit instrument, and capable of measuring horizontal angles to fractions of a second. To the same ingenious optician is also due the invention of the survey measuring chain, superseding at once the varying deal-rod, and rivalling even the glass-rods as a measuring line.

The importance of the base-line in triangulation, for the purpose of calculating unknown distances, is stated with as much simplicity as the subject permits, by the writer of an article on the "Cadastral Survey" in the "Edinburgh Review," vol. 118. In substance it is this: If the distance between two given points is accurately known, all that is necessary, in order to ascertain the distance of any point that can be seen from both of them, is to observe successively from each end of the known base, the angle subtended by the other end of the base and the point to be determined. The length of the unknown sides may then be calculated by the formulæ of plane trigonometry, and the distances so determined become, in their turn, bases for the determination of fresh unknown distances. By constantly constructing new triangles on the sides successively determined, the whole country is at last covered by stations, the positions of which are known with the nicest accuracy. The whole of the principal triangulation which has consumed so many years of anxious toil, has been simply a series of repetitions of this proceeding. The simplest instruments will suffice to do this work roughly—the levels, the screws, the verniers, the reading microscopes of the theodolite, are only inventions to secure precision otherwise unattainable. To secure approximate accuracy would be easy enough, but to do it in such a way that the whole area of Great Britain—nearly 122,000 square miles—no point fixed by the triangulation shall be more than three, or at most four, inches out of its true position, involved an amount of care and calculation not easy to be imagined. The greatest inaccuracy which can possibly be laid to the charge of one of the modern Ordnance Survey Maps, is far smaller than the breadth of the finest line that the engraver can make upon the copper plate—smaller even than the discrepancy discoverable in two measurements on the same map on two successive days, when some variation of temperature has stretched or contracted the paper on which it is printed.

Working in harmony with the French surveyors, General Roy proceeded at once to carry his series of triangles from Hounslow to the coast of Kent and Sussex, and from thence westward to the Land's End. At his lamented death (to be afterwards referred to) in 1790, the burden of the work fell on Captain Mudge, of the Royal Artillery, and Isaac Dalby. Their "Account" of the Trigonometrical Survey contributed to the "Philosophical Transactions," and published separately, 1799, was long the standard work of authority on the interesting project with which they were so thoroughly acquainted. Among their earliest proceedings was to test anew, with most satisfactory results, the original Hounslow measurement, and to lay down a new base line on Salisbury Plain of 36,574·4 feet. This new line, on being triangulated in due course with Hounslow, was found not to vary more than an inch from the actual measurement made on the Plain. A third base was more recently laid down at Lough Foyle, primarily in connection with the Irish Survey, but with the extremely pleasing secondary result that, in tracking across the country for the purpose of determining what ought to be the Salisbury base, the discrepancy with actual measurement was found to be not more than four inches and a-half in a distance of over four hundred miles. It is now possible to measure an arc of parallel extending from Valentia, on the south-west coast of Ireland, to the town of Orsk, on the extreme east of European Russia, the longest ever likely to be measured.

The ingenious contrivances for perfecting the undertaking devised by General Roy are endless, and can only be referred to here by a brief example or two. Mention has already been made of the deal rods, glass tubes, and steel chains used to secure accuracy in measurement. But the expansion and contraction of glass, as well as iron, introduced an element of doubt in the nicer calculations; and, although it was known that the rate of expansion might be ascertained and allowed for, provided the exact temperature of the bar all through was ascertained at the time of observation, yet this could not always be done in out-door work. Availing himself of the ascertained principle that, while metals contract or expand differently at varying temperatures, they always bear to each other the same proportion, Colonel Colby solved the difficulty by clamping together a bar of iron and a bar of brass of the same length at a given temperature, with silver plates let in to transverse bars for the purpose of marking certain immovable points. Again, the heliostat, or revolving mirror, familiar now to newspaper readers from its use by the armies in Afghanistan and Egypt, is in constant use by Ordnance surveyors for flashing from point to point a knowledge of relative positions, even although the extremities might be one hundred miles apart. Then it is necessary to make the triangulation all over the kingdom consistent with itself—that is to say, that the sum of the three angles in every triangle should be 180 degrees, and the sum of all the angles round every station 360 degrees. Three unknown quantities in an equation is generally considered a near enough approximation to the truth. The intrepid calculators of the Ordnance Survey face the solution of equation with thirty-six unknown quantities.

The principal triangulation of the kingdom commenced, as we have seen, by Roy in 1784, was carried on at intervals till 1858, when it may be said to have been practically completed. This survey was extended to Scotland in 1809, and continued with several breaks till 1823, when it was suspended for fifteen years. The survey is now finished, and maps on the 6-inch scale have been published of the whole country, and for the most part also on the 25-inch scale. The useful 1-inch map is far advanced in two styles—contours only, and hills. Nearly all towns and populous places have been issued on the 5-feet or 10-feet scale. Regarding the battle of the "Scales," fought in the House of Commons for over twelve years—1851–63—with a pertinacity hardly surpassed by the battle of the "Guns," it is neither seasonable nor necessary to enlarge on now or here. Nor can further room be occupied by any description of the delicate processes employed before maps can be submitted to the public for acceptance in all their beautiful and accurate details. To the present Director of the survey, Sir Henry James, R.E., belongs the high honour—first, of connecting the triangulation of the United Kingdom with France and Belgium; second, calling in the aid of, and almost inventing, the art, known as Photozincography, by which the maps, with all their delicate outlines, are transferred through a simple method to such a permanent surface as has given us the best copies yet produced of many precious ancient records—Domesday-Book, Saxon Charters, and the most suggestive "National State Papers," illustrating the history of England, Scotland, and Ireland.

Mention has been made of the remarkable care taken to preserve General

Roy's wonderful Theodolite. With another of his survey inventions Fortune was less favourable; his Standard Yard, used for measuring the Hounslow base line, and afterwards placed in Exchequer Chambers, Westminster, being burnt in the great fire which in October, 1834, consumed the Houses of Parliament. In this case a Royal Commission on Weights and Measures had luckily provided some years earlier that, if the General's standard measure was lost, it would be lawful to renew it by means of the length of the seconds pendulum. General Roy's death was of startling suddenness. Having prepared for the Royal Society, by command of the King, an elaborate series of papers concerning the exact latitude of Greenwich and Paris Observatories, he was revising the printed sheets at home after a day's work in the office, June 30, 1790, when he was seized with an illness of which he died in two hours. Besides being a Major-General, at this time the great military engineer was Deputy Quartermaster-General, Colonel of the 30th Foot, Surveyor-General of Coasts and Batteries, and a Fellow of the Royal Society, as well as of the Society of Antiquaries. In 1793 the latter learned body issued the General's "Military Antiquities" as a posthumous volume, folio, profusely illustrated with drawings. One year after his measurement of the Hounslow line a paper on the subject, contributed to "Transactions of the Royal Society," secured to Roy the Copley gold medal. The most eminent mathematicians of his day—Ivory and Leslie among the rest—did not fail to do justice to his great merits, nothing more censorious being written of him than that he had somehow failed to appreciate to its full extent a theorem first propounded by his friend Adrian Legendre, the theorem being to the effect that, if each of the angles of a small spherical triangle be diminished by one-third of the spherical excess, the sines of the angles thus diminished will be very nearly proportional to the length of the sides themselves; so that the computations with respect to such spherical triangles may be made by the rules of plane trigonometry. Aided by this theorem, drawn from the newer mathematics, it was thought that General Roy might have simplified many of his calculations, and in the case of a few—only a very few—been more exact than he arrived at by the old system of calculation.

Still, it was universally admitted that General Roy possessed a strong and vigorous understanding; was an excellent draughtsman, and a profound natural philosopher, as was abundantly established in his paper on the measurement of heights by the barometer, printed in the "Philosophical Transactions," 1777. Nor was it judged to be less to the General's credit that he pursued his abstruse studies at a time when the British army afforded few instances of the kind either to encourage him by example or rouse him by emulation, and when the connection between mathematical science and his military art was but imperfectly understood.

BURNS AND "HIGHLAND MARY."

BURNS incense is now offered up with such profusion each January as to make the poet's joke about his own reputation rather a matter of history than prophecy. Writing to his friend, Gavin Hamilton, on the occasion of the first Edinburgh visit, he remarks—"I am in a fair way of becoming as eminent as Thomas à Kempis or John Bunyan, and you may expect henceforth to see my birth-day inserted among the wonderful events in the Poor Robin's and Aberdeen Almanacs along with the Black Monday and the Battle of Bothwell Bridge." Popularity naturally incites inquiry, and many occurrences turn up for discussion which in lesser or more obscure reputations would be allowed to pass unnoticed. One of the unconscious services rendered by the warm admirers of Burns is the inquiry they compel into facts and surmises associated with his life, and so establishing more or less of what is clearly historic. The poet's connection with "Highland Mary" has long had an interest of this kind for plodding inquirers—an interest in no degree lessened, but rather strengthened, by a mystery Burns has himself thrown around the story, quite out of keeping with his usual candour in such affairs. The attachment has been described as the purest and most elevated ever formed by the poet, and the songs in praise of the simple Highland girl are justly ranked among the most finished efforts of his muse. The "banks and braes and streams around the Castle o' Montgomery" has become classic ground to thousands who never heard of the wooded slopes of Parnassus; Doon has been found more inspiring than Castaly; and to the Coilsfield dairymaid has been vouchsafed an immortality rivalling the Laura of Petrarch or the Beatrice of Dante. On her merits and her fame public opinion has long since set its seal. It is so far as the subject touches the poet that it has an interest for inquirers. Recent research would almost lead to the conclusion that the "Highland Mary" attachment, instead of being a thing standing apart in the poet's life as a permanent or earnest feeling, was but an episode in a wider domestic drama—only an accident—almost the accident of an accident. Burns may be permitted in the first instance to tell the story in his own way. In the course of a few notes on some of the Scottish songs printed in the "Museum," prepared for his neighbour the Laird of Friars' Carse some time after 1788—probably about 1794—the poet writes of the "Highland Lassie" as "a composition of mine in *very early life* before I was at all known to the world. My Highland lassie was a warm-hearted, charming young creature as ever blest a man with generous love. After a pretty long tract of the most ardent reciprocal attachment we met by appointment on the second Sunday of May in a sequestered spot on the banks of Ayr, where we spent the day in taking a farewell before she should embark for the West Highlands to arrange matters among her friends for our projected change of life. At the close of autumn she crossed the sea to met me at Greenock, where she had scarce landed when she was seized with a malignant fever before I could even hear of her illness." In a similar strain the poet writes to Thomson in 1792, enclosing the song "Will you go to the Indies, my Mary?" "In my *very early years*, when I was thinking of going to the West Indies, I took the following farewell of a dear girl." It is now necessary to set down a few dates, in order to avoid being misled by the poet's phrases about "very early life," and "very early years." It is known to all acquainted in even a slight degree with the life of Burns, that the West Indies project occupied his mind only once, and that was in the summer of 1786, when the Kilmarnock edition of his poems was passing through the press, and when—and this bears closer on the inquiry—when Jean Armour's father was threatening the hapless bard with the terrors of a jail in order to compel him to provide for his illegitimate offspring. Burns at this time could hardly be described as very young. He had quite completed twenty-seven on his last birth-day—not an early age in affairs of gallantry for him who, at seventeen, addressed "Handsome Nell" to his girl neighbour in the harvest field. If the surmise is correct, and no other theory fits in so well, or fits in at all, with ascertained facts, the romantic parting on the banks of Ayr took place in the summer of 1786—"the second Sunday in May" being the 14th of the month. But the surprise does not end here. Some months before this Burns had placed in the hand of his friend Aiken an irregular but legal certificate of marriage with Jean Armour; nor, as appears from one of the poet's own letters, was it destroyed till some day between the 3rd and 17th of the preceding April. What the poet calls the "pretty long tract of ardent reciprocal attachment" comes, therefore, within thirty days of being inconveniently near formal obligations to his earlier love. Destroyed though the declaration was, Burns was none the less bound by its contents—a responsibility he appears to have overlooked or been misinformed about when he presented Mary Campbell with the famous Bible that summer afternoon. In one of the volumes may yet be seen in the poet's handwriting, "And ye shall not swear by my name falsely—I am the Lord" (Levit. xvi. 12); in the other, "Thou shalt not forswear thyself, but shalt perform unto the Lord thine oath" (St. Matt. v. 33). According to Dr. R. Chambers, sound lawyers have already given it as their opinion that the destruction of the informal declaration in no way altered the relative position of the parties, but only introduced an element of difficulty, had it been necessary to establish the marriage by evidence in Court. The verbal testimony of any who had seen or even heard of the document would have gone far to fix the conditions it was originally intended to establish. When Burns became first acquainted with Mary Campbell cannot be fixed with great precision. It is not likely to have been earlier than 1784, when he went with the rest of the family to reside in her neighbourhood. Mary Campbell is presumed at this time to have been in the service of Burns' friend, Gavin Hamilton, in Mauchline, but removed, it is thought, afterwards to Coilsfield, where, it is also surmised, she resided during the summer of 1785. Wherever living, she would seem to have left Ayrshire about Whitsunday, 1786, the term day that year being the day following the parting with Burns—"the second Sunday in May." The date of this parting can otherwise be fixed with reasonable accuracy. The Bible itself is of date 1782, and, in addition to the verses quoted, bears the signature, "Robert Burns, Mossgiel," a place with which Burns had no connection till 1784, as mentioned above. In the absence of positive information about the closing days of Mary Campbell, the Bibles are not the least important link in the chain of evidence. Their history has been singular enough. On the death of "Highland Mary" at Greenock, as we think in October, 1786, the volumes were treasured by her mother, Burns being a forbidden subject with her father. Mrs. Campbell died in extreme poverty at Greenock, in 1828. Some time before this date the old woman had presented the Bibles to her daughter, Mrs. Anderson, from whom they passed through two sisters to her son, William Anderson, mason, Renton, Dumbartonshire. On emigrating to Canada, in 1834, the volumes were taken with him, and for a time lost trace of; but, being heard of accidentally by a few of the poet's admirers in Montreal, the precious relics were secured for £25, and handsomely restored to the old country for the purpose of being placed in the monument at Brig o' Doon, where they are now to be seen in fitting company with other memorials of the bard. There are other discrepancies not easily reconciled in the account given by Burns of Highland Mary. He writes of her as proceeding to the Highlands "to arrange matters among her friends for our projected change of life." Very little appears to have been known about Mary in the household at Mossgiel. Mrs. Begg recollected no sort of reference being made to her more than once when the poet remarked to John Blane, gaudsman, that Mary had refused to meet him in the old castle—the dismantled tower of the priory near Coilsfield House. Even presuming that Burns as well as the Armours acted under a sincere though erroneous impression that a complete and valid separation had been effected, it is difficult, from what we know of Mary's character, to see how the sad position of Jean Armour— a position as painful as it was notorious—could be accepted by her as a reason for hastening on in any way a union to which she was previously averse. With his passage taken out, his chest on the road to Greenock, and the sails filling with the breeze that was to waft him from old Caledonia, matrimony, one would have said, was the last thing likely to be thought of by the poet, either for his own advantage or the comfort of her on whom he had again set his changing affections. There is still another particle of proof militating strongly against a marriage at this dark period in Burns's history. On the 22nd July of the year in question—1786—the poet executed a deed investing his brother Gilbert with all his "goods, gear, and moveable effects," profits from poems included, to be held by him in trust for the upbringing of his illegitimate daughter, known as "Sonsie, smirking, dear-bought Bess." In particular, provision was made by the same deed for continuing his daughter's exclusive interest in the copyright after she had reached the age of fifteen years. With what then was he going to endow Mary Campbell in the way of worldly goods? Marriage in such circumstances was as indiscreet as after events proved it improper. Months after the first blast of the Armour strife was over, early in January, 1787, when being caressed by the rank, fashion, and learning of Edinburgh, he wrote to his friend Hamilton at Mauchline, "To tell the truth, among friends, I feel a miserable blank in my heart for the want of her," referring to Jean Armour. All these relations and responsibilities are alluded to in the touching "Farewell," wherein, however, Mary, whom he may be presumed to have just asked if she would "go to the Indies," is not once mentioned :—

Farewell, old Scotland's bleak domains,
Far dearer than the torrid plains
  Where rich annanas blow;
Farewell, a mother's blessing dear!
A brother's sigh! a sister's tear!
  My Jean's heart-rending throe!
Farewell, my Bess! though thou 'rt bereft
Of my paternal care,
A faithful brother I have left,
  My part in him thou 'lt share.
    Adieu, too, to you too,
    My Smith, my bosom frien',
    When kindly you mind me,
    Oh then befriend my Jean!

What bursting anguish tears my heart!
From thee, my Jeanie, must I part!
  Thou weeping answer'st "No!"
Alas! misfortune stares my face,
And points to ruin and disgrace—
  I, for thy sake, must go.
Thee, Hamilton and Aiken dear,
  A grateful warm adieu,
I, with a much-indebted tear,
  Shall still remember you.
    All hail then, the gale then
    Wafts me from thee, dear shore!
    It rustles and whistles—
    I'll never see thee more!

Instead of returning from the Highlands after arranging, as the poet writes, "for our projected change in life," Dr. R. Chambers (to whom all inquirers on this point are under great obligations), thinks Highland Mary had agreed, at the recommendation of a former patroness, to accept for the Martinmas term a new situation at Glasgow in the family of Colonel M'Ivor. This careful biographer also mentions as a tradition that the illness under which the fair girl suffered at Greenock was superstitiously believed to have been inflicted by the cast of an evil eye, and friends, therefore, seriously recommended her father to go to a spot where two burns met, select seven smooth stones from the channel, boil them in new milk, and give her the same to drink. Mary's illness was far too serious for either charms or skill. Burns's "Highland Lassie" sickened of fever, died in a few days, and was buried in a lair at the West Church belonging to a distant relative of her mother, thus closing what the impassioned poet described in after years as "one of the most interesting episodes of my youthful days."

KILMARNOCK.

A HANDY and useful addition was made to local literature by the issue of a new or fourth edition of the late Archibald M'Kay's well-known "History of Kilmarnock." It was somewhat over thirty years since the first appeared, and two have been issued in the interim. Admirably arranged as the book is, and full of information, it is yet hardly full enough, and not quite so fresh in details as the year on the title-page would lead one to infer. The new preface is dated last June, yet among the worthies who figured in "Auld Killie," of whom brief—too brief—notice is given, no mention is made of the fact that John Kelso Hunter died so far back as February, 1873. It is just between seven and eight years since J. K., "John Kobbler," otherwise "The Cobbler Artist," was taken away from his "last" as well as his easel, to the regret of many friends, aged a little over seventy. Neither the "Retrospect" nor "Life Studies of Character," nor "Memorials of West Country Men and Manners," is so much as mentioned, and yet it is not to be disputed that Hunter's writings have fully more to do with such fame as he enjoys than any labour he ever undertook in connection with the "Kilmarnock Drawing Academy," important as that institution might be in the history of art. Hunter's portraits were in the main looked upon as wonders, the feeling generally being, not that they should be done so well, but that in the circumstances they could be done at all. His books, on the other hand, were the man all over, surrounded by portraits of another kind, coloured like those on canvas, with the airy imagination of the artist. These must long continue to be enjoyed by all who esteem graphic accuracy with a strong dash of Doric tincture. James Paterson, too, another Kilmarnock worthy by residence, thoroughly Ayrshire also by birth and work, receives only a brief mention, suggested apparently by his experiences on the local "Chronicle." And yet

James Paterson wrote the "History of Ayr," and transcribed "The Obit Book of St. John the Baptist," not to speak of much miscellaneous work in the way of compilation. Neither is it indicated in any way that such an industrious labourer in the literary vineyard has been dead for two or three years. Nobody can grudge the ample space devoted to Sir James Shaw, an exceptionally prominent and worthy native of the town; but one pre-eminent duty of a local historian, and one on which even readers beyond the bounds of the locality look to him as an authority, is to give a reasonably complete account of those who in the world of enterprise or thought did some good work in their day, but probably not sufficient to merit any reminder in the way of a public monument. The prominent can easily be held in remembrance; but local history, to be properly written, must be made up of many people not reaching a very high standard of effort, just as on the other it must deal with many events having only a parochial significance. The general historian requires so often to be indebted to the special or local that disappointment is experienced when details are found to be less full than might be reasonably expected, especially when opportunity has been afforded for increased care by four editions. As slips occur in the way of omitting to mention death, so on the other hand persons still living might have been described. An otherwise excellent notice of Mr. Templeton, vocalist, is slightly marred by an absence of any information that he is still (1880) living, and must be about, if not over, eighty years of age. The date of birth, instead of being only an inference from certain other facts, should have been stated with distinctness. In the mere arrangement of his matter no less than in simple directness of expression, Mr. M'Kay must be judged to merit very high praise. There is some mention of the earliest notices of the burgh, though, from the absence of ecclesiastical or municipal records, these cannot be expected in very great detail, nor might they be considered as adding to the usefulness of the book for popular purposes. The town books extend no further back than 1686, and the earliest entry in the register of baptism is of date 1644. For its erection as a parish, for the date of its first church, or even for the period of the reputed St. Marnock, only stray references of second or third rate value, so far as age is concerned, can now be had. For the "Locartt" vassals of the great De Morville, who are presumed to have placed the parish under the protection of Kilwinning, that ancient mother of many fraternities, Time has preserved but little until a period is reached so recent as hardly to be history when judged of in connection with the event itself. Early in the seventeenth century—probably 500 years after a village had begun to cluster round the church—Pont wrote of Kilmarnock as having a weekly market, and "a faire stone bridge over the river which glides past by the toune till it falls into the river Irvine. It hath a pretty church, from which the village castle and lordship takes its name. The Lord Boyd is now lord of it, to whose predecessors it hath belonged for many generations." It was only a few years before this date, or in 1591, that Kilmarnock received its first charter, being erected into a burgh of barony by Thomas, fifth Lord Boyd. In 1672 a second charter, conferring additional rights and privileges on the town, was granted by Charles II. in favour of William, ninth Lord Boyd, and first Earl of Kilmarnock, great-grandfather of the unfortunate William, fourth Earl, executed on Tower Hill for his share in the Rebellion of 1745. From the third Earl Kilmarnock received a grant of the common greens of the town, certain shops under the Tolbooth, the tron and weights, with the customs of the burgh, including all connected with the fairs and weekly markets. When this grant was made the Magistrates were elected by the Lord of the manor from a list presented to him annually. So far as Parliamentary representation or municipal government was concerned, Kilmarnock continued in this condition till 1832, when under the Reform Bill of that year it was included among the fifteen towns in Scotland, not royal burghs, which were to join with others in sending a member to the Commons. Gradually increasing in enterprise and population, Kilmarnock came to be a place of considerable importance in the West Country, and throughout the perilous times of the Covenant and Rebellion lent a consistent and substantial support to the cause of religious and civil liberty. Whig by conviction no less than by tradition, several sons of Kilmarnock occupy an honourable place in the roll of Covenant martyrs, while several barbarous executions took place within the burgh for the avowed purpose of overawing its inhabitants. The moorlands of Ayrshire were too near, as they were too well known, to the dragoons for Kilmarnock to be kept free from their unwelcome presence. In January, 1682, Captain Inglis complains that the countrymen will neither sell corn nor straw to the troops, but shut up their doors on seeing the soldiers. So far as the last rising in favour of the House of Stuart was concerned, although its titular chief, through some personal resentment of his own, it has been said, cast in his lot with the young Pretender, the townsfolk were prominently active in support of the House of Hanover. In his petition to the King, the Earl of Kilmarnock affirmed that he influenced neither tenant nor follower to assist or abet the rebellion, but that, on the contrary, between the time of the battle of Preston and his own unhappy junction with the rebels, he went to the town of Kilmarnock, and pleaded the cause of His Majesty with such effect, that 200 men were soon in arms, and remained most of the winter in Glasgow or elsewhere. As might have been expected from his long familiarity with local men and events, Mr. M'Kay furnishes much interesting information concerning Burns and his Kilmarnock friends, many of his "howfs" being minutely described, and the men whom he mixed with or satirised noticed in a pleasant informing manner. As indicating the extension of the town caused by carpet weaving, engineering, and other industries, the population, it may be mentioned, has increased within the present century from 8,079 in 1801 to 24,071 in 1871. At present the total valuation of the burgh proper, including railways, is £83,722, and of the landward portion, also including railways, is £22,392. Mr. M'Kay's "Kilmarnock" is not a book of events only—although all the more important are given, including fires and floods—but he very properly deals with the pastimes of the people, their churches and schools, and all the recent improvements for which the burgh has been so worthily distinguished in recent years. Regarding all these points, and many more, on which space will not permit us to dilate, Mr. M'Kay's book may be confidently taken in hand as a trustworthy guide and authority, subject to such small exceptions as are mentioned above.

ST. MICHAEL'S, DUMFRIES.

Since even the memory of the just "smell sweet and blossom in the dust," what high consideration should be meted out to those Old Mortality's who so far defy "Decay's effacing fingers" as to keep the departed in green remembrance by gathering together their memorials for wide and permanent respect? The quaint old Knight of Norwich, Sir Thomas Browne, writes of unsatisfied affection as receiving some pleasure from being neighbours in the grave, "to lie urn by urn, and touch but in their names." In his "Memorials of St. Michael's," the historian of Dumfries, following up, and indeed partly completing, his previous labours, brought whole generations side by side, enabling survivors at home, or it may be in distant parts, to recall old associations and renew forgotten friendships. He has discharged his somewhat mournful task with feeling and judgment. Grave without being gloomy, informing but never dull, minute and yet discriminating, the reader will find in M'Dowall's meditations among the tombs much that will enlarge the understanding as well as touch the heart. Names, he says, that appear of little note to strangers may be precious to some humble household, as having belonged to those who, in happier days for the survivors, were its chief prop or pride. All burial grounds—even the unconsecrated —are counted sacred; but as a rule each bereaved mourner counts that spot the dearest and most hallowed of all which contains the gem of his own circle. Of some graves, half-neglected as obscure, noticed in the volume, the observation naturally arises, "Sombody's darling slumbers here." Without presenting anything in the way of extreme antiquity, or even of that grotesque character which has made epitaphial literature quite lively reading, having no pretensions to great splendour or high historical associations, the burial ground of St. Michael's, Dumfries (the "Auld Kirkyard," as it is familiarly spoken of), yet calls up recollections wide and deep peculiar to itself. For a provincial burial-place, it is unusually large and yet unusually crowded with memorials. It has been for centuries the grave of magistrates and burgesses, conveners and deacons, not to speak of old country families of repute like the Maxwells, Sharpes, and Fergusons. It is even hallowed as the grave of martyrs, one granite memorial, renewing the testimony of an earlier but humbler stone, recording that "near this spot were deposited the remains of William Grierson and William Welsh, who suffered unto death for their adherence to the principles of the Reformation, January 2, 1667. Also of James Kirk, shot on the Sands of Dumfries, 1685. "Rev. xii. 11." But magistrates and even martyrs are to be found in other churchyards. The special interest of St. Michael's, Dumfries, is its connection with the memory of Burns. The poet worshipped in the church, and in the ground adjoining his dust, and the dust of his wife and family, rests under the stately mausoleum designed by Turnerelli for the poet's admirers. Here, too, and not far distant, is the grave of Jessie Lewars (afterwards Mrs. Thomson) to be enrolled by fate "with native worth and spotless fame." As a near neighbour in the street, and the daughter of a brother exciseman, Burns had addressed to her the song, "Here's a health to ane I lo'e dear," and it is pleasing to remember that his closing sickness was soothed as far as it could be by her tender attention. John Lewars himself is buried not far off, as is John Bushby of the "Election Ballads," and James Gracie, banker, that "man of worth"—helpful when help was most needed. More still. Within St. Michael's the graves are still to be seen of Gabriel Richardson, "Brewer Gabriel" of the epitaph, but known also as the father of Sir John Richardson, an intrepid Arctic voyager; and of Colonel de

Peyster, "My honoured Colonel, deep I feel your interest in the poet's weal." This officer of the Dumfries Volunteers survived Burns more than a quarter of a century, having been spared to the long age of ninety-six. With a reputation for severity, acquired in the American war, the colonel appears to have been in reality a modest, warm-hearted man. A few days before his death he wrote, and it has been appropriately placed on his monument :—

> Raise no vain structure o'er my grave,
> One simple stone is all I crave,
> To say, beneath a sinner lies,
> Who died in hopes again to rise,
> Through Christ alone to be forgiven,
> And fitted for the joys of heaven.

It will thus be seen that Burns and his contemporaries furnish matter unusually attractive for the "Memorials;" nor can it be said that the industrious compiler, Mr. M'Dowall, has in any case failed to set forth in an attractive way the most important facts necessary to be known of their personal history and the associations naturally called up by the mention of the poet or his friends. He is directly referred to or used in illustration between thirty and forty times :—

> All ask the cottage of his birth,
> Gaze on the scenes he loved and sung,
> And gather feelings not of earth,
> His fields and streams among.

> They linger by the Doon's low trees,
> And pastoral Nith and wooded lyre,
> And round thy sepulchres, Dumfries—
> The poet's tomb is there.

The plan adopted to bring the "Memorials" into something like order is simple and natural, and wrought out in a way well suited to make the book useful for family or general reference. The work is divided into thirty-one chapters, each taken up with a separate walk or section, in which all the memorials of departed worth are passed under review, the inscriptions in many cases being given in full, and in all as much interesting collateral information presented as keeps the book from being a mere dull or monotonous chronicle of the tombs. He does not claim, nor was it well possible, even if desirable, to give the names of every member of the great company resting within the area of St. Michael's, but from his minuteness, and the care with which for years he is known to have passed through its quiet walks, it may be assumed that no family burial-place with any memorial or noteworthy member has been passed by unnoticed. The book has thus an interest for friends far distant and long absent distinct from relatives nearer who may wish to renew their memories by a personal visit to the graves, book in hand. Whenever, writes Mr. M'Dowall, the persons commented upon figured in history or were connected with important events, local or national, a brief biography or descriptive sketch has been given. To town councillors and trades, with the provosts and bailies, conveners and deacons—many of them heroes of John Mayne's "Siller Gun" —considerable prominence has been given, as is the case also with those who bore rule in spiritual things, or ministered to the bodily health, or looked after the legal business of the lieges. The Latin epitaphs have in translation had the benefit of the rare scholarship of Dr. Cranstoun, rector of the Burgh Academy, whose "Catullus" and "Tibullus" most readers of old classics in an English dress are familiar with. In the tenth chapter the walk naturally leads our author to the cholera mound, and this in turn suggests an account of the grievous pestilence referred to in the inscription:—"In this cemetery, and chiefly within this enclosure, lie the mortal remains of more than 420 inhabitants of Dumfries who were suddenly swept away by the memorable invasion of Asiatic cholera A.D. 1832. That terrible pestilence entered the town on 15th September, and remained till 27th November, during which period it seized at least 900 individuals, of whom 44 died in one day, and no more than 415 were reported as recovered. That the benefit of this solemn warning might not be lost to posterity, this monument was erected from collections made in several churches in this town." Among the oldest monuments in St. Michael's is one erected by "a grateful spouse and pious children" to commemorate the virtues of Francis Irving, merchant and magistrate, who died November, 1633. In addition to a Latin Inscription, the following lines have been added as expressing the personal opinion of the old citizen :—

>King James at first me Balive named
>Drumfreis oft time me Provest clamed
>God hast for me ane crowne reserved
>For King and Countrie have I served.

We should not omit to mention that a fair index of names and subjects permits Mr. M'Dowall's book to be turned up with the utmost readiness by all wishing to know what can be known about the work done while it was day by the now silent occupants of the old burying-place of St. Michael's, Dumfries.

DUMFRIES ROOD FAIR.

WHILE nothing is easier to note than the mere market or trade aspect of fairs, there is a difficulty sometimes in accounting for the vitality of old customs, which has helped to raise certain gatherings of this kind almost to the dignity of national institutions. Fairs in Scotland have originated in various ways. In days when the Church was learned as well as powerful, she invariably flung her protecting arm round the little community gathered near the monastery or cathedral, and even conferred upon them special privileges in the way of trade, or exemption from dues. Glasgow and Paisley, Dunfermline and Brechin, all owe their fairs to the Church. Ayr and Stirling, again, with Perth and Inverness, are of civil or royal origin. A third class, such as Falkirk, Muir of Ord, and Carman, may more properly be set down as "trysts," or markets originating from the ordinary necessities or conveniences of stock trading. Civil in origin, yet with a brotherhood of Grey Friars in their midst, and possessed at the same time of special "tryst" or market features, Dumfries Rood Fair may be said to present features belonging to all three classes. The gathering itself is of old date, in all probability coeval with the foundation of the burgh by William the Lion. His character of erection is not in existence, nor has any copy of it been seen in modern times. The usual form observed was for the sovereign to declare to all concerned that the town or "vil" described, had been raised to the dignity of a burgh, and possessed all the liberties enjoyed by the King's other burghs. The burgesses were freed from tolls throughout the kingdom, and a certain cohesion was given to their corporate existence, by a grant of lands contiguous to the town. Stated fairs as a rule were also permitted to be held in the course of the year, and toll and customs due to the burgh, fell to be collected at places set forth in the charter. A second charter of King Robert III., dated at Glasgow, 1395, confirms all previous customs and privileges, with the addition of Nith fishings, excepting only such portion as had been granted by predecessors out of Divine charity to the Minorite Brethren. A formal but apparently uncompleted precept for a new charter by King James VI., in 1621, purports to confer upon the Magistrates and Council authority "to have and use within the burgh upon ilk Monday and Friday, ane publick mercat day, togidder with twa fairis in the year, the ane thereoif to begin upon the [blank] day of Apryle, and the aither upon the fourtene day of September yearlie, and aither of them to continue for the space of aucht days theireafter." Influenced, apparently, by the festival day of the burgh's patron, St. Michael the Archangel (Sept. 29), the autumn or Rood Fair was fixed at a stated period between this date and the other Church festival known as the Exaltation of the Holy Cross or Rood, " Exaltatio Sanctæ Crucis." St. Michael himself composedly trampling the dragon under foot, may still be seen, as graven by a cunning hand, in front of the midsteeple buildings, the Town's Chamber for many years before removal to Buccleuch Street. About this St. Michael much amusing literature, diverting at any time, but especially suitable at fair time, has been written by grave clergymen. In the "New Statistical Account" one reverend gentleman, ignorant apparently of the traditions gathering round the name of him who in Heaven made war against the Woman, describes St. Michael as "a Popish saint of extreme sanctity," while another identifies his "Kirkmichael" with the burial-place of the archangel. In early days, and in accordance with what was known as " The Laws of the Four Burghs," after the peace of the fair was proclaimed, it was not lawful to capture or attack any wrong-doer within the burgh, unless he had broken the peace of the fair, or was a traitor to the King, or had been guilty of some misdeed for which Holy Church itself could not give "gyrth" or sanctuary. None have as yet been able to trace the "Pied Poudre" Court in Scotland, but from the readiness with which appeals could be made to "the bailies of the fair" in the case of articles lost or stolen, it may be inferred that such magistrates formed a ready court of reference in all disputes between the burgesses and the "dustyfoot" or travelling merchant. As a salutary warning to evil-doers, market or fair days were generally fixed upon for carrying out extreme sentences of the law. It is mentioned in M'Dowall's excellent "History of Dumfries" that in April, 1659, nine unfortunate women, condemned as witches, were inhumanly strangled and burnt at the usual place of execution, on a Wednesday afternoon. The local clergy, on this occasion, being unable to overtake the task of spiritual consolation, was assisted on the day of execution by brethren from Galloway. In the face of all the changes in trade caused by railways, the Rood Fair gathering in the south has, from generation to generation, been considered the event of the year. Young and old have been alike interested in the return of the welcome season; and to it in troops they flock from every point of the compass—from the green holms of Annandale to the solitary Glenkens—from breezy Kyle to Solway shore—all direct their journey to "Maggie, by the banks of Nith." Then they are of all classes. In the space between Church Place and Assembly Street, there may be seen the laird and the factor, the farmer and the cottar, wives and daughters, man-servant and maid-servant. Elderly fair-goers have a habit of contrasting the splendour of the fair nowadays with what it was in past times, when the seven incorporated trades turned out with their gaudy trappings on the Thursday, or town's holiday, and a glimpse might even have been obtained of King James' famous gift, "the Siller Gun," as it was borne in triumph to their own hall. In "the shows," especially, the falling off is described as a local calamity. And certainly with Jerry Wombwell on the White Sands, and old Ord on the Green, a poor substitute is presented by a gaudy show of shooting ranges and a ricketty caravan or two, even though they do happen to contain Peruvian Pangythans. David Street, too, has been shorn of its crockery display, and all the china or Staffordshire ware to be seen there might be packed within the space of a common crate. Burwell's Bazaar, a very Cave of Aladdin, with its sanded floor and gay contents, not to speak of the desperate excitement of the lottery, was first removed from its time-honoured stance in Buccleuch Street, and now seems to be altogether improved out of existence. These are, no doubt, drawbacks of a kind, but the real spectacle happens to be the people themselves—the lads and lasses—and here they have been in abundance, exuberant yet orderly, gay as holiday attire can make them, but richer still in stores of health and strength won in the harvest field. They gather to see each other, and care for little else. Mere town sights are of little moment. Not an extra score of people find their way to any of them. Burns, as he at one time wrote to Grose was likely, might as well be lying in the quiet solitude of Alloway. The Observatory, made of easier access from the Dumfries side, by the new and elegant suspension bridge across the Nith at the Dock, may attract a few specially curious, but they are mostly townsfolk or visiting friends of townsfolk. The hostelries adjacent to High Street supply the bulk of the entertainment wanted, and their resources are taxed to the utmost. Royal Oaks and Crowns, Globes and Georges (the hack "Supple Sam," in "Guy Mannering," belonged to the George) have all been too little for the demands made on them by our lively south-country Jocks and Jennies.

RENFREWSHIRE RECORDS.

IN issuing a new series of selections from the Judicial Records of Renfrewshire, Mr. Hector added a useful and entertaining volume to the historian's library, and presented a series of details regarding the administration of law in the county, as well as of the manners and condition of the people, interesting far beyond the bounds to which the different papers specially refer. In drawing from those Renfrewshire records, of which as Sheriff-Clerk he was official custodier, Mr. Hector was in reality illustrating the history of Scotland in general, and that on points whose preceding writers of far higher pretensions were neither very full nor very accurate. A list of rents, prices, and valuations may present a dry, forbidding appearance to readers caring only for amusement or passing the time; but they form the material out of which history must be constructed, if we really desire to know how our ancestors lived at home or were controlled by civil authority. In Mr. Hector's hands the various documents submitted become something more than mere material for history. It is history itself, the Muse unrolling the historic scroll in her own way. In addition to the "libel" as presented to the Court for discussion and settlement, Mr. Hector has always a few introductory remarks to offer in the way of explanation, sometimes by way of contrast or comparison with things judicial in our own time. These remarks as a rule are not only made with brevity and intelligence, but are full of suggestive matter likely to occur only to a mind familiar with the details of legal practice and trained in the strict application of general legal principles. Nor are such details by any means as a rule of a dry statistical character; in like manner to the first volume there is in the second something for the merely curious to beguile a half-hour, and something also for those who have earnestly laboured in modern times to bring about some improvement in the local judicial business of the country. In this respect the attractive qualities of Mr. Hector's book gives ground for hope that similar collections may soon be issued illustrating the history of other counties in Scotland. Renfrewshire is not richer than others in ancient judicial records; nor does Mr. Hector say so. Rather otherwise. In all Scottish counties such records have been accumulating rapidly since 1748, when the earlier records of hereditary officials and Bailies of Barony were abolished by the Heritable Jurisdiction Act, and their records transferred to the new Sheriffs. From the absence of sufficient accommodation, as Mr. Hector justly observes, or through want of due appreciation of their value, the earlier as well as the more recent records were improperly buried and injured in obscure corners where such portions as can be preserved still await the attention of Government for publication, so far at least as the documents might be judged historically important. So late as 1873, the judicial records of Renfrewshire were for the most part huddled on the damp stone floor of the record room at Paisley—no inventories, covered with dust, many missing, and all going to decay. So serious did matters look in this department, that when Mr. Hector was appointed Sheriff-Clerk in that year he found it necessary to decline taking possession of the records, or to be held responsible in any way regarding them, so long as they were permitted to remain in their then condition. Through the active exertions of Sheriff Fraser and others funds were at length procured for putting the record room in order, and steps taken to arrange and inventory such documents as remained. In carrying out this congenial duty the Sheriff-Clerk naturally came across many papers relating to the old hereditary courts and illustrative of the social condition of the people. Believing that some of them might still interest the public, he selected, annotated, and published portions in the press weekly during the last three years. The result was the first volume of records issued from the tasteful press of the Messrs. Cook, Paisley, early in 1876. The second, with which we are now dealing, has just been submitted to subscribers by the same careful publishers. This series would appear, for the present at least, to close the publication. Mr. Hector explains that his chief object has been to prompt other custodiers of county records to follow his example, believing it to be a duty which they should not shrink from; and to press at the same time the duty laid upon those in authority to provide sufficient accommodation for the safe and careful preservation of official documents. The new volume is divided into eight convenient sections:—1, County Representation, Freeholders, &c.; 2, Old County Families and Estates; 3, County Courts; 4, Social Condition and Manners; 5, Prisons and Prisoners; 6, the Burgh of Paisley (with a Plan, of date about 1545, and View of the Old Abbey "Yett House"); 7, Miscellaneous; 8, Rents, Prices, &c., 1730-50. In addition to the illustrations just mentioned, a number of well-executed facsimilies are presented of certain of the more important documents described and inserted in the text. The volume formally bears to be dedicated by permission to Sir William Stirling-Maxwell, Bart.—" Eminent as a legislator and author, and representative of one of the oldest and most distinguished families in Renfrewshire;" but during its passage through the press Sir William died at Venice. In accepting the dedication the accomplished Baronet wrote that he had read the "records with great pleasure, and tendered his thanks to Mr. Hector for the instruction and amusement they had afforded him." The volume is to be had in two sizes—a handy octavo for use, and large paper for book-fanciers inclining to luxury or display.

Curious rather than important, the gleanings of the late Mr. Hector from the record room of his county have been strung together in a narrative of such historic interest as entitles him to the thanks of readers far removed from the circle of mere local antiquaries, and fully justifies the desire expressed that he would gather into a neat, convenient book-form what was at first intended to serve a more ephemeral purpose in the columns of a local newspaper. From the Sheriff-Clerk's familiarity with Renfrewshire and his local knowledge of most record repositories in the county, it is to be wished he could have seen his way to have enlarged his scheme so far as to include not only records of older date than he has referred to, but documents other than those which naturally fell under his own official custody. It would have been well, for instance, to have had set forth with some local colouring that remarkable dispute described in the Abbey Cartulary as occurring between the abbot and convent on the one hand and a contumacious layman, known as Gilbert the son of Samuel of Renfrew, on the other, concerning certain church lands on the north side of the Clyde, one property being minutely described as the great house made of wattles—"domus magna fabricata de virgis" —intended for the entertainment of pilgrims journeying to the Shrine of St. Patrick. It presents what is probably the earliest specimen furnished by ecclesiastical law of trial by jury, and is, besides, interesting as settled by evidence taken on oath of witnesses familiar with the localities and persons described in the process. The abbot and convent of Paisley appealed to Pope Gregory the Ninth to vindicate the rights of their house, and His Holiness so far espoused their cause as to issue at Spoletum, 8th June, 1232, a commission to the Deans of Carrick and Cunningham and the master of the schools of Ayr within the diocese of Glasgow, to redress, without appeal, the grievances complained of. The commission is afterwards described as sitting at Ayr on the Sabbath immediately following the Lord's-Day on which is sung "Quasi modi genite," 30th April, 1234. Then a search, say in the town-clerk's office under a trained eye like Mr. Hector's, might be made to reveal something concerning that preposterous riot on the part of Renfrew, referred to in a letter addressed by James IV., 23rd December, 1490, to John, Earl of Lennox, and Matthew Stewart, his son, commanding them, at the instance of the abbot, to make inquisition for the discovery and punishment of divers persons of the burgh of Renfrew, who, animated apparently by ill-will and jealousy against the town of Paisley, shortly before erected by the Sovereign into a free burgh of barony, had during the night-time riotously destroyed the stones and hewn-work of the market cross of that town. Some more reference also to the old families of Renfrewshire and their residences would have been a pleasant feature in a collection of records relating to a county so famous for its antiquarian interests in these respects. Documents, judicial or municipal, public or private, are always welcome when they can be connected with the traditions of such houses as the Montgomeries and Cunninghams, Maxwells and Stewarts, or even with those of lesser estate, though equally distinguished, like the Dennistouns, Napiers, and Mures. Crawford, too, of Jordanhill, a daring soldier of the reign of James VI., connects himself intimately with Paisley, by appearing early in 1570 before the Abbey to take over the fabric on behalf of the King, along with the body of Robert, Lord Sempill, under an assurance that all persons in the Abbey and Place would be set at liberty, excepting only those under suspicion of being concerned in the murder of Henry, Lord Darnley, his Majesty's father. An unlucky ordination dinner at Inchinnan, where "the meat was not nyce," and the ale only "twopenny," as set forth with graphic vigour by Mr. Hector, hardly requires the pleasant fancy of the author of "The Pen Folk," or even the antiquarian enthusiasm of the historian of "Saint Mirin," to connect itself with a record known as "The Inventure of the graithe in Inchinane, with the auld rotten

Papistrie thairin." "Item (says this record of about 1570) in chapell, 2 mess buiks. Item, ane ymage of the babe Jesus. Item, kaist ymage of our Lady, and ane grit ymage witht ane ymage of Sanct Ann. Item, ane little ymage of ewir bane that stud upone ane chandlar," &c.

Thankful, however, for even the comparatively recent records of his office, and glad to know that under his care they were lately arranged with a view to reference as well as preservation, it is a more pleasant part of our task to indicate Mr. Hector's own plan of arranging his materials, and to describe how successfully he touched upon the various topics embraced in the volume issued in such excellent taste from the Paisley press. Section first is taken up with documents illustrating that period generally described in Scotland as "The Persecution;" sections two and three relate to the manners and customs of the people from about the time of the Revolution to the end of last century; section four recalls to readers the administration of law during the same years, and shows by many well-selected cases how severely it bore upon all charged with crime—young and old, woman or child—and what gross irregularity then characterised the administration of justice in provincial courts. The closing portion of Mr. Hector's very interesting volume is made partly up of a few miscellaneous papers relating to some Renfrewshire families of note, and a valuable, though rather dry series concerning rents and prices prevailing over the county during the seventeenth and eighteenth centuries. Each legal document produced from the archives of the Sheriff-Clerk is accompanied by a page or two of explanatory matter, setting forth its main features and obviating any necessity for non-professional readers losing time or patience over the somewhat crabbed originals. In order, however, that these may be consulted by the careful scholar with as much exactness as possible, a few excellent drawings in *facsimile* have been introduced into the work. As was befitting the official chief in an office where Motherwell wrote, Mr. Hector has been fortunate enough to disinter a new Jacobite song out of a very unpromising bundle of law papers; but whatever zeal the author may have intended to show on behalf of the exiled house, the merits of the piece are so very ordinary that James M'Alpie, Sheriff-Clerk, and for some time Substitute, can hardly be said to add to the interest of that department of literature which includes such lyrics as "Will ye no come back again?" and "Waes me for Prince Charlie." The inconvenience and loss occasioned by "Black" or counterfeit Irish coins is touched upon in the form of a complaint at the instance of the Procurator-Fiscal, of date 1727. The grievance unfortunately was too common in those days, and neither swift nor severe punishment could prevent fraud in the currency. In June of the following year (1728), Patrick, second Viscount Garnock (of whom something may be learned in Dobie's "Examination of the Claims of John Lindsay Craufurd") writes to Hunter of Hunterston from Kilbirnie:—"Please lett me know, in answer to yrs. what i ou you o borrowed money, which I think is a shilling sterline, and two or thereby halfpence." While the general ignorance of the people and the uniform severity of those who sat in high places are brought fully enough out in Mr. Hector's book, there is a deficiency we did not expect in documents illustrating the darker superstitions of the district—a matter to be wondered at all the more from the somewhat evil eminence enjoyed by Renfrewshire in the annals of witches and warlocks. Recent, historically speaking, though most of the documents are, some of them almost touch the time when clergy and judges sent poor creatures to the gallows or the stake for imputed crimes not possible to be committed. Some of the victims, indeed, got a taste of the bitterness of death in both forms, being first partly "wirrit to death" at a stake and then burnt. This sad chapter in the history of ignorance and superstition is just touched upon in the case of Perhie and others libelled in 1692 for the "unnatural, barbarous, and unchristian" crime of drinking the health of the devil, and scandalising in connection therewith certain good citizens of Paisley. The punishment in this case was simply exposure at the Cross. There is nothing about Mary Lamond and the other Innerkip witches of 1662, who had been taught by Katherine Scott in Murdistane to get milk from her neighbour's cow, "bidding hir goe out in mistie mornings, and tak with her a hairie tedder, and draw it over the mouth of a mug, saying, in God's name send us milk and meikle of it. Be these wayes she and the said Kathrine got muckle of thair neibours' milk, and made butter and cheise thairof." Her experience, first at Ardgowan and then at Kempock, was that "The Deil, for ordinar in the shape of a black man with cloven feet, sang to them, gave them wyne to drink, and wheat bread to eat. When thay dancit they war all verie merrie, and he kist them, ane and all, when thay skaillit," except once when his sooty highness nipt her on the right side, "but thairafter straikit it with his hand and healed it." There is nothing even about "Auld Dunrod," another graceless son of Innerkip, who

---------muntit his stick,
His brumestick muntit he,
And he flychter't twa three times about,
Syne o'er the Firth did flee.
But he forgot the rowantree
At the Rest-and-be-Thanfu' stane,
His magic brumestick tint its spell,
And he daudit his head thereon.

It is possible that any official documents ever called into existence by such cases may still exist in the record room of the Lower Ward, or, what is more to be dreaded, they may have been withdrawn from the custody of officials not so careful as Sheriff-Clerks nowadays to permit private friends to illustrate narratives like the famous Bargarran imposture.

What mercy might be expected in those dark days by the victims of a wicked superstition may be illustrated from what happened so late as 1770 to Jean Montgomery, a married woman, who, on a charge by no means established in evidence, of stealing a cut of a piece of lawn of less value than ten shillings, suffered four months' imprisonment before trial, one month after trial, and, in addition to being banished from the country, was sentenced, under form of law and justice, to be stripped naked to the middle, marched through the streets of Paisley in charge of the common hangman, and to be by him publicly whipped on the bare back at four places, all duly yet inhumanly set forth in the deliverance—ten lashes at the Townhead, ten at the head of the New Street, ten at the foot of the New Street, and a final ten lashes at the Cross, after being marched down the Causeyside and up Saint Mirren's Wynd, with her hands tied, as they had been all through her dismal progress. This terrible sentence, it is to be recollected, stands recorded not as witnessing against a distant age or a savage race—not in Dahomey or among black people at all—but at home, in a community reputed to be civilised, and near enough our own time to have been witnessed by the fathers of the present generation. From the fact of Jean Montgomery being described as a married woman, wife of John Storie, weaver, there is a presumption that she must at some time of her life have received in a kind of way the benefit of clergy, yet no voice is raised for mercy on her behalf in pulpit or on platform. Even the members for the county and burgh of Renfrew sit dumb in parliament, and this at a time when the one was represented by a gentleman so well known as Wm. M'Dowall of Castlesemple, and the other (embraced in the Glasgow group) by an official of such eminence as Lord Frederick Campbell, third son of John, fourth Duke of Argyll, afterwards a most efficient Lord Clerk-Register, and much talked of even earlier, from his marriage with the widow of that Laurence Earl Ferrers, executed at Tyburn for the murder of his land-steward. Had such a sentence stood on record against either man or woman in the time of the Persecution— say for "rabbling." some poor indulged curate or the like—there is no end to the illustrations it would have furnished the Kirk with of the patience manifested by the Covenanted opponents of a system only possible to be upheld by "the Boot" of Lauderdale and the sword of Dundee. Even in Boston at the time, where the struggle for independence was just assuming precise form, a mere black slave, George by name, for half-murdering a white man in his own house, and then tarring and feathering him, received only two years' imprisonment with the addition of forty stripes save one of the number meted out to poor Jean

Montgomery for her alleged guilt in stealing a cut of a piece of lawn. In Hogarth's Bridewell scene, the uplifted cane of old Inspector Suspercoll has sometimes been described as out of place; but there Kate is tightly laced up, and in the newspapers of the day special mention is made that Mary Moffat, the type in her "Progress" of many a Hackabout, was then in confinement, "beating hemp in a gown very richly laced with silver." The only alleviating circumstance in the Paisley case is that the sentence might not, or could not, be carried into effect. Mr. Hector, it is but right to state, gives no indication of this being possible, and rather leaves the reader to infer that such an outrage as the sentence indicates was not perpetrated. He writes of the deliverance as being a disgrace to "our" records and to all concerned in carrying it out; and so in every sense it is, but we fear that "our" records may be designed to indicate a wider area than Renfrewshire. There is no reason we know of for believing the people of Paisley to have been more blood-thirsty than their neighbours, or their rulers to have been more Draconian. What occurred in Paisley a century since need not be considered exceptional so far as Scotland is concerned. The fact of the flogging may be a matter of certain and easy proof. Whipping half-naked women through the streets, under form of law, could never be so common even in Paisley but that it must have fixed itself in the memory of some inhabitants likely to speak of the fact to many still living. No doubt there were other important matters exciting discussion in the burgh that week—the trial, among others, of Mungo Campbell for shedding in a poaching squabble the blood of another Montgomery, Alexander, tenth Earl of Eglinton. But even he had such a measure of fairness shown to him in the Justiciary Court that it could not altogether blot out of memory this humiliating case of Jean Montgomery or Storie. Some countenance is given to the merciful theory here suggested as to its being a mere formal sentence from the circumstance that in May, 1735, a certain infirm old Mary Black and her daughter, for what was described as "accession to fire-raising" in a stackyard, were sentenced in the same county to be banished the district, but previously to suffer twelve months' imprisonment, and every fourteen days each of them was to be taken from prison, stripped naked to the waist, and flogged by the common hangman at five different places, all duly set forth, in the streets of Paisley, the younger prisoner in addition to be burnt on the face. The flogging in this case was officially authorised to be administered with "a lash of small cords, consisting of five lashes knit at the ends." For the sake of humanity, one is glad to be able to state that not even a hangman could be found to carry out the merciless decree, and the prisoners were liberated on promising to banish themselves from the county. Thanks to that progress of knowledge based on experience which has led in modern times to the necessity of tempering justice with mercy and punishment with decency, it is no longer necessary to rely on the sensitive feelings of the common executioner for avoiding such outrages on nature.

THE RENFREWSHIRE WITCHES.

IN his now forgotten play of "The Drummer," Addison unconsciously anticipates by way of a joke a sentiment which a few years later than his time continued to be widely and sincerely entertained. When Truman explains that poor Dobbin is bewitched neither by Goody Crouch nor Goody Flye, "Then, exclaims the coachman, it must be by Goody Gurton, for she is the next oldest woman in the parish." The great humourist makes Sir Roger himself a sort of half believer in the popular superstition. He would apparently have committed Mother White for trial had his chaplain not been present, and though he openly acquitted her of any concern in the wind which blew down his barn a month after her death, he still betrayed by his manner a lurking suspicion that it was she after all who brewed the blast. The reprint of a once popular West Country tract (Gardner, 1877) affords an excuse for referring to a tragedy in which it is hard to say whether superstition or imposture played the most prominent part. A small old mansion in Erskine parish, known as Bargarran, has earned the evil reputation of being the scene of one of the maddest of all the mad delusions concerning witchcraft which stain the judicial annals of Scotland. At Bargarran, in the summer of 1696, resided John Shaw, a man of moderate landed estate, with his wife and a few young children—one in particular, Christian by name, being noticed as of an unusual lively and open disposition. While the "True Narrative of the Sufferings and Relief" of this young girl makes reference to occurrences in August of the above year, its composition is of date many months subsequent, and among the few really contemporary documents bearing on the case which have been saved, it is satisfactory to find a series of minutes so complete and official as is furnished by the records of the local Presbytery. The Kirk, as was usual in such cases, took the earliest steps to set the civil law in motion. The first note sounded openly in the case came from the Rev. Andrew Turner, minister of Erskine parish, who at Paisley, on the 30th December, 1696, represented to the Presbytery the "deplorable case" of Christian Shaw, with details so minute as almost to supersede the necessity of referring to the pretended experiences of the girl herself as made in the so-called "Narrative." Since the beginning of September last (it was reported) she had been under a very sore and unnatural distemper, "frequently seized with strange fits, sometimes blind, sometimes deaf and dumb, the several parts of her body sometimes violently extended, and other parts as violently contracted, and for several weeks past she hath disgorged a considerable quantity of hair, folded up straw, unclean hay, wild-fowl feathers, with divers kinds of bones of fowls and others, together with a number of coal cinders burning hot, candle grease, gravel stones, &c., all which she puts forth during the forementioned fits, and in the intervals of them is in perfect health, wherein she gives an account of several persons—both men and women—that appear to her in her fits tormenting her, all which began with her upon the back of one

Kathrine Campbell, her cursing of her; and though her father hath called physicians of the best note to her during her trouble, yet the application of medicine to her hath proven ineffectual, either for better or worse, and that they (the Presbytery) are ready to declare that they look upon this distemper as *toto-genere* preternatural." Failing the powers of physicians to do anything in the way of alleviating the "distressed damsel," fasting and prayer was now enjoined by the Presbytery; and with a view of ulterior proceedings, a deputation was appointed on the same day to proceed to Edinburgh, in order that the whole affair might be laid before the Lords of His Majesty's Privy Council. Soon after this date a portion of Christian Shaw's "Narrative" is likely to have been put together; but whatever she may have said was shaped and influenced so much by different members of Presbytery, that it may be said to be rather the production of the reverend court than a genuine account of personal experiences. In due course the Privy Council granted a Commission to Lord Blantyre and other gentlemen in the neighbourhood for the taking of evidence, and so preparing matters that a formal trial, if necessary, might be made of any alleged to be concerned in the mysterious visitation. In the course of their sittings at Renfrew during February, 1697, the Commissioners obtained the "confession" of three people—two lads named Lindsay and an Elizabeth Anderson—as accessories with at least seven others in the bewitching of Christian Shaw. The Lindsays, who testified against their grandmother, were only striplings of twelve or fourteen years of age, while Anderson, who implicated her own father, was but seventeen. The testimony of these witnesses was judged to be of such importance that on the last day of meeting the Commissioners desired they should be severally kept by turns in the houses of members of Presbytery, that the ministers might have an opportunity of dealing with their conscience till further steps could be taken by the authority. A report, to be afterwards referred to, was presented to the Privy Council, and a commission appointed for trial in March. Meanwhile spiritual efforts were not neglected. On the 24th of that month the Presbytery of Paisley, "considering the great rage of Satan in this corner of the land, and particularly the continued trouble of Bargarran's daughter, which is a great evidence of the Lord's displeasure so to let Satan loose among us," the Presbytery therefore judge it necessary to set apart a day of solemn humiliation and fasting to "wrestle with God in prayer, that he may restrain Satan's rage, and relieve that poor afflicted damsel." The new Commission, made up of the best known gentlemen in the West Country, with the accomplished Sir James Stuart as King's Advocate, commenced their sittings at Paisley in April, when business was preceded with a sermon by the Rev. Mr. Hutcheson from the suggestive text, "Thou shalt not suffer a witch to live." An illegal deputation from the Presbytery was also associated with the Commissioners for "dealing with the conscience of those on whom the insensible marks are found, in order to their being brought to confession, as they shall with the Commissioners concert the method of the same." Following the course usually observed on such occasions, the Commission would send a report of the evidence taken to the Privy Council, but no trace of the document has been found in recent years. Some help as to the nature of its contents may be found in an informal "Abbreviate of the Precognition and Report," made by the first or preliminary Commission for taking evidence. The occurrences there spoken to were of the usual marvellous and impossible description. The deluded maid Anderson affirmed that she had seen Satan speak to her grandmother in the likeness of "a black, grim man," with a very cold hand; that she had been repeatedly at witch-gatherings on Kilmalcolm Moor, above the village of Kilpatrick, and in the manse garden at Dumbarton, Satan being always present, and engaging freely in conversation. In particular, Anderson confessed to being present in Bargarran orchard when the destruction of Christian Shaw was contrived. Some, she said, were for stabbing, others for choking, and a third for hanging her; but fearing they might be taken before next morning, their lord, as they called him—"the black, grim man"—gave them a piece of unchristened child's heart to eat, telling them that though they were apprehended they should never confess. So far as confession was concerned, witness was threatened with being torn to pieces, especially by Maggy Lang, or "Pinched Maggy," as she was called. After two hours, or thereby (the witness gravely concluded) the whole party disappeared in a flight, but she herself went home on foot. The testimony of the two Lindsay lads was so similar in detail as to afford strong presumption that the monstrous story was concocted by some person equally credulous but more experienced than themselves. From the want of any official record of the court's proceedings it is impossible to say how many were indicted, or "deleted," as it was called, for these imaginary and impossible crimes. Even the victims who suffered can only be indicated in a doubtful way. The number, according to all accounts, would appear to have been seven, and from a note appended to the reprint by Mr. D. Semple their names would seem to have been—John Lindsay, cottar, Barloch; James Lindsay, cottar, Bilboe; John Reid, smith, Hapland; Margaret Lang, Cartympen; Margaret Fulton, Dumbarton; Catherine Campbell, servant, Bargarran; and Agnes Naismith, probably of Old Kilpatrick. On what strict principle of law these seven could be found either more or less guilty than the other panels on charges so preposterous as to be incapable of proof by evidence of any kind is never likely to be ascertained. If the slightest reliance could be placed on the incoherent ramblings of the girl Anderson, some of the women at least may be presumed to have been well up in years—possibly old and wrinkled, poor and friendless—in all these respects, unlike the witches of modern days, who cast their spells over poor humanity under quite different conditions. There is not only a want in the way of documents concerning the proceedings of the Commissioners, but it would appear as if even the municipal records of Paisley failed to furnish any reference to this extraordinary series of executions which may be presumed to have been carried out under authority of the burgh magistrates. As the Kirk introduces us to the case, so is it from the Presbytery records we get the last glimpse of the victims. The burning was fixed for the 10th June. On May 19, three ministers of the Presbytery were appointed to converse as frequently as they could with the seven persons condemned to die for witchcraft, and two were appointed to preach special sermons on the day preceding the execution.

A few days after this date, the prospect of the horrid end at the Gallowgreen induced one of the prisoners to commit suicide in the Tolbooth of Paisley. The final note in the tragedy is sounded in a minute of date June 9, when the Presbytery "did appoint the whole members to spend some time this night with the condemned persons who are to die to-morrow, and did allot to each one or two of the brethren one of the sentenced persons to be dealt with by them, AND WAITED UPON TO THE FIRE." The threatened sacrifice of six victims would not appear to have rid the country as yet of the Evil One. He was now at large—indeed, under form of law, more jubilant than ever, and in appearance not unlike the Bargarran invention—"a black, grim man." And yet the Kirk must not be made to bear all the blame. Belief in witchcraft was a feature of the age, and that too in highly accomplished circles, legal and medical, as well as clerical. Even in enlightened England, and fifty years after this Paisley case, Ruth Osborne, aged seventy, was drowned in Herefordshire by a disorderly mob for the imputed offence of bewitching her neighbours. One of the ringleaders was certainly hanged for his share in the riot, but the occurrence at Tring is sufficient to show how widely and recently the delusion prevailed. So far as the Renfrewshire case was concerned, the King's advocate would appear to have spoken as if he sincerely judged the stories in his brief to be capable of verification, and were in point of fact verified by the witnesses produced. Nor can it be said that, in comparison with other trials of the kind, he pressed unduly for a conviction. The law recognised the imputed offence, and it must therefore be held as capable of proof. Judging from such "Accounts" and "Abbreviates" as have been preserved, the Court may be said to have looked with clear enough eyes on the case, but unhappily with lesser light to guide them than shines in our better days. The most that may be inferred from the case is that no profession of faith, however orthodox, nor any form of belief, however sincerely entertained, can secure either just judgment or merciful conduct. From a case raised in the local courts soon after the trial, it would appear that Neil Snodgrass, writer, was subjected to some abuse for the part he had taken in defending the witches. Trials for witchcraft, or at least a belief in the superstition, still exist in the Highlands. The last execution for witchcraft in Scotland took place at Dornock, Sutherlandshire, in 1727. Although the month was June, it has been handed down by tradition that the weather was very severe, and the poor old woman victim, after being brought out to get tied to a tar barrel, sat composedly warming herself by the fire prepared to consume her, while the other instruments of death were being made ready. The Acts of Queen Mary and King James authorising such executions were formally repealed by the Parliament of Great Britain, in June, 1736. It became from that time incompetent to institute any suit for "witchcraft, sorcery, enchantment, or conjurations," and only a crime to pretend to exercise such acts, liable to be punished by imprisonment and pillory. So far as the Bargarran family is concerned, it is pleasant to know that they came to distinguish themselves more honourably in what is now one of the most extensive industries of the district, the Lady Bargarran and her daughters being the first to engage in the spinning of a fine linen thread, "cheap and white, and known by experience to be much stronger than the Dutch," and the reputation of which they sought to protect by a trade-mark made up from the family armorial bearing of three covered cups.

PAISLEY ABBEY.

In noticing the "Judicial Records of Renfrewshire," occasion was taken to point out how few of those gathered together by Mr. Hector bore in even an indirect way on the history of the grand old Clugniac Abbey so intimately associated with the ecclesiastical renown of the county. Soon after, a neat quarto volume was issued from the Paisley press (Parlane, 1876), dealing exclusively with the Abbey, and illustrating many noteworthy occurrences which took place within or around the monastic fabric reared and endowed by the piety of the early Stewarts in the cradle of their race. While nothing but fair words need to be set down regarding either the design or execution of the work, it still leaves large spaces in the historic canvas to be filled in by some patient antiquary less intent on what records suggest than on what they describe. The author is mentioned as gathering some scanty lichens—antique, yellow, or gray, as they may happen, encrusted through seven centuries in the Gothic mouldings of the Abbey. To preserve some fragmentary leaves, too obscure it may be for the general historian, yet precious, because history is a mosaic, and composed in its finest pictures of infinitesimal details which are apt to be overlooked—to diverge where divergence is useful, to linger where delay is sweet; this, and no more, do these pages propose; no more do they offer to the reader; and, to avoid disappointment, for no more should the reader look. With the delicious ease of a practised writer, a hand at once firm and delicate, and an eye careless a little of things near or common, but fond of setting forth affinities or relations, dim at first, apt to be overlooked, but never quite inappropriate—the writer passes down through century after century of the Abbey annals, reflecting a very large portion of the country's ecclesiastical history. The rise of the first Stewards and the arrival on the White Cart of the monks from Wenlock are illustrated by the foundation and other charters of the Abbey. Of the founder himself much interesting information is given in a series of chapters relating to Walter the Steward and his wife Marjory, daughter of King Robert Bruce. In the early days of the Abbey, when the Cart stole softly among lilies and reeds, when the outer land waved with corn-fields, and the near land was white and red with orchard blooms, nothing, says the writer, could have been fairer or more sweet to see than the rich and low land set in its upland frame. But it is a picture of the past. Orchard and corn-fields are historical. "In the black and slow winding water a cress, or a lily, or a reed would now be as great an anachronism as if the Crusading Steward who gave gifts to the Abbey long ago were to appear with cross upon his armour in the dull, modern streets." Of Marjory it is remarked the people will have her a Queen—a monument of unknown origin must be "Queen

Blearie's Stane." Marjory (so the story is told) on an autumn day was following the sport she loved, chasing the fallow deer in her husband's oak forest of Paisley, when she was thrown from her horse, not far from her own castle, and lifted, with dead young face, from among the drifted leaves. They raised the cross of stone on the spot where the Princess fell. Long after every vestige of the oak forest was gone, among the low tufts of broom and wild roses stood this old solitary cross. If ever inscription was carved upon it, it was long worn away, but the fond tradition of its name lingered tenaciously around it, not to be dispelled by any reasoning that Marjory was not a Queen. After having been preserved for four centuries the cross was demolished. Some hundred years ago, when Pennant wrote, part of it formed the lintel of a neighbouring barn—a vandalism not to be wondered at when the Abbey itself was despoiled, and its images, even then, lay broken in the open cloister among the rank neglected grass (p. 110). Imagination, it is mentioned elsewhere, can hardly realise the despoiling of the Abbey by commmand of the reforming lords—how the monks fled from their convent through the eager streets, gray old men who had almost forgotten how the outside world fared, whose grandfathers remembered Paul Crawar, the Bohemian, and his burning at St. Andrew's Cross; and men in their early prime, who were youths when Wishart, the gentle laird, preached on the Mauchline Moor among the broom and the May flowers; and as vainly, it may be asked, how the young Abbot Claude demeaned himself among his flying monks— how he brooked to see the crowd of townsmen assail his convent gates, and to hear his voice derided and ignored within his own Abbey walls— how he saw with helpless hands all the wealth of the shrines scattered, and scorned by the meanest there as an unholy thing—scorned by poor weak men and women who had often crept to the gate of the monastery, taken their dole from the hands of the monks, and asked their blessing and their prayer. The work of that August day laid choir and north transept in ruins, shattered the house of the abbot, the guestan-house, library, scriptorium, filled the cloister-court with the *debris* of the beautiful still retreat; but it left the nave entire, desolate, profaned indeed, but with no mark of violence. It left a church for the people —a church for worship in the new form amidst the ruins of the old (p. 270). Under some such conditions were the sacred shrines thrown down, and the pleasant gardens laid waste. The splendour of the fabric may be inferred from the circumstance that the mason work was held in charge by the same craftsman who looked after Melrose and Glasgow—that Melrose, whose chroniclers gave their old abbot no undue praise when they wrote—"Jocelinus episcopus sedem episcopalem dilatavit et Sancti Kentegerni ecclesiam gloriose magnificavit." The work of the despoiler in these days was authorised by a missive commanding certain of those to whom it was addressed to pass incontinent to the kirk, "and tak' doun ye haill images yrof, and bring furth till ye kirkyard, and birn them oppingly, and syklyk cast doun ye alteris and picturis, and purge ye said kirks of all kinds of monuments of idolatry." For much pleasant gossip concerning those who bore rule in the Abbey, Abbot Shaw among the rest, for the erection of the chapel dedicated to St. Mirren, and for the early burghal life of Paisley, the "lichens" themselves must be turned over and the old-world fragrance inhaled. Less is made of some of the Abbey benefactors than might have been expected—pre-eminently of the great House of Lennox—Saxon most likely in origin, but swarming in a century or two with Celtic Donalds and Gilchrists. In consideration of various pious motives set forth in charters, certain Earls of the first Lennox succession granted lands in different parts of their wide domain to the stately Abbey on the Cart, and gave the monks beside many valuable fishing rights within the rivers Clyde and Leven. By one charter, dated on the day of St Valentine the Martyr (14th February), 1273, Earl Malcolm granted to the Abbey and Convent of Paisley certain fishings in the Leven, with land adjoining the highway to Dumbarton; also wood from his grove of Bonhill, pasture for eight oxen, and such wood and stone as might be required to carry on the fishing. Other charters provide for the protection of the monks when passing through lonely places to look after their Leven or other fishings.

To readers who care about contrasting times past with times present, Paisley Abbey has an interest apart from even its own old chronicles. It is not only one among the few ecclesiastical foundations spared from pre-Reformation times, but it presents the still rarer distinction of preserving some measure of its seemliness amid all the noise, activity, and change incident to that modern commerce by which it is so closely hemmed in and overshadowed. With most other old abbeys this is not the case. Lincluden, Dundrennan, and New Abbey, in the south, are only so many charming ruins in their still wooded solitudes; Crossraguel, a former dependency of Paisley, is as undisturbed by trade as when Abbot Allan was roasted "quick" by Gilbert, the wicked Earl of Cassilis. A transept gable at Kilwinning, the masonic glory of Hugh de Morville—the honoured mother of a wide-spread family—still represents, amid quiet graves, the crafts concerned in the rearing of that temple where

> No workman steel, no ponderous axes rung,
> Like some tall palm the noiseless fabric sprung.

Cambuskenneth still flings its lone shadow across the quiet links of Forth; the mouldering cloisters of Tironensian Lindores may still be seen on the edge of the majestic Tay looking out from her own sequestered hamlet of Newburgh across to the sylvan quietness of Errol; Dryburgh and Melrose, Kelso and Jedburgh, all exist more or less amid the pastoral surroundings in which they were first planted. With Paisley Abbey all is changed—nothing but contrasts between what was and is. The once rippling and silvery Cart now a sluggish and pestilent drain; the trim gardens of the monks, the richly-laden fruit trees, the waving grain and rich pasture land, the browsing cattle and frisking lambs, have all been edged out of the scene by such modern conditions of life as made their existence impossible. At Paisley Station any railway passenger may take in at a glance from the train the most important elements in the past and present forces of social life. On one side the ruined Abbey, rich with the memory of portly abbots, and still fragrant in imagination with the good cheer of the refectory; on the other a typical illustration of the triumphs of modern science—an iron shipbuilding yard full of noise and bustle, and requiring ingenious appliances in the way of machinery, none the less that room is scarce and the situation unfavourable. Closer still to the traveller there is (1880) on one side of the bridge a prison, rendered partly necessary by the want, misery, and temptation which may be presumed to exist low down on the other side. When the last School Board fight was at its keenest the poor and weary denizens at this point on the Cart might have been seen basking with their bairns in that late spring sunshine, visiting them as bountifully as when abbots bore sway, and enjoyed as gratefully as when there was no prison to control their liberty or school board to vex their ignorance. The Abbey fabric itself presents much of the contrast we are indicating between the past and present. The zeal of the Reformers spared the nave, still used on Sundays, but the choir and transept, the library and scriptorium, the abbot's house and the guests' chamber, were all so far destroyed as only to be useful in reminding the student of days when churches could be filled without "Revivals," and no part of the graceful fabric be considered useless or unnecessary in the service :—

> Behold a stately fane, by pious builders
> Raised of old, for worship of Jehovah;
> Within its long, withdrawing aisles
> Attendant monks in slow procession go,
> Chanting praise of Him who died upon the Cross.
> On festal days the people crowd its sacred courts,
> And join in that triumphant hymn of Praise
> To "God the Father," and to "Christ the King of Glory,"
> Which still swells the heart of gladdened worshippers,
> And sends them home renewed in vigour for their daily life.

With a minuteness not likely to be thought tedious by any connected with Paisley, the enthusiasm of ex-Provost Brown in the cause of his old "Pedagogue" incited him to draw up a history of the Burgh Grammar School, not more remarkable for accuracy of detail than profusion of illustration and order in arrangement. From the old charter of foundation to a record so ephemeral as a prize list; from a portrait of King James to a portrait of the janitor, not omitting the author; from a statement of old endowments to speeches by new subscribers —all have been gathered into a volume certain to be treasured by many as a memorial of days when they "were boys together," and useful to others at the same time as a book of reference on all matters relating to the school. Nor is it the least praise due Mr. Brown to mention that, while the teachers are introduced to the reader primarily, of course, in connection with their work, he also takes frequent occasion to notice their private or social accomplishments, so that old pupils may renew acquaintance with a master and not be quite overwhelmed by that severe dignity naturally associated with a real rector in office like Peddie, or Hunter, or Brunton. Of James Peddie, an English school pupil so distinguished as "Christopher North" describes his jubilee dinner as only a fitting reward to a man as blameless as he was useful, and whose whole life had been devoted to the training of youth in habits of decorum and rectitude. Most others also appear to have shown the utmost consideration for their pupils, or, like Goldsmith's teacher, "if severe in aught, the love they bore to learning was in fault." Paisley Grammar School, to which the larger portion of Mr. Brown's volume is devoted, was founded by King James VI., in 1576, the tenth year of his reign and the tenth of his birth, this being probably due to the mediation of the Rev. Patrick Adamson, first Reformed minister of the Abbey Parish, but at the date of the grant acting as chaplain to the Regent Morton. The deed provides for the government of the school by the magistrates and councillors of the burgh, and for its erection and support grants to their successors for ever, the altarages of St. Mirren and Columba, of St. Ninian, of St. Mary the Virgin, St. Nicholas, St. Peter, St. Catherine, and St. Anne, the chapel of St. Roque or St. Rollox, and seven roods of ground adjacent, with the pittances of money, obit silver, and commons formerly possessed and lifted by the monks of Paisley monastery, as appears from a stone still preserved but removed from time to time as the building was changed. The first fabric was erected in 1586, and the site Mr. Brown concludes, after some hesitation, was on the south side of the Old

School Wynd, then a vennel or passage leading to the Barnyard, where there was a port, and to Oakshaw, on the site of the Chapel of St. Nicholas. There appears to have been two class-rooms, one used for the Grammar School proper, the other as a singing or "sang school." The patronage, although formally vested in the council, appear to have been practically exercised at a very early period by the Church. In 1604 the magistrates remitted a candidate for the office of master to the minister of the burgh and Presbytery of Paisley, for the purpose of making trial of his doctrines and ability to teach. In 1626 another was appointed after being found qualified by the Presbytery; and in 1689 a William Stewart, who had become the subject of Church discipline, was apparently dismissed by the council at the instance of the Presbytery. The magistrates, however, appear to have been active enough in doing what was then judged wise to keep up the reputation of the school. In 1647, when John Tannahill was to be appointed, if found qualified, for his further encouragement the council conclude that all men children shall go to the Grammar School, that all woman schools be discharged from receiving boys under pain of censure, and that no woman whatever keep a school from All-Hallowday next but such as upon their petition might be allowed by the council. This resolution was proclaimed over the burgh next year by "de tuck of drum." Formal visitations would seem to have commenced in 1646, when the council appointed the school to be visited once a month by the bailies and ministers. One instance of undue severity occurs in the records this year, and may have something to do with the "visitation." In June of that year "Doctor" Lawson was to be absolutely discharged, that "he strike nane of the scholars within the school of Paisley hereafter, and that he shall take no such authority on him; and if he do in the future contrary, the first bairn he strikes it is concluded that he be removed from the school." It is to be feared the warning was useless, as dismissal followed within a few months. In immediate connection with his subjects, and extremely interesting besides on their own account, are the extracts gleaned by Mr. Brown from the records of his own and other burghs, especially in so far as these throw light on the two great calamities of war and pestilence. In December, 1645, the bailies and council of Glasgow, "taking to their consideration the lamentable estate and condition of the poor people within the town of Paisley, and of the hard straits they are brought to by God's visitation of the plague of pestilence lying upon them now for this long time, for this present supply they have condescended to bestow upon them twenty bolls of meal." During the January following John Park, mealman, Causeyside, for falsely asserting that the bailies of Paisley had acted unfairly in dividing this meal among the rich and not among the poor, was fined three dollars and laid six hours in the stocks. Leprous persons could only be abroad two days of the week for two hours at a time, "and not to go into any house, but to have clappers to call the people out, under pain of punishment." At the close of 1650, when Cromwell's troops were marching on the burgh, "the council appoint that the shire's arms that are in the Tolbooth shall this night be transferred thereof, and carried to come convenient place where the same may be hidden from the enemy. The Royalist defeat at Worcester appears to have led to an entire abolition of local courts. In April, 1652, the council agreed, "because there may not be a head court holden, in respect that the English by their declaration have discharged all courts, it is concluded that upon Thursday next, the penult of this instant, which should be the head court day, the bailies and council shall meet in James Alexander's, bailie, his heich hall, and there shall elect a new treasurer for the affairs of the town, and shall create any burgesses that shall happen to be, and receive resignation if any be, and book those having right into common lands." As became a body of patrons who as far back as 1620 had subscribed to encourage "a pleasant Invention or Play," the council in 1702 made a grant of twenty pounds Scots towards expenses incurred by the scholars in acting "Bellum Gramaticale," and the then "Doctor" was allowed seven pounds two shillings Scots (10s. 6d.) to buy a new hat with, "towards his farther encouragement, for pains in attending to the school by and attoure his salary." Other town schools undertaken with a view of completing the work of education, or called into existence by some passing inefficiency in the Grammar School, are carefully treated by Mr. Brown in separate chapters. In this there is set forth in a way at once pleasant and instructive all necessary details concerning the origin, history, and teachers of the English, Commercial, and Low Parish Schools. By "town's schools," Mr. Brown means schools over which the council exercised more or less control, or at least in which they took some special interest. Denominational schools are not referred to, nor is the question raised how they came into existence, what they have done, or what they have cost. This field is still open, and open in other quarters than Paisley. Another chapter of Mr. Brown's book relates the more recent history of the Grammar School and Academy, this necessarily involving an account of the praiseworthy efforts made by the author, as chairman of the committee of subscribers, to carry out the erection of a suitable new fabric in Oakshaw Street, in which such a curriculum would be observed as might fit pupils for proceeding direct to the University, or entering upon the business of life. The period embraced by this chapter extends from September, 1864, when the building was opened, till the examination of June, 1873, when it ceased to be under the management of the Town Council and subscribers, and came under the control of the local School Board in terms of the Education Act.

ALEXANDER WILSON, ORNITHOLOGIST.

"PAISLEY reprints" being as a rule rather superior in appearance to the original editions, it is pleasant to record (1876) that no falling off is presented by two volumes containing the writings of a native so humorous as the author o "Watty and Meg," and famous afterwards in the far different field of American Ornithology. A reprint (Gardner) is hardly the word to describe the result of

Mr. Grosart's labours, nor, it is but fair to say, is it used by editor or publisher. It is only a reprint in the very limited sense of presenting some matter which had been in print before, and much which might have been but never was gathered together in any orderly form. For the main facts in Wilson's life, reliance up to this time had to be placed on two distinct authorities, domestic and scientific. For the early home, or Paisley days, the unwearied labours of Thomas Crichton, Master of the Town's Hospital, gave welcome help to the reader. Such outline as was given of American experiences had to be sought for in the "Sketch" prepared by his friend Ord for the closing volume of the "Ornithology," or in still more fragmentary notices written for new editions of that work by Sir William Jardine, Prince C. L. Bonaparte, and Dr. W. M. Hetherington. Under Mr. Grosart's care, Wilson's letters and miscellaneous writings are now made to tell the story of Wilson's life. Of ninety-six letters, forming by far the largest portion of the first volume, thirteen are here printed for the first time, and as many as seventy-four carefully corrected and edited. This should surely satisfy the ambition of even a labourer so zealous and a scholar so exact as the editor of the "Fuller Worthies." The first five letters written in 1788-9 are addressed to David Brodie, schoolmaster, Quarrelton; the other long and deeply interesting series—sent, some to Brodie, some to his father, others to his friends, Bartram, Orr, and Duncan—extends from 1794, the year of his arrival in the States, to 1813, the year of his death—the last, from Philadelphia, in July, describing the writer as far from being in good health. "Intense application to study has hurt me much. My eighth volume is now in the press, and will be published in November. One volume more will complete the whole." The letters are preceded by what Mr. Grosart calls a "memorial introduction" from his own pen—throughout which he is very far from following the charming simplicity of Wilson's style—and is most appropriately closed with various essays, prefatory or descriptive, from the "Ornithology."

Before dealing with the second or poetical volume, a word or two on

Wilson's early life is necessary to let the reader fully understand the great merit of Mr. Grosart's work. Born in what is still known as the Seedhill of Paisley, 6th July, 1766, Wilson's father, also Alexander, and his mother, Mary M'Nab, a native of Row, Dumbartonshire, appear at a very early period to have entertained an ambition that their "Alic" should enter the Church. This at least may be inferred from the ornithologist's own account in his "Solitary Tutor":—

> His parents saw, with partial fond delight,
> Unfolding genius crown their fostering care,
> And talked with tears, of that enrapturing sight,
> When, clad in sable gown, with solemn air,
> The walls of God's own House should echo back his prayer.

It is not clear, however, that his training at the Grammar School (then presided over by John Davidson) had any special reference to Church work, or that his attendance there was anything else than limited, interrupted, and imperfect. As his fame was to be won later in the woods, so was he sent early to the fields, being employed as a herd laddie at the farm of Bakerfield in the neighbourhood. The tradition is that he was a very careless herd, busying himself too often with a book to keep the kye out of the corn. In his thirteenth year, as appears from the original indenture in Paisley Museum, Wilson entered upon a three years' apprenticeship as a weaver to his brother-in-law, William Duncan, and on its termination wrought for about four years at the loom as a journeyman, residing over that time partly in Paisley and partly in Lochwinnoch and Queensferry. At this latter place, and in conjunction with his first employer, Duncan, Wilson commenced business as a pedlar or travelling merchant, and availed himself at the same time of such opportunities as this line of life offered to obtain subscribers for a small volume of poems, then ready for publication. To his experiences as a packman readers of Scottish poetry are indebted for "The Loss of the Pack," "The Insulted Pedler," and kindred pieces, some of them read in the first instance by the author to a promiscuous audience in the Pantheon, Edinburgh. The "Poems" appeared in 1790, and a second edition, with some alterations, the following year. "The Spouter," included in the second of Mr. Grosart's volumes, seems below Wilson's average style, and may be the work of some other hand. The inimitable and ever fresh "Watty and Meg" appeared anonymously as a chap-book in 1792. Tradition of a sort has identified the two principal characters in the drama with a certain Watty Matthie and Meg Love, of Lochwinnoch; but more exact inquiry fixes upon the Seedhills, Paisley, as the exact locality, "Mungo Blue" being a certain William Mitchell, keeper of a change-house there; "Dryster Jock," a John Campbell employed in the cornmill; and "Pate Tamson," a tanner in the same place. "Watty" and "Meg" also, Crawfords by name, were well known to Wilson. Shortly after the poem appeared, "Meg" is reported to have said to her husband, "D'ye ken what lang Sandy Wilson, the poet, has done? He has 'poemed' us." It is yet open to an artist familiar with old Paisley life to make a reputation by setting forth that exquisite street scene—

> Folk frae every door came lamping,
> Maggy curst them ane and a';
> Clappit wi' her hands, and stamping,
> Lost her bauchles i' the snaw.

Like many other enthusiasts, Mr. Grosart, to elevate Wilson, is somewhat less than fair to others. Hector Macneil, for instance, the author of a kindred ballad to "Watty and Meg," known as "Scotland's Skaith," or "Will and Jean," is spoken of as a vapid, watery imitator; and this, although the common people for whom they were written, and who in such a case are the real test of popularity, are known to have purchased them gladly at the rate of 10,000 in one month. Neither should it be forgotten that Wilson himself never again came up to the mark of "Watty and Meg;" while Macneil wrote such songs as "Saw ye my wee Thing?" "My Boy, Tammy," and "Come under my Plaidie," with none of which can any of Wilson's songs be compared. Even "The Disconsolate Wren," his next best piece, is only in the second or third rank of Scottish ballads. The incongruous combination of "snaw" and "sawing" in the first verse of "Watty and Meg" has been frequently pointed out, and many ingenious theories started touching the kind of "sawing" in which the hero was engaged, but none fits so well as the necessity occasionally laid on poets far higher in reputation than Wilson of using words which simply rhyme or rattle without much reference to fitness in other respects. A rhyme was wanted for "blawing;" "snawing" was ready, even in seed time, and so "Watty" was left to waste his treasure on the white drift till wearied, when, if the record is to be followed, he

Dauner'd doon to Mungo Blew's.

Sometime about 1792 Wilson had resumed the loom in Paisley, but chafing under ungenial restraint, in a time of great local excitement he launched the shafts of his satire against certain well-known neighbours, described as "The Shark," "Light Weight," &c. The hapless poet was in consequence adjudged guilty of libel, and thrown into prison. A painful letter to his friend Brodie, marked as not printed before, reveals the sad straits to which he was reduced at this time:—

"PAISLEY JAIL, 21st May, 1793.

"DEAR SIR,

"When I last wrote you nothing but absolute necessity would have prevailed on me to make the requisition I then did, and sorry I was that that necessity should ever have cause to exist. I sincerely thank you for the token of friendship which you sent me, which I will repay as soon as Providence shall open the door for my release from this new scene of misery—this assemblage of wretches and wretchedness—where the rumbling of bolts, the hoarse exclamations of the jailor, the sighs and sallow countenances of the prisoners, and the general gloom of the place require all the exertions of resolution to be cheerful and resigned to the will of fate, particularly those who have no prospect or expectation of liberty. Being perfectly unable to pay the sum awarded against me, which is in toto £12, 13s. 6d., I yesterday gave oath accordingly, and had the comfort to be told that Mr. Sharp was resolved to punish me, though it should cost him a little money. However, I shall know after a little more confinement of two days or so. Meantime, to have a line or two from you would be an additional favour to,

"DEAR SIR,

"Your obliged Servant,

"A. WILSON."

Poor, discontented, looked upon as a suspicious character, and with no encumbrance beyond what he recognised as existing towards his father's household, when liberty came, Wilson turned his gaze across the Atlantic to the States where some friends had preceded him. Along with a nephew, William Duncan, he left Belfast Loch in the ship "Swift," 23rd May, 1794, with a mixed body of passengers, 350 in number, and arrived off Cape Delaware, 11th July. A long and affectionate letter was despatched to his father in a few days from Philadelphia. Wilson's first employment was in a copper-plate printer's office, a trade for which he is not known to have received any special training; then the pack was resumed for a short time, and finally he settled down as a schoolmaster in the township of Kingess, about four miles from the Quaker city. This fixed Wilson's career. From early life, as may be seen in his poetry, he had been fond of all feathered creatures. With the mavis and the blackbird, the robin and the wren, and pigeons of all kinds, he was on the most familiar terms. At Philadelphia was the garden of William Bartram, an experienced botanist and naturalist, and a warm friend of Wilson's to the close of life; and there, too, was Lawson the engraver, who willingly seconded his efforts at self-instruction and drawing from nature and etching. The beginning of Wilson's great work appears to have been simple enough. In June, 1803, he writes to his old friend Crichton:—"I have had many pursuits since I left Scotland—mathematics, the German language, music, drawing, &c., and I am now about to make a collection of all our finest birds." Henceforward, writes Mr. Grosart, Wilson devoted himself to this casually announced collection of all America's finest birds "with a consecration of intellect and heart, scrutinising observation, and beautiful enthusiasm that thrill one across half the century and more. North and south, east and west, he journeyed, gun in hand, in forest, brushwood, reeded swamp, river, lake, mountain, everywhere, with a burning passion, combined with a modest patience of research very wonderful." In the fall of 1804, he undertook a two months' pedestrian tour to Utica, making in some days forty-seven miles, and traversing in all upwards of 1,200. 1809 saw him as far south as

Carolina, during which excursion, as he wrote to his father, he visited every town within 150 miles of the Atlantic coast, from the River St. Lawrence to St. Augustine in Florida. Towns were visited chiefly from the facilities they afforded for obtaining subscribers to the "Ornithology," not always a welcome mission to the author. One entry in his diary runs—" Visited a number of the literati and wealthy of Cincinnati, who all told me they would think of subscribing." They are (Wilson dryly adds) a very thoughtful people. Another thought such a book should not be encouraged, as it was not within the reach of common people, and therefore inconsistent with Republican institutions. Worse still from the Governor of Staten Island: "He turned over a few pages, looked at a picture or two, asked my price, and, while in the act of closing the book, added—' I would not give a hundred dollars for all the birds you intend to describe, even had I them alive.'" Pleasant exceptions now and then occurred to such treatment. One merits special mention, a landlord bearing the honoured name of Isaac Walton refusing to take anything for keeping either the wanderer or his horse:—"You seem (the diary records) to be travelling for the good of the world, and I cannot and will not charge you anything. Whenever you come this way call and stay with me—you shall be welcome." The great journey to Pittsburg is referred to in a letter to his father, February 1811:—

"My last route was across the Alleghany Mountains to Pittsburg, thence to the falls of the Ohio—720 miles alone in a boat—thence through the Chickasaw and Choctaw country (nations of Indians), and West Florida to New Orleans, in which journey I sustained considerable hardship, having many dangerous creeks to swim, and having to encamp for thirteen different nights in the woods alone. From New Orleans I sailed to East Florida, furnished with a letter to the Spanish Governor there, and visited a number of the islands that lie to the south of the peninsula. I returned to Philadelphia on the 2nd of September last, after an absence of seven months. In prosecuting this journey I had sometimes to kindle a large fire; I then stripped the canes for my horse, ate a bit of supper, and lay down to sleep, listening to the owls and cheekwills and to a kind of whip-poor-will that are very numerous. On the fourteenth day of my journey I arrived at Natchez, Mississippi, after having overcome every obstacle alone, and without being acquainted with the country, and, what surprised the boatmen more, without whisky."

During this Southern journey Wilson picked up his famous Carolina parrot, described with much minuteness in the third volume of the "Ornithology." "When at night (he writes) I encamped in the woods I placed it on the baggage beside me, where it usually sat with great composure, dozing and gazing at the fire till morning. In this manner I carried it upwards of a thousand miles in my pocket, where it was exposed all day to the jolting of the horse, but regularly liberated at meal times and in the evening, at which it always expressed great satisfaction. In passing through the Chickasaw and Choctaw nations, the Indians, wherever I stopped to feed, collected around me, men, women, and children, laughing, and seeming wonderfully amused with the novelty of my companion." Poor Poll was drowned in the Gulf of Mexico.

HUMANITY OF WILSON.

The following reminds one of Burns' "wee sleekit, cow'rin', tim'rous beastie":—

"One of my boys caught a mouse in the school a few days ago, and directly marched up to me with his prisoner. I set about drawing it that same evening, and all the while the pantings of its little heart showed it to be in the most extreme agonies of fear. I had intended to kill it in order to fix it in the claws of a stuffed owl, but happening to spill a few drops of water near where it was tied, it lapped it up with such eagerness, and looked in my face with such an eye of supplicating terror as perfectly overcame me. I immediately untied it, and restored it to life and liberty. The agonies of the prisoner at the stake, while the fire and instruments of torment are preparing, could not be more severe than the sufferings of that poor mouse; and insignificant as the object was, I felt at that moment the sweet sensation that mercy leaves on the mind when she triumphs over cruelty."

Wilson appears to have obtained 250 subscribers to his "Ornithology," but the total number printed is not exactly stated. A list of the names and Institutions is given in the second volume of Mr. Grosart's work, and among them it is gratifying to observe the University of Glasgow and the Hunterian Museum. The first volume appeared in 1808, the eighth in 1814, with the sorrowful announcement of the author's death. The end was characteristic of the man. While sitting in the house of one of his friends, enjoying the pleasures of conversation, he chanced to see a bird of rare species, for which he had long been in search. With his usual enthusiasm he ran out, followed it, swam across a river over which it had flown, fired at, killed, and obtained the object of his pursuit; but caught a cold, which, bringing on dysentery, ended in his death, 23rd August, 1813. His remains were deposited in the burial-ground of the Swedish Church, Southwark District, Philadelphia. While in good health he is said to have expressed a wish to be laid in some rural spot where the birds might sing over his grave. It is in a business district of the city, but on paying a pilgrim visit Mr. Grosart heard an ariole piping softly and sweetly a few yards from the resting-place of the ornithologist. The two volumes with which we have been dealing present by far the most complete picture yet sent forth of Wilson the poet and Wilson the ornithologist. Here he appears as he lived—a man possessed of genuine gifts and tender feeling, allied to indomitable perseverance, unflagging power of endurance, and the still rarer virtue of thorough simplicity in character. The memorial statue erected within the enclosure of Paisley Abbey was a fitting tribute to the genius of one of the most distinguished natives of the old burgh, and a recognition no less of the increasing fame which Time is sure to gather round the memory of Alexander Wilson.

MOTHERWELL AND CUNNINGHAM.

SIMILARITY in taste, something in style, more in experience, and a great deal in the form of contributions to the minstrelsy of Scotland, make it convenient to notice Motherwell and Cunningham together. So far as the work known as Cromek's "Remains of Nithsdale and Galloway Song" is concerned, a note prefixed to the latest edition, makes no apology necessary for continuing to treat it as has been generally done since its first issue, over seventy years since, as substantially the work of Allan Cunningham. Cromek himself was a fussy yet useful man in his day, and, although somewhat credulous, did good service to the ballad literature of Scotland, albeit he was a native of Yorkshire. In his memoir of Blake as an artist, Cunningham writes of his early patron, the engraver, as having skill in art and taste in literature, although "honest Allan's" latest editor sets him down as a sharp man of business, no way averse to take advantage of artists working for him. The history of the "Remains," in a published form, is given with substantial accuracy in the prefatory note already referred to. When the songs of Burns had been given to the world with judicious care by Dr. Currie, Cromek became so attracted by their delineations of Scottish life that he made a pilgrimage to the North, and collected material for his "Reliques of Robert Burns," published in 1808, and for which he was made a member of the Antiquarian Society of Scotland. After its publication he again came North, and it was during this second visit he met Allan Cunningham, and secured the material which appears in the Nithsdale and Galloway "Remains." Cunningham was at the time working as a mason in Dumfriesshire, but neglected trade in his ardent pursuit of literature; and it was partly through Cromek's advice and influence that in the very year when the "Remains" appeared he went to London and became connected with the newspaper press. It is said that Allan presented some of his poetry to Cromek, but received only feeble praise for his productions, until the thought occurred to him that he might secure more favourable criticisms if he appealed to Cromek's weak side by saying they were traditionary remains. The bait took; the patron became enthusiastic, and the result was "The Remains of Nithsdale and Galloway Song."

Certain general similarities between Cunningham and Motherwell have already been pointed out, but it may be proper to mention in connection therewith that they overlapped each other in their lives as well as their writings. Born in 1784 the boy Cunningham was just beginning to scribble his first lines when Motherwell was born in 1797. The first survived his brother poet seven years, dying in 1842, at the age of fifty-eight, while the younger, born in 1797, the year after Burns's death, was just spared to exceed the age of Burns by one year, being laid with honour in our Necropolis in 1835 at the early age of thirty-eight. Cunningham commenced rhyming young, although his more important printed pieces did not see the light till the "Remains" were printed in 1810, when the poet had reached the mature age of twenty-six. Motherwell's earliest work, in the "Harp of Renfrewshire," appeared in 1819, when he was about twenty-two. Each forsook his first business in life for journalism, Cunningham contributing to the London press between the period when he abandoned the mason trade in Scotland, when he became connected with Chantrey; while Motherwell forsook his clerkly duties in the Sheriff's office to assume editorial work, first in connection with the Tory "Advertiser" in Paisley, but latterly, and with greater prominence, because in his best known days, on the Tory "Courier" in Glasgow, from 1830 till his death. Cunningham was nothing of a politician. Motherwell, on the other hand, was both zealous and informed in the cause he espoused; and, though it may seem a strange transition to pass from the serene heights of poetry to the noisy jostling of party strife, the author of Sigurd's "Battle Flag" was early embroiled in the Reform excitement, and there is no reason for doubting that he wrote on politics with as much sincerity, and even with as great a measure of contentment, as he brought to bear on his ballads and songs. There was still other kindred work engaged in by the two poets. Cunningham issued his collection of "The Songs of Scotland, Ancient and

Modern," in 1825, and Motherwell his Scottish "Minstrelsy, Ancient and Modern," in 1827, each having followed out in his own way the lines laid down by Scott in his Border "Minstrelsy," issued from Ballantyne's Kelso press in 1802. Again, both poets were ardent admirers of Burns, and each issued an edition of his works, which appeared the same year (1834), Motherwell being associated in his task with James Hogg. Each of them also imitated the ancient ballads, and amused friends with them as genuine antiques. In gifts they were not far removed. It may be, and indeed it is certain, that there is nothing in Cunningham quite up to the level of "Jeannie Morrison," or "My Heid is Like to Rend, Willie;" but, as in the case of his townsman, Alexander Wilson (see p. 296), it should be remembered that Motherwell himself nowhere else rises to the same height. So sound a judge as Miss Mitford doubted if even among all the writings of Burns there was anything so exquisitely finished, so free from a line too many or a word out of place as these two lyric ballads. In other pieces, whether they be songs or ballads, the advantage will often be found to lie with the author of "A Wet Sheet and a Flowing Sea." For a landsman, never familiar with the sea beyond an occasional trip in a Margate hoy, to have written such a song at all is in itself a marvel. "The Mermaid of Galloway," and "Bonnie Lady Ann," both included in the "Remains," are quite equal to either "The Master of Weemys" or "The Song of the Danish Sea King." But where so much is excellent in both, further distinction or parallel may appear invidious. The old words used by Motherwell in dedicating the "Poems" to his friend Kennedy may be applied to each—"A posie of gilly-flowers, each differing from other in colour and odour, yet all sweete." The claim made by Dr. M'Connechy to a distinguished place for his friend among the minor poets is not likely to be disputed, as he has undoubtedly enriched the language with many noble specimens of song. The Doctor's carefully written memoir of his friend, whom he succeeded in the editorial chair of the "Courier," is prefixed to Mr. Gardner's "Reprint," as prepared for the edition of 1846. "Christopher North" found concentrated in Motherwell clearness in perception, soundness in sense, and fine but strong sensibilities, all leading him to the true haunts of inspiration—the woods and glens of his native country, and the music of her old songs. The closing verses of "Wearie's Well" are inexpressibly touching—

> Farewell, and for ever,   In sorrow and sadness
> My first love and last;   This hour fa's on me;
> May thy joys be to come—   But light, as thy love, may
> Mine live in the past.   It fleet over thee.

Then there is that plaintive touch of humble life in "Oh, wae be to the Orders," which Motherwell placed first among his songs:—

> I never think o' dancin', and I downa try to sing,
> But a' the day I speir what news kind neibour bodies bring;
> I sometimes knit a stocking, if knittin' it may be,
> Syne for every loop that I cast on, I am sure to let doun three.

In a dedication to his friend, W. Kennedy, Motherwell writes of his Norse legends as intended only to be a faint shadow of Norse poetry:—"All that is historical about them is contained in the proper names. The first, 'Sigurd's Battle Flag,' does not follow the story as given in the Northern Sagas, but only adopts the incident of the Magic Standard, which carries victory to the party by whom it is displayed, but certain death to its bearer. 'Jarl Egill Skallagrim's Wooing Song' is entirely a creation, and nothing of it is purely historical, save the preserving of the name of that warrior and Skald. From the memorials, however, he has left us of himself, I think he could not well have wooed in a different fashion. As for 'Thorstein Raudi,' or the Red, that is a name which occurs in Northern history; but, as may well be supposed, he never said so much in all his life about his sword or himself, as I have taken the fancy of putting into his mouth."

THE BARNS OF AYR.

THE Marquis of Bute's lecture on the "Burning of the Barns of Ayr" places the history of this event in the clearest possible light before the reader, divested alike of the fierce prejudices manifested against Scotland by early English chroniclers, and of the equally misleading credulity swarming over the pages of native rhymers of the "Blind Harry" order. That a representative member of the Royal Stuart family so personally popular as the present Marquis of Bute, connected moreover with Ayrshire by descent no less than possessions, should address the people of the county on an event so interesting as the "Burning of the Barns" by Wallace and his ancestor, Bruce, will be generally accepted as an occurrence not more interesting than it was appropriate. The list of royal and noble authors has in recents days got so much enlarged that Walpole's once famous "Catalogue" of the order is now useful for little beyond purposes purely antiquarian. Since his day there falls to be added, in English literature alone, names no less important than Her Majesty, the Prince Consort, and— to mention only a few others—living representatives of the houses of Argyll, Keppel, Lennox, Mandeville, Wellesley, and Stuart. To Scotch audiences the young Marquis of Bute has addressed at least two lectures—one to his neighbours at Rothesay in the winter of 1875 on the "Daily Life of King Robert I. at Cardross," and a second at Ayr in the February of 1878, concerning that event in the War of Independence known as "The Burning of the Barns of Ayr." The *brochure* differs a little from the lecture as delivered. It contains some matter which the Marquis had not before him at the time, and a good deal also which he had written but omitted, in order, as he modestly explains, not to be even more burdensome to a patient audience than the extreme dryness and intricacy of the inquiry demanded. Second, the original lecture has been altogether pulled to pieces, and arranged anew under the six following heads:—

THE BARNS OF AYR.

(1) The Capitulation of Irvine, July, 1297, with a sketch of the events leading to it, being the epoch to which Lord Hailes believed that the burning was to be assigned; (2) a sketch of the English invasion of 1298, which the Marquis believes to be the time when any event possible to be identified with the "Burning of the Barns" really took place; (3) a discussion as to who the burners were; (4) a notice of King Edward's residence at Ayr and retirement from Scotland after the burning; (5) the account of the burning in Blind Harry; (6) the executions connected by Blind Harry with the burning. Disappointed with his campaign in Flanders, chafing under the limitations imposed upon him by his Parliament at Westminster, and incensed beyond endurance by the renewed hostile attitude of the Scottish patriots, King Edward would appear to have crossed into Scotland by way of Berwick, during the summer of 1298, in a mood boding but slight mercy to those concerned in resisting his usurped authority. His army was great beyond all precedent —magnificent, it has been said, and overwhelming. Burton, following contemporary authorities, writes of 7,000 mounted men-at-arms as being in the muster, 3,000 of them in coats of mail; and this host, overwhelming as it was in numbers, was joined by 500 other horsemen from Gascony. After this, footmen might be reckoned of little moment, but the number has been put down at 80,000, among them being many auxiliaries from Wales and Ireland. The disastrous defeat at Falkirk followed on the 22nd. Wallace contrived to convey a small body of his troops off the field, and made an attempt to hold Stirling. Finding this useless, they destroyed what food could not be used, and marched, it has been said, nobody knows whither, the commander and his followers alike disappearing from the history of the war. In July of the preceding year (1297), Wallace, according to the noble lecturer, would appear to have entirely dissented from the conduct of those who swore allegiance at the capitulation of Irvine. The patriot and his friends left the army and retreated into the forest of Selkirk, as a great part of the centre of Scotland south of Forth was then called. On July 17, eight days later than the last documents of Irvine, it was proposed at Roxburgh "that an attack should be made upon William Wallace, who lay there

then, and does still, with a large company, in the forest of Selkirk, like one who holds himself against your Majesty's peace." Citing Hemingford as an authority, Lord Hailes steps in at this point, with his explanation of the "burning," expressing it as his belief that the story took its rise from the pillaging of the English quarters, about the time of the treaty. Silent altogether as to the burning of barns either at Ayr or Irvine, Hemingford's statement may yet be accepted as evidence of a kind, that the English invaders treated the native population with hardly a degree less severity than the Canaanites experienced at the hands of the remorseless Jew:—"When our people (the English) returned to Irvine, it was told them that many of the Scotch and Galloway men had plundered their baggage, after the manner of enemies, and killed more than fifty men, women, and children. So they followed them, and slew about a thousand of them, and came back with the prey doubled." Erroneous as the Marquis thinks it by about a year, a brief paraphrase of Blind Harry's account of the burning may be given as embodying the popular belief as early at least as the fifteenth century. On the suggestion, he writes, of Aymer de Valence, and in spite of the protests of Henry Percy, a Court of Assize was proclaimed to be held at Ayr on June 18, 1297, under the auspices of a judge named Arnwlf. To this Court the leading persons of Ayrshire were summoned, with the secret intention of putting them to death; and it was to meet in four great barns which at the time stood in Ayr, and which had been built for the King when his lodging was there—(not till 1298). One of the beams was furnished with abundance of running nooses; the entrance was strongly guarded by armed men, and none were allowed to enter but as they were summoned. Sir Reginald Crawford was called first to do homage. Passing in he was immediately lifted off his feet, a noose slipped over his head, and hoisted up to the beam, where he died. In like manner died Sir Brice Blair, Sir Neill Montgomery, with various Crawfords, Kennedys, Campbells, Berkeleys, Boyds, and Stuarts. The minstrel reports the barns as being burnt the same night, Wallace and his party looking on from a safe point, known ever after as Burn-weill-hill. In explanation of various discrepancies in Blind Harry, and between him and Barbour, the Marquis ventures with considerable caution to submit an hypothesis, that between the burning of Lanark and the attack on the bishop's palace at Glasgow, Blind Harry found that Wallace had made an attack on an English judge at an "Aire," which he took to be the town of that name (instead of a Justice Aire), especially as he also knew that Wallace was famous, among other things, for having burnt the English quarters in that town. So he mixes up three things—the executions in the barns, the attack on the judge, and the burning—working the whole into a fancy narrative, with probably a good spice of plagiarism out of Barbour. The lecturer describes himself as conscious that, applied to the myth which finds its wildest development in the "Wallace," his treatment may be styled a destructive criticism. He would, however, rather claim for the lecture a constructive tendency. His aim has been to place, or rather perhaps suggest, a way of placing upon a sound historical basis an event in national and local history, the obscurity of which has made it the victim alternately of credulity and scepticisim. The authorities quoted throughout are, as far as possible, contemporary. Some of them, it is mentioned, have not yet been published, and of those that have been, many are translated by the Marquis for the first time. A map, illustrative of the marching and countermarching of King Edward in Scotland, accompanies an inquiry full of interest in itself, and not without importance as bearing on the development of popular beliefs.

RAMBLES IN GALLOWAY.

VALUABLE for what is suggested more than for what is completed, Mr. Harper's "Rambles in Galloway" were thought seriously defective as a guide to the pedestrian. Even better writing and fuller historical knowledge would not have atoned for the want of any table of distances or any map of the district traversed. It is no doubt open for travellers to ramble at their own will, gossiping when they please and as they please about the traditional associations or physical aspects of the hills and dales traversed; but it is different when, as in the present case, the writer is desirous of making his district more widely known, and of impressing on travellers the important, but by no means exaggerated truth that he might fare worse by going further from home in search of scenes of soft lowland beauty, or the stern and wild in mountain landscape. In such circumstances the Rambler takes the place of a Guide where a map is essential. The volume itself presents a most attractive appearance, so far as printing and illustrations are concerned. The matter, if not so fresh or full occasionally as one would like, is on the whole presented in a quiet, business like fashion—altogether free from the vice of exaggeration so apt to beset local chroniclers. Its merits, indeed, in this respect tend rather to cross the reader's temper by presenting what is attractive and useful, but compelling him at the same time to search elsewhere for distances and routes. The "Rambles" are arranged under thirty-three distinct chapters, treating of so many different journeys or localities, but little help is furnished to the reader whether the country traversed from point to point was six miles or sixty. Castle-Douglas to Auchencairn, eight miles, forms one chapter or route; Castle-Douglas over Cairnsmore to Newton-Stewart, about thirty miles, forms another. A brief index, of proper names at least, would also have been useful. The want of minuteness in the itinerary is the more to be regretted, as Mr. Harper's own pages show that Galloway, or the two south-western counties of Kirkcudbright and Wigtown, even since opened up by railways, still possesses special attractions for the pedestrian, whether his taste runs in the way of historical or traditionary lore. It is not easy in dealing with works of this kind to cease wondering at the prolific genius and rare powers of Scott. Not a county or bit of coast-line in Scotland but has been touched by the Enchanter's rod. From Kirkwall to Caerlaverock, from Colonsay to the Bass, not an old castle, church, or mansion but has had a new interest added to it by his writings. Galloway presents no exception to this rule, nor could it well occur with a correspondent of the novelist in the district so exact and enthusiastic as Train. Endless scenes and incidents in the romances are associated with Galloway. That "Young Lochinvar, who came out of the West," belonged to the gay Gordons of Kenmure line. Helen Walker, who practised in real life the virtues with which fiction has invested the imaginary character of Jeanie Deans, lies buried in Irongray churchyard, with a memorial-stone set up by the novelist to mark her humble grave. On a tragical incident in the history of the Stair family Scott founded "The Bride of Lammermoor." Robert Paterson, prototype of "Old Mortality," was a Galloway wanderer, and set up his first stone at Caldons, Wigtownshire. The creeks of Warroch often sheltered Dirk Hatteraick; and at Ravenshall the Smugglers' Cave is still pointed out. Still earlier associations of importance are rife in the district. At Tongland lived the Italian friar whose ridiculous attempt at flying drew down the satire of Dunbar; and there, too, within the old castle of Comstone, Montgomery is supposed to have written his famous "Cherrie and Slae." Grounds now included within the Maitland property are thought to be referred to in the verse—

> How every blossom, branch, and bark,
> To pen the pleasures of that park,
> Against the sun did shyne.
> I pass to poets to compile
> In high, heroic, stately stile,
> Whase muse surmatches myne.
> But as I looked myne alane
> I saw a river rin
> Out owre a steepy rock of stane,
> Syne lighted in a lin,
> With tumbling and rumbling
> Among the rocks around,
> Devalling and falling
> Into a pit profound.

To the Kenmure family mentioned above an interesting reference is made in the form of a letter to John Gordon, seventh Viscount, son of William, attainted, written by the Young Pretender during his short stay at Holyrood, Oct., 1745:—

"The continued loyalty of your family, with your father's unhappy suffering in 1715, and the repeated assurances I have received from all hands of zeal and attachment to my family, leaves me no room to doubt you will take the first opportunity to appear in the cause of your King and country. Being determined to make no longer stay in these parts than to give time to some friends who are now on their way from the Highlands to join me, I judge it proper you may repair to the army with what men you can get together, without delay, when you may be assured of meeting with particular marks of my favour and friendship." It was the old story:—

> At length the news ran through the land—
> The Prince had come again;
> That night the Fiery Cross was sped
> O'er mountain and through glen;
> And our old baron rose in might,
> Like a lion in his den,
> And rode away across the hills
> To Charlie and his men.

In 1824 the Kenmure dignities were restored in the person of Viscount William's grandson, to the great joy of the family bard, who exultingly wrote—

> The Gordon hath his father's name, renowned in love and war;
> Hail him, Kenmure's noble Viscount, and Lord of Lochinvar.

The title became extinct in 1847 on the death of Adam, eighth Viscount. Church matters, especially such as relate to the Covenanting period, but suggested, naturally enough, by graves in lone moorland places, or, as at Wigtown, indicating a great judicial crime, appear frequently in Mr. Harper's volume. For the earliest settlement of all, St. Ninian's at Whithorn, he cautiously follows the excellent memoir prepared by Bishop Forbes. Dedicated to St. Martin of Tours, from whom craftsmen were obtained to shape its walls after the Roman fashion, the White House on the promontory became the burying-place of St. Ninian himself, and was for ages famous as a sanctuary not only in North Britain, but throughout the whole Anglo-Saxon Kingdom, and among the races of

Ireland. Even from Gaul, Alcuin, the counsellor of Charlemagne, sent epistles to the brethren at Whithorn, while in later times the ancient shrine continued renowned as a pilgrimage whither princes, churchmen, and warriors came from distant parts by sea and land to pay their devotions. In days nearer our own, and for another form of piety, a second shrine was found at Anwoth, in the church of the "Godly Rutherford." "Blessed birds" he described the sparrows and swallows to be who built their nests there. On removing to St. Andrews, and when known to be on his death-bed, he was summoned with impotent malice to appear before the Privy Council. "Tell them," he said, "I have got a summons already before a superior judge and judicatory, and it behoves me to answer that summons first. Ere your day arrives I will be where few kings and great folks come." When the messengers returned to the Council and intimated that the author of "Lex Rex" was dying, Parliament, with a few dissenting voices, voted that he should not be allowed to die in the College. "Yes," remarked Lord Burleigh, "you have voted the honest man out of his College, but you cannot vote him out of heaven." Crocketford, near Dalbeattie, has an interest of a different kind—an interest centering not in piety but in delusion—possibly fraud. Here Luckie Buchan and her crazed followers set up their camp on being removed from Closeburn parish, and here the cunning old prophetess died (1791), and so late as 1846 was buried in the same grave with the last of her followers. In expectation of her direct translation to heaven, the body had for many years been secretly kept above ground among her own people. She described herself, as most readers know, to be the Woman clothed with the Sun mentioned in the Revelation, and blasphemously pretended to have brought forth, in the person of the Rev. Hugh White, the manchild who was to rule all nations with a rod of iron. "I never heard (wrote Scott in 'St. Ronan's Well'), of alewife that turned preacher except Luckie Buchan in the West." According to Mr. Harper, their fame as wheelwrights and spinners extended all over the South of Scotland. The Buchanite women introduced into Galloway the two-handed spinning-wheel, and found employment in preparing linen yarn for families in the neighbourhood. They possessed a community of goods, and appeared to live comfortably and peaceably together, each in turn, as they paid the debt of nature, being interred within a small plot of ground behind their dwelling-house in the village of Crocketford. On visiting the spot, fourteen graves were pointed out to our author by an old woman now occupying the premises, still owned, he was given to understand, by a descendant of this strange sect of Buchanites. Among the old ecclesiastical foundations within the Stewartry, Mr. Harper gives short but appreciative notices of Dundrennan, the last resting-place in Scotland of Queen Mary after her flight from Langside; of Sweetheart, or New Abbey, the burial-place of the munificent Devorgilla, daughter of Alan, Lord of Galloway, and mother of John Balliol, for a short time King of Scotland; and of Lincluden, now more emphatically than even in Burns' time a "roofless tower, where the wa'flower scents the dewy air." Here the rambler may recall scenes associated with the most stirring periods of Scottish history; and here, too, he is brought in presence of the last resting-place of Lady Margaret, eldest daughter of Robert III., Countess of Douglass and Lady of Galloway and Annandale. She died at Threave Castle about 1440, and was interred in a magnificent tomb built into the north wall of the choir, near the altar, when that part of Lincluden Abbey was erected by Archibald the Grim. The fabric, with lands around, has for generations formed part of the patrimonial inheritance of the old Catholic house of Terregles, but munificent supporters, as they have always been, of the new foundation of St. Andrews, at Dumfries, only little was laid out, and that at distant intervals, to keep up a ruin so intimately associated with the ancient faith as the Abbey of Lincluden. Drawings, however, are now (1876) being made with the view of something being done to prevent the fine choir at least from crumbling to dust. Mr. Harper, our readers may be informed, does not enlarge unduly upon, far less confine himself in rambling to what is old or ecclesiastical. Threave and Bombie, Maxwells and MacLellans, Kircudbright Castle and Town, Black Morrow Wood and Buchan Forest—from Nith to Dee, from Dee to

Portpatrick—all places, families, and customs, are made to render up their quota of entertaining matter. About things new and industrial he has also much pleasant gossip. At Arbigland, the birth-place of Paul Jones, and at St. Mary's Isle, which he plundered, the rover of the Solway naturally turns up in the character of an American privateer. In his own neighbourhood of Dalbeattie, again, the author has many fresh and informing notes to set down about the granite works carried on there, and the important part such industry has played in the erection of docks at Liverpool and embankments on the Thames. We could have wished even more about that wandering minstrel, William or "Wull" Nicholson. M'Diarmid's edition of his pieces is not very widely known nowadays; and when insipid watery versifiers are so rife it is not desirable, however odd or thriftless he may have been, to let writers like the author of "The Brownie of Blednoch" slip into forgetfulness.

THE HERRIES PEERAGE.

ONE of the three noblemen recently (April, 1884) called to the Upper House as a Peer of the United Kingdom is Marmaduke Constable-Maxwell, known in the Peerage of Scotland as Baron Herries of Terregles. The new Peer, who was born in 1837, is eldest son of that William Constable-Maxwell of Everingham, Yorkshire, declared by the House of Lords, in 1858, entitled to the Barony of Herries of Terregles (Kirkcudbrightshire) as lineal heir of the body of Agnes Lady Herries, daughter and co-heir of William Lord Herries, son of Andrew, who sat as a Lord of Parliament in Scotland, 1505-6, and was slain at Flodden 9th September, 1513. Agnes, Lady Herries, became the wife of Sir John Maxwell, afterwards called of Terregles, second son of Robert, fifth Lord Maxwell. Judged to have claimed the dignity of a Peeress in her own right, by this marriage the Herries barony passed into that powerful branch of the Maxwell family so prominently mixed up in their day with all the events which have become historically associated with Nithsdale, Annandale, and the southern counties generally. The formidable fortresses of Caerlaverock and Threave indicate but partly the baronial splendour of the Maxwells. In quite recent times at least two other interesting properties have fallen into the Herries branch of the Maxwell family. Through the marriage of William Maxwell, only son of the attainted or fifth Earl of Nithsdale, with Catherine, daughter of Charles, fourth Earl of Traquair, their descendant, Henry Constable-Maxwell of Scarthingwell Park, Yorkshire, uncle of the new Peer, succeeded to the Traquair property in 1875 on the death of the venerable Lady Louisa Stuart, whose name he assumed. By his marriage with Mary Monica, only daughter of Hope-Scott, Q.C., Joseph Constable-Maxwell, younger brother of the present Lord Herries, succeeded to the romantic Tweedside property of Abbotsford, and adopted, like his father-in-law, the name of Scott. The Galloway property of Terregles has been kept in the family by the succession of Alfred Constable-Maxwell, second surviving son of Peter, another brother of the late Peer, and nephew of Marmaduke Constable-Maxwell, so long distinguished for the refined hospitality with which he kept up the fame of a beautiful property, naturally looked upon in some respects as the cradle of the race from which he sprung. Constable-Maxwell died July, 1872, and is 'fittingly commemorated by an exquisite memorial chapel within the walls of that Roman Catholic Church in Dumfries which during life he had supported with princely munificence. The recently erected convent crowning the eminence known as Corbelly Hill, on the opposite side of the Nith, and the establishment of the Marian Brothers in a fabric long occupied as the Royal Infirmary, may serve to indicate the zeal with which the Herries Maxwells supported the ancient faith, from which they never swerved.

The earliest Maxwell of Caerlaverock mentioned in history is Sir John, Great Chamberlain of Scotland, 1231, whose son, Aylmer or Emereus, also Great Chamberlain, acquired the barony and castle of Mearns by his marriage with Mary, only daughter and heiress of Roland, feudal possessor of the barony. A younger son of this marriage acquired from his father the barony of Nether-Pollock, and founded the family now represented by the young Stirling-Maxwells. The eldest, Sir Herbert de Maxwell, was grandfather of that Sir Eustace who defended Caerlaverock against Edward I., as described in the curious contemporary Norman-French poem, edited during the present century by Sir Harris Nicolas. From this point the Caerlaverock Maxwells divide themselves into two distinct and well-defined branches—the Maxwells, Lords Herries of Terregles, and the Maxwells, Earls of Nithsdale. By the line last mentioned the Herries honours were carried into the Yorkshire family of Constable, Lady Winifred Maxwell, daughter of the attainted Lord Nithsdale, marrying in 1758 Haggerston Constable of Everingham. Their grandson, Marmaduke-William Constable, was father of that William who established his right to the Herries honours, which are now about to receive an augmentation in the person of his son Marmaduke, the present Peer. The latter, as mentioned above, was born in 1837, and educated at Stonyhurst Roman Catholic College. In 1875 he married the Hon. Angela Mary Charlotte Fitzalan Howard, second daughter of Lord Howard of Glossip, and has issue two daughters, Gwendoline and Angela Mary, both born in 1877.

It is uncertain when the Herries barony was created. Herbert of the name is known to have sat as a Lord of Parliament in 1489. But a still earlier reference to the family, if not to the dignity, occurs in the person of a certain William de Heriz, who witnesses various charters in the reign of William the Lion. The first described as of Terregles (or Church lands of Lincluden) is Sir John "Herice," who obtained a charter of the lands from David II. on the resignation of the same by Thomas, Earl of Mar, in 1359. Nine years later this same Sir John would appear to have received a grant of the lands of Kirkgunzeon, within the Stewartry, which had previously belonged to the Abbey of Holmculteram, in Cumberland. The most prominent of his descendants was John Maxwell (Lord Herries), the friend and adviser of Queen Mary, who accompanied her in the flight from Langside, entertained her, it is thought, at least one night in his mansion of Terregles, and, much against his advice, saw her sail across the Solway from Dundrennan for the purpose of submitting her case to her sister Sovereign, Elizabeth of England. The tenure of the barony is not free from doubt during its occupancy by Sir John Maxwell. In right of his marriage with Agnes Lady Herries, he became possessed of one-third of the baronies of Terregles and Kirkgunzeon, and subsequently acquired the two-thirds which had belonged to her sisters. On 8th May, 1566, King Henry and Queen Mary granted a charter to Sir John Maxwell of Terregles, and Agnes Herries, his wife, and their heirs-male, whom failing, to the heirs-male of the said Sir John Maxwell. This charter was ratified in Parliament on 19th April, 1567, when, as a favour, the holding of the lands was changed from ward and relief to blench. Previous to this, and at least as early as 12th March, 1566-7, he had taken the title of Lord Herries. Sir James Balfour (Lord Lyon), writing, however, long after the time, states that he was created Lord Herries at the baptism of Prince James, on 17th December, 1566. It was inferred from this statement, and other circumstances, that a new peerage was created in the person of Sir John Maxwell, and limited to heirs-male. This, however, after a lengthened investigation, the House of Lords found not to have been the case (23rd June, 1858). They thought the original peerage created in the person of Sir Herbert Herries in 1489 was to heirs general, and that Agnes Lady Herries, the eldest daughter of William Lord Herries, was a peeress in her own right. She was found to have been often called by herself and others Agnes Lady Herries. There is no instance of her being called Lady Terregles from her husband's title, although her sisters are found to have been called Lady Garlies and Lady Skirling.

William Maxwell, fifth Earl of Nithsdale and Lord Herries, married the Lady Winifred Herbert, youngest daughter of William, first Marquis of Powis. The Earl having taking part for the Stuarts in the rising of 1715 was, 9th February, 1716, found guilty of high treason, and had sentence of death pro nounced against him. His Lordship, however, through the heroic aid of his devoted and incomparable Countess, escaped from the Tower of London after his conviction, and died at Rome, 20th March, 1744, leaving issue an only son William, who married, as mentioned before, Catherine Stuart of the house of Traquair, with issue Winifred Maxwell, who married, also as mentioned before, William-Haggerston Constable of Everingham, Yorkshire, whose grandson William established his right to the Herries honours. He petitioned in the first instance for a reversal of the attainder and for the title of Lord Herries, as the lineal descendant and heir of Herbert, first Lord Herries. An Act of Parliament being passed in 1848 reversing the attainder as regards the descendants of William, Earl of Nithsdale, forfeited in 1716, he again claimed the title of Lord Herries, which was decided in his favour, June 23, 1858, by the House of Lords, William Maxwell of Corruchan, the heir-male, having opposed. William Constable may therefore, but for the attainder, be considered the thirteenth Lord Herries. He married Marcia, daughter of Hon. Sir Edward M. Vavasour, Bart., of Hazlewood, Yorkshire, and had issue a large family of sons and daughters, the eldest being the present Lord Harris, Marmaduke Constable Maxwell, fourteenth Baron. On at least three different occasions during the present century the ancient but still stately ruin of Caerlaverock has been, the scene of festivities on a great scale, which revived for a time the memory of its former greatness. On the first occasion, in 1827, the tenants of Caerlaverock and other friends dined in the ancient hall, when Wm. C. Maxwell came of age; on the second occasion, in 1858, they met in the same place to hail him as Lord Herries; and in 1859 his Lordship acknowledged the compliment by treating his tenantry to a grand banquet and ball within the walls of the Castle. The local historian (W. M'Dowall) seems to have had pleasure in mentioning that the best of feeling existed in ancient times between the Maxwells and their retainers, and continues down till the present day.

A GALLOWAY CHARACTER.

"KELTONHILL, that fechtin Fair," written of by Mayne and drawn by Faed, is likely to come again to the front in connection with the republication of Mactaggart's amusing "Gallovidian Encyclopædia." Born at Plunton, in the parish of Borgue—about 1800—"The Friday night before Keltonhill Fair was the night in which I, 'gommeral Johnnie,' first opened my mouth in this wicked world." The design of his work is to set before the reader the original, antiquated, and natural curiosities of the South of Scotland, with sketches of eccentric characters and curious places, and explanations of singular words and phrases, interspersed with poems, tales, and stories, illustrative of the ways of the peasantry. How and when the notion of such a production arose the author describes himself as at a loss to say :— "I am inclined to imagine that it is mostly the work of instinct, that the conception of it was created in my skull when that thick skull itself was created, and afterwards expanded as it expanded; for, from my youngest days, I have been a wanderer amid the wilds of nature, and keenly fond of every curious thing belonging to my native country, while Providence has surely been very kind to me in this respect, for casting my lot in a nation among a rare and singular class of mankind." These few words of personal explanation furnish the key-note to balance in critical scales the humorous yet grave absurdities, the grotesque confusion exhibited in etymology and folk-lore, and the calm contented self-appreciation of the writer. If some books are valuable as warnings on account of their very badness, others again are doubly welcome when they unconsciously reflect all the droll twists and queer fancies characterising the imagination of an enthusiastic but ill-trained son of genius. No Advocate's Library was flung open to him; no Auchinleck MS. aided his researches; the whole is the work of habit and memory, of learning seized by snatches, and a few hints received from others. Scampering along in this way, as he calls it, "ram-stam," the author's expectation is in a fair way of fulfilment, in so far at least as the production of a book is concerned never likely to create much noise, yet not forgot in a hurry, and to be found in the same "bole" with Burns, Allan Cunningham, Nicholson, Peden's Prophecies, and Rutherford's Letters. Over Nicholson, indeed, "a wandering wicht of Homer's craft," and author of "The Brownie of Bledpoch," not noticed in the work, Mactaggart waxes quite eloquent. There is about him, he says, a melancholy and an independence that will ever cause him to be admired by true Caledonians. "And should all mankind desert him I hope he will never find me far away; whatever I can do for the good of that man so shall it be."

In arrangement, the "Encyclopædia" partakes of an alphabetical character, but, like the author's philology, it is only alphabetical after a kind. Under "Borgue," for example, we do not get Deacon Macmin, the Borgue philosopher. The word "Deacon" must be looked up for that. Nicholson is not under Nicholson, but under "Wull," as is also the joyous Gracie of the Tanaree at Millburn, Kirkcudbright; and Ross Island is neither under "Ross" nor "Little," but "Wee," a matter more to be wondered at, as the author not only notices "Janet Richardson," but appends a sad ballad on the wreck of Captain Ormonby:—

> So on did steer young Ormonby before the furious wind,
> The tide being out along the shore, no harbour could he find;
> The Little Ross no shelter was, the anchors would not hold,
> So our noble tar upon the bar among the foam was rolled.

Deacon Macmin, as drawn by Mactaggart, is well worth taking a little trouble to find out. When the minister of Borgue died, some friends designed to erect a monument in memory of his reverence, but ere proceeding far they thought there would be no harm in taking the Deacon's opinion about the business. "I ken na (said he) what ye wad say about him but that he's *there*," indicating that his body lay there, and that no more in justice required to be said. "So (remarks our author, gravely) the idea of a monument was blasted by the Deacon's sarcasm." In some other respects the Deacon appears to have been a kindred spirit with the "Miller of Minnieive"—

> I'm but ane humble, dusty miller,
> No unco fond of grubbing siller,
> Nor steering wi' a steady tiller
> Through life's queer sea;
> But tak my dram wi' a care killer,
> My Joke like thee.

Under the heading "Naturalls," a tender subject for the author to meddle with, will be found graphic descriptions of several of the unfortunate class well known in Galloway—among the rest Davie Eddie, Wull Gourly, who played tunes on his nose; Jamie Neilson, famous for "the plan" or "not the plan;" and Girzey Whay, of Kirkcudbright, with her

> Pocket napkin on a staff,
> To make the burgess bodies laugh.

Laird Cowtart, the "obstinate man," who refused to avail himself of light from Harris' candles on account of a slight quarrel, will also repay perusal. In some respects our author has anticipated certain recent epics of later days. Carrol's "Hunting of the Snark; an Agony in Eight Fits," is yet quite fresh. Mactaggart quotes from a poem of his own, fortunately never published, "The Rustic Madman, in Six Tornadoes." A Carlylean flavour is also thrown over the account of Paul Jones—"A Gallovidian, I am rather sorry to say; but he was a clever devil, and had strong talents of the infernal stamp." At other times our poet appears to have taken his pleasures sadly, if one may judge from the style of his address, "Mac is Major," written on reaching twenty-one, and after he had been a little time at Edinburgh University—

> Now Mac upon the Solway shore,
>   Whar seamaws skirl and pellocks snore,
>   And whilks and mussels cheep;
>   Whar puffins on the billows ride,
>   And dive adoon the foaming tide
>   For siller fry sae deep.
>   Puir chiel, his ane-and-twentieth year
>   He entereth upon;
>   My merry days are past, I fear,
>   And sad anes coming on.
>   Nae matter, I'll batter
>   As weel's I can through life;
>   Aye dash on, and brash on,
>   Throughout this worldly strife.

To refer to the "Encyclopædia" in terms of more exact criticism might appear ungracious and unnecessary—ungracious, because there is no end of good things within the book, and unnecessary, because the author has said that the work is presented just as he wished it. As for errors, "let them rest on my own broad back. Works of this kind are always fuller of errors than any others; also, should any be displeased because I have not taken notice of some curiosity which was a favourite of theirs, be it told that I was either not of their way of thinking or that I knew nothing about it." In the face of such a direct disclaimer it would be of little use trying to show that "Hogmanay" could hardly be derived from "hug-me-now," or that "Effie," not "Eppie," is the endearing contraction of Euphemia. So at least Scott thought, Eppie being, probably, rather allied to Elspeth. One story might have been given, seeing it lay at our author's own door. His treatment of the "Laird of Coul's Ghost," and of ghosts generally, makes it matter for regret that Mactaggart did not try his hand on "A true Relation of an Apparition, Expressions and Actings of a Spirit which infested the house of Andrew Mackie, in Ringcroft of Stocking, in the Parish of Rerrick, in the Stewartry of Kirkcudbright, in Scotland, 1695, by Mr. Alexander Telfair, minister of that parish, and attested by many other persons who were also eye and ear witnesses. Ephesians vi. 11—'Put on the whole armour,'" &c.

DRUMLANRIG AND THE DOUGLASES.

By slow degrees, and at uncertain intervals, the antiquaries of the South of Scotland are making up for their remissness in illustrating various sections of local history, so thoroughly overtaken by the superior zeal of their brethren in the North. It cannot of course often happen that a single corner of Scotland so prolific as Aberdeenshire or Moray in great names can send out within one generation scholars of such rare culture as Robertson and Innes, Stuart and Burton; but, putting for a moment great names aside, the common rank and file of the antiquarian force have shown infinitely superior industry and enthusiasm in dealing with such a tract of country as lies between the Grampians and the Murray Frith. Here was the land of Barbour, who sung so well of the hero-king, even although he was a Southerner; of gossiping old Spalding, who lights up the sombre page of his "Troubles" with dashes of genuine humour, entitling him to the warm commendation of the most recent historian of that agitated period. The pious Bishop Elphinstone, the Parson of Rothiemay, the "gay Gordons," the valiant Keiths, not to speak of municipal records, and the very "Breviary" of the old Church, have all found painstaking and loving commentators. The "Spalding Club" was mainly instituted to illustrate the history and antiquities of the north-east counties, and the useful series of volumes issued under its auspices make it plain that it may serve as a model for some kindred association in the neglected South. There matters are improving, but still far behind. With the exception of M'Diarmid's "Picture of Dumfries," avowedly light and sketchy, though full at the same time of his inimitable graces of style, and a few dry and not very accurate "Statistical Accounts," there was hardly any literature in existence relating to this part of Scotland, till M'Dowall set himself with cultivated ardour to put into continuous historic shape the existing traditions clustering round "The Queen of the South." The part taken by the burgh in events so recent as Mar's Rebellion, or the entry of the young Chevalier on the retreat from Derby, could seldom be encountered except in the imperfect pages of Peter Rae, or in the loose talk of some old burgess of the Johnny Gas type, who might be spoken of as having at a very uncertain period the felicity of encountering some plundering Celt "out" in the perilous '45. The notes to Mayne's "Siller Gun" were thought to present as many genealogical and traditionary facts as people in those neglected times needed to care about. Of charter lore, municipal records, or ecclesiastical history, there was absolutely none. Public documents of that kind were neither read nor cared for. Even yet in this respect the southern antiquaries are but on the threshold of their work. Lincluden and Dundrennan, neither of them possibly rivalling in magnificence the stately fane at Elgin, so roughly handled by the "Wolf of Badenoch," or the surpassing beauty of the lonely Kirkwall, saved by its isolation from the despoiler—still even Lincluden, Sweetheart, and Dundrennan have all a story to tell. Why are they permitted to remain dumb? Why is no cunning hand engraving in detail the crumbling fragments ere they pass from sight. Is it never to be known how the monks of the South lived when the Church was independent without being rebellious, zealous without being intolerant, the guide and home of the scholar, the patron and instructor of the craftsman. Of "sweet Lincluden's holy cells," which struck even the robust Burns with plaintive tenderness, little more is on record than that there was interred Margaret, Countess of Douglas, daughter of Robert III.; and there, also, in later and evil days, the barons assembled to decree the code known as "Grim Lord Archibald's battle laws." Dundrennan, again, is chiefly known in connection with the hurried flight of Queen Mary after the disastrous overthrow at Langside, and to a few in modern times, who have not forgotten how often the bench of this country has been adorned by the scholarly taste and courtly bearing of its occupants, as giving an honoured title to the owner of the Abbey ruins, the genial and gifted Thomas Maitland. Holywood also, with its Druidical cromlechs, should be made to reveal something, unless, indeed, as some students deem probable enough, the reputed Abbot of Sacrabosco is a sort of doubtful creation. Then for family records. With the exception of the Maxwells and Scotts, finished with such fine taste by Mr. Wm. Fraser, the charter-rooms of the old houses in the South are almost virgin ground for the student. Drumlanrig itself must contain priceless treasures in the way of national, territorial, and family lore. Even a good catalogue or calendar would be an acquisition to the working antiquary. A little gleaning— hardly one sheaf out of the harvest, and this relating to a single historic season, but certainly of exceptional interest—makes up a most interesting portion of the "Memoirs of Viscount Dundee," by the late Mark Napier, Sheriff of the County. Raehills, again, must be full of memories of Johnstons, as Jardine Hall is of Jardines, and Hoddam of the Sharpes—one member of the last, the accomplished but odd "C. K. S.," being in himself alone worthy of the most delicate treatment. Bonshaw and Wyseby, Robgill and Stapleton, might all be made to render up interesting details of many a long line of Irvings and Bells, Edgars and Flemings. The distinction indicated above between North and South, so far as antiquarian study is concerned, cannot be explained by any deficiency of interest in the annals of the latter. Mr. M'Dowall has already shown that these are full of unfailing interest, while the natural peculiarities of the district—its crops and minerals, its breezy uplands and rich vales, its luxuriant woods and fairy gardens, its winding streams and trouting pools, its linns and haughs and fertile holms, the brawling Annan, storied Liddle, and, greater still, the sweeping Nith, "whose distant roaring swells and fa's"—the very sough of the Caul—all go to furnish material to the student of physical science, as rich as the floating traditions are to the novelist or the poet. Nor are the sons of the soil naturally unfitted for dealing with such attractive specialities. Were the honours of the eightieth birth-day not so recent (1875), Mr. Carlyle might be referred to as able to speak for Annandale. Telford, "Eskdale Tam," knew a century since all the traditions then current about Langholm and Canonbie. So long as Mr. Carruthers reigned in Inverness, it would take a bold man to plead that there was anything in the air of Dumfriesshire, disqualifying its natives from dealing with the higher elements of literary criticism or chilling sympathy with the engrossing traditions of their birth-place. Long since Arthur Johnstone wrote of the district—

> Florida tot pingues hic tondent prata juvenci,
> Gramina quot verno tempora fundit humus.
> Illius externas saturant pecuaria gentes,
> Et mensas onerant Anglia sœpe tuas.

Pleasantly paraphrased by Rev. Mr. Bennett, Moffat, as—

> Full many a sleek and seemly steer enjoys the flowery fields;
> Full many an herb, in genial spring, the soil ungrudging yields.
> To distant lands her fruitful farms their produce oft convey,
> And load the board in England's halls on many a festive day.

But, better than all reasoning on such a point, here is Dr. Ramage, with his little book confined to three parishes, and these not of supreme importance, showing how every little corner has its pleasant record, when the eye has been properly trained to decipher, and the ear to hear, the floating traditions of the past. Having rather exceeded our limits with remarks designed to stir up friends in the South to good work in the field of antiquarian study, it is hardly possible to give extracts showing the extreme value and fidelity manifested all through Dr. Ramage's very enticing work. But this is the less to be regretted, as by far the larger portion has already found a wide audience in the pages of the "Dumfries and Galloway Courier," and where, at the present time (1875), another series of interesting topographical and genealogical notes are appearing from week to week. Dr. Ramage has endeavoured, and fairly succeeded, in bringing together about as much information as can at present be obtained regarding the three parishes selected for illustration—Durisdeer, Closeburn, and Morton. Tumuli, cairns, stone and bronze celts, coins, remains of ancient camps, place-names—the most enduring and probably the most important of all the means of illustrating the occupation of a country—have been pressed into the service, though, with a modesty almost unnecessary in his case, he explains that such studies demand a more varied knowledge than is commonly possessed by one person. In connection with Durisdeer parish—the burial-place of the Queensberry and Buccleuch family—we naturally hear much of the Douglases, and of the high state kept up by them at Drumlanrig, and much also about the fabric itself, with its spacious apartments, and grounds around rivalling in magnificence the fabled gardens of Almira. "One Douglas (says Burns) lives in Home's heroic page; but Douglases were heroes every age." In the pages of the master of Wallace Hall, the old House appears to have been as turbulent and discontented as their neighbours of lesser note, and equally unscrupulous about the method of obtaining such "guids, geir, and plenishing" as they might require. Minute genealogical details of the House of Douglas are given, the change in the succession indicated with exactness, many letters and charters quoted, and a brief but quite intelligible account of various criminal trials in which the House was concerned. One of these, Barbara Napier, sister-in-law of Douglas, of Coshogle, tried and sentenced to be burnt for witchcraft in 1591, illustrates the old story of the charmed ring used to induce love, and obtained by the poor victim, so it was said, from another notorious witch. Still more attractive matter is set before us in Closeburn parish, visited frequently by Burns, and the residence of "Lovely Polly Stewart," whose unfortunate story is here told with even more minuteness than it merits. Dalgarnock, too, close at hand, has had a new interest added to it by the poet as the tryst or fair frequented by that faithless wooer, taunted there and then by his discarded Phyllis as improperly

> Gaun up the lang loan to my black cousin Bess;
> Guess ye how the jaud I could bear her.

Again, in Morton parish, the reader is pleasantly introduced to another celebrity, Robert Paterson, the "Old Mortality" of Scott, and tenant for a time before he commenced his wanderings of the quarry at Gateley-bridge. To turn out students so distinguished in after life as the present Archbishop of Canterbury is no doubt a high honour to any educational institution, yet on the whole Wallace Hall bulks rather large in Dr. Ramage's volume. When a new edition is issued, a map of the district would also be an improvement. It might assist some unlettered tourist, used to gad about French watering-places, losing his time and vexing the hearts of waiters, to know that the Pass of Enterkin is amongst the most solitary and beautiful spots in this southern county. So good a judge as the author of "Rab and his Friends" found this out, and has written a pleasant paper thereon. We will be glad to meet Dr. Ramage again in the field of parochial antiquities. Should his leisure from graver responsibilities permit, he no doubt knows where to find suggestive localities not far from home. Sanquhar and Wanlock are full of Covenanting memories, and some noteworthy things in the way of modern industry. Or he may turn his steps westward, passing under the shadow of Tynron Doon, and enter Glencairn parish, where he will find at one end those who in modern times represent "Sir Robert, the lord of the Cairn and the Scaur;" and at the other memories of the old historic house of Craigdarroch—

> A line that had struggled for freedom with Bruce;
> And patriots and heroes must ever produce.

THE SCOTTS OF BUCCLEUCH.

NEVER quite so common a name, even in Southern Scotland, as natives are apt to imagine, the Scott clan have yet been distinguished and powerful as far back as either records or tradition can be safely followed. The novelist Sir Walter fixes upon a certain Uchtred Fitz Scott, who flourished at the Court of David I., as the earliest who can be properly identified with the fortunes of the family; but he was not inclined to dispute the accuracy of the tradition which carried the ancestors of Uchtred to the reign of Kenneth III. (973-996) —when they are said to have possessed the barony of Scotstoun, Peeblesshire. It is to some date approaching this that the not over-careful Satchells in his "True History" of the family of Scott would refer the origin of the Buccleuch name to a narrow escape of the King from the fury of a stag at bay which he had pursued through a large portion of the Royal hunting grounds in Ettrick. A certain John of Galloway, living in concealment at Buccleuch, or rocky "cleft," on Rankleburn, overcame the stag, and, after slaying it, carried the carcass up the steep side of the "heugh" and laid it at the feet of the King. The monarch is said thereupon to have made the doubtful remark—

> And for the buck thou stoutly brought
> To us up that steep heugh,
> Thy designation ever shall
> Be John Scott in Buckscleuch.

In addition to the lonely farm of Buccleuch, situated among the overhanging hills, there is lower down Rankle Glen, the site of the old church of Buccleuch, and also the ruins of the family tower, the latter within three miles of Tushielaw, ere reaching which the burn has found its way into Ettrick water at Cacrabank. Even before the close of the fifteenth century the family historian finds himself on solid ground for indicating the descent of the Buccleuch family. Sir David Scott of Branxholm took a prominent part in public affairs during the reign of James III., and sat in the Parliament of 1487 as "Dominus de Buccleuch." Sir David would appear to have been the first of the family so designated. At least one tower still remains of that old castle of Branxholm, which he strengthened and enlarged to accommodate those "nine-and-twenty knights of fame," with their squires and yeomen, so vividly described in the "Lay of the Last Minstrel" as hanging their shields within the fortalice, to "carve out their meal with gloves of steel, and drink the red wine through the helmet barred." Branxholm, greatly modernised, and now used as a residence for the Duke's "Forest" Chamberlain, was in those days one of the most important fortresses between Cumberland and the Tweed—a centre of princely Border power and festivity in harmony with the lofty bearing of the baron who led to the field that strong array—

> All knights of metal true,
> Kinsmen to the bold Buccleuch.

Walter, a grandson of Sir David, was Warden of the West Marches, and celebrated in his day for valour and magnanimity during the minority of James V. To Sir Walter's period belongs the story of the "Lay," the Baron himself making a narrow escape when attempting to release the King from the custody of Angus. He afterwards distinguished himself at Pinkie, 1547; but five years later, as recorded in the poem, lost his life in the streets of Edinburgh when engaged in an encounter with Kerr of Cessford. A grandson, Sir Walter of Buccleuch, was also Warden of the West Marches, and otherwise celebrated in Border song as making at the head of his clan a successful sally on Carlisle Castle for the rescue of "Kinmont Willie," seized and confined by Lord Scrope on a certain day of truce in the spring of 1596. And he asks in anger—

> Have they taken him, Kinmont Willie,
> Against the truce o' Border tide;
> And forgotten that the bauld Buccleuch
> Is keeper here on the Scottish side?

Kinmont "Willie's" residence became in modern times the Annandale seat of the Queensberry family. After the succession of James to the English throne, Buccleuch was very active in quieting the Borders, and, to accomplish this end, raised a regiment of resolute soldiers, whom he afterwards carried over to fight against the Spaniards in Holland. Having obtained considerable renown in the Netherlands as a commander under Prince Maurice, he was raised to the Peerage of Scotland, with the title of Lord Scott of Buccleuch. He married a daughter of the old foe of his house, Sir William Kerr of Cessford, sister of Robert, first Earl of Roxburghe, and died in 1611. An Earldom of Buccleuch, with the secondary title of Eskdale, came into the family with Lord Walter (1619), whose son Francis acquired Dalkeith from the Morton family, 1642.

Of two daughters born to Earl Francis by his wife of the house of Rothes, the eldest, Mary, became Countess of Buccleuch in her own right; but, dying without any issue from her marriage with Scott of Harden, she was succeeded in the family honours and wide estates by that amiable Countess Anne, who, as the wife of the illegitimate but favourite son of Charles II.—

> ——— Had known adversity,
> Though born in such a high degree;
> In pride of place, in beauty's bloom,
> Had wept o'er Monmouth's bloody tomb.

On his marriage in 1663, the Buccleuch dignity was elevated to a Dukedom, and the name of Scott assumed by Monmouth. After the execution of her husband for levying war against his half-brother, King James (1685), Duchess Anne resided for the most part at Dalkeith or in the stately tower of Newark on Yarrow, now a romantic ruin, but included within the beautiful grounds surrounding Bowhill, where, in April, 1884, Duke Walter breathed his last. It was at Newark, the reader may remember, the "Last Minstrel" sung his "Lay" to please the hospitable lady and her high-born dames. Wordsworth refers to the place as—

> That region left, the vale unfolds
> Rich groves of lofty stature,
> With Yarrow winding through the pomp
> Of cultivated nature.
> And, rising from these lofty groves,
> Behold a ruin hoary—
> The shattered front of Newark's tower,
> Renowned in Border story.

To the last, even after she had made a second alliance with Charles, third Lord Cornwallis, the Duchess kept up the style of a Princess of the blood, being served by pages on bended knee, and under a rich canopy, which none were permitted to approach without permission. To prevent the Scotch titles becoming extinct at her death, the Duchess resigned them into the hands of the Crown, and obtained, 1687, a regrant to herself, and after her death to James, Earl of Dalkeith, her eldest son, and his heirs-male and taillie. The second son became Earl of Deloraine. The Duchess survived till 6th February, 1732, when she was a little over eighty years of age. The Earl of Dalkeith having predeceased his mother, 1705, the succession on her death opened up to his eldest son, Francis, born 1695. In 1743 he obtained by Act of Parliament a restoration of the Earldom of Doncaster and Barony of Scott of Tynedale, two of the English honours of his grandfather, the Duke of Monmouth. He married, first, 5th April, 1720, Lady Jane Douglas, eldest daughter of James, second Duke of Queensberry, by whom he had a son, Francis, Earl of Dalkeith, who predeceased his father, and, secondly, Miss Powell, but by that lady had no issue. On the approach of the Pretender to Edinburgh in 1745, Duke Francis sent his tenantry to assist in defending the City. He died 22nd April, 1751. His son, the Earl of Dalkeith, had married Caroline, eldest daughter and co-heiress of the famous John, Duke of Argyll and Greenwich, by whom he had four sons and two daughters. His eldest son, Henry, succeeded his grandfather. One of the daughters, Frances, married to Archibald, Lord Douglas, was a posthumous child.

Henry, third Duke of Buccleuch, was born 13th September, 1746. In March, 1764, his Grace and his brother, the Hon. Campbell Scott, set out on their travels, accompanied by the learned Dr. Adam Smith. The brother was assassinated on the streets of Paris on the 18th October, 1766, in his nineteenth year. His remains were brought home by the Duke, and deposited in the family vault at Dalkeith. On the commencement of the war with France in 1778, Duke Francis raised a regiment of Fencibles chiefly among his own tenantry, and, by his attention to the wants of the service, secured the affection and esteem of all under his command. He married, in 1767, Elizabeth, daughter of the last Duke of Montague, by whom he had three sons and four daughters, viz., George, who died in infancy; Charles William Henry, Earl of Dalkeith;

Henry James Montague, who succeeded as Lord Montague in 1790, on the death of his grandfather, the Duke of Montague, but died in 1845, without male issue, when the title became extinct; Mary, married to James George, Earl of Courtown; Elizabeth, to the Earl of Home; Caroline, to the Marquis of Queensberry; and Harriet, to the sixth Marquis of Lothian. On the decease of William, fourth Duke of Queensberry, "Old Q," without issue, 23rd December, 1810, Duke Henry succeeded to the Dukedom and to considerable estates in Dumfriesshire. It was to the influence of this Duke of Buccleuch that Sir Walter Scott was indebted for his appointment in December, 1799, to the office of Sheriff-depute of Selkirkshire, and afterwards in 1806 to that of one of the principal clerks of the Court of Session. His Grace died 11th January, 1811.

His eldest son, Charles William Henry, fourth Duke of Buccleuch, and sixth of Queensberry, was born 24th May, 1772, and in 1807 was summoned to the House of Peers as Baron Tynedale. He married, 23rd March, 1795, Harriet Katherine Townshend, youngest daughter of Thomas, first Viscount Sydney. Her Grace died in 1814. There is a touching correspondence on this event between the Duke and Sir Walter Scott in Lockhart's life of the poet. The Duke was a constant friend and correspondent of Sir Walter, and at an early period of money difficulties gave his name as security for a loan of £4,000. He also bestowed on the Ettrick Shepherd the life-rent of the farm of Altrive, on the favourite braes of Yarrow. By his Duchess he had two sons, Walter Francis, Earl of Dalkeith, who succeeded him as fifth Duke of Buccleuch, and died April, 1884, as before mentioned, in his forest retreat at Bowhill, aged seventy-eight; Lord John Douglas Scott, an officer in the army, and six daughters. Earl Charles died at Lisbon, 20th April, 1819. The present Peer, William Henry Walter, better known as Earl of Dalkeith, is the sixth Duke.

ST. COLUMBA.

"ALTUS Prosator, Vetustus Dierum, et Ingenitus"—so opens that magnificent hymn which the unbroken tradition of thirteen centuries connects with the name of Columba, but of engrossing interest otherwise, in so far as it indicates modes of thought prevailing in the early Church at a time when creeds, as we now have them, were barely formulated. Athanasian only in so far as it expresses opinions known to have been valiantly defended by Athanasius, certain prominent doctrines embodied in the famous creed were expressed in language almost identical to the brethren of Iona by the Apostle of our Western Highlands. "Patris, et Filii, et Spiritus Sancti una est Divinitas æqualis gloria, co-æterna Majestas," declares the creed; so in like manner Columba—"Cui est Unigenitus Christus et Sanctus Spiritus co-æternus in gloriâ Deitatis perpetua." Subject or not subject to Rome, here is belief, expressed at least as early as the Council of Nice (A.D. 325), set out in language almost identical with what the Church put into form some centuries later—probably not far removed from Columba's own day. Welcome on its own account at any time, the student of our early poetry will find a new interest added to the hymn through the care and scholarship of its latest editor. Naturally inclined to such studies, and frequently engaged in them, it occurred to the present Marquis of Bute that there were many persons who would hail with pleasure a new handy edition of the "Altus" of St. Columba, as well from veneration for the memory of the author as from appreciation of the intrinsic merits of the work, and of its interest as a specimen of ancient Celtic Latin poetry. The text has been taken from the edition, unhappily uncompleted, of the "Liber Hymnorum," prepared for the Irish Archæological and Celtic Society by the late Dr. Todd, author of the well-known "Memoir and Mission of St. Patrick." To the words of the poem the noble Marquis has added a most useful kind of double commentary. First, a paraphrastic translation into

English prose; and, secondly, a series of notes designed chiefly, though not exclusively, to assist the reader by placing before him the passages of Scripture cited or alluded to in the text, so far at least as could be done for the work of a writer who was using a Latin version other than the present. The hymn itself is not so widely known as to make a brief account of it altogether unnecessary. After the first chapter or section, in which, as may be seen from the extracts above, God is praised as He is in Himself, the thought of the author of the "Altus" passes through three phases, in each of which he praises the Most High for a special class of His works. The first is dedicated to the angelic world, the second to the material cosmogony as understood by the writer, and the third to the things which shall or may be hereafter. Each section comprises seven chapters of twelve short lines each, with the exception of the prelude, which runs out two lines extra. Here occurs the phrase noted before, "Ingenitus," "Unbegotten," yet natural or strictly in the course of nature. The editor properly explains that no such expression is found in Scripture; but in the Athanasian creed there is "Pater a mullo est factus, nec creatus, nec genitus"—"The Father is made of none, neither created, nor begotten;" and the word also occurs in such Church Offices as the Trinity Sunday Antiphon at "Magnificat," in the Roman Breviary "Te Deum Patrem Ingenitum"—"Father unbegotten." "Vetustus dierum" is evidently the "Antiquus dierum," or "Ancient of Days" of Dan. vii. 9, 13, and 22. The section relating to the angelic hosts partly repeats views set out at greater length in that division of Adamnan's life of the Saint known as "The Apparition of Angels," from which the reader gathers that in Ireland, especially in and around his favourite Derry, as well as in Iona, legions of these ministering spirits were seen and conversed with. Montalembert makes repeated reference in his life of the Saint to the encouragement and aid derived through the angelic attendants—"Sed haberat cælestia in quibus privilegia ostenderet magnopere possibili fatimine"—"Heavenly creatures wherein to show graces as great as any utterance can express." The chapter on "Heaven," which is given at length as a fair specimen of this early Celtic poem, would seem, as the Marquis writes, to imply that Columba regarded as identical that Paradise in which God placed Adam with that Paradise which is the home of the saints, still existing in some part of the world—

Plantatum a prooemio	Cujus et situm florido
Paradisum a Domino	Lignum vitæ est medio,
Legimus in primordio	Cujus non cadunt folia
Genesis nobilissimo;	Gentibus salutifera;
Cujus exfonte flumina	Cujus inenarrabiles
Quatuor sunt manantia;	Deliciæ ac fertiles.

The first eight lines are, of course, founded upon Genesis ii. 6–14; the next on Rev. xxii. 2, where mention is made of the tree of life and the leaves "for the healing of the nations;" and the last two probably on Ezek. xxviii. 13— "In deliciis Paradisi Dei fuisti"—"Thou hast been amidst the pleasures of the garden of God;" or, as our authorised version has it, "Eden, the garden of God." With the chapter commencing "Quis ad condictum Domini Montem conscendit Sinai?" the poet passes to the third and last part of his work. Having described the work of God in the creation and preservation of angels and men, of the intellectual and material components of this planet and her sphere (which to him was nearly, if not quite, the same thing as the Kosmos), he projects thought forward to the time when this planet will be changed. Then, continues his editor, a pause is made for a moment to consider that there has been but one whose drawing near to God, when revealing Himself in terror, can ever have enabled him to know, however imperfectly, what the terror of the end will be. To follow this chapter with wisdom, it is therefore necessary to read in connection Exodus xix., particularly from ver. 16—"Et ecce cæperunt audiri tonitrua ac micare fulgura, et nubes densissima operire montem, clangorque buccinæ vehementius perstrepebat"—"And behold the thunders began to be heard," &c. In this portion of the poem the Marquis naturally detects a certain inclination to dwell upon the terrible, recalling so far that element in Columba's character which sometimes cast shadows on the brightness of his life, and infused with a certain awe the veneration which surrounded his memory after death. When King Dermot, sitting enthroned on Tara, gave judgment against him in the dispute concerning the O'Donnell Psalter, which had been transcribed with his own hand, Columba exclaimed in wrath, "I shall tell my brethren and my kinsfolk how the rights of the Church have been violated in my person, and the wrong shall be wiped out in blood. My humiliation shall be followed by yours in the day of battle. Cursed be he who does evil. The thing which he sees not comes upon him, and the thing which he sees vanishes from his grasp." Columba afterwards found a friend in St. Brandan, of Bute, who, having seen the column of fire which went before Columba and the angels walking by his side, besought his brethren at Teilte to revoke the sentence passed on one thus manifestly singled out for some high purpose. But Columba by that time was getting disquieted in conscience. He had, it is said, begun to doubt, not that victories had been won by his prayers, but whether he had been right in applying so potent an engine to the discomfiture of mortal adversaries. "I beseech you," he said to a holy monk named Abban, "to pray for the men who have been slain in the wars waged by me for the honour of the Church. I know that if you intercede they will obtain mercy, and the angel with whom you daily converse will reveal to you the will of God concerning them." The monk, prompted by a feeling of modesty, long refused his request. At length he prayed, and when his prayer was ended, the angel gave him the assurance that all should be admitted to the bliss of heaven. Dr. Reeves interprets the piece commencing "Causa quare voluit Deum laudare," as a prayer to be forgiven for three battles he had occasioned in Ireland. On the whole, the Marquis judges the intrinsic merits of the "Altus" to be very great, especially in these latter and more imaginative chapters, some of which he thinks would not suffer by comparison with even the famous "Dies Iræ." It is by these, indeed, he hopes the poem may commend itself to many who may not have been aware of its existence, or may not have had no opportunity of consulting it in a convenient form. As the editor has not judged it necessary to refer to the different legends regarding the composition of the "Altus," or the supernatural advantages claimed for its recitation, it may interest readers who turn over its pages for the first time to be reminded of its connection with Pope Gregory the Great, an ancient tradition fixing its composition at Iona in acknowledgment of gifts sent to the monastery by his Holiness, who is further said to have listened to its recitation, standing, out of respect for the author, whom he knew not only as a great missionary, but as possessed also of rare gifts in poetry and oratory, with which he adorned his long, adventurous, and self-denying life.

CUNNINGHAM.

THE work done by the Maitland Club in its day was so thorough, varied, and scholarly that high expectations are naturally raised when a new volume is submitted as practically one of the series, and prepared by a member with a view to presentation when the club was in its palmiest days. Nor is it the least praise due Mr. Dobie's "Pont" to say that it is entitled to take its place beside some of the most useful volumes of the series. We miss indeed the old familiar title-page, and also the roll of members so suggestive of the pleasant weaknesses incident to a taste for tall folios and scarce quartos. But in other respects—in its printing and binding, the compact yet clear page, a margin broad enough to be agreeable to the eye, yet avoiding the error of unseemly waste, and the time-honoured boarding—all tend to commend it to members as a fit addition to a series of works not more remarkable for good taste than solid learning. To readers composing a far wider circle it will be found an enticing addition to the library of the working student or the topographical collector. Mr. Dobie, sen., well known as a sound authority on certain West Country pedigrees, commenced his labours on "Pont" in 1825. It was afterwards repeatedly referred to in

"Maitland" Reports as a contribution in preparation, but the sudden death of the annotator in 1853 prevented the fulfilment of his design when on the eve of completion. Fullarton's "Account of Cunningham," issued nearly twenty years since, went over the same ground with, it is said, a rather free use of the result of Mr. Dobie's inquiries. The MS., however, was preserved with fair care; and on the return to this country of Mr. J. S. Dobie, jun., in 1870, the present publication was undertaken. While the notes and illustrations of the annotator remain intact the latest editor has endeavoured to supplement his notices of places and families where they appeared deficient, and, what was equally essential, has brought down the information to quite a recent date. Of Pont himself a word or two is necessary. A son of Robert, minister of Edinburgh West Church, Timothy matriculated in St. Leonard's College, St. Andrews, in 1579–80, and from 1601 to 1608 was minister of the parish of Dunnet, in Caithness. His taste, however, lay in mathematics and kindred studies, and he is said to have been the first projector of an atlas in Scotland. Having given up his parochial charge, Pont personally surveyed all the counties and isles of Scotland, and made drawings of such monuments of antiquity as tended to illustrate his descriptive notes. The year of his death has not been ascertained with certainty, but Pont's papers are known to have been placed under the charge of Gordon of Straloch, himself an eminent geographer and antiquary. At the instance of Charles I. these papers were afterwards of great service to the Blaeus of Amsterdam in the publication of that portion of their great work, "Geographia Blaviana," relating to Scotland. The preface mentions the fifth part as a child of which the parents were Pont and Gordon and the nurse Sir John Scot of Scotstarvet. The map of Cunningham given in Blaeu's work has been reproduced in the original size for Mr. Dobie's volume.

Cunningham, famous in rhyme for its corn and bere, would seem to have been the most complete of Pont's surveys. He appears to have gone over the district with leisure, as he enumerates about 350 places. He omits, indeed, few of any importance, but is occasionally inaccurate in fixing the exact locality.

Making up, as readers are aware, with Carrick and Kyle, the more modern electoral division of North and South Ayrshire, Cunningham itself may be best realised under three geographical divisions. The first or north part bending westward to the Firth on one side, and marching with a large portion of South Renfrewshire on the other; the second lower to the south-east, comprehending the parishes of Stewarton and Dunlop; and the third to the lands on the banks of the Irvine, which separates the northern division from Kyle—lands described by Pont as "fertill and full of profitt," and so populous in his day that "at the ringing of a bell in the night a few houres ther has beine seen conveine 3000 men weill horsed and armed." Mr. Dobie's work has been so arranged as to do the utmost possible justice to this interesting tract of country. Following an editorial note by the editor, and a brief introduction by the annotator, Pont's notes are given in a continuous form precisely as they appear in the Balfour MS., transcribed by the late Professor Cosmo Innes. These notes are again repeated, followed in each separate instance by such additions, corrections, and explanations as the researches of Mr. James Dobie had brought to light in his day, this new matter making up by far the larger portion of the volume. Regarding many places curtly dismissed by Pont in a word or two new information is presented, at once curious, minute, and interesting. Beith, for example, mentioned by the old topographer simply as "a parochiall church situated neir the laick of Kilburny," is made to reveal quite a history of Scottish provincial life during the sixteenth and seventeenth centuries. "Kilburny Castle, a fair bulding weill planted, the heritage of Johne Craufurd, laird thereof," introduces the reader to the Garnock family, and, as might be expected from Mr. Dobie, to the desperate claim of succession set up in 1810 by the so-called John Lindsay Craufurd. In connection with the Church of Kilbirnie a lengthy notice is given of that Captain Thomas Crawford concerned in the capture of Dumbarton Castle, 1571, whose monument is still conspicuous among the humbler memorials scattered round the churchyard. Cunninghamhead, "a stronge old dunion seatted on ye brinke of ye River Annock veill planted," is followed by a history of lairds, eminent some of them in the cause of the Reformation, and others in the Revolution Settlement. Wodrow gives an anecdote of Sir William of the last-mentioned period. In 1695 he had occasion to obtain an audience of the King and Queen in presence of the favourite Portland:—"The King (writes the minister of Eastwood) cast his eye on Sir William, and said, soe as he heard him, to Portland, I know Sir William is a Scotsman, but, pray, from what part of Scotland is he? Portland answered, Sir, he is a West-country gentleman. The King, looking to him, touched his nose with his finger, and, smiling, said, Sir William, I warrant you, is a great Whig; and went out to his coach. Portland on going out said, Sir William, yon was as much as if the King had called you his sweetheart." Glengarnock has been identified by some as the residence of that Hardyknute referred to in Lady Wardlaw's famous ballad. Rowallan, "a stronge ancient dwelling belonging to ye surname of Moore, weill neir 400 yeirs. With them K. Rob. 2nd allayed," opens up the history of a family too proud to claim descent from kings, because kings had come from them, Elizabeth, wife of Robert II., being a daughter of Sir Adam Mure by Joanna, daughter of Sir Hugh Dennistoun of Dennistoun. Nor is Caldwell, with its classic associations, quite forgot, although it happens to be a little beyond the boundary of North Ayrshire. Giffen Castle, a heritage of the almost Royal house of Douglas of Liddisdale, naturally suggests many details concerning the resident branch of Montgomeries to whom the estate fell "in days when good King Robert rang." Francis, one of the representatives for Ayrshire in the Union Parliament, was sufficiently prominent to be obnoxious to the satirists of the day, and is described in certain coarse pasquils which the Jacobites were not ashamed to circulate as "ambling like any paced horse;" another shares with him the unhappy distinction, "For rebellion engrained you may each bear the bell." The Union was a sore subject in other places besides Cunningham. In his life of Peden, Patrick Walker, "packman of Bristo Port," mentions that one of the evil consequences of that backsliding step was the mingling of ourselves with a people who, among other abominations indulged in, trained their children to say Papa and Mamma instead of Father and Mother, which custom the author deprecated as one of the causes of God's wrath to Scotland, evidenced in his day by the prevalence of burning fevers and agues previously unknown. With Kilwinning Mr. Dobie appears to have taken special pains, one view being given of the ancient doorway, and another, presented by the Earl of Eglinton, of the somewhat dull, modern church, but introducing effectively the remaining gable of the Abbey south transept. The letterpress presents as fair a history of this important foundation as it is possible to prepare in the absence of the Abbey Cartularly, lost apparently since Pont's time. Records connected with the Lodge of Mother Kilwinning are not known to exist of earlier date than 1642. A French poem somewhat vaguely refers to James Lord Stewart as receiving into his Lodge at Kilwinning the Earls of Gloucester and Ulster. The Abbey was then ruled by Abbot William, who sat in the Parliament held at Brigham in 1289. Ecclesiastical records connected with the Presbytery of Irvine do not exist of older date than 1646, and those of the Regality Court of Kilwinning, now in the General Register House, Edinburgh, commence a few years later.

LEADHILLS AND WANLOCK.

TIME redresses grievances in its own way, all the fuller in appearance sometimes because redress comes in an unexpected form. Between forty and fifty years since, when the Disruption controversy was embittering the social life of Scotland, few noblemen were held up to greater obloquy than the late Duke of Buccleuch. He not only insisted that the Established Church was the real Church of the people, but refused to recognise the Seceders even to the extent of permitting them to build places of worship on his land. For Thornhill a door of relief was opened by the magnanimity of old Janet Fraser of Virginhall. To Free

Church miners in the dreary uplands of Wanlock no tenderness was shown. The land quaintly described in old writings as "God's Treasure House in Scotland" was to them a house of bondage. The gold of that Havilah might be good, yet it was to them mere earthly treasures which thieves might break through and steal, and of small account compared with the spiritual riches dispensed under the most untoward circumstances generally by their own pastor, Mr. Hastings, but occasionally by divines so distinguished as Chalmers, Candlish, and Guthrie. Time has now changed all this. Under the above title an account of this auriferous region, written by the successor of Mr. Hastings, was respectfully dedicated to the same Duke of Buccleuch, as "The generous patron of Art, Literature, and Agriculture, whose benevolence as a landlord is universally esteemed (even by the men of '43), and who, with the Duke of Argyll, gave a noble example to the proprietors of Scotland in the gift of the patronage of his numerous parishes to the people, without compensation." City charges like Maitland Street need not, therefore, be looked upon as the only indications going of changes in thought and feeling. The greater part of Mr. Porteous' interesting little volume appeared from time to time in the columns of the "Dumfries Courier;" but, it being deemed advisable to gather the detached papers into a more permanent and accessible form, the opportunity was taken of extending what was mainly an account of the parish of Sanquhar so as to include Crawford, Crawfordjohn, Leadhills, and Wanlockhead, with some notice of the geology and mineralogy of the district, extended information as to the gold, silver, and lead workings, details as to properties, owners, and workmen, and some useful facts connected with the Church history of the district from the Reformation to the present time. The first chapter describes "The House"— its geological formation, pasturage, streams, and temperature. The second commences with "The Treasures," and the men who have wrought in gold, silver, and lead, from Bevis Bulmer, in the sixteenth century, to the exceptionally high-class mining population for which Leadhills is famous in our own day. Of "The Treasure House" itself, or earthen vessel, not much can be said, so far as outside beauty is concerned. After travelling through the district, Dr. John Brown describes Leadhills as a dreary, unexpected little town, but, like all natives of such forlorn, out-of-the-world places, the people cannot understand how any one can be happy anywhere else; and when any of them leaves the wild unlovely place they accompany him with wondering pity to the outskirts of their paradise, and never cease to implore and expect his return for good. They are known to be thoughtful and solid, make good use of an extensive library, gathered mostly by themselves, and are unwearied in their attendance on ordinances. This deep religious feeling has no doubt received a colouring from the memory of many Covenanting struggles floating about the district. Here in an especial manner was the preaching ground of Cargill and Renwick, of Alexander Peden and Richard Cameron. Only a few years since, "Black Joan frae Crichton peel, a carline stoor and grim," celebrated the bi-centenary of the famous Sanquhar Declaration, in terms of which first Cameron and then Renwick denounced and disowned Charles II. as a tyrant and persecutor. Memories of a more pleasant nature are called up by the remembrance that within a year after Renwick had closed the long line of those who in Scotland sealed their testimony with blood, Allan Ramsay, the poet, was born at Leadhills. His father was manager of the mines, and there did the author of "The Gentle Shepherd" continue to live till 1701, when he removed to Edinburgh to commence, at the age of fifteen, an apprenticeship to a wig-maker. Another literary memory is associated with Wanlockhead. A few years after Ramsay's death, and while residing with his sister, Mrs. Telfer, in what is now known as the Duke's shooting lodge, Smollett wrote his inimitable "Humphrey Clinker," a novel, we regret to say, of which Mr. Porteous thinks but lightly. Tabetha and Lismahago, Matthew Bramble and Jerry Melford, might have excited the humour of even a Free Church divine in the bleak solitudes of Wanlock. Among other names of some distinction associated with the district are James Taylor, John Hutcheson, and William Symington, all concerned in the early experiments of steam navigation undertaken by Patrick Miller of

Dalswinton. More remarkable, in some respects than even scientific reputation, was the fame acquired by the grandfather of the Taylor above-mentioned as the very oldest person who must ever have lived in those parts. Born in 1637, the year of Jenny Geddes' exploit in St. Giles', and when Charles I. was yet King, a tombstone in Leadhills Churchyard records that John Taylor, miner, died there "at the remarkable age of 137 years." To "lie like a tombstone" is proverbial; and to prevent disappointment on the part of those curious in such inquiries, it may be as well to mention that there does not appear to be much other than tombstone evidence for the remarkable longevity of John Taylor. The succession of owners and lessees is described with much exactness by Mr. Porteous. In 1562 a Royal grant was made to John Achisone and John Alsowand, burgesses of Edinburgh, "to wark and wyn in the lead mynes of Glengonar and Wenlock," and to transport the ore to Flanders; that the silver may be there extracted, paying to the Queen "fortie-five unce of uter fyne silver for every thousand stane wicht of lead." Thomas Foulis, goldsmith in Edinburgh, succeeded; and his niece, Ann, marrying her advocate, James Hope, after a successful defence of her claims, the Leadhills workings passed to the Hopetoun family, who have held them ever since. Last year, the company working the mine raised about 1,200 tons, or 24,000 bars of 1 cwt. each, selling for the most part at £22 per ton. The lordship is one-ninth to the Earl of Hopetoun, with fixed rent of £52, 10s., the company having all minerals, gold, silver, and lead at its command. The Wanlock mines are wrought by a manager in the interest of the Duke of Buccleuch. Miners work five days a week, and earn on an average all the year round fully £4 per month. Mr. Porteous' book is illustrated by a geological map of the district known as the "Treasure House," and a few engravings by typographic process from the author's drawings. A ghastly view is also presented of what he calls the "Tree of the Christian Church in conflict with Papal fire," and a perplexing diagram of the divisions and unions in the Church of Scotland since the Reformation. This last puzzle is described as elucidated in the author's earlier work on the invincible position of Presbytery, concerning which he holds strong Covenanting principles, and quotes approvingly:—

> The braid blue bannet still may cleed the pows in green Glencairn,
> The laverock wake the mavis yet in howes o' auld Carsphairn;
> But waes me for the Covenant psalm that echoed aince amang
> The wastlin' hames o' Scotland, mair sweet than mavis sang.
>
> For noo nae mair amang the glens, nae mair amang the hills,
> The simple strains o' Covenant times the moorland shepherd trills;
> Ye'll wander far afore ye hear the e'ening psalm ava;
> The bonnie flowers o' Scotland's faith are nearly wede awa.

THE FULLARTONS OF FULLARTON, &c.

TRADITION of a kind fixes Fullartons in Ayrshire as early as the beginning of the twelfth century, the first possessor of the barony so named, near Irvine, being probably a follower of Walter, son of Alan, ancestor of the High Stewards who obtained from the Crown grants of broad lands in the counties of Ayr and Renfrew when the family left their Shropshire home to settle at the Court of David in the North. The name has been set down, although not without challenge, as derived from one of two employments—a "Fuller," or cleaner of woollen cloth, and a "Fowler," an important hereditary officer in the Royal household largely concerned in supplying the king's table. Nisbet, in his "Heraldry," seems to have preferred the last-mentioned derivation, and appeals for corroboration to a certain charter in the Haddington collection; later writers rely with equal confidence on an ancient washing-green or "bleachfield" on the south-west bank of the Irvine over against the Royal burgh. The industrial origin of the name is further accounted for by the circumstance that "Fowl" in Saxon is "fugel," "fugel-bono," a fowl-killer. Adam, son of Alam, received a charter of

Fullarton lands from James, High Steward of Scotland, about the close of the thirteenth, or early in the fourteenth century. A son, Reginald, who was also infeft into the family lands, accompanied David II. to Durham, and being taken prisoner with the king in that disastrous battle, was one of twenty hostages left in England for payment of his Sovereign's ransom. Succeeding Fullartons were—Rankin, first of the Dreghorn branch; George, designed of Corsbie; and at a long interval of time, James and Robert, brothers, the last thought to have founded the Bartonholme family in the early years of the seventeenth century. John, second son of the above James, served with honour in the French and German wars, and acquired late in life the estate of Dudwick, Aberdeenshire, which remained in his family till the close of the eighteenth century, when it passed to the family of Udny of Udny. A third son, William, became minister of St. Quivox, Ayrshire, and ancestor of two branches of this prolific house—the Fullartons of Thryberg Park, Yorkshire, and of Carstairs, Lanarkshire, one of whose successors sold the property to the late Henry Monteith, Esq. James Fullarton's eldest son, also James, was Sheriff of the Caillary of Kyle-Stewart, and Commissioner for the shire of Ayr in the Scots Parliament of 1643, having also the distinction of being sharply fined by both Charles and Cromwell for his zeal in the Presbyterian cause. He died in 1667, leaving by his wife, of the house of Cunninghamhead, three sons and three daughters. The eldest of the family, William, was apprehended on suspicion of being concerned in the affair of Bothwell Bridge, but so far kept the fortunes of his family together as to obtain a charter from Queen Anne (1707), constituting Troon a free port and harbour, and erecting the town of Fullarton into a burgh of barony. On the death of William, without issue, the succession in the estate opened up to his next surviving brother, George of Dreghorn, father of Patrick, who practised as an advocate at the Scottish bar, and predeceased his father, 1709. George's grandson, William, built Fullarton House, and otherwise greatly improved the family estate. He died in 1758, leaving an only son, who became the well-known Colonel Fullarton, but was little over four years of age when his father died.

Colonel Fullarton received his academical education in Edinburgh, and at the age of sixteen was placed under the care of Patrick Brydone, whom he accompanied in his once popular Tour over Sicily and Malta. In 1775 (as mentioned in the "Scottish Nation," young Fullarton was appointed principal secretary to the embassy of Lord Stormont at the court of France. In 1780 he proposed to government the plan of an expedition to Mexico against the Spaniards, which being approved of, he raised the 98th regiment of infantry, of which he was appointed colonel, though not previously in the army. He and Lieutenant-colonel, then Major Mackenzie Humberstone, raised two thousand men, at their own expense, with unusual despatch, and involved their estates to a very large amount, by preparations for the expedition. The unexpected breaking out of the Dutch war, however, caused it, instead of Mexico, to be sent upon an attack on the Cape of Good Hope; and ultimately it was employed in the war in India. Colonel Fullarton, with the troops under his command, served at first on board Commodore Johnston's fleet, but in May, 1783, he received the command of the southern army on the coast of Coromandel, a force consisting of upwards of thirteen thousand men. His campaigns and operations with this army, in that and the succeeding year, were attended with a rapidity and brilliancy of success previously altogether unknown in that country. On his return to Europe, Colonel Fullarton published "A View of English Interests in India," together with an account of his campaigns there, 1782-84. He was frequently a member of the House of Commons, and was twice returned for his native county of Ayr. In 1791 he was served heir of line and representative of the family of Cunninghame of Cunninghamehead, baronet. (See vol. i., p. 746.)

At the breaking out of the French war in 1793, he raised the 23rd light dragoons, then called "Fullarton's light horse," and also the 101st regiment of infantry. The same year, at the request of the President of the Board of Agriculture, he wrote "An Account of the Agriculture of the County of Ayr, with Observations on the Means of its Improvement," which was printed and generally circulated. In 1801 he also wrote an essay, addressed to the Board of Agriculture in England, on the best method of turning grass lands into tillage. The same year he was appointed governor of the island of Trinidad, but returned home in 1803, when he preferred a charge against Sir Thomas Picton, the former governor, for authorising torture on a female slave, which led to the trial of that gallant officer. Colonel Fullarton died at London, 13th February, 1808, at the age of 54, and was interred within the church of Isleworth, where a marble monument, with an appropriate Latin inscription, was soon after erected to his memory. The Fullarton estates at Irvine was purchased in 1805 by William Henry, fourth Duke of Portland, and still remains in possession of that family.

The family of Fullarton held, from an early period, lands in the Island of Arran. A cadet of the principal family, said to have sprung from a second son, named Lewis, settled in the island, and his descendants have always been distinguished by the patronymic of M'Lewie, or M'Lewis. When Robert the Bruce landed in Brodick Bay, whilst upon his peregrinations through the Western Highlands, one of the Fullartons directed him to a place where some of his adherents had taken shelter, and were employed in making a temporary fort. For this and other services, the king granted to Fergus Fullarton a charter, dated at Arneale Castle, in Cunningham, 29th November, in the second year of his reign (1307), of the lands of Kilmichael and others, with the hereditary office of coroner of the bailiedom of Arran. The estate of Kilmichael and Whitefarland, in the parish of Kilbride, worth about £800 a year, still remains in possession of the family, the rest of the island being the property of the Duke of Hamilton. Alexander Fullarton (brother of Lewis Fullarton of Kilmichael and Whitefarland) married Miss Macduff, Perthshire, whose mother was a Menzies of Culdares. Charles Fullarton, daughter of Alexander, married Mr. Bowden, father of Menzies James Bowden, Fullarton; Robert Bowden, and Miss Eliza Bowden, of Newton Place, Glasgow.

The present Menzies of Culdares is thought originally to be a Stewart whose ancestors assumed the name of Menzies. Old Menzies, the original family, entailed the estate, having ten sons and three daughters. The lawyer who drew the deed, said, in joke, "After the ten sons and descendants you might put me in." This was done, and strange to say, the lawyer's family ultimately got possession—all the sons of the real laird and descendants having died out. The Beresfords of Ireland made a move as next male-heirs to dispute the family succession of the lawyer, but the deed was so clear that they did not push their claim.

Colonel Fullarton, of the Skeldane family, another officer of high repute in the Indian Army, and who took a leading part in the overthrow of Tippo Saib, was some years subsequently taken prisoner in India by a chief of high caste and great wealth. All overtures and money bribes for the release of the colonel proved unavailing, but in time his liberty came about in a romantic and remarkable way. Colonel Fullarton, who was a man of splendid appearance and perfect manners, and knowing the native language fluently, became quite a favourite with his captor, so one day this chief took a very beautiful daughter to see his prisoner; both then parted feeling a mutual and instinctive admiration for each other, and ere many days passed the "princess" found her way back to the prisoner's quarters. In time their attachment for each other became great, and culminated in a marriage by the rites of her creed; this secured the colonel's liberty, when he was soon afterwards married by the rites of his Church. The lady received a handsome dowry, and both set out for England and Scotland. On arrival at Leith they were met by his relatives and friends, and the handsome couple were carried in state befitting her rank to Edinburgh, where, after a short stay, they proceeded to his property in Ayrshire, where both lived long, happily, and popularly. From this family of Skeldane were also descended the Fullartons of Burnside, Largs, Overtoun, and Kerrelaw, Ayrshire. This last property is now possessed by the sister of Mr. Gavin Fullarton, Helensburgh, in life-rent and in fee to her son, who is heir to the baronetcy now held by Sir Henry Kingston James. The original Fullartons were of French origin—(see Scott's "Lord of the Isles" and Notes); and, besides their once vast estates in Ayrshire, held lands in Arran from the days of the Bruce. To that branch Bruce was much attached. The Arran estates were entailed by the father of Dr. Fullarton of Ayr, cousin of Skeldane, whose son, John, a dashing naval officer, long resided in Campbeltown, having built the house of "Rosemount," near the residence of his brother-in-law, Captain Beatson. Colonel James, the second son, a Knight of Hanover and Companion of the Bath, married Miss M'Laverty of Keil, Campbeltown, but died without issue. Major Archibald, who lost his leg at Salamanca, in the Peninsula, succeeded when quite an old veteran to the Arran estates, and the male-heirs of his family predeceasing him, the property passed to his daughter (Mrs. Bowden Fullarton, of Glasgow), by his marriage with Miss Peebles of an old Glasgow family.

Mrs. Bowden Fullarton, dying in 1875, was succeeded by her half sister, Miss Jessie Spottiswoode Fullarton, now heiress of Kilmichael, Brodick, and Whitefarland, Loch Ranza. It was Colonel James Fullarton, already referred to, who first placed his cousin (by the female side), the present Lord Napier of Magdala, in the British Army—a mark of gratitude the gallant field-marshal has in many ways recognised to the family. Margaret, daughter of Dr. Lewis Fullarton, of Kilmichael, who died about 1859, was well known and esteemed in Ayr. Another daughter, Isabella, was the widow of Dr. John Mackinnon, D.D., of Tyree, early in this century and for many years tutor to the Argyle family. Their son, Campbell, Inspector General of Hospitals, who took a conspicuous part at the siege of Delhi, for which he received the decoration of the Bath, married Miss Beatson, Campbeltown, and by her left an only son. Another son, the Honourable Lewis Mackinnon, of the Legislative Assembly, died at Jamaica in 1882.

John Fullarton, second son of William of the Carstairs branch, passed advocate 17th Feb., 1798, when in his 23rd year, and on 17th Feb., 1829, was elevated to the bench in the room of Lord Eldin, when he took the judicial title of Lord Fullerton. He died 3rd Dec., 1853, about three weeks after resigning his seat on the bench.

INVERKIP TO WEST KILBRIDE.

WITH a fairly straight road running north to south, of little, if anything, over twenty miles in length, there is nothing, of course, to prevent a pedestrian in ordinary "form" from accomplishing in one day the entire distance between "Auld Kirk" on the Kip and the more southerly parish, named, like its church, after the pious St. Bridget. But if he desires, as most intelligent travellers do, to linger over the supreme beauties of the locality through which he is travelling, and to make himself acquainted at the same time with even a few of those historic remains associated with stirring scenes in Scottish history, he must deviate so frequently from the main path as to make a break, for one night at least, all but necessary. This our friend, who may be presumed as tramping along the shore road, knapsack on back, will be found, can most conveniently be done by resting about the centre of the parish lying between Inverkip and Kilbride, or say in the pleasant watering-place of Largs itself. Here he may profitably spend an odd hour or two of a long summer day by examining localities easily identified with that famous battle through which, over six hundred years since, the victorious Alexander III. freed Scotland once and for ever from the tyranny of Northern Sea Kings or Vikings, not unworthily represented by Haco and his plundering Norsemen from Norway, Denmark, and Sweden. Even otherwise, a day's leisure would not be misspent among the richly-wooded glens which open up every here and there eastward, or by the side of one or other of the many sparkling yet secluded streams which find their way through the valleys, rushing and leaping with joy till lost in the waters of the opening Firth. Beautiful as Clyde is admitted to be at all points of its journey—some 106 miles—to the sea; beautiful when it begins to show itself in the upland pastoral solitudes of Crawford, when it is winding round the base of Tinto, or overshadowed by the dark chasm of Cartland, or leaping over huge Falls like Cora Linn, or winding gently, yet with majesty, among the orchards and broad meadows and fair woodlands of Lanarkshire—none of these features in the route of our noble river surpasses in beauty what borders its banks as the river gets lost in the Firth, and the Firth in the sea. Here the attractions are at once varied, interesting, and informing. Leaving behind us the princely splendours of Ardgowan, as already faintly described in these pages (see 119); and even without troubling ourselves for a moment with the reflection that Inverkip, as a parish, stretched as far eastward in pre-Reformation times as Greenock, where the Church of St. Lawrence stood, there is within little more than a mile north-east from the parish church the ruins of that old Castle of Dunrod, famous in the annals of Renfrewshire as the resort of both wizards and witches, and not very far off—indeed, not quite so far away—an old arch crossing the Kip burn known as the Roman Bridge, and which, in name at least, may have been an antiquity when the battle of Largs was fought.

About a mile south from Inverkip village, the traveller enters the north or Wemyss portion of Kelly or Bannatyne property, held by that family, it is thought, for over 300 years. In 1792 the old Kelly property was purchased by John Wallace, of Cessnock, Ayrshire, one of the leading Glasgow West India merchants. He built the larger and older part of the present Kelly mansion within the next year or two, and here he died, 4th June, 1805, when the property passed to his son, Robert Wallace, of Postal Reform fame, to be afterwards referred to. By various contracts of excambion the original Wallace purchase was extended southward beyond Kelly burn to Auchindarroch, and northward to Wemyss Bay, the port of Ardgowan, in exchange for the lands of Finnock conveyed to the then Sir Michael Shaw Stewart. Shortly after entering Parliament, as first member for Greenock, under the Reform Bill of 1832, Robert Wallace was obliged to part with that Kelly estate which he had done so much to extend and adorn. The purchaser in the first instance was a Mr. Alexander, an Australian merchant, but he was able to retain the property only a few years, when Kelly fell into the hands of Mr. James Scott, of Dalmonach Print-works, and the Wemyss portion passed to Charles Wilsone Brown, Glasgow.

In 1860, the Wemyss portion of Kelly was sold for Mr. Brown in two portions, Wemyss Bay falling to the now venerable (1885) George Burns, Esq., one of the founders of the great Cunard Steamship Company, who built Wemyss House on the property from designs by Mr. Salmon, Glasgow, and erected also the beautiful Episcopal Church near by, in memory of Mrs. Burns. Wemyss Castle property passed to his son, Mr. John Burns, presently (1885) Chairman and Managing Director of the Cunard Steamship Company (Limited)—a company which in its early days he did more to develop and consolidate than any other single person. To Wemyss Castle, as built for Wilsone Brown from designs by Billings, Mr. John Burns has made important additions, and otherwise rendered the surrounding grounds a feature of attraction, even to travellers who only see them at a distance from a Clyde steamer. In 1867, the estate of Kelly proper was purchased from Mr. Scott by James Young, Esq., of Durris, F.R.S. and LL.D., a chemist of such high repute that he may almost be said to have created the shale oil trade in this country as well as in America. Rising from but a humble position as an apprentice cabinetmaker to his father in Glasgow, Dr. Young first availed himself of what little leisure he had in taking lessons at the Andersonian Institution, where, by assiduity and intelligence, he attracted the attention of Professor Graham, who first made his young pupil assistant in Glasgow, and then took him to London, when the Mastership of the Mint opened up to the older accomplished chemist. After that came a few years' service, first in the laboratories of Messrs. Muspratt, St. Helens, Liverpool, and next of Messrs. Charles Tennent & Co., in Manchester. It was while discharging duty at this latter place that Dr. Young's attention was drawn by Sir Lyon Playfair to the subject of oil of high quality flowing from a pit at Alfreton, near Manchester. The discovery of the Torbanehill mineral was not long in bringing Young's careful researches to a practical issue. The works were established at Addiewell and Bathgate, which prospered so greatly that in 1866, when his patent expired, they were sold to a Limited Company for £400,000. When these works were undertaken the yearly produce of oil in Scotland was not more than 6,250,000 gallons. At the date of his death (13th May, 1883, when Dr. Young was in his 72nd year), the production had risen to 15,000,000 gallons, of which the Young Company produced about one-third. Dr. Young continued on terms of the closest intimacy with Graham, to whose memory he caused a most effective statue by Brodie, to be set up in George Square, Glasgow, besides joining with a young friend, Dr. Angus Smith, in editing several of his scientific treatises. To Dr. Livingstone Young was also much attached, unwearied, first in promoting his discoveries, and finally in ascertaining his sad fate. A model of the hut in which the intrepid traveller died was erected within the grounds of Kelly by two of the African attendants who had remained with their kind master to the last.

Continuing the shore road southward from Kelly, the next important property in this part of Cunningham is Skelmorlie, noted in modern times for its excellent Hydropathic Establishment, but still more famous for that old castle of the Montgomeries, restored in 1852 by John Graham, Esq. (born 1805), a prominent Glasgow merchant, renowned in art circles as a munificent judicious patron, and the happy possessor of a collection of pictures unrivalled in the West Country, if not in the kingdom, for interest and value. Generous in all matters connected with art, Mr. Graham may be said to have made his private gallery public in the best sense of the term, so that thousands have had opportunities in this way of studying the finest examples of painters so celebrated as Gainsborough, Ary Scheffer, Rosa Bonheur, Wilkie, Turner, and Holman Hunt. A little south, but close at hand, is Bridgend House, also occupied by Mr. Graham, and the mysterious Serpent Mound which has excited so much discussion among antiquaries. From this point a walk of about an hour and a-half lands the traveller in Largs, where unending scenes of interest may be enjoyed, even if he should not have leisure to examine the curious Skelmorlie aisle and monument, or the graceful memorial set up in honour of the gallant and learned Sir Thomas M'Dougal Brisbane, whose family patrimony lies to the north-east of the town. Omitting Kelburne, as already noticed (p. 91), Lord

Glasgow's village of Fairlie, with its castle, glen, and yachting industry, is soon in sight, as is also Hunterstone, of high historical repute centuries before anything was ever heard of its Runic Brooch; and lastly, on a ledge of rock standing well into the Firth, Portincross, one of the oldest fortresses in Kilbride parish.

Within West Kilbride parish also, but backward a little from the shore, is Carlung, purchased in 1877 from the trustees of James A. Anderson, Union Bank, by the late James Arthur, Esq. of Barshaw, near Paisley. When Mr. Arthur died in the summer of the present year (June 17, 1885), it was felt that no unnecessary compliment was paid in describing him as in many respects one of the most remarkable men connected with Glasgow enterprise during the last half-century. Born at Paisley in 1819, he commenced business in a small way while quite a young man. From the outset prosperity attended all his efforts, but he was not long contented with the restricted field which Paisley afforded for his unwearying energy. Removing to Glasgow, he began a similar business in Argyle Street under the firm of Arthur & Fraser, now Fraser & Sons, and here also his labours were crowned with growing success. But it was not until a few years later, when he founded the firm of Arthur & Company, that his proper sphere was found. Mr. Arthur had not been many years in Glasgow when he was discovered to be a man of great sagacity, singular acuteness and swiftness of judgment. Combined with these characteristics were a mastery of detail and powers of organisation and arrangement rarely to be found, while, as has been already indicated, his energy and enterprise were unbounded. All these qualities he brought to bear on the management of the business which he now established, and to the building up of which the remainder of his life was devoted. From comparatively small beginnings it has grown to be one of the largest, if not the largest, establishments of the kind in Great Britain. In addition to a home trade of vast extent, the firm has large business connections abroad. In South Africa, Australia, New Zealand, and the Dominion of Canada, it is directly represented; and its agents are as well known in each of these colonies as they are over the length and breadth of the United Kingdom. In most of these fields of enterprise Mr. Arthur may be said to have led the way, others following his example, and reaping the benefit of his far-seeing sagacity. Besides the gigantic establishment in Queen Street, where almost every description of merchandise may be found, the firm have extensive factories in Glasgow, Leeds, and Londonderry. Though assisted by able coadjutors, Mr. Arthur to the very last took an active personal interest in the management of the business of which he was the founder, and had daily placed before him, until laid aside by illness, statements showing the position of the numerous departments into which it is subdivided. Some years ago the firm was converted into a Limited Liability Company, but it is understood that the membership is confined to Mr. Arthur's own family and his former partners. In addition to his own business, Mr. Arthur was largely interested in various other important commercial undertakings connected with the West of Scotland. He was one of the promoters and original directors of Young's Paraffin Company, and continued a member of the board down to the time of his death. He was also chairman of the "Loch Line" of ships sailing between this country and Australia; and latterly, along with several leading capitalists in the West of Scotland, he originated the "Clan Line" of steamers. A good many years ago he purchased the small residential estate of Barshaw, near Paisley, and more recently he acquired the estate of Carlung, near West Kilbride, where during a considerable part of the year he resided. Mr. Arthur was a Liberal in politics, but never took any prominent part in public business. A member of the Chamber of Commerce, he, on several occasions, was appointed to the board of Directors, and his counsel in all matters affecting trade and commerce was highly valued. Mr. Arthur was a member of the Free Church, but by no means narrow in his sympathies; and, besides being a liberal supporter of the denomination to which he belonged, gave largely to all worthy religious and benevolent objects. He left a widow, whose name is honoured in the town of Paisley, to which she belongs, for the interest she takes in all good work; and a family, consisting of four sons and one daughter.

West Kilbride parish appears in the "New Statistical Account" as having been originally a dependency of the Abbey of Kilwinning, but since the Reformation considerably altered and extended. In 1650 Southanan and Crosby were annexed from Largs, and a little later Montfode, Knockewart, and Boydstone were disjoined from Kilbride for the purpose of extending Ardrossan. Strictly speaking, the modern parish may be described as made up of the following seven baronies:—Southanan, the most extensive, and once the property of the Sempills; Crosby, associated with the Crawfords of Loudoun, Sheriffs of Ayr; Kilbride proper, long held by the Boyd family, Earls of Kilmarnock; Ardneill, or Portincross, also once a Boyd property; Carlung, with Drumilling, both Church lands; and Hunterstone. It has often been stated, but the proof is not altogether satisfactory, that among the distinguished natives of Kilbride parish were Professor Dr. Robert Simson, of Euclid fame, and General Robert Lord Boyd, Lieut.-Governor of Gibraltar, under Lord Heathfield, during the memorable siege of 1782. West Kilbride parish is about six miles in length, with an average breadth of three miles, or an area on the whole of 8,650 acres Scotch measure. The coast line, including many indentations, between Largs and Ardrossan, may be set down at from seven to eight miles, for the most part low and sandy, except at Portincross, where it presents a rocky front, steep and bold.

FINIS.

BELL AND BAIN, PRINTERS, GLASGOW.

INDEX

----, Phyllis 328
ABERCORN, Earl Of 161 Lord
    James 100
ABERCROMBY, 191 George Ralph
    97 Montagu 97 Ralph 187
ABERUTHVEN, Lord 181
ACCOCHAR, Andrew Chief Of 18
ACHISONE, John 346
ADAM, Robert 36
ADAMNAN, 336
ADAMSON, Patrick 290
ADDISON, 278
ADGYLL, Caroline Daughter Of
    Duke John 333
AIKEN, 252 255
AINSLIE, 244
AIRE, Justice 309
AITCHISOUN, James 201
AKEMPIS, Thomas 250
ALBANY, Duke Robert Of 69 Regent
    183
ALBERT-EDWARD, Prince Of Wales
    112
ALCUIN, 313
ALEMARE, Lord 165
ALEXANDER, Boyd 122 James 222
    292 Janet 222 John 124 Mr 354
ALEXANDER, King Of ? 110
ALEXANDER II, King Of 125 196
ALEXANDER III, King Of 92 109-
    110 182 353
ALISON, 234 Archibald 232-233
    235-237 Capt 234-235 Gen 234
    Lady 233 Maj 235 Sheriff 232
ALLAN, Abbot 288
ALLANTON, Baron James 52
ALLARDYCE, Mr 187 191-192
ALPIN, 160
ALSOWAND, John 346
ANDERSON, 281-282 David 234
    Elizabeth 280 James A 357 Mrs
    253 William 253
ANDERSONE, George 198
ANGUS, 331 Earl Of 3 100 169 Lady
    Margaret 161 Lord Archibald 161
    Lord William 161
ANNAN, 214
ANNANDALE, Lord 109
ANNE, Queen Of ? 79 90 348
ANNE, Queen Of England 43
ARBUCKLE, Katherine 104
ARBUTHNOT, Adm 189
ARCHIBALD, Lord 325 The Grim
    314
ARDROSS, Euphame 100 Scott Of
    100
ARDROSSAN, Baron 106
ARGYLE, 87 352
ARGYLL, 9 46 57 149 169-171 306
    Bishop Of 97 Countess Of 3
    Duchess Of 61 Duke John 333
    Duke John Of 276

ARGYLL (Cont.)
  Duke Of 61 189 344 Earl Of 17
  147 154-155 Lord 142 Lord
  Archibald 19 148 175
ARMOUR, James 203 Jean 252 254
  Mr 252
ARMSTRONG, Christie's Will 79
  Willie 79
ARNWLF, 308
ARRAN, Earl Of 17 196
ARTHUR, James 357 Mr 357-358
  Mrs 358
ARUNDELL, Louisa-Alice 65 Robert
  Arthur 65
ASHBURNHAM, Earl Of 173
  Jemima-Elizabeth Daughter Of
  Earl Of 173
ASHTON, Lucy 84
ATHANASIUS, 335
ATHOL, 142 Duchess Jane 47
ATHOLE, 86 170
AUBIGNY, Lord 64
AUCHINLECK, John 23 Lord 24 29
  165
AULDHOUSE, Annabella Of 128
  George Of 128
AULDOCHY, Patrick 156
AYRSHIRE, Francis Of 342
BACON, Lord 159
BAILLIE, Andro 198 Col 137
  Principal 170 Robert 205
BAILLIE-COCHRANE, A D 114
BAIN, 359
BAKERFIELD, 295
BALCARRES, Earl Of 174 176 180
  Lord James 181
BALDOON, 85 David Of 84
BALFOUR, 20 James 318
BALIOL, Edward 99 John 110
BALLANTYNE, 304
BALLIOL, John 314
BALMERINOCH, Lord 93
BALMUTO, 12-13 Lord 28

BALVENY, Douglas Of 183
BANNATYNE, 12 354 Dugald 209
BARBOUR, 44 309 324
BARGARRAN, 281 Lady 284
BARJARG, Lord 165
BARNES, Thomas 102
BARTLEMORE, 74
BARTRAM, 294 William 298
BASTIAN, 9
BATES, Hugh 127
BATTLE, Sarah 34
BEATON, 183 Archbishop 30
  Cardinal 72 James 17 196 John
  16
BEATOUN, 219 James 220
BEATSON, Bazill 104 Capt 352
  Henry 104 Miss 352
BECKET, 224
BEGG, Mrs 253
BELHAVEN, Lord Robert 52
BELL, 326 359 Provost 197
BENNETT, Rev Mr 327
BERESFORD, 351
BERKELEY, 308
BERZELIUS, 238
BETHEL, Mr 180
BETHUNE, Archbishop 226
BEZA, 225
BILLINGS, 355
BIRREL, 156
BLACK, Mary 277
BLACKADDER, Bishop 71 Robert 70
BLACKWOOD, Sall 57
BLAEU, 340
BLAIR, Anne 35 Brice 308 Bryce
  120 David 115 Dorothea 94
  Edward Hunter 94 J Hunter 35
  Louisa 115 Robert 10
BLAKE, 302
BLAKENEY, Lord 244
BLANDY, Mary 16
BLANE, John 254
BLANTYRE, Lord 280

INDEX. 363

BLEARIE, Queen Of 285-286
BLIND, Harry 306-309
BLORE, 15
BODLEY, Thomas 67
BOGLE, 215 George 209
BONAPARTE, C L 294
BONHEUR, Rosa 356
BONTINE, R C 123
BOQUHONENE, Laird Of 156
BORTHWICK, 28 Lord 17
BOSWELL, 22 25 76 Alexander 24 26-29 145 165 David 120 Elizabeth 23 James 23-24 26 29 62 166 Jamie 24 Jessie Jane 29 Lady 29 Margaret 120 Miss 29 Thomas 23
BOTHWELL, 5-7 9 17 Erle 8
BOUILLE, Gen 212 Marquis 212
BOUNAPARTE, 187
BOWDEN, Charles 350 Eliza 350 Menzies James 350 Mr 350 Robert 350
BOWMAN, Provost 37
BOYD, 308 James 196 Lord 198 Lord Robert 196 359 Lord Thomas 258 Lord William 258 Zacharias 198 Zachray 205
BOYLE, 91 Earle James 97 Agnes 92 128 Anicia 92 Ann 93 Augusta 96 David 92 94 Diana 96 Dorothea 94 Elizabeth 92 94 96 103 George 93 96 George Frederick 93 96-97 101-102 Gertrude 95 Gertrude Julia Georgiana 97 Grizel 92 Helen 94 Isabella 96 James 96 Jane 93 John 92-94 96 128 Julia 96 Lady Gertrude 101 Lady Gertude 102 Lady James 96 Lord John 103 Lord-Justice Clerk 28 Margaret 93 Marion 92 Montagu 97 Mr 97 Muriel Louisa Diana 97 Patrick 93-94 Richard 92

BOYLE (Cont.)
William 92 96
BRACKLEKEN, Clerk Of 104 Margaret 104
BRAMBLE, Matthew 345
BRAXFIELD, Lord 62 166
BREADALBANE, 90 Alma-Carlotta Wife Of Earl Of 173 Earl Of 147 173 Lord 87
BRIDPORT, Lord 190
BRINDLEY, 39
BRISBANE, Thomas M'Dougal 356
BRODERICK, Adm 186
BRODIE, 242 297 356 David 294
BROUGHAM, 239
BROWN, 74 Charles Wilsone 354 Ex-Provost 289 George 166 John 345 John Jr 209 Mr 290-291 293 355 Wilsone 355
BROWNE, Thomas 260
BRUCE, 45 77 112 306 329 352 Alexander 23 David 99 Edward 44 113 Eleanor 44 Elizabeth 23 King Of 168 182 Lady Matilda-Harriet 131 Lord Alexander 111 Lord Edward 111 Lord Robert 111 Lord Thomas 111 Marjory 99 285 Robert 99 109-110 165 Robert King Of 175 285 Robert The 350 Thomas 131
BRUNTON, 290
BRYDONE, Patrick 349
BUCCLEUCH, 328 330 Countess Anne 95 Countess Mary 332 Duchess Harriet Katherine 334 Duke Charles William Henry 334 Duke Henry 167 333 Duke Of 162 334 343-344 346 Lady Francis 167 Lord Scott 331 Walter Of 331
BUCHAN, 79 Earl Of 55 Luckie 313
BUCHANAN, 7 148 174 197 206-207 215 224 226 Catherine 216

BUCHANAN (Cont.)
  George 143 John 214 216-217
  Marquis Of 181 Maurice Of 176
  Walter 209
BULLER, Miss 57
BULMER, Bevis 344
BUNTEIN, Ritmaster 203
BUNYAN, John 250
BURKE, 133
BURLEIGH, Lord 313
BURN, Mr 214
BURNET, 83 197
BURNETT, James 166
BURNLEY, W F 209
BURNS, 103-105 107 113 250-252
  259 261-262 268 300 303-304
  314 321 325 328 Bess 254 Dr
  224 George 355 George Mrs 355
  Gilbert 254 J W 221 James 222
  James Mrs 222 John 355 John
  William 187 222 Mr 223 Robert
  253 302 Sonsie 254
BURTON, 307 324
BURWELL, 267
BUSHBY, John 261
BUTE, Lord 32-33 Marquis John 32
  Marquis Of 29 306 335
BUTTERFIELD, 97
BYRON, Lady 237
CADE, 68
CAIRN, Robert Of 329
CAIRNCROSS, 119
CALDERWOOD, Bishop 229 James
  Of 127 Mr 54 Mrs 54-59 William
  Of 127
CALDWELL, 29 33-35 Easter 30
  Laird Of 6 Margaret 130 Wester
  31
CALLANDER, Col 174 Fanny 174
CAMDEN, 63 166
CAMERON, 23 Richard 345
CAMPBELL, 75-76 89 215 308
  Archibald 52 Catherine 282

CAMPBELL (Cont.)
  Colin 234 236 Coline 160 Cornet
  74 Daniel 37 41 63 Eufame 198
  George 70 Ilay 10 34 Islay 62 J
  209 J C 207 James 93 Jane 93
  139 John 70 165 296 Kathrine
  280 Lady Frederick 276 Lord
  Frederick 189 276 Mary 105
  252-254 Mr 96 Mrs 34 253
  Mungo 74 104 277 Of Ardkinlass
  155 Of Clathick 230 Richard 139
  Thomas 49 135 203
CANDLISH, 344
CANMORE, Malcolm 168
CANNING, 236
CAPRINGTON, Laird Of 128
CAR, Andrew 20
CARGILL, 221 345
CARLILE, William 209
CARLYL, Mr 326
CARLYLE, Dr 40
CARMICHAEL, 183 Elizabeth
  Daughter Of Lord John 3 Grizel
  113 John 130 Lady Ann 130
  Lord John 3 Walter 113
CARNEGIE, Margaret 172
CARNWATH, Earl Of 79 George Of
  79-80 Lord 77
CARRICK, Alexander 111 Andrew
  113 Countess Eleanor 44
  Countess Marjory 109 Lady
  Christian 111 Lord Duncan 109
  Lord Edward 111 Lord Neil 109
  Lord Nigel 109 Lord Robert
  Bruce 110 Malcolm Of 82
  Margaret 109 Marjory Of 110
  Neil 111 Robert 207 Thomas 111
CARROL, 322
CARRUTHERS, Mr 326
CARSTAIR, 348
CARSTAIRS, 86 Baronet Of 95
CARTULARY, Abbey 125
CASSILIS, Lord Gilbert 288

INDEX.

CASSILLIS, Earl Of 17 20 Lord 142 144 Lord Gilbert 143
CASTLEMILK, Margaret Of 120 Stewart Of 120
CASTLEREAGH, 237
CATHCART, Alan 44 Baron 45 Charles Alan 47 Col 45 Eleanor 44 Eleanora Daughter Of Lord Charles 121 Frederick 48 George 48 Jane 47-48 Lady 122 Lady Elizabeth 49 Lady Elizabeth Mary 48 Lady Jane 46-47 Lady Marion 43 46 121 Lady Sarah 43 46 Lord Alan 45 48-49 Lord Alan Frederick 48 Lord Alan-Frederick 121 Lord Charles 43-46 48-49 121 Lord Charles Murray 47 Lord John 45 Lord William Shaw 47 Mary 47 Shaw 46 Viscount 47 Walter 44 William 47
CECIL, 6 8
CESSNOCK, 70
CHAFIN, Carol 13
CHALMERS, 344 Isabella 70 Marion 70
CHAMBERS, R 252 255
CHANTREY, 133 242
CHARLEMAGNE, 313
CHARLES, Edward Pretender's Son 37
CHARLES, King Of 23 79 83 112 201 203 221 348
CHARLES I, King Of 53 120 161 169 340 346
CHARLES II, King Of 22 83 100 129 160 171 173 185 201 243 258 332 345
CHARLES V, King Of 131
CHARLES, Prince Of 188
CHARLOTTE, Princess Of 114
CHIESLEY, John 79 Mrs 79
CHRISTIE, Mr 116
CHURCH, 359

CLARKE, Gen 190
CLAUDE, Abbot 286
CLEGHORN, 118 Stephen Of 113
CLERK-MAXWELL, 238
CLINTON, Henry 101
CLIVE, 133
CLOUSTON, Lord Provost 236
CLYDE, Lord 135 235
CLYDSDAILL, Johne 198
COALSTON, Lord 166
COATES, Wm 209
COCHRANE, 92 Alexander 101 Basil 101 Charles 101 Euphame 100 Ex-Provost 38 Gertrude Julia Georgiana 97 Gertrude 101 Grizel Winifred Louise 102 J D 102 James 101 Jane 101 John 100 Lady Gertrude 102 Lady Grizel 100 Lord 102 Lord Archibald 101 Lord Douglas Mackinnon 102 Lord Thomas 101 122 Lord Thomas Barnes 102 Lord William 100-101 Louisa Gertrude 102 Louisa Harriet 102 Mr 102 Mrs T 95 T 95 Thomas George Frederick 102 Thomas H A E 97 Thomas Horatio Arthur 102 Winifred 102
COCKBURN, 10 28 Adam 85 George 187
COCKERELL, R H 108 Theresa 108
COIL, Old King 103
COLBY, Col 247
COLONNA, Cardinal 68
COLQUHOUN, 147-148 152 Adam 153 230 Alexander 149-150 153-154 Archibald 42 Dr 209 232 Frances 122 130 James 205 230 John 153 Lord Provost 209 229 Lord-Advocate 14 Matthew 200 Miss 230 Mr 230-231 Mrs Patrick 230 Patrick 209 229-230 Robert 130 Walter 153

COLTNESS, Baronet Of 51
COMYN, 91 John 182 Of Buchan 182 Red 182 Walter 92
CONDE, 172
CONDORCET, 12
CONSTABLE, Haggerston 317 Marcia 319 Marmaduke-William 317 William 319 William-Haggerston 319 Winifred 317
CONSTABLE-MAXWELL, Alfred 316 Angela Mary 317 Angela Mary Charlotte Fitzalan 317 Gwendoline 317 Henry 316 J 116 Joseph 316 Marmaduke 125 315-317 319 Mary Monica 316 Peter 316 William 315 317
CONYNGHAM, Margaret 127
COOK, Mr 270
COOTE, Maj-Gen 187
COREHOUSE, Lord 14-16 52
CORNWALLIS, 15 Lady Anne 332 Lord 137 Lord Charles 332
COSPATRICK, Alexander 167 Lord Charles Alexander Douglas 167 Lucy-Elizabeth 167
COURTOWN, Lady Mary 334 Lord James George 334
COVENTRY, Countess Of 57 Lord George William 57
COVINGTON, Lord Alexander 80
COWAN, Robert 209
COWBROCHE, Eune 159
COWCADENNIS, 198
COWDEN, 221
COWTART, Laird 322
CRAFT, 203
CRAIG, Lord 12
CRAIGCROSTEN, Laird Of 160
CRANSTOUN, 14 Dr 263 George 10-11 52 Jane Ann 15 Lord 11 Lord James 15 Margaret 15 Mr 12-13 W H 16
CRAUFURD, John Lindsay 274 341

CRAUFURD (Cont.)
  Johne 341
CRAWAR, Paul 68 286
CRAWFORD, 7 121 184 194 272 296 359 Andrew 96 Anne 120 Capt 6 Earl Of 163 174 176 180 Elizabeth 126 Hew 126 Jane 126 John 93 120 130 Lord Alexander 179 Lord Alexander William 181 Lord David 176-181 Lord David Edzell 179 Lord James 181 Lord John 179 Margaret 93 Mary Lindsay 93 96 Patrick 35 93 Reginald 308 Robert 126 Thomas 341
CRAWFORD-POLLACK, Hew 126
CRAWFURD, 132
CRICHTON, 298 Thomas 294
CROMARTIE, Lord George 42
CROMEK, 302-303
CROMPTON, Elizabeth Mary 48 Samuel 48
CROMWELL, 24 83 161 202-204 292 348 Oliver 80
CROSBIE, Andrew 62 166
CRUM, Walter 240
CULCREUCH, Laird Of 149
CUMBERLAND, 46 244 Duke 57
CUMBERNAULD, 184 David Of 183
CUNNINGHAM, 105 272 303-304 Alexander 32 Allan 302 321 Dame Margaret 128 Elizabeth 121 Frances 130 J 16 J Montgomery 29 Jessie Jane 29 John 121 130 Margaret 15 92 William 15 36 92 William Of 342 Wm 209
CUNNINGHAME, 349 Anne 121 William 111 121
CUNNINGHAMHEAD, 348
CURRIE, Dr 302
D'ACRE, Saint Jean 122-123
D'ADHEMAR, Count 245

D'ARCY, Helen 15
D'EU, Count 32 Countess 32
DALBY, Isaac 246
DALE, David 206-207 209
DALGLEISH, 7
DALKEITH, Lord John Douglas
   Scott 334 Caroline 334 Duchess
   Jane 333 Duke Francis 333
   Elizabeth 334 Frances 333
   George 333 Harriet 334 Henry
   333 Henry James Montague 334
   Lady Caroline 333 Lord Charles
   William Henry 333 Lord Francis
   162 Lord James 333 Lord Walter
   Francis 334 Lord William Henry
   Walter 334 Mary 334 Mrs
   Francis 333
DALRYMPLE, 81 83-84 86 89
   Charles 85 David 62 165
   Elizabeth 45 49 Hew 24 Janet
   84-85 John 82 85 91 Lord 91
   Lord-President 54 121 Margaret
   121 Marion 121 Miss 54
   Secretary 88 Viscount 91 William
   82
DALTON, 238
DALZELL, Henry Burrard 80 Lord
   Robert 80
DARNLEY, 1 5-8 184 194 Lord 196
   Lord Henry 3-4 9 183 272
DAVID I, King Of 48 109 126 195
   329
DAVID II, King Of 99 111 168 317
   348
DAVID, King Of 141 347
DAVID, Agnes 55 Earl 55 Erskine
   55 Henry 55
DAVID, Prince Of 182 Prince Of
   Cumberland 126
DAVIDSON, John 295 Principal 225
DAVY, 238
DAYIS, Ryall 198
DEANS, Jeanie 311

DECIES, Caroline Agnes Daughter
   Of Lord Decies 173 Lord John
   173
DEHERIZ, William 317
DELBURNE, Agnes Of 92 John Of
   92
DELORAINE, Earl Of 333
DEMAXWELL, Aymer 125 Eustace
   317 Herbert 317 John 125
DEMORVILLE, 258 Hugh 288
DEMPSTER, 146
DENHAM, Wm Lockhart 113-114
DENHOLM, J Stewart 64
DENNISTOUN, 272 Elizabeth 126
   Hugh 342 James 57 James Sr
   209 Joanna 342 Robert 126
DEPEYSTER, Col 261-262
DERBY, Earl Of 174 Lord 108
DERMOT, King Of 338
DEVALANCE, Aymer 308
DHOONDEE, King Of The Two
   Worlds 139
DICK, James 243
DILLY, Mr 25
DIN, Donald 99
DINWOODIE, Elizabeth 114
DOBBIE, W H 209
DOBIE, 274 J S Jr 340 James 341
   Mr 340-341 343 Mr Sr 339
DONALD, 287 C D Jr 42 Dun 99
DOUGLAS, 26 60 142 324 328 342
   Archibald 5 164 166 Countess
   Margaret 325 Duchess Of 61
   Duke Archibald 61-62 161 166
   Duke Of 164-165 Francis 166
   George 21 James 77 Jane-
   Margaret 167 Janet 128 John 28
   Lady Ann 169 Lady Frances 333
   Lady Jane 61 161-162 164-165
   333 Lady Lucy 166 173 Lady
   Mary 161 Little 16 Lord 63 Lord
   Archibald 167 173 333 Lord
   Charles 167 Lord James 167

DOUGLAS (Cont.)
  Lord William 111 Margaret 61
  161 163 Marquis Archibald 161
  Marquis James 161 Marquis Of
  161 Mr 61-63 164-166 Robert
  201 Wilhelmina 167 William 161
DOUGLASS, 215 Lady Margaret 314
DOW, M'Innis 155
DRAGON, Bob 206
DRUMMOND, Annabella Daughter
  Of Lord Drummond 169 John
  147 Lord 169
DUGALD, 169
DUMFRIES, Lord William 91
DUNBAR, 142 311 Archbishop 218
  David 84 Gavin 72 218-219
  James 220 Janet 84 Jannet 219
  John 219 William 220
DUNCAN, 109 294 Earl Of Fife 121
  William 295 298
DUNDAFF, Viscount 181
DUNDAS, George 11 Henry 11 231
  Lord 39 Lord-President 62 165
  Robert 10-11
DUNDEE, Viscount 168 326
DUNDONALD, 221 Adm 102 Earl Of
  100 Lord Thomas 102
DUNLOP, 215 Colin 38 John 96
  Matthew 126
DUNMORE, Robert 209
DUNNING, 60 63 166
DUNROD, 124 Auld 275
DURHAM, Philip Calderwood 55
DURIE, Lord 79
EDDIE, Davie 322
EDGAR, 13 326
EDGEWORTH, 43
EDMONSTONE, Archibald 169
  Janet 169 Marjory 128 William
  128
EDMONSTOUNE-CRANSTOUN, C E
  H 16
EDWARD I, King Of 111 317

EDWARD (Cont.)
  King Of England 110 I King Of
  Scotland 182 King Of 307 309
  Prince Of England 110
EGLINTON, 73 103 Countess
  Susannah 76 Earl Of 17 20 343
  Lady Susannah 72 Lord 75 107-
  108 Lord Alexander 72 74 76
  277 Lord Archibald 76 Lord
  Hugh 104
ELCHO, Lord 54
ELDIN, Lord 352
ELDON, Lord 236
ELGIN, Lord 237 Lord Thomas 131
ELIBANK, Lord 164
ELIZABETH, Queen Of 8 15 21 184
ELIZABETH, Queen Of England 1
  22 318
ELIZABETH, Wife Of Robert II 342
ELLIOCK, Lord 165
ELLIOT, 127 Hugh 139
ELLIOTT, Mrs W F 29 W F 29
ELPHINSTONE, 134 Adm 190
  Bishop 324 Capt 189 Charles
  186 189 George Keith 186 Hester
  Marie 186 James 93 Keith 189
  Lady 191-192 Lady Clementina
  186 Lord 106 Lord Charles 186
  188 Lord George Keith 188 Lord
  John 186 Lord Keith 190-191
  Margaret 191 Margaret Mercer
  186 William 186 189
ERROL, Augusta Daughter Of Lord
  James 96 Lord James 96
ERSKINE, 10 David 24 James 165
  Mrs Henry 134
EUGENE, King Of 168
EWING, Barbara 130 Greville 130
FAID, 320
FAIRSERVICE, Andrew 227
FALLISDAILL, Bailie 154 David 153
  James 153 Thomas 153
FARADAY, 238

FARQUHAR, Elizabeth Mary 123
  Robert 123
FAULDS, Andrew Wilson 76 James
  76 Janet 76 Robert 76
FERGUSON, 261 Adam 60 62 Prof
  240
FERGUSSON, Adam 106 George 14
  James 85 166
FERRERS, Laurence Earl 276 Mrs
  Laurence Earl 276
FIFE, Earl Of 99
FINLAY, 206 James 209 Kirkman
  212
FINTRY, Lord 181
FITZCLARENCE, Augusta 96
  Frederick 96
FLAHAULT, Count 191 Countess
  Margaret 191
FLAUHAULT, Count 186 Countess
  Margaret Mercer 186
FLEET, James 43 Sarah 43
FLEMING, 21 326 Adm 186 Baldwin
  181 Cornwallis 186 Lady 184
  Lady Clementina 186 188 Lord
  17 184 Lord Charles 186 Lord
  John 18 183 185-186 Lord
  Malcolm 183 Lord Robert 183
  Malcolm 182 Mary 183 William
  185
FLESHER, 205
FOLEY, E T 173 Emily 173
FORBES, Bishop 312
FOULIS, Thomas 346
FOX, Mr 245
FRANCE, Dauphine Of 1-2 4
FRANCIS I, King Of 183
FRANCIS II, Dauphine Of 7
FRANKLIN, 40
FRASER, 357 Janet 343 Sheriff 270
  W 180 Wm 326
FRAZER, Alex 165
FREDERICK II, King Of Prussia 46
  The Great 46

FREDERICK II (Cont.)
  The Great King Of Prussia 189
FRENCH, Wm 209
FROISSART, 168
FULLARTON, 340 Adam Of 347
  Alam Of 347 Alexander 350
  Charles 350 Col 348-351 Dr 352
  Fergus 350 Gavin 351 George
  348 Isabella 352 James 348 352
  Jessie Spottiswoode 352 John
  348 352 Lewis 350 352 Margaret
  352 Miss 351 Mrs Alexander 350
  Mrs Bowden 352 Patrick 348
  Rankin Of 348 Reginald Of 348
  Robert 348 William 348 352
FULLER, 68
FULLERTON, 10 Col 106 Lord 352
FULTON, Margaret 282 Robert 209
FYVIE, Alexander 159 Lord 157
GADGIRTH, Chalmers Of 82 Marion
  Of 82
GAINSBOROUGH, 356
GALBRAITH, Malcolm 121
GALLOWAY, Devorgilla Daughter Of
  Lord Alan 314 John Of 330 Lord
  64 Lord Alan 314 Lord Alexander
  61 Lord Archibald 182
GAMBIER, Adm 101-102
GARDEN, Francis 62
GARDENSTON, Lord 62
GARDENSTONE, Lord 166
GARDINE, Francis 166
GARDINER, Hannah-Anne 130
  Richard 130
GARDNER, 278 293 Mr 304
GARLIES, Lady 318
GARNE, Thomas 198
GARNOCK, 341 Patrick 274
  Viscount 93 274
GAS, Johnny 325
GEDDES, Jenny 346
GEMMELL, James 209
GEORGE, King Of 91

GEORGE I, King Of 93 173 I King Of
    England 43
GEORGE II, King Of 57-58 King Of
    England 43
GEORGE III, King Of 54 73 147
    King Of England 43 160
GEORGE IV, King Of 50
GIBBON, 235
GIBSON, 27 193 Alexander 79
    Elizabeth 114 John 114-115
    Miss 115
GIBSON-CRAIG, W 97
GIFFORD, 116
GILBERT, 109 King Of Carrick 113
GILCHRIST, 287
GILLAN, Dr 115
GILLESPIE, James 81
GILLIES, John 114 Neil 223
GILMOUR, Mr 107
GILSON, Provost 223
GLASGOW, Countess Of 94
    Dowager-Countess 97 Earl Of 95
    Lord 97 356-357 Lord David 93
    Lord George 95-96 Lord John 39
    92
GLASSFORD, 206 215 Henry 42
    James 36 42 John 36-39 41-42
    209 Margaret 42
GLENCAIRN, Lord 142
GLENCOE, 87 90
GLENGARIE, 87
GLENGARY, 90
GLENLUCE, Lord 83
GLENURQUHY, Laird Of 160
GLOUCESTER, Earl Of 343
GOLDSMITH, 290
GORBAL, 203
GORDON, 142 324 340 Adam 312
    Duchess Of 55 J E 130 John 311
    Lady Mary 161 William 311-312
GOURLY, Wull 322
GOWRIE, Earl Of 169
GRACIE, James 261

GRAHAM, 175 177-178 239 241
    Agnes Caroline 173 Alexander
    168 Alma-Carlotta 173
    Annabella 169 Archibald 209
    Beatrice-Violet 173 Christian
    173 David 168 Douglas 113
    Duke Douglas-Beresford-Malise-
    Ronald 181 Edgidia 168 Emily
    173 Fanny 174 Frederick Ulric
    174 George 173 Georgiana-
    Charlotte Caroline Lucy 173
    Isabel 173 James 168 172-174
    Jane Hermoine 174 Janet 169
    Jemima-Elizabeth 173 John 42
    356 Lady Ann 169 Lady Lucy
    166 Lady Margaret 169 Lady
    Mary 168 Lord David 173 Lord
    Douglas Beresford Malise Ronald
    173 Lord James 169 Lord John
    169 171 Lord Thomas 168 Lord
    William 169 173 Lucy 173
    Margaret 172 240 Marquis Of
    181 Mary 47 Matilda 168
    Montague William 173 Mr 356
    Mungo 169 Patrick 168-169 Prof
    355 Robert 168 Thomas 47 238
    242 Violet Hermoine 174 William
    168
GRAHAME, 49 Allister 159 John
    159
GRANGE, 18-20
GREENOCK, Baron 47 Lady 48 Lord
    47-48
GREENWICH, Duke John 333
GREGORY, 233 Pope 339 The Ninth
    Pope 271
GRENVILLE, 14
GREVILLE, Algernon W F 173
    Beatrice-Violet 173 Lord 173
GREY, Lord 236
GRIERSON, William 261
GROSART, Mr 294-296 298 301
GROSE, 268

INDEX.

GROSVENOR, Lady Octavia 124
  Richard 124
GUELDRES, Mary Of 82
GUISE, 2 21
GUNNING, Maria 57 Miss 57
GUNNINGS, Miss 61
GUTHRIE, 344
HACO, 353
HAILES, Lady 85 Lord 62 85 165
  307-308
HALL, Basil 15
HALLIBURTON, David 137
HAMILTON, 18 57 63 73 86 142
  161-162 164 243 254-255
  Archibald 47 Basil 104 Bazill
  104 Bishop Of St Andrews 184
  Claud 3 17 19 100 Duchess Of
  61 Duke James 60 Duke James
  George 61 Duke Of 60 62 165
  350 Elenora 107 Emma 47 Gavin
  105 250 253 Gilbert 209 Jane 47
  John 20 104 Katherine 104 Lord
  Archibald 123 Lord Douglas 61
  165 Lord Margaret 104 161 May 183
  Patrick 72 Robert 107 William 47
  215
HAMILTOUN, Marqueis Of 198
HAMILTOUNE, James 204
HAMMILTOUN, Malcolm 198
HAMPTON, Lord 96
HANOVER, 259
HARPER, Mr 309-310 312-314
HARPSFIELD, Nicholas 67
HARRINGTON, Louisa-Alice 65
  Robert 65
HARRINGTON-STUART, Charlotte
  65 Lt Col 65 Robert Edward 65
HARRIS, 322 E Cranstoun Charles
  16 Lord 137
HARTE, Emma 47
HASTIE, Alexander 223
HASTINGS, 133 Mr 344
HATTERAICK, Dirk 311

HAY, Edward 96
HEATHFIELD, Lord 359
HECTOR, Mr 268-274 277 284
HEMINGFORD, 308
HENDERSON, Alexander 197
HENDERSONE, James 155
HENRY, King Of 183 318
HENRY King Of Scotland 4
HENRY VIII, King Of 183
HENRY, R 4
HEPBURN, 9 17-18
HERBERT, Lady Winifred 318
HERDMAN, James 210-211
HERICE, John 317
HERIZ, William 317
HERMAND, Lord 12 14
HERRIES, 21 116 Baron 315
  Herbert 318 Lady Agnes 315 318
  Lady Winifred 318 Lord 17 22
  316 318 Lord Andrew 315 Lord
  Herbert 317 319 Lord John 317
  Lord William 315 318-319 Lord
  Wm C 319 Mary Daughter Of
  Roland 317 Roland Of 317
HERSCHEL, John 238
HERTFORD, Lord 33
HESKETH, Robert Bamford 102
  Winifred 102
HETHERINGTON, W M 294
HEWITT, Mrs 62 162 164-165
HIGHLAND, Mary 103 105 250-251
  253 255
HILDEBRAND, 224
HILL, Col 88 James 49
HOFFER, Mr 240
HOGARTH, 277
HOGG, James 304
HOLYROOD, Prince Of 50
HOME, 170 179 328 Earl 161 Earl
  Of 334 Henry 165 Lady Elizabeth
  334 Lady Lucy-Elizabeth 167
  Lord Alexander 167 William 203
HOOD, Lord 190

HOOK, Theodore 117
HOPE, Ann 346 Charlotte 116 Dr
  241 J R 116 James 346 John
  237 Thomas 112
HOPE-SCOTT, Mary Monica 316
HOPETOUN, Earl Of 346
HORNER, 11
HOTSPUR, 104 127
HOULDSWORTH, Henry 51 James
  51 Thomas 51 William 51
HOUSTOUN, Anne 121 Eleanora
  121 Elizabeth 127 G L 100
  George 123 Helena 121 Helenor
  120 John 120-121 Lady 122
  Lady Margaret 121 Laird Of 6 Lt
  123 Margaret 120 Patrick 127
HOUSTOUN-STEWART, Adm 122-
  123 Capt 122 Lt 124-125 Martha
  123 William 123-125
HOWARD, Angela Mary Charlotte
  Fitzalan 317 Lord 317
HUITSCHAW, Mungo 200
HUMBERSTONE, Mackenzie 349
HUME, 18 20 Baron David 12 David
  32-35
HUNT, Holman 356
HUNTER, 274 290 John Kelso 256
  Robert 210
HUNTINGDON, Earl Of 109 Isabella
  109 Margaret 110
HUNTLY, 9 18 220 Marquis Of 161
  171
HUSS, John 68
HUTCHESON, 202 222 John 120
  345 Margaret 120 Rev Mr 281
HUTCHESONS, 203 205
HUTCHINSON, Gen 187
HYDER, Ali 137
INGLIS, Capt 259 Violet 114
INNES, 324 Cosmo 180 341
IRVING, 326 Francis 264
ISLES, Bishop Of The 9
IVORY, 249

JACKSON, 135-136
JAMES, King Of 82 150 154 157
  226 264 267 284 290 332 King
  Of England 7 331
JAMES I, King Of 27 70 111 174
JAMES II, King Of 95 104 118 168
  186 196
JAMES III, King Of 44 92 113 169
  178 330 King Of Scotland 180
JAMES IV, King Of 23 70 169 177-
  179 183 272 IV King Of Scotland
  181
JAMES V, King Of 3 27 112 183 219
  331
JAMES VI, King Of 120 146 175 185
  228 266 272 290
JAMES, Prince Of 5 119 183 219
  318
JAMES, Dr 67 Henry 248 Henry
  Kingston 351 High Steward Of
  Scotland 348
JARDINE, 326 Prof 31 William 294
JARVIE, Bailie Nicol 40
JEFFREY, 10-11 28
JERVIS, John 189
JOANNA, Consort Of Prince David
  182
JOCELINE, Bishop 195
JOHN XXIII, Pope 67
JOHNSON, 25 62 166 Dr 23-24 76
  165 192 Samuel 26
JOHNSTON, 127 326 Commodore
  349 Mr 240 Prof 240
JOHNSTONE, Arthur 327
JONES, Paul 315 322
JORDANHILL, Crawford Of 184 194
  272
KAMES, Lord 165
KAYE, David 198
KEIR, Mary 120
KEITH, 324 Adm 101 188 191 Adm
  Lord 187 Baron 191 Bishop 229
  Lord 188 192 Marshal 189

INDEX. 373

KEITH (Cont.)
   Viscount 186
KEITH-ELPHINSTONE, 187
KELBURNE, Lord 96 Viscount 96
KELLY, 354 356 Fitzroy 180
KEMPIS, Thomas A 250
KENMURE, 311 Viscount 312
KENNEDIE, 113
KENNEDY, 304 308 Abbot 143-146
   Gilbert 143 Malcolm 82 Margaret
   82 Quentin 27 143 145
   Susannah 72 Thomas 72 W 305
KENNEDYJANNET, 82
KENNET, Lord 165
KENNETH III, King Of 330
KEPPEL, 306
KEPPOCH, 87 90
KER, Robert 42
KERR, 20 162 Mary 95 Of Cessford
   331 Robert 95 William 95 331
KETHCART, Rainaldus 44
KILKERRAN, Helen 85 Lord 85
KILKONATH, Adam 110 Countess
   Marjory 110
KILMARNOCK, Earl Of 258-259
KILWINNING, Mother 343
KINCAID, James 203
KINCARDINE, Earl Of 181 Lord
   Alexander 23 Lord Thomas 131
KINMONT, Willie 331
KIRK, James 261
KITTOCHE, Gilchrist 154
KNELLER, Godfrey 223
KNOX, 69-72 141 143-144 146
   John 3 27 140 145 Mrs 144
KOBBLER, John 256
KOCHLIN, 240
LABRUNE, Madame 165
LABRUNNE, 162 Madame 62
LACY, 104
LAINSHAW, 41
LAMARRE, Pierre 163
LAMMERMOOR, Bride Of 55 83

LAMOND, Mary 274
LAMONT, J 97
LANG, Maggy 282 Margaret 282
   · Pinched Maggy 282 William 209
LANSDOWNE, Dowager-
   Marchioness 192
LAPLACE, 239
LATIMER, Hugh 72
LAUD, 31 201
LAUDER, 225
LAVOISIER, 239
LAWRENCE, 136 Dr 115
LAWRIE, John 209
LAWSON, 298 Doctor 291
LECONFIELD, Constance Elizabeth
   36 Lord 36
LEE, 113 Lord 79-80
LEECHMAN, William 31
LEGENDRE, Adrian 249
LENNOX, 6 30 41 306 Charles Duke
   Of 174 Countess Margaret 3
   Duchess Isabella 174 Duke Of 9
   93 160 Earl Of 5 154 Lord
   Donald 176 Lord John 272 Lord
   Malcolm 175 287 Lord Matthew
   3 Lord Robert 196 Regent 184
LEPRAIK, Robert 145
LESLIE, 249 Alexander 170 197
   David 171 202
LESLY, 71
LETHINGTON, Maitland Of 183
   Mary Wife Of Maitland 183
   Secretary 5
LEVEN, Anne-Maria Daughter Of
   Lord David 131 Lord David 131
LEWARS, Jessie 261 John 261
LIEBIG, 239-240
LINCOLN, Bishop Of 68
LINDSAY, 5 20 142 280 Earl Of 163
   Isobel 126-127 James 126 176
   282 John 282 Lord 181
LINLITHGOW, Sheriff Of 20
LINNAEUS, 238

LIOLF, Son Of Macus 126
LIVINGSTON, 88 Thomas 87
LIVINGSTONE, 21 Lord 17
LOCHIEL, 87
LOCKHART, 63 334 Alexander 80
    Allan 78 118 Allan Eliot 118
    Charles 80 Charles Macdonald
    80 Charlotte 116 Col 115
    Cromwell 80 David Blair 115 118
    Dr 114 Elizabeth 80 114 Emilia
    Olivia 80 George 79 Grizel 95
    113 J G 118 James 78 80 94
    John 80 114-115 John Gibson
    115 Katherine 115 Lawrence 115
    118 Lawrence Archibald
    Somerville 115 Lawrence William
    Maxwell 115 Louisa 115 Marion
    115 Mrs John 115 Norman 80
    Norman Macdonald 80 Philip 80
    Robert 114-115 Robina 80
    Simon 77-78 Simon Macdonald
    80 Sophia 116 Stephen 113
    Union 79 Violet 114 Walter 114
    William 79-80 113-115 William
    Eliot 118
LOGAN, 50
LONDONDERRY, 237 Marchioness
    236-237
LORNE, Lord 172
LOTHIAN, Harriet Wife Of Marquis
    334 Marquis Of 334
LOUDOUN, Earl Of 74 93
LOUIS, Napoleon King Of 191 46
LOUIS, Phillippe King Of 191
LOUIS XIV, King Of 32 79
LOUIS XV, King Of France
LOUIS XVIII, King Of 236
LOVE, Meg 296
LOYOLA, Ignatius 141
LUCAS, 190
LUCRETIUS, 239
LUS, Laird Of 150
LUSS, Laird Of 6 155-156 159-160

LUSS (Cont.)
    Lord 157
LUSSIS, Laird Of 154
LUTHER, 70 Martin 141
LYLE, Manasses 203
LYNCH, W 63
LYNDOCH, Lord 168
LYNEDOCH, Lord 47
LYON, Lord James 318
LYOUN, James 198
M'ALPIE, James 274
M'ALPINE, Alex 209
M'AULAY, Aulay 154
M'AULEY, Aulay 148
M'CALPPINS, 148
M'CLERICH, Donald 155
M'CONDOCHIE, John Dow 159
    John M'Coneill 155
M'CONNECHY, Dr 304
M'CRIE, 144 146 Dr 224
M'DIARMID, 315 324
M'DONALD, Gillespie 155
M'DOWALL, 41 260 267 324 Mr
    262-264 326 W 319 William 122
    Wm 276
M'GAVIN, William 23
M'GREGOR, Dugall 155 James 209
    John Dow M'Oncoalich 155
    Nicoll M'Pharie Roy 155
M'GREGOUR, 158
M'HISSOCK, Gilliemichell 155
M'INTNACH, Allan Oig 153
M'IVER, John 211
M'IVOR, Col 255
M'KAIL, Hugh 53
M'KAY, Archibald 256 Mr 257 259-
    260
M'KERRELL, Mr 130
M'KIE, Allister 154
M'KNACHTANE, Lair Of 156
M'LACHLAN, Mrs 238
M'LAVERTY, Miss 352
M'LEAN, Findlay Dow 154

M'LEWIE, 350
M'LEWIS, 350
M'NAB, Mary 295
M'NEILL, Duncan 237
M'PHATRICK, Duncan 159
MACADAM, Frederick 48 Jane 48
    Quentin 48
MACALLUM, Archibald 211
MACARTNEY, 45
MACAULAY, 33 66 84 88 238
MACDONALD, 89 Alexander 80
    Elizabeth 80 John 80 104
    Macian 88 Reginald 52
MACDUFF, Miss 350
MACFARLANE, 18 20 147
MACGREGOR, 147 149-151 153
    157 160 Alexander 148 Allister
    152 154-156 James 148 John
    152
MACGREGOUR, 149 Laird Of 155
MACGUIRE, Col 43 Hugh 43 Sarah
    43
MACINTOSH, George 207
MACKENZIE, George 42 83
    Margaret 42 Miss 96
MACKIE, Andrew 323
MACKINNON, Campbell 352 Isabella
    352 John 352 Lauchlan 148
    Lewis 352 Louisa Harriet 102
    Mrs Campbell 352 W A 102
MACLEHOSE, Mr 214 217 223
MACLELLAN, 314
MACLEOD, 171
MACMIN, Deacon 321
MACNEIL, Hector 296
MACQUEEN, Robert 10 62 166
MACRAE, 207
MACTAGGART, 320-323
MACUS, 126
MAGINN, 118 Dr 117 William 117
MAHDI, 125
MAIDMENT, James 113
MAITLAND, 5 10 Capt 187

MAITLAND (Cont.)
    Thomas 325
MALCOLM, Capt 137 John 137
MALONE, 26
MALYN, Sarah 43 46
MANCHESTER, Caroline-Maria
    Daughter Of Duke Of 173 Duke
    Of 173
MANDEVILLE, 306
MANNING, Mr 139
MANSFIELD, Chief-Justice 166 Lord
    60 63
MAR, 18 46 72-73 79 93 170 189
    325 Lord Thomas 317
MARCH, Earl Of 219
MARIE, Theresa Queen Of 46
MARISCHAL, Earl 189
MARSHAL, James 219
MARTIN, V Pope 68
MARWICK, Dr 199 Mr 192-196 198
MARY, Dowager Of France 1
    Princess Of 128 Princess Of
    Cambridge 236 Queen Of 5-9 16-
    19 21 45 127 147 183-184 194
    225 284 314 317-318 325 Queen
    Of England 43 Queen Of France
    2 Queen Of Scotland 1 3-4
MASSENA, 190
MASSON, Prof 228
MATHIE, Annabil 129 Janet 128
MATTHIE, Watty 296
MAURICE, Prince Of 331
MAXWELL, 30 32 261 272 314 326
    Agnes 92 128 315 Annabel 120
    Archibald 131 Aylmer 316 Aymer
    125 127 Barbara 130 Caroline
    131 Catherine 122 316 319
    Elizabeth 126-127 130 Emereus
    316 Eustace 317 Frances 122
    130 George 120 126-130
    Hannah-Anne 130 Harriet-Anne
    130 Herbert 91 125-126 317
    Isobel 126-127 James 122 130

MAXWELL (Cont.)
　Janet 222 Johannes 126 John 9
　17 32 48 92 123 125-132 200
　209 315-318 Lady Ann 130 Lady
　Matilda-Harriet 131 Lady
　Winifred 317 Lord Robert 315
　Margaret 92 127 130 Marion 115
　Marjory 128 Mary 125 317
　Robert 126-127 130 Walter 130
　William 115 122 127 316 318-
　319 Winifred 318-319 Wm C 319
　Zecharias 130
MAYNE, 320 325 John 263
MAZARINE, 79
MCGREGOUR, Callum 158
　Duelchay 158 Duncan McEwne
　158 Johne Dowe McAllister 158
　Mcrobert 158 Robert Abroch 158
MEADOWBANK, 12
MEARNS, Mary Of 125 Roland Of
　125
MELBOURNE, Lord 236
MELFORD, Jerry 345
MELVIL, Andrew 226-227
MELVILL, 19-21 Gen 213
MELVILLE, 226 228 Andrew 197
　223-224 G 180 James 225
　Richard 225 Viscount 11 231
　Whyte 108
MENOU, Gen 188
MENZIES, 350
MERCER, Miss 186 191 William 186
MERSE, Barons Of 20
METCALFE, 134
METHVEN, Lord 12
MHOR, Dugald Ciar 153
MILBANKE, Miss 237 Mr 237
MILLAR, Bailie 220 John 218
MILLER, Catherine 216 Martha 123
　Patrick 39 345 Thomas 62 165
　William 123
MILNES, Monckton 236
MILTON, 83

MILTON-LOCKHART, 113
MITCHELL, John Oswald 217
　William 296
MITFORD, Miss 304
MOFFAT, Mary 277
MONBODDO, Lord 166
MONK, 83
MONMOUTH, 95 332 Duke Of 333
MONRO, Colonell 198
MONTAGUE, Duke Of 333 Elizabeth
　Daughter Of Duke Of 333 Lady
　167 Lord 167 334 Lucy-Elizabeth
　Daugher Of Lord Montague 167
　Mary Wortley 54
MONTALEMBERT, 336
MONTEITH, 206 Henry 348 John
　207
MONTGOMERIE, 272 342 356 Hugh
　104-106 Lady 105
MONTGOMERY, 63 72 103 311
　Alexander 104 277 Alexander
　Seton 104 Archibald 104 Elenora
　107 Hugh 104 107 James 104
　186 Jean 275-277 John 104
　Katherine 104 Lady Sophia 108
　Lord Alexander 106 Lord
　Archibald 105 107 Lord
　Archibald William 106 108 Lord
　Hugh 105 107-108 Maj 202
　Margaret 121 Neill 308 Theresa
　108
MONTGOMERY'S, Peggy 105
MONTROSE, 9 42 53 168 171 174-
　175 184-185 Duke 167 173
　Duke James 176 Duke Of 166-
　167 169 178 180-181 Earl Of
　169 Lord John 177 Marquis Of
　170 172
MONTROSS, Lord William 177
MOODY, Hugh 209
MOORE, 29 342 John 135
MORAY, 19-20 Lord Randolph 219
　Regent 18

INDEX.

MORE, 29
MORNINGTON, Lord 137
MORRISON, Helen 94 William 94
MORTON, 5 19 332 Fletcher 166
   Isabel Daughter Of Lord William
   173 Lord William 173 Regent
   290
MOTHERWELL, 273 302-305 Mr
   193
MUDGE, Capt 246
MUGDOCK, Lord 181
MUIR, 11 James 93 Quintein 198
MUNGO, Saint 219
MUNRO, Alexander 136 Campbell
   140 Capt 137-138 Col 135 139
   Daniel 135-136 Gov 133 Jane
   139 John 136 Lady Thomas 140
   Lt 137-138 Maj 139 Maj Gen 134
   Miss 134 Thomas 133 136-137
   140
MURAT, 237
MURDOCH, George 39 218
MURE, 91 272 Adam 30 342 Anicia
   92 Baron 35-36 38 61 Col 123
   Constance Elizabeth 36 David 97
   Elizabeth 29 64 99 342 Gilchrist
   30 92 Hector 30 Jane 93 Jean
   121 Joanna 342 John 30 35 Mrs
   34-35 Robert 31 William 31-33
   35 38 61 93 123-124 Wm 36
MURE-CAMPBELL, James 93
MURRAY, 7 Earl Of 4 220 James
   167 Lord 184 Regent 45 193
   Wilhelmina 167
MUSCHETT, Gilbert 185
MUSPRATT, Mr 355
MYRETON, Andrew 60 Elizabeth 60
NAISMITH, Agnes 282
NAPIER, 171 272 Barbara 328 Lady
   172 Lord 352 Lord Francis 38
   Mark 326 Patrick 152 Peter 152
   W 118
NAPOLEON, 102 191

NAPOLEON (Cont.)
   III Emperor Of 237
NEILSON, 105 Jamie 322
NELSON, Lord 47
NETHER-POLLOK, Laird Of 17
NEWCOMEN, Theresa 108
NEWTON, Isaac 242
NICHOLSON, 122 321 Eleanor 120
   Thomas 120 William 315 Wull
   315
NICOLAS, Harris 317
NICOLSON, Eleanor 121 Thomas
   121
NISBET, 347
NITHSDALE, Earl Of 316 Lady
   Winifred 318 Lord 127 317 Lord
   William 318-319
NORTH, Christopher 209
NORTHESK, Christian Daughter Of
   Lord Northesk 173 Earl Of 173
NORTON, Caroline 131 Fletcher 63
   131 George Chapple 131
NORVELL, Thomas 204
NOTTINGHAM, 87
O'CONNELL, Daniel 236
O'DONNELL, 338
OCHILTREE, 20 Baron Of 100 Lord
   144
OGILVIE, 169 Lord 170
OGILVY, 18
OLIPHANT, 168
ORANGE, William Of 86-87
ORD, 294
ORKNEY, Lord Robert Of 112
ORMONBY, Capt 321
ORR, 206 294
OSBORNE, Ruth 283
OSMAN, Digma 125
OSSORY, Countess 43
OSWALD, Elizabeth 126 James 39
   Richard 39
OUTRAM, 136
PAISLEY, Baron Of 100 Mr 270

PAKINGTON, Diana 96 John 96
  John Slaney 96
PALATINE, Countess Euphame 168
PALMERSTON, 236 Lord 236
PARK, John 292
PARLANE, 284
PATERSON, 106 222 James 256-
  257 Robert 311 328 William 103
PEDDIE, James 290
PEDEN, 23 321 342 Alexander 345
PEDIE, Provost 223
PEEBLES, Miss 352
PEEL, Robert 234
PENN, William 54
PERCIVAL, 101
PERCY, 104 111 Henry 308 Ralph 127
PERHIE, 274
PEYSTER, Col 261-262
PICTON, Thomas 350
PIOZZI, Mrs 192
PITCAIRN, 149
PITFOUR, Lord 166
PITT, 11
PLAYFAIR, Lyon 355
POLKELLIE, Lady 70
POLKEMMET, 12-13
POLLOK, John Of 127 Robert Of 127
POLMAISE, Agnes Caroline 173
  Murray 173
PONT, 258 339 341 343 Robert 340
  Timothy 340
PORTEOUS, Mr 344-346
PORTERFIELD, Boyd 122 George
  202 Margaret Of 122
PORTLAND, 342 Duke William
  Henry 350
POWELL, Miss 333
POWIS, Edward Earl 173
  Georgiana-Charlotte Caroline
  Lucy 173 Marquis William Of
  318

POWIS (Cont.)
  Winifred Daughter Of Marquis
  William 318
PRAGUE, Jerome Of 68
PRIMROSE, Jean 104 William 104
PRINGLE, Andrew 165 Judge 211
PROMPHREY, W 51
PRUDACHE, Neil M'Gregor 155
PURGSTALL, Countess Jane Ann 15
QUEENSBERRY, 90 328 331
  Caroline Wife Of Marquis 334
  Duchess Harriet Katherine 334
  Duke Charles William Henry 334
  Duke James 333 Duke Of 164
  Duke William 334 Marquis Of 28 334
QUEENSBURY, Old Q 334
RABAT, Deacon 194
RAE, Peter 325 William 234
RAMAGE, Dr 327 329
RAMSAY, Allan 73 345 Miss 345
RAMSAYE, Barbara 198
RAMSDEN, 245
RANKEN, Alexander 114
RATTRAY, John 55
RAWLINSON, Henry 236
RAYLEIGH, Lord 239
READ, Alexander 137 Capt 137 Col 137
RECTOR, Lord 35
REDESDALE, Lord 180
REEVES, Dr 338
REID, Adam 70-71 John 282
RENFREW, Gilbert Of 271 Samuel Of 271
RENFREWSHIRE, Barons Of 20
RENNIE, 106
RENWICK, 345 Mr 198
REPINGDON, Cardinal 68
RESEBY, 69-70 John 68
RETZ, Cardinal 172
RICHARDSON, 33 Brewer Gabriel
  261 Gabriel 261 Janet 321

RICHARDSON (Cont.)
  John 261 William 115
RICHMOND, Charles Duke Of 174
  Duke Of 9
RIDDELL, Henry 207 209 Mr 180
RIDLEY, Master 72
RITCHIE, 38 James 36
RIZZIO, David 5
ROBERT, King Of 99 111 182
ROBERT I, King Of 111 306
ROBERT II, King Of 29 99 342 King Of Scotland 64
ROBERT III, King Of 99 111 119 124 128 168 183 265 314 325
ROBERTSON, 324 J 182 195 John 207 209
ROBIESTOUN, 205
RODGER, 105 113
RODNEY, 15
ROGERS, Samuel 192
ROLT, Mr 180
ROSS, Agnes 92 Alexander 151 Baron 94-95 Charles 80 Countess Elizabeth 95 Dame Margaret 95 Earl John 95 Elizabeth 92 94 103 Euphemia 64 Grizel 95 John 63 Lady Grizel 101 Lord 17 20 92 Lord George 91 94 101 103 Lord James 95 Lord John 92 Lord William 95 Margaret 45 83 Matthew 14 Olivia Emilia 80 William 94
ROSSALYN, Earl Of 166
ROSSLYN, Earl Of 28
ROTHES, 332 Christian Daughter Of Duke John 173 Duke John 173 Earl Of 17 Lord 142
ROTHESAY, Duke Of 111
ROUET, William 37
ROXBURGHE, Earl Of 95 171 Isabel Wife Of Lord Robert 173 Lord Robert 173 331
ROY, 245 Col 244 Dr 243

ROY (Cont.)
  Gen 242-243 246-250 Rob 153 160 William 243
RUPERT, Prince 46
RUSSELL, James 115 Jerome 72 Katherine 115
RUTHERFORD, 313 321 Lord 84
RUTHVEN, 5 Lady Margaret 169 Lord William 169
RUTLAND, Duke Of 173 Lucy Daughter Of Duke Of Rutland 173
RYALL, Mary 4
SABINE, Capt 43 Mrs 46 Sarah 43
SAINTJOHN, 44
SAINTMAUR, Lady Jane Hermoine 174
SAINTVINCENT, Earl Of 189 Lord 190
SALMASIUS, Claudius 83
SALMON, Bailie 220 Mr 355
SANDFORD, D K 130
SATCHELLS, 330
SAWTREY, 68
SCAUR, Robert Of 329
SCHEFFER, Ary 356
SCHLOMBERGER, 240
SCOT, John 340
SCOTLAND, Queen-Mother 2
SCOTT, 11 27 29 45 62 77 83-84 127 166 227 304 310-311 313 323 326 328 351 Campbell 333 Dame Margaret 95 David 330-331 Duchess Anne 332 Duke Walter 332 Euphame 100 Hope 180 J 116 J R 116 James 354 John 116 330 Joseph 316 Katherine 274 Lady 15 116 Lady Wife Of Lord Francis 332 Lord Francis 332 Lord Henry John 118 Lord Walter 95 Mary 332 Mary Monica 316 Mary-Monica 116 Mr 355 Sophia 116

SCOTT (Cont.)
  Uchtred Fitz 329 Walter 15 51-52 115-116 118 148 228 329 331-332 334
SCROPE, Lord 331
SEATON, 183 Lord 16 20
SELKIRK, Charles 218 Lord 61 165
SEMPILL, 45 153 359 Gabriel 48 Lord Robert 272
SEMPLE, D 4 282
SETON, 52 Alexander 104 Christopher 111 Hugh 104 James 104 Jean 104 Lady Christian 111
SETON-MONTOLIEU, Hugh 108
SHAKESPEARE, 159
SHANTER, 113
SHARP, Mr 297
SHARPE, 261 326
SHAW, 119 122 122 Abbot 287 Andrew 70 Christian 128 279-281 Eleanor 120-121 James 121 257 Jean 121 Joanna 121 John 43 46 120-121 163 279 Lady 163 Margaret 120-121 Marion 43 46 121
SHAW-STEWART, Catherine 122 Elizabeth Mary 123 Frances 122 Houstoun 122 John 119 122 Margaret 122 Michael 122-124 Octavia 124 Patrick Maxwell 123 Robert 123
SHERIDAN, Caroline 131 Thomas 131
SHEWALTON, Lord 93
SHORTRIDGE, James 222 John 222 Mr 222 Mrs James 222 William 222
SHOUSTER, Robina 80
SIGISMUND, Emperor 67
SIMSON, Robert 359
SINCLAIR, John 96 Julia 96
SKALD, 305

SKALLAGRIM, Jarl Egill 305
SKELDANE, 351 Archibald 352 James 352 John 352 Miss 352 Mrs Archibald 352 Mrs James 352
SKELMORLIE, Hugh Of 106
SKIRLING, Lady 318
SLAVE, George 276
SMEATON, 39
SMITH, 255 Adam 54 211 333 Angus 239-240 356 Dr 240-242 Gabriel 200 John 192 John Guthrie 217 Sydney 11
SMOLLETT, 37 121 345 Tobias 152-153 230
SNODGRASS, Neil 283
SOMERSET, Duke Edward Adolphus Of 174 Protector 2
SOMERVILL, James 209
SOMERVILLE, 50 77 79 118 James 114 Lord 17 Mary 239 Mrs 239
SOUTHESK, Earl Of 172
SPALDING, 324
SPEIRS, Alexander 36 Archibald 39
SPIERS, A A 124
SPOTTISWOOD, 227 229 Archbishop 224 226 228
SPREULL, Ann 222 Bass John 221-222 James 222 Janet 222 John 221-223 Miss 222
STAHL, 239
STAIR, 46 81 86-89 311 Dame Margaret 84 David 85 Earl John 85 Earl Of 90 Elizabeth 45 49 Hew 85 James 85 Jannet 82 Lady 70 83 Lord 83 85 Lord John 45 90-91 Lord William 91 Lord-President 70 Margaret 45 83 Viscount 49 54 83 85 Viscount James 45 82
STANHOPE, Earl 170
STEUART, Archibald 54 Gen 54

INDEX.   381

STEUART (Cont.)
  Gospel Coltness 53 Henry 51-52
  Henry B 51 Henry James Seton
  52 James 50 52-54 James
  Denham 54 Lady Frances 54
  Marion 92 Provost 53 Thomas 53
  William 92
STEVENSON, T G 113
STEWARD, Alan Ancestor Of 347
  Marjory 285-286 Walter Ancestor
  Of 347 Walter The 285
STEWART, 9 29 64 100 284 350 A B
  97 Adm 123 Agnes 55 Allan 143
  Andrew 165 Andro 200 Annabel
  120 Annabella 128 Annabil 129
  Anne 120 Archibald 61 120 124
  128 163-164 Barbara 130 Capt
  163 Donald 155 Dugald 15
  Edgidia 168 Elizabeth 99 120
  George 162 206 Helen 15 Helena
  121 Helenor 120 Henry 15
  James 54 111 120 Janet 128
  Jannet 219 John 62 112 119-
  120 122 124 128-129 162 164-
  165 272 Lady Jane 62 162-165
  Lady Mary 168 Lord James 343
  Lord John 111 Lord Robert 111
  Margaret 109 120 Marjory 99
  Mary 120 Matthew 272 Michael
  120-122 Michael Shaw 354
  Michael-Shaw 122 Miss 54 Mr
  163 206-208 212-213 Mrs John
  164 Patrick Maxwell 123 Polly
  328 Robert 64 120 Sholto 163
  Thomas 185 Walter 48 99 109
  120 125 130 William 153-154
  204 291 William Houstoun 123
STEWART-NICOLSON, Alice 124
  Michael Hugh 124
STIRLING, 171 206-207 215
  Elizabeth 130 Archibald 39 130-
  131 John 209 Margaret 65
  Walter 209 230

STIRLING (Cont.)
  William 65 130-131
STIRLING-MAXWELL, 317 John
  Maxwell 132 William 130-132
  270-271
STONEFIELD, Lord 165
STORIE, Jean 276-277 John 276
STORMONT, Lord 349
STRAFFORD, 31
STRANRAER, Lord 83
STRATHAVEN, Earl Of 29
STRATHERNE, Earl Of 168
STRICHEN, Lord 165
STUART, 37 62 99 165 259 306 308
  318 324 Alexander 60 65 Andrew
  59-61 63-65 Andw 64 Archibald
  60 101 Catherine 319 Charlotte
  64-65 Christian-Anne 64
  Elizabeth 60 64 Gen 134 137
  Henry 316 J 63 James 27 65 80
  281 Jane 101 John 64-65 99
  Louisa 316 Margaret 65 Mr 28
  60 63-64 William 64
SUSPERCOLL, Inspector 277
SUTHERLAND, 151 Duchess Ann
  42
SWINTON, Lord 12
SYDNEY, Harriet Katherine
  Daughter Of Thomas 334
  Viscount Thomas 334
SYMINGTON, William 345
TAMSON, Pete 296
TANAREE, Gracie Of 321
TANNAHILL, John 291
TARBAT, 87 90
TAYLOR, James 345 John 346
TELFAIR, Alexander 323
TELFER, Mrs 345
TELFORD, 77 106 Eskdale Tam 326
TEMPILL, Arthour 204
TEMPLETON, Mr 257
TENNANT, 206 Charles 207 Robert
  218

TENNENT, Charles 355
TERREGLES, 314 Agnes 315 John 315 Lady 318
THOMSON, 251 C 240 Dr 241 James 240 Mrs 261 Peggy 105 Robert 218
THORNTON, Cyril 215
THRALE, Hester Marie 186 Miss 192 Mr 192 Mrs 192
THURLOW, 63
THYNNE, Lady Alice 124
TIPPO, Saib 351
TIPPOO, 138 Saib 134 137
TODD, Dr 335 Mr 222
TOWNSHEND, Harriet Katherine 334
TRAQUAIR, Catherine Daughter Of Lord Charles 316 Lord 79 Lord Charles 316
TUDOR, Margaret 3
TURENNE, 172
TURGOT, 12
TURNBULL, Bishop 196 225
TURNER, 356 Andrew 279 Dr 241 Edward 238
TURNERELLI, 261
TYNEDALE, Baron 334
TYTLER, 17 20 P F 234
UCHTRED, 109
UDNY, 348
ULSTER, Earl Of 343 King Of 111
UNDWYN, Father Of Macus 126
URE, 238
VALANCE, Aymer 308
VAUTROULLIER, 70
VAVASOUR, Edward M 319 Marcia 319
VEITCH, James 165
VERNON, Mr 236
VILLEGAIGNON, Adm 2
WALDEN, Netter Of 67
WALKER, Helen 311 Patrick 342
WALLACE, 34 44-45 306 308-309

WALLACE (Cont.) John 354 Robert 354 William 307
WALPOLE, 33 91 306 Horace 43 Secretary 236
WALTER, The Great Stewart 125 The High Steward 127 The Stewart 77
WALTON, Isaac 226 299
WARDLAW, Lady 342
WASHINGTON, 40
WATSON, Gen 244 West 193
WEDDERBURN, 60 63 Alexander 166
WELLESLEY, 306 Col 139 Marquis 137
WELLINGTON, 47 234 237 Duke Of 48 139
WELSH, William 261
WEMYSS, 121 Earl Of 54
WHAY, Girzey 322
WHEWELL, Dr 236
WHIST, 33
WHITE, Hugh 313
WHITWORTH, 39
WICKLIFF, 66-69
WIGTOWN, 185 Earl Of 170 182 186
WILKIE, 356
WILLIAM, Abbot 343 King Of 85-86 88-90 129 King Of England 43 The Lion 77 109-110 181-182 265 317 The Lion King Of 195
WILLOCKS, 225
WILSON, 294 298-300 A 297 Alexander 293 295 301 304 Alic 295 Andrew 76 Janet 76 John 209 Mary 295 Mr 76 Prof 237 Sandy 296
WINTON, 108
WISCHART, Robert 182
WISHART, 286 George 225 James 80 Lockhart 80

WODEFORD, 67
WODROW, 342
WOLFE, 38
WOLLASTON, 239
WOMBWELL, John 267
WOODROW, 120 221-222
WORDSWORTH, 332
WORTLEY, Mr 180
WYLIE, Hugh 230
WYNTOUN, 69
YARBOROUGH, Earl Of 108

YARBOROUGH (Cont.)
   Lady Sophia 108
YARKE, 166
YESTER, Lord 17
YORK, Cardinal 64 Duke James 95
   Duke Of 50 83 221
YOUNG, 358 Alexander 52 Dr 239
   355-356 James 242 355
   Livingstone 356 Margret 198 Mr
   242
ZETLAND, Lord 108

www.ingramcontent.com/pod-product-compliance
Lightning Source LLC
Chambersburg PA
CBHW072130220426
43664CB00013B/2200